Goddesses in Myth and Cultural Memory

Also Available from Bloomsbury

The Roman Mithras Cult, Olympia Panagiotidou with Roger Beck
Sacrifice in Pagan and Christian Antiquity, Robert J. Daly SJ
Ten Gifts of the Demiurge, Emilie Kutash

Goddesses in Myth and Cultural Memory

Emilie Kutash

BLOOMSBURY ACADEMIC
LONDON • NEW YORK • OXFORD • NEW DELHI • SYDNEY

BLOOMSBURY ACADEMIC
Bloomsbury Publishing Plc
50 Bedford Square, London, WC1B 3DP, UK
1385 Broadway, New York, NY 10018, USA
29 Earlsfort Terrace, Dublin 2, Ireland

BLOOMSBURY, BLOOMSBURY ACADEMIC and the Diana logo are trademarks
of Bloomsbury Publishing Plc

First published in Great Britain 2021
This paperback edition published 2023

Copyright © Emilie Kutash, 2021

Emilie Kutash has asserted her right under the Copyright, Designs and
Patents Act, 1988, to be identified as Author of this work.

All rights reserved. No part of this publication may be reproduced or transmitted in any form or by any means, electronic or mechanical, including photocopying, recording, or any information storage or retrieval system, without prior permission in writing from the publishers.

Bloomsbury Publishing Plc does not have any control over, or responsibility for, any third-party websites referred to or in this book. All internet addresses given in this book were correct at the time of going to press. The author and publisher regret any inconvenience caused if addresses have changed or sites have ceased to exist, but can accept no responsibility for any such changes.

A catalogue record for this book is available from the British Library.

Library of Congress Cataloging-in-Publication Data
Names: Kutash, Emilie, author.
Title: Goddesses in myth and cultural memory / Emilie Kutash.
Description: London ; New York : T&T Clark, 2021. | Includes bibliographical references and index. |
Summary: "How have the goddesses of ancient myth survived, prevalent even now as literary and cultural icons? How do allegory, symbolic interpretation and political context transform the goddess from her regional and individual identity into a goddess of philosophy and literature? Emilie Kutash explores these questions, beginning from the premise that cultural memory, a collective cultural and social phenomenon, can last thousands of years. Kutash demonstrates a continuing practice of interpreting and allegorizing ancient myths, tracing these goddesses of archaic origin through history. Chapters follow the goddesses from their ancient near eastern prototypes, to their place in the epic poetry, drama and hymns of classical Greece, to their appearance in Platonic philosophy, Medieval allegory, and their association with Christendom. Finally, Kutash considers how goddesses were made into Jungian archetypes, and how contemporary spiritual feminists made them a counterfoil to male divinity, thereby addressing the continued role of goddesses in perpetuating gender binaries"– Provided by publisher.
Identifiers: LCCN 2020055146 | ISBN 9780567697394 (hardback) | ISBN 9780567697417 (pdf) | ISBN 9780567697400 (epub)
Subjects: LCSH: Goddesses.
Classification: LCC BL473.5 .K88 2021 | DDC 202/.114–dc23
LC record available at https://lccn.loc.gov/2020055146

ISBN:	HB:	978-0-5676-9739-4
	PB:	978-0-5676-9737-0
	ePDF:	978-0-5676-9741-7
	eBook:	978-0-5676-9740-0

Typeset by Integra software solutions., Pvt, Ltd.

To find out more about our authors and books visit www.bloomsbury.com
and sign up for our newsletters

To three talented and creative women: Anne, Charlotte, and Danielle

Contents

Preface		viii
Acknowledgments		x
1	Introduction: "To Whom Death Never Comes"	1
2	Goddess Prototypes: The Classical Literature	17
3	The Goddesses of Philosophy: The Literature of Later Antiquity	37
4	Virgin, Erotic Temptress, Mother and Cosmic Womb	53
5	Dualism and the Mediating Goddess	73
6	"The Goddess of the Triple Ways": Triads and Trinities	89
7	Naming the Goddess: Geopolitics and the Intertranslation of Names	107
8	Asherah, Sophia, Shekhinah: Are They Hebrew Goddesses?	123
9	Did Christianity Make the Goddess Disappear?	139
10	Personifying Nature and Wisdom: The Medieval and Early Modern Goddess	155
11	New Mythologies of Gender: Feminists, Psychoanalysts, Epistemologists	171
12	The Goddess Interpreted	189
Notes		196
Select Bibliography		225
Index		232

Preface

Phiroze Vasunia, in his preface to Brooke Holmes' book on gender and antiquity, points out that "reception studies" is a growing field and that cultural debates today can be illuminated through the lens of Greco-Roman antiquity. In 2011, I delivered a paper, "Theogonic Mythology Reinvented: Goddesses and Late Antique Ontogony" to the International Society for Neoplatonic Studies. The paper discussed how the goddesses of Hesiod's *Theogony* became *the* goddess of philosophy in the texts of the Platonists and Neoplatonists. Many of my colleagues wanted to know more about this intriguing subject. Harold Tarrant, in a discussion we were having after the talk, suggested that I might consider writing a book on goddesses and I thank him for that suggestion. As time went on, I became engaged with the fascinating work of Jan Assmann on cultural memory, or what he calls "mnemohistory," Gerald Bruns's book *Hermeneutics Ancient and Modern*, Robert Lamberton's *Homer the Theologian* on allegorical readings of the epic tradition, and Luc Brisson's *How the Philosophers Saved Myths*. That there is continuity between ancient and modern thought, I came to realize, can be augmented by Assmann's idea that cultural memory is an abiding and lasting influence and that allegorical and symbolic reading of ancient myth can move its reception forward in time. In every period of history, including the present, it seems that goddesses and their ancient mythical epic presence have never succumbed to oblivion. It is the scholars and writers of every generation who have made goddesses immortal.

"Memory," according to Walter Benjamin, "creates the chain of tradition which passes a happening on from generation to generation. It is the Muse-derived element of the epic art in a broader sense and encompasses its varieties. In the first place among these is the one practiced by the storyteller. It starts the web which all stories together form in the end" (*Illuminations*, p. 98). With a better understanding of how allegorical and hermeneutical, and philosophical interpretation can preserve and enhance collective memory, I also came across studies of goddesses that were philosophical and hermeneutical. Spyridon Rangos' study of Artemis and Tuomo Lankila's study of Aphrodite, Sarah Iles Johnston's evocative *Hekate Soteira*, are prime examples. I had been impressed before this project began by Johnston's exploration of the goddess Hekate, recognizing the *Chaldean Oracles*' influence on creating a mediating goddess in Platonist ontology. Pierre Hadot, in the *Veil of Isis*, studied, among other things, the sixteenth to nineteenth centuries and the use of the imagery of Artemis/Isis and the veiled goddess of antiquity in icon and idea. All such investigations allowed me to place the study of goddesses within the much wider purview of hermeneutics, historiography, and cultural memory. A further realization emerged during my research when I found that every era also had in common the deployment of gender binaries along similar lines. This confirmed, for me, that there is continuity between very diverse interpretive communities in relation to a cultural code that is embedded in the very long common history they share. It is a history that is sometimes "known" but sometimes operates without awareness as an "unknown known." Male gender is treated as an exemplar of logic, ideas, and transcendent spirituality, while female gender is associated with the maternal, indeterminate, nature, receptivity, and even with the presymbolic in discourse. Although each period of history has transformed goddesses according to its own priorities, whether political, theological, philosophical, or literary, all the assumptions concerning gender remained the same. For late Platonists, the goddess's shameful activities could only be sanitized by treating them as food for allegory. For the later theologized philosophy of the Gnostics and Neoplatonists, goddesses as "metaforms" became placeholders for the highest metaphysical truths. For the Christians, they signified sinful female presences that should be excluded from the canon, but to some spiritual feminists of our own time, they constitute a newly revivified object of worship and antidote to the male-only divinity of the Judeo-Christian legacy. Gender essentialism, however, played a role throughout. This code appears ubiquitously today evidencing its intransigence, even if only in the fact that it has needed and received widespread criticism by current scholars.

That Hesiod's phantasmagorical dreamlike "vision of the whole" could contribute to both the known and the "unknown known" of a whole culture is striking. Thus while this book is about goddesses, in fact it is equally about hermeneutics, the persistence of myth as an important feature of normative discourse, about how goddesses became the metaform "goddess," about cultural memory, and about the historicality of interpretation and the reception of ancient texts. It is also about a certain kind of forgetting which Slavof Žižek has called the "unknown knowns": the influences of certain ideas are so embedded in a culture that they operate out of the awareness of those that have fallen under their sway. Such are the so-called binary oppositions of gender. They appear in Near Eastern myth, in Hesiod, in Homer, in the Pythagorean table of opposites, in medieval allegory, and remarkably in some contemporary psychoanalytic and feminist scholarship, even if only to reverse the valuation of female characteristics in a presumably biased history. I hope the book helps to support the idea that there is no such thing as a de-historicized reading of a text, that indeed "the past is not a natural growth but a cultural construction," as Jan Assmann has elaborated. In addition, I am hoping that my book will serve to increase appreciation of the fact that myth is an integral and dominating feature of our collective imagination.

Acknowledgments

I want to thank all my Neoplatonic and Classics friends who encouraged my work and whose examples I follow: my good friend Sarah Pomeroy for her pioneering work on women in antiquity, and especially for our very productive sessions and discussions, furthering my understanding of late antiquity, while translating Plutarch's *Isis and Osiris*, Eunapius' *Life of the Sophists*, and Iamblichus' *The Life of Pythagoras*, something we did for our own edification. Svetla Slaveva Griffin; John Finamore, Harold Tarrant, all important influences and interlocutors, John Turner, with gratitude for his extensive work on Gnosticism, specifically on Hekate and female goddess prototypes within Gnostic literature, Christina Manolea, for her understanding of allegory and symbolic argument in relation to interpretive reading of Homer through the lens of late Neoplatonists, Robert van den Berg on the Proclus hymns; Luc Brisson for his invaluable work on mythology and philosophy; and John Dillon, the founding father and originator of so many scholars' continued work on Platonism, early, middle, and late. Zeke Maazur was a friend whose work on Gnosticism and erotic imagery in Neoplatonism was a source of mutual interest and discussion. I hope that mention of this work here will help to memorialize him as he so deserves. I am also grateful, as always, to James Davis who is unceasingly supportive of all my work and to Deborah Blake.

I gratefully acknowledge permissions to use portions of a previously published article of mine that apears here in Chapter 10 and previously appeared as an article in *The Internarial Journal of the Platonic tradition*, "Review Essay: Wendy Elgersma Hellerman: *The Female Personification of Wisdom. Journal of the Platonic Tradition*" #2, 2013 and permissions to use portions of my article, "The Prevailing Circumstances: The Pagan Philosophers of Athens in a Time of Stress." In *The Pomegranate* 10.2 (2008) 184–200, in Chapter 6.

1

Introduction: "To Whom Death Never Comes"

In the second century of the common era, in the town of Autun in Gaul, the people of the town still held processions to honor their beloved goddess Berecynthia (also known as Cybele). After a martyred Christian saint was killed because he would not bow down to Cybele, in a dramatic scene, the bishop threw the image of Berecynthia, an idol carried in this procession, to the ground. When she was unable to be re-erected despite all efforts of prayer and sacrifice, the people began to doubt her power. All the onlookers converted on the spot to the Catholic Church. Incidents like these document the long struggle between Christianity and the Roman "Magna Mater" (the Great Mother) as an object of veneration.[1] This second-century incident illustrates how the reception of a goddess, an object of devotion in the world of the ancient Greeks and early Roman Empire, could alter with a changing geopolitical circumstance. The bishops who railed against goddesses and particularly despised Aphrodite for her blatant eroticism would have been quite alarmed to live in the twentieth and twenty-first centuries. In a rather lengthy article in *The Atlantic* (January 2001), titled "The Scholars and the Goddess," Charlotte Allen writes about Wicca and Goddess spirituality, describing it as a fast-growing religion in Neopagan circles. Aside from neopagan goddess worship, in Greece there are now followers of Hellenism who wish to return to their ancient cultural roots by worshipping the ancient gods.[2] Carol Christ, in 1978, gave a keynote address at a conference called "Great Goddess Re-emerging" at the University of Santa Cruz. It was attended by 500 people and later published as an article "Why Women Need Goddesses." The first women's spirituality conference, held in Boston in 1978, was attended by 1,800 women. Now, in the early years of the twenty-first century, these movements are still growing, and it seems that goddesses are still among us. Not only are they the object of scholarly and popular attention, they are characterized in ways that still gain traction from the very old "muse inspired" narratives of ancient epic poets.

Goodison and Morris point out that it is the feminist quest for "reshaping and transforming symbols of divinity which validate women's experience" that has fueled much of the goddess movement of today.[3] Philip G. Davis's book *Goddess Unmasked: The Rise of Neopagan Feminist Spirituality* and Lynn Meskell and Cynthia Eller's

The Myth of Matriarchal Prehistory, as well as the work of Mary Lefkowitz, provide skeptical accounts of such modern goddess revivals,[4] mostly on the basis of a flawed view of history. On the other hand, in Brooke Holmes words, "[t]he wild interpretive potential coiled in myth is nowhere clearer than in the polyphony of feminist readings and appropriations."[5] These two examples, one that is wary of anachronism and the other respectfully "receptive," illustrate both the failings and strengths of our collective memory of the past. Despite the new-found allegiance to goddesses, the history of goddesses and how they survived the centuries, retaining a presence far beyond the Christian dismissal, are largely unknown. Some of the appropriation of goddess mythology has enhanced feminist literature in a positive way while some is a result of misreading based on unexamined assumptions. What I have intended to provide, in *Goddesses of Myth and Cultural Memory*, is an account of the remarkable but actual fact that goddesses have a presence in a wide range of literature, philosophy, and theology in such divergent contexts as Hermeticism, Gnosticism, Neoplatonism, Kabbalah, Medieval allegory, and in feminist and psychoanalytic literature of our own time. The history that emerges through this diachronic presentation will allow readers, ranging from undergraduate students, graduate students, nonacademic readers to research scholars, to find their way through an incredible series of diverse settings within which goddesses have featured. It will enable them to think critically about what may have been a matter of curiosity and/or fascination, but which can now be viewed as a comment upon the times, places, and gender norms that are reflected in texts of the time. Furthermore, it will enhance the readers appreciation of the fact that this history has contributed to the stereotyping that is often the "unknown known" in our thinking about gender.

Jan Assmann, building upon the work of the French sociologist Maurice Halbwachs on the social frame of collective memory, suggests that "[t]he past only comes into being as far as we refer to it."[6] Cultural memory, he suggests, persists over millennia, and can define the memory horizon of a society.[7] He contends that

> Just as an individuals form a personal identity through memory, maintaining this despite the passage of time, a group identity is also dependent on the reproduction of shared memories. The difference is that group memory has no neurological basis. This is replaced by culture: a complex of identity-shaping aspects of knowledge, objectified in the symbolic forms of myth, song, dance sayings, laws sacred texts, pictures.[8]

Furthermore, collective or bonding memory is a social and cultural phenomenon that can last hundreds and possibly thousands of years.[9] In his book *Moses the Egyptian: The Memory of Egypt in Western Monotheism*, Assmann establishes the premise that cultural memory is an all-pervasive explanatory paradigm.[10] Moses and the Golden Calf, and other canonical memories of the Jews leaving Egypt, are still celebrated by the Jewish people though basically only documented in the biblical text. The organizing myths of other religions and cultures also document the power of this form of remembering. Similarly, the "memory" of goddesses is a direct result of the ability of later texts to incorporate "previous signifying systems" and "reconstruct pre-existing sign-functions."[11] *Goddesses in Myth and Cultural Memory*, then, is arranged diachronically to facilitate the reader in developing a sense of the evolution and reception of goddess mythology as it impacted on a variety of interpretive communities. At the same time, the reader will be able to get a sense of the thematic constancies that seem to endure regardless of changing geopolitical and cultural context. The diachronic approach illustrates group memory within diverging interpretive communities through the centuries, while the thematic approach reveals the commonalities across these communities. One which is striking is the preservation of a certain type of codified binary gender opposition. I also hope to make it clear that almost everything that is known of goddesses is "literary" and hence subject to reader response and historical context. While statues and aretalogies attest to the presence of goddesses as objects of worship to long-gone cultures, goddesses command a still more powerful presence in the Archaic and Classical literature of Greece and in the texts that span all the centuries that follow.

One can go as far back as Sumer and find that gods and goddesses not only represent the power in the universe and control the natural elements of sky, sun, moon, and storms, but also watch over the *polis* (city-state).[12] Every city-state in ancient cultures had its own divine pantheon and a ruling divinity that served to ensure peace and prosperity and who was in a close relationship with the city ruler. Goddesses, as well as gods, served these functions. Our knowledge of these histories is solely dependent on archeological finds and deciphered manuscripts, themselves subject to reception and interpretation. A certain caution must be observed, then, in making too facile assumptions about the mysterious figures that preceded the epic poems and hymns that date from the archaic period. Goodson and Morris point out that scientific objectivity, in current approaches to archeology, has given way to the notion of a participant observer. The influence of Orphism, Hesiod's *Theogony*, Homer, and the Homeric hymns as sources for iconic goddess prototypes, on the other hand, is our source par excellence, for what we know of goddesses and this fact should not be underestimated. In these texts, one finds a chthonic deity, a goddess of the crossroads, of fertility, of the wild, a queen of night, and a guide between the underworld of the dead and the world of the living. There are wives, mothers, and virgins, and a celebrated goddess of love. Separately named, politically unattached, each of these goddesses embodies a diverse set of functions. Athena, born from the head of her father Zeus, is a virgin and is known as the goddess of wisdom and war. Hekate is an honored Titan who guides Persephone from the world of Hades. Hera, the wife of Zeus and a mother goddess, possesses life-giving fertility, as do Kybele and Rhea. Artemis is a goddess of the wild and Gaia the sole origin of most of the progeny that populate the theogonic genealogy that follows her. These figures are forever after known to be the traditional goddesses of the archaic and classical ancient world, and it is these figures that have been taken as objects of devotion in certain contemporary settings. This is powerful evidence that the prototypes found in ancient literature have taken a strong hold on our collective memory. It is these very goddesses that inhabit the texts of current scholarship, arouse the passionate attention of popular culture, and prove their legendary immortality by capturing an everchanging but perennial interest.

Jenny Strauss Clay has pointed out, "The study of the gods in early Greek poetry is not merely of antiquarian or academic interest but is justified as a necessary foundation for an understanding of the roots of Western thought."[13] In *Goddesses in Myth and Cultural Memory*, I have emphasized the fact that most of what is known about goddesses has little to do with the archaic original cultural settings within which goddesses were worshiped and mythologized and much to do with perennial reception and re-interpretation of these myths. I agree with Jean-Pierre Vernant, who has written extensively on Greek mythology in his claim, that "It is no longer possible for us today to reconstruct a prehistory of Greece starting from a tribal community or even a previous matriarchal society."[14] The book will proceed by tracking a trajectory that was initiated in the archaic period, but which culminates in the contemporary world. Much of extant scholarship has held fast to the conviction that goddesses, whose personae are essentially constructed by the epic poets, originated in the elusive space of archaic history. The goddesses of the people of the archaic past, however, are shadowy figures at best. The goddesses that commandeered ritual and votive practice in archaic civilizations are long gone. Knowledge of what they might have been like can only be accessed when ancient manuscripts and archeological finds are interpreted.

When we turn to the Greek dramatists in the Golden Age of Greece, we find one of the first settings for a "reception" of epic mythology. Here the traditional gods and goddesses retain their archaic resumes but carried out new functions. In this genre, they take part in dramatic narratives, inciting humans to action and intervening in human affairs. Many commentators consider this usage to be a *deus ex machina*. Certainly, it is difficult to separate the artist's need for a facilitator in the action of the drama and the presumed theology the god or goddess represented. Mary Lefkowitz, however, does not consider the gods' presence in these dramas as external to the action. She suggests that they are central to it, and to the idea that justice is done in the end and that the gods ultimately control human destiny. In theogonic mythology, gods and goddesses play a role in super-cosmic events and in the creation of the world. In the *Iliad* and *Odyssey* and in Greek drama, they do so in human lives.[15] Greek drama, then, is a transitional literature, extracting the gods and goddess from the context of myth and rendering them "forces" in human events. In this milieu, gods and goddesses have already been utilized in roles that go beyond the horizon within which they were originated.

The Archaic Sources

Ancient votive, ritual, and regional practices related to the worship of a goddess, then, must be differentiated from the archaic and classical texts that mythologize her. Acknowledging this difference allows a full appreciation of how textual innovations both reflect and transform their surrounding culture. Charles Martindale, whose pioneering work on reception theory and classics is widely followed, calls the desire of a classicist to experience Homer as untouched by any taint of modernity "deluded."[16] While deluded may be too strong a word here, it points to the fact that caution must be applied to any project that would aim at reconstructing the originating historical situation within which goddesses were part of the lives and ritual practice of archaic societies. It may be equally treacherous to assume we can fully decode Homer or

Hesiod in terms of original source material. The question of the influence of ancient Near Eastern mythologies remains an open issue, but all references to a goddess that follow the archaic and classical periods began and remain literary. That there was a "myth itself" is very often a product of romantic imagination.

What do we know about the earlier cultures that may have preceded and influenced Hesiod and Homer? "In all likelihood their origins are heterogeneous," as Strauss Clay tells us, "some may belong to the pre-Greek Aegean substrate, whereas others are unquestionably Indo-European in origin; yet others may be imports from abroad, especially the East."[17] In recent scholarship, even the East-West binary has been seen to be simplistic and has given way to an emphasis on historical and comparative studies of mythology and religion.[18] With an Indo-European orientation, the statuary and texts found throughout the ancient world have given us artifacts that amaze and inspire, and one thing is indisputable. Goddesses were very important to ancient societies as were gods. Archeological finds, inscriptions, and aretalogies add to our inherited artifacts and are tributes to the extra-textual importance of gods and goddesses to early societies. They provide direct knowledge of ritual and of traditional burial practices, as does evidence of telestic and/or mystery rites.[19] Walter Burkert, Carolina López-Ruiz, M. L. West Jenny Strauss Clay, G. S. Kirk, and others have found precursors to Hesiod, Homer, and the Homeric hymns in Mesopotamian and Near Eastern (e.g., Ugarit-Phoenician) texts.[20] M. L. West points out that in 1929 when the excavation of Ugarit began, literature of the bronze age began to be deciphered. Akkadian cuneiform, Sumerian and Hittite texts, as well, subsequently became accessible.[21] As Semitic-Ugarit texts became available, they allowed a greater appreciation of earlier influences. Burkert cites Franz Dornseiff as the first to give credit to the impact of the Near East on classical Greece, as well as Albin Lesky.[22] The deciphering of Hittite mythological texts revealed connections that document a common heritage and texts of Semitic Ugarit, Greek fragments of Philon of Byblos dealing with Phoenician mythology, and other sources have received increasing scholarly attention. Similarities between the Hurrian creation myth and the Greek mythology of Ouranos, Kronos, and Zeus have also been widely appreciated for at least fifty years.[23] Goddesses too have ancestors, Inanna in Sumer, Ishtar in Akkad, Anath in Canaan, etc., whose characters are similar to the Hesiodic and Homeric figures.[24] Love and war, virginity, promiscuity, bloodthirstiness, and theogonic fecundity did not originate with Hesiod. The oldest of them known to Western scholarship was Inanna, the great Sumerian goddess of love and war.

Jan Assmann points out that an ancient text is in need of as much philological labor as it does "because the context within which it was formerly understood has now disappeared."[25] Whatever preexists Hesiod's or Homer's literary masterpieces despite Near Eastern influence would be impossible to recover. The "tautegorical" level of myth in its regional and cultural significance has been refigured and received within a changed cultural milieu. Although Hesiod is an early and archaic source for goddess mythology, the style in which he presents these myths is well on its way to metaphor and allegory.[26] Kirk discusses his predecessors Francis Cornford, W. K. C. Guthrie, and Martin Nilsson, who assumed that there was an identifiable break between rational scientific thought and mythology in regard to the epic poets and the Presocratic physicists. In opposition to these views, myth in a pure form "may have lain thousands of years in the past."[27] Hesiod's presumed date, according to modern scholarship, is somewhere between the second half of the eighth century and the first quarter of the seventh.[28] Whether Hesiod preceded Homer or was his contemporary is not known. In any case, Hesiod had already taken a large step along the way to "demythologizing" the traditional myths and turning them into literary masterpieces.

Robert Lamberton points out that Greek poetry is "characterized by a certain style, a style perhaps best understood in terms of the exclusion of a vast range of possibilities rather than in terms of a specific internal creativity. The most nearly authoritative Greek theogony—Hesiod's—is a magnificent example of this."[29] Malcolm Wilcock, in an influential article on the subject of myth in Homer, proposes that Homeric myths and Homeric characters are a matter of ad hoc personal invention by the poet.[30] Wilcock concludes, "If Homer invents so freely, it must be dangerous for us to use the *Iliad* as if it were a handbook of mythology."[31] Jasper Griffin sides with Wilcock, agreeing that the poet of the *Iliad* invents archaic-sounding myths.[32] Gregory Nagy calls his own revision of this theory a "paradigm shift."[33] They are, in his estimation, variations on themes of earlier myths of which Homer makes selective use. They are, therefore, a "mythological exemplum," bypassing any mythology vs. truth (*mythos/aletheia*) distinction that the post-Homeric treatment of myth produced.[34] In view of these considerations, I consider the works of the epic poets to clearly be works of art, composed by authors who already see their historical cultural artifacts through a new lens. The prototypes which are encountered in these works, and the narratives that they present, limit the extent of comparison that can be made to earlier sources. In the eighth century BCE, as Voyatzis points out, when these works were composed, the pace quickened in all spheres.[35] Prosperity, rapid population growth, increasing contacts with the outside world, development of the Greek alphabet, and the epic poetry of Homer and Hesiod coincided with the rise of the Greek polis. Regional myths, converted to a later usage, become more sophisticated, are often allegorical, and are contextualized by literary priorities. The themes that these authors use as raw material are in the service of creating literature and not religion.

Historical Change

The goddesses conceived by the authors of ancient epic poetry, hymn, and drama are not regional, are not embedded in cultural practice, and transcend both time and place. Jenny Strauss Clay reminds us that early literary works such as those of Homer and Hesiod are products of "the Pan-Hellenic Olympian orientation,"[36] a time of geopolitical change that consolidated Hellenic culture in general. Homer and Hesiod produced "cultural texts" that possess a special normative and formative authority for a society as a whole, whereas the earlier texts may have been linked with magical effects to invoke divine presence and support votive rituals.[37] Robert Lamberton claims that Hesiod "might be the most important of ancient authors,"[38] and as Athanassakis points out, "the oldest repository of Western Culture when it comes to the origin of the cosmos and the many divinities in it."[39] It is Hesiod who created the template that constitutes the Titanic and Olympian pantheon. His formulaic descriptions provide some of the most potent and authoritative myths that survive and change with the centuries. Jean-Pierre Vernant calls this template "a system of classification, in which categories are established and hierarchies and delineations and definitions of spheres of influence among the gods are put in place."[40] Chapter 2 of *Goddesses in Myth and Cultural Memory* describes the prototypes of the goddesses present in archaic and classical literature and the speculations that scholars have made concerning their pre-classical Near Eastern origins.

In Late Antiquity, mythology had a second coming. The imperialism of Alexander and the conquests of the Roman Empire brought about widespread geopolitical and intellectual change. Appropriation of regional cultures in the service of ecumenical universalism was one result of expanding empire. These centuries saw the use of Archaic and Classical literature undergo considerable transformation. During the first and second centuries CE, in particular, a fusion of exotic literature and Platonic philosophy, so-called Egyptomania, and a backlash against Stoic and Epicurean skepticism resulted in a resolute turning away from the pure rationalism that had dominated philosophy in Plato's academy. Plato had disparaged myth in favor of reason, while in the Hellenic and Greco-Roman periods, mythology was revived and was omnipresent. Esoteric and mystical literature was widely disseminated in later antiquity. It found its way into the texts of Platonist philosophers as well. Through the unlikely fusion of Platonism and theology based on myth, goddesses were revived and became goddesses of philosophy.

Geopolitical change has a profound effect on cultural priorities. Alexander's ecumenical imperialism was a deliberate effort to establish a two-way street between the hegemonous empire he was creating and local lore and practice. Regional cultures, as they assimilated to Hellenic and later to Roman influence, were encouraged to assimilate their own deities to those of their conquerors, and vice versa. Transposing separate and regional names of gods and goddesses and finding equivalences of function and description fostered the allegiance of the people of these regions and reduced their resistance to foreign influence. Paradigm shifts occurred in contemporary philosophy and literature as well. An iconic "goddess" figure emerged in many spheres of both ritual, art, and philosophy fusing the formerly separate goddess types. Roman artworks attest to the interest in such goddess figures and there are many examples of sculpture dating from the first and second centuries CE along these lines. A Demeter-Io-Isis statue, for example, that dates to the Roman imperial period (160–200 CE) can be seen in the Boston Museum of Fine Arts. The Greco-Roman goddess Isis, whose lore originated in Egypt but who was widely worshiped throughout the Greco-Roman world, came to have many features in common with Demeter and other Greek goddesses. She found her way into Platonist literature of the second century, most notably Plutarch's *Isis and Osiris* and Apuleius's *Metamorphoses*. Thus, during a time when Greek culture was disseminated throughout the Mediterranean world, goddesses acquired a new importance not only to the constituent populations, but to the literary and philosophical world as well. In Rome itself, gods and myths were recast in terms of Greek mythology, as were Egyptian myths, as "the Romans made the support of Greeks and Greek culture the lynch-pin of their rule of the region."[41] Chapter 3 describes these events and the influential exotic literature, particularly the *Chaldean Oracle*s and Gnostic texts, that enabled the transformation of myth to philosophy.

The Hellenist and Greco-Roman Platonists treated the original goddesses of classical literature more as a "metaform" than as a cultic or mythological artifact.[42] Myth becomes "saved," as Luc Brisson suggests, by being treated as an allegorical vehicle to represent and support theological and philosophical ideas.[43] One result of the cross-fertilization of myth and Platonist philosophy is that the male and female prototypes that were featured in Hesiod and were known to classical Greece became increasingly formulaic. One influence was the revival of Pythagoreanism which resulted in the protypes becoming imbued with Pythagorean binary oppositions. This syncretism, I suggest, had a lasting effect on gender opposition in Western cultural memory. As I studied the transformations of goddess mythology across future centuries, though the settings may have been radically different, I was struck by the fact that an essentialist gender opposition remained the same.

Interchangeable Goddess Names and Descriptions

In the pagan world, going back to early Mediterranean history, divine names were freely assigned and interchanged according to usage and geopolitical context. In late antiquity, the names of the gods become interchangeable in both popular practice and scholarly literature. As Assmann suggests, "The gods are given a semantic dimension by means of mythical narratives and the cosmological speculations," allowing the names to be translatable.[44] Names and resumes of the goddesses of ancient mythology were associated with one another and the individual identities and characteristics of certain goddesses were now applied to figures that served as "simulacra" of their cultic or ritual counterparts (this was particularly true in aretalogies of the time). Furthermore, for the philosophers of these times, both the gods and goddesses became associated with gender-specific philosophical traits, along the lines of the Pythagorean table of opposites. The binary oppositions of male and female divinity became more pronounced, while the separate identities of individual gods and goddesses became less distinct. Gods and goddesses became iconic figures that were composites of traditional characteristics from a variety of earlier more distinct figures. Hekate, never mentioned in Homer, was given a unique and important role in Hesiod. Hekate had a share in the earth, sky, and sea, and possessed powers to help a wide range of mortals. In later antiquity, she features prominently in such widely disseminated exotic second-century literature as the *Chaldean Oracle* where she acquires a role in world creation. The very popular Isis became an iconic figure and widespread object of worship and devotion. While she had been identified as early as Herodotus in his *Histories* (2.59.156) as the equivalent of the Greek Demeter, she gained prominence in later antiquity, most notably in the Ptolemaic period. Evidence for the ecumenical nature of Isis can be found in the aretalogies or encomia of Isis derived from archeological finds such as the Memphis Stele (Ptolemaic period).[45] These prove Isis to be the epitome of syncretism. R. E. Witt describes her polyonymous ("many-named") nature as a consequence of the Hellenization that allowed her to take on many of the characteristics of the Greek goddesses.[46] In the early Common Era, Isis is found to be a widespread geographical presence. In many towns, including the birthplace of Paul of Tarsus, and in most of the cities where he proselytized the newfound Christian gospel, she was an established and renowned object of worship. Cleopatra identified herself with Isis, an example of her widespread popularity. When Plutarch, a second century CE philosopher, constructs a complex and lengthy account of the Isis and Osiris myth, discussed here in Chapter 3, he takes the further step and identifies Isis with philosophical concepts derived from Platonist philosophy.

In the hands of the philosophers of these times, many of whom accessed widely disseminated revelatory literature, such as the *Chaldean Oracles* and Gnostic gospels, theogonies changed character. In a peculiar and fascinating process, theogony contributed its structure to an entirely new genre. Analogous to the hierarchy of generations of gods and goddesses that Hesiod presents, the latter-day Platonists conceived of hypostatic levels of reality proceeding from a transcendent source and emanating down to nature producing levels of reality in the process. In the classical literature, earlier generations of gods and goddesses multiply and reproduce the later generations of divinities. Now philosophers give the gods and goddesses roles in the creation of the intelligible and the natural world.[47] Middle (second to fifth centuries CE) and later Neoplatonic philosophers fused the names of gods and goddesses with philosophical concepts and gods' names and activities became interchangeable. Platonic accounts of the origin of the universe and the anatomy of being became theology: gods and goddesses became agents in elaborate ontologies. The Neoplatonists (fourth and fifth centuries CE), building on this heritage, theorized that the descent from higher transcendent levels of reality to the psychical and material world was a spiritual process. With a precedent in the *Chaldean Oracles* where a goddess (Hekate) is described as "the bestower of life-bearing fire" (Frag. 52) or later in Proclus' *Commentary on Timaeus* where he mentions "life bearing goddess" in several places (II. 151. 7-10 for example),[48] the goddess as "Life" became a powerful operant, providing agency in ontologies that would otherwise be static. The Platonist philosophers envisioned the intellectual world to be at rest and beyond physical materiality consequently lacking the ability to move and change. The only way this transcendent level of reality could supply ideas and formal structure to the material world was through an intermediary. In the archaic epic, mating and childbearing on the part of goddesses produced a genealogical succession. Now a goddesses' fertility becomes a world-creating power which allows the production of nature. Her reception in future allegorical and literary rhetoric will reflect these innovations particularly her association with nature.

Transforming the Goddess: The Literature of Antiquity

Athanassakis asserts that in most of the epic poem "it is the mother who matters." Chapter 4 elaborates upon Hesiod's precedent for one of the most predominant of the goddess prototypes: the goddess as fertile mother. The male partner is much less prominent or altogether absent.[49] Hesiod had provided numinous, almost hallucinogenic, visions of the erotic coupling of heaven and earth, god and goddess, and of the birth of immortal beings of luminous beauty and terrifying monstrosity. The life-giving reproductive function and the erotic attraction to the male feature prominently in myth.⁵⁰ Even virgin goddesses have a connection with this role. Fertility and the mothering and nursing of offspring, as an identity marker for many of the goddesses of Hesiod, are a prime example of how earlier prototypes can transform with geopolitical and philosophical context. Conceiving and birthing progeny transmute into general life-producing powers. In Neoplatonic hierarchies, for example, the higher hypostases (a hypostasis is a substance, essence, or underlying reality) are eternally at rest in inviolable unity. They are gods. Life, motion, and change are left to the goddess who intervenes in the creation of nature from higher principles. She helps to produce the universe through her longing for a liaison with the higher world and her interaction (mating) with it. Reproductive generation transmutes into emanative or processive production.

Chapter 4 discusses the extensive erotic imagery associated with the goddess as well. Plato (429–347 BCE), in his dialogue *Phaedo* (75AB), describes how all becoming yearns for true being and strives to become like it. Later, Aristotle (384–322 BCE), in *Physics* (192a 15–25), says that matter desires form. Aristotle decrees that God moves *hôs erômenon* (erotically). This background enables the analogy between erotic coupling and the combining of form and matter in creating nature that is found in later Platonists. Plutarch's second-century *Isis and Osiris* is an example of reproductive analogies as templates for philosophical ideas. The love of Isis for Osiris, in this text, unites matter and form. Osiris provides matter with order when to create the world, he sows in matter (Isis) *logoi* from himself (372f).⁵¹ In another of Plutarch's works, *De Animae Procreatione in Timaeo* (1014b–1015f), a male and female deity enact the love affair that causes form to inject itself into matter.⁵² As these examples illustrate, the goddess of antiquity is now an operative in metaphysical schemes. Her capacity as "mother" and her erotic longing to possess "form" bestowed by a male deity will empower a life-producing force that allows the physical world of nature to come into existence. These characteristics, reproductive fecundity and an engagement with nature not mind, become a deeply enmeshed theme that will impact upon future instances of the binary oppositions of gender from antiquity to the present.

The evolution of the goddess, from her traditional prototypes to her debut as a life-giving principle, continued after the second century CE culminating in the work of Proclus and the other pagan philosophers of the late Athenian school. Chapter 5, leading up to this, takes up a theoretical discussion: dualism and gender binaries become fused with one another as philosophical oppositions. The philosophical categories, for example, form and matter become conflated with female and male divinities in Platonist accounts of the first and second centuries CE. Brooke Holmes has documented the many instances in contemporary texts where philosophers have discussed the association of "matter" in ancient philosophy, with female gender, and this will be taken up in Chapter 11 here.⁵³ Influenced by the Pythagorean table of opposites where female is associated with multiplicity and matter and male is associated with unity and form, this binary becomes firmly entrenched. In Chapter 6, Proclus (fifth century CE) the Neoplatonist who was the leader of the later empire Athenian School, a revival of Plato's academy will proliferate this template. Proclus was determined to elevate the classical tradition in an empire in which Christianity was fast eclipsing his own tradition.⁵⁴ One of the ways he preserved the Hellenic tradition was to make elaborate rhetorical use of the goddesses, as did his cherished text, the *Chaldean Oracles*. He equated Hekate with Artemis, Soul with Persephone, and Virtue with Athena, and turned the goddess into a life-giving female principle who assumes an active intermediating function in cosmic creation. Divinizing categories of Platonic ontology, he systematized them in a manner more baroque and complex than that of any of his predecessors. In this chapter, the reader will encounter triads and trinities and develop a sense of the elaborate intricacies of the goddesses' role in Neoplatonist ontology. In this context, she is a member of a triadic superstructure that permeates all levels of reality. Chapter 7 takes up the complex issue of god naming. Goddesses often carry the names of their cultic predecessors, while their descriptions are transformed and do not commensurate with the ancient sources that created their porotypes.

The Persistence of Goddess Imagery

The remaining chapters of *Goddesses in Myth and Cultural Memory* document the persistent presence of goddesses mythology in the changing cultural landscapes of the centuries that follow late antiquity. These chapters will provide evidence that meanings stemming from the interpretation of texts are always historically mediated. Chapter 8, on Hebrew literature, shows that it too is not exempt from mythical iconography and it is not unrelated to the pagan mythological history documented in the earlier chapters. Although not in mainstream Hebrew liturgy, a "goddess of wisdom" in the form of "Sophia" can be found in the apocryphal wisdom literature. In the medieval period and its aftermath, the Kabbalist "Shechinah," a female principle, is an instance where deification and personification appear in Jewish religious literature that otherwise eschews imagery in relation to deity. This usage will be shown to incorporate ideas that also appear in Gnostic and Neoplatonic coinages, discussed in earlier chapters. Chapter 9 documents the influence of Platonic and Neoplatonic literature in relation to Christian theology. In Gnostic and Neoplatonist literature, for example, a female presence mediates the philosophical triad. In Christian theology, a neutered Holy Spirit mediates the Trinity. Scholars continue to debate the possible connections between the literature of the church fathers and that of Gnosticism. One analogue that can be documented, when it comes to Christianity, is that between Christ and Sophia. Other scholars associate Mary, mother of Christ, with goddess prototypes.

Chapter 10 describes the use of allegory in medieval literature where the enduring presence of the prototypes discussed earlier reappears. Although goddesses were expunged from all Christian settings, medieval allegorists recreate them in the form of "Natura" and "Sophia." Artemis, goddess of the wild, the fertile earth mother Gaia, the progenic fertility of Hera and Rhea, the dark fecundity of Nyx, all contribute to the persona of the goddess Natura. This literature is an exemplary demonstration of how the idea of nature, associated with matter, motion, and change, devalued by religion and philosophy in favor of the spiritual and transcendent, plays a role in allegories of world creation. Female divinities are associated with nature and the material world while male divinities are the purveyors of form and ideas. Sophia, also discussed in Chapter 10 and who appeared in the wisdom literature of Ancient Judaism, Hellenistic

Platonism, Neoplatonism, Gnosticism, Orthodox, and Esoteric Christianity, is particularly prevalent in medieval allegory. This prototype has been a persistent perennial interest of theological and rhetorical history up to the present day. She has inspired architecture, as in the famous church of Hagia Sophia, and featured in Jakob Böhme's sixteenth-century German Christian mysticism and Russian sophrology. Sophia is among us even today, given adulation by modern neopaganism and new age spiritual movements that seek a female deity.

Chapter 11 considers the ways in which goddess mythology has been received in the twentieth and twenty-first centuries. This chapter, in many ways, is the culmination of the central thesis of *Goddesses of Myth and Cultural Memory*: historicity is important as the diachronic sequence has shown but critical attention must be paid to thematic "cultural memory" as well. Much of the contemporary reception of goddess mythology continues to promulgate gender binaries along the same lines as it did in the past. The ancient associations of gender with nature and movement and fertility and change, etc., appear, as an "unknown known," in contemporary literature. Jung's anima and animus, for example, specifically incorporate goddesses, while other psychoanalysts and feminist philosophers employ the same binary oppositions of gender that featured in the many instances discussed in earlier chapters here. The French philosopher Julia Kristeva is an example. She assumes that the female gender is associated with semiotic, indeterminate, and changeable poetic language, while the male is associated with "phallo-logo-centric" and fixed symbolic language. She attempts to reverse the valuation, but still preserves the persistent myth that supports it, assuming the premise that these categories are associated with gender. Feminist epistemology in its earliest forms deployed gender essentialist prototype, implicating Plato, Aristotle, and Descartes as unjustly valuing male "logocentric" forms of knowing. The assumption of an unquestioned association of the feminine with nature, as well, has fostered an earlier phase of ecofeminism, even using goddesses as exemplars in promoting this association. Cultural memory even when operating as an unknown, then, influences the reception of previous cultural artifacts. In the final chapter (12), the history of goddesses is summed up emphasizing the divergent meanings they represented to different interpretive communities. Goddesses became placeholders for the highest philosophical truths or examples of shameful behavior; mother of the gods or counters to hegemony of male divinity, etc., but all the while retained the attributes of indeterminacy, closeness to nature, and maternal fecundity. This final chapter again reiterates the importance of cultural memory and ends with a mention of the collusion of political motivation with goddess scholarship.

The Myth of Binary Opposition According to Gender

In Assmann's words, "The past is not a natural growth but a cultural construction."[55] The diachronic sequence that has been presented here illustrates the capability of historiography to identify supervening themes over long time spans. My hope is that this narrative will increase the readers appreciation for the fact that a critical examination of source material can cast light on our present unexamined assumptions.

Daniel Chandler, a semiotician, claims, "It is a feature of culture that binary oppositions come to seem natural to members of a culture, even if some of them may be regarded as 'false dichotomies.'"[56] Gender dualism is a binary opposition that seems to be all but impossible to dislodge from Western rhetoric. It features in late antique Platonism and is found throughout Gnostic literature, Neoplatonism, and medieval and later literature. Influenced as they were by the Pythagorean table of opposites and the gender attributions of epic poetry, the close relationship between dualism in philosophy was seen to fuse, in the minds of the philosophers of Late Antiquity with the binary oppositions of gender. When the gods and goddesses are made to function as actors in philosophical scheme, these oppositions are crucial to their roles. Platonist and Neopythagorean esoteric philosophical texts may seem an obscure area of interest only to scholars but, in fact, these texts have influenced the entire history of philosophy as well as other related scholarship. In them, the traits associated with female gender are the ones that are devalued in the hierarchy of being. The male gender is associated with light, permanency, intellect, and aloof and exempt unity, and the female with darkness, reproductive fecundity, change, and motion. The less valued, but necessary, traits of movement and change entail discontinuity, disunity, and are associated with nature; the eternal, unmoving, unmixed principle area a higher more valued reality. This opposition has left an indelible mark on the history of idea. One of the claims, then, of *Goddesses in Myth and Cultural Memory* is that we need to understand that mythology persists and continues its long life, in many contemporary settings, precisely along the same lines as it did in the texts of its ancient predecessors.

The Power of Goddesses

One thing that working on this project has made me aware of is how meanings are always mediated. Searching for an originary moment for any given historical theme or truth may not be possible. In the area of studies of classical reception, one must avoid the slippery slope of projecting anachronist meanings onto historical facts. The question that always stays with anyone doing this type of research is what an historical fact is and when it is important to respect the "truths" of a particular interpretive community which brings its own unique horizon. Jan Assmann's concept of "cultural memory" helps to mitigate this dilemma. While the parameters of the resume of each goddess were established in the epic poetry and hymns of early periods, and while these accounts themselves drew upon near Eastern sources, her continued survival was the result of re-appropriation by means of literary, allegorical, and symbolic interpretation. Following the goddess, then, through all her textual and iconic incarnations documents the remarkable fact that ancient mythology has survived the centuries. Tracking the ever-changing contexts within which goddesses appear and reappear demonstrates that certain root prototypes have an enduring life. The goddesses that disappear in their original forms reappear in strange and esoteric ways, changing form with ever-new engines of interpretation. When goddesses disappear entirely, that is a commentary, too, on the culture from which female deity is absented. Anthropomorphizing God is long out of the picture, yet the Judeo-Christian God is still referred to as male. Monotheism may avoid attributing physical characteristics to the deity, but no such restrictions seem to apply to gender.

It is important to avoid motives that are political or ideological. The power of the goddess as an abiding icon documents the recurring presence of gender essentialism but also some glaring misappropriations in the interpretation of goddess history. Although *Goddesses in Myth and Cultural Memory* is primarily a history of how ancient sources of goddess mythology have affected later texts, it also explores some of the "distortions" of this history that seem to persist. Lucy Goodison and Christine Morris, for example, in their book *Ancient Goddesses*, dedicated to some of the findings and essays of archeologists, soberly assess the claims of the so-called goddess movement, which was started by the archeologist Marija Gimbutas.[57] Goodison and Morris characterize the main themes of this movement, based on female figurines unearthed throughout the cities of the ancient world, as "a central hypothesis" that there was a peaceful, goddess-centered culture which existed in the distant past in many places, especially in ancient Europe, Greece, Malta, Egypt, and the Near East. Priestesses officiated and the goddess was ostensibly the primary ruling deity. This matriarchal culture was allegedly taken over by warlike Indo-European males in around 3000 BCE. Goodison and Morris give a complete review of this literature and contend that it is the feminist quest for "reshaping and transforming symbols of divinity which validate women's experience" that has fueled this movement.[58] In a later article Goodison and Morris state that "Gimbutas' work has promoted a moral fable in which humanity deteriorated from the innocence and peace of the Neolithic, a utopian society paralleling the Biblical Garden of Eden, except that the original sin now lay with men, who spoilt the party."[59] They point out that terms like "Mother Goddess" and "Great Goddess" have been used without question while in fact these were polytheistic cultures. Great Goddess interpretations have come to be rejected by most scholars.[60] Brooke Holmes provides a detailed account of this shibboleth including a discussion of the new archeological data which has debunked the original interpretations supporting this narrative.[61] Helen Foley, in her *The Homeric Hymn to Demeter*, also discusses so-called spiritual feminists who are interested in drawing on pagan traditions to (re)create a more female-centered religion.[62] They have been particularly attracted to the *Hymn to Demeter*. Furthermore, contemporary goddess revivalists have created rituals of passage and transformation, in attempts to make goddesses "live" again in a new milieu based on characteristics that accrue to a fertile, mothering, earth-centered, female presence. This too is not "new." Helena Blavatsky called upon Isis, in her book *Isis Unveiled*, in her addresses to the theosophists of the nineteenth century, in an attempt to repackage pagan spirituality as ancient wisdom.

John Deely's claim that "At the heart of semiosis is the realization that the whole of human experience, without exception, is an interpretive structure mediated and sustained by signs" is certainly borne out by the history of the goddess in text.[63] Berecynthia, thrown to the ground by a bishop in the second century, was only made of marble or clay. The goddesses of literature have been far more durable. Goddess worship as it was practiced in archaic antiquity is unknown to us and will forever remain so. Lost in the mists of history, she can never reappear, nor will her true and original devotees. Whether a goddess was ever a principal deity in the minds of early religious devotees is unproven. Objects do not speak and cannot explain themselves. Ancient literature will never repossess the meanings to which its intended readers subscribed, and archeology does not provide answers about social context. Texts, on the other hand, can be interpreted, but interpretation is already itself allegory. Examining the many transformations of goddess lore helps us to understand the limitations of our own contemporary discourse and to formulate questions pertinent to our own time. Why has the memory of female deities persisted and/or disappeared depending on cultural context? What is the impact of geopolitics and rhetoric on the interpreting of ancient texts? What are the myths of our own time regarding deity and gender? What distortions in our own historiographic approach to ancient artifacts and texts need to be brought to scholarly attention? Finally, what is the mysterious power possessed by ancient myth that allows it to prevail even in face of all attempts to devalue it as improper scholarly discourse?

2

Goddess Prototypes: The Classical Literature

The sets of descriptions of the gods and goddesses found in Homer, Hesiod, the Homeric hymns, Callimachus, the Orphic hymns, and the various types of Orphic documents are the originating sources for an enormous body of subsequent literature. It is to this literature we must look to competently understand the basis for the "cultural memories" that have persisted. They are the product of a very specific time and place. As Strauss-Clay reminds us, "The Olympus of Hesiod and Homeric poetry is a Pan-Hellenic construct that elevates the gods beyond their local attributes. The evolution of most major gods from most major cities into the integrated family at Olympus amounts to a synthesis that is not just artistic but political in nature, comparable with the evolution of the Pan-Hellenic games known as the Olympics."[1] She tells us that the Panhellenic Olympian religion that swept through the Aegean region around the eighth century BCE radically changed the culture of Greece. This phenomenon resulted in the great shrines at Olympia, Delphi, Delos, and Eleusis, and the great Panhellenic epics of Homer and Hesiod. These events facilitated the subsequent reinvention of the goddesses of the polis, of ritual, and of votive offerings. Once objects of worship at local sites over which goddesses presided, they became widely known through the "great stories" told at Panhellenic festivals and other means of transmission. The epic poetry of Hesiod, Homer, and the Homeric hymns invoked universally recognizable figures who could have widespread appeal. Formerly each goddess held a singular identity and a set of characteristics consisting of regionally specific traits. In the epic poem, although each goddess still possessed a distinct prototype, she was encapsulated within a taxonomy structured as a genealogical series. This prototype became formulaic and set for all time, a fact supported by the similar descriptions appearing in the Homeric and Orphic hymns, as well as later in those of Callimachus and the playwrights, and many other antique sources. The epic, in particular, embeds the goddesses within a text that held her unique résumé but delineated her relation to other deities in carefully crafted narratives.

In the Hesiodic epic, Homeric hymn, and Homer's *Odyssey* and *Iliad*, the stories told of the gods and goddesses are intertwined. The "pantheon" holds a conceptual unity wherein the identities of individual deities are crafted within a genealogical series, a history that is one of a family tree. The individual identities form a "set" of deities, a "henotheism," in terms of a single bigger picture, which encapsulates them within a shared narrative. ("Henotheism" derives from the Greek "*kath' hena theon*" meaning "according to one divinity.") The distinct prototypes that emerge from this literature are descriptions and epithets that have stood the test of time. A goddess of wisdom and war, of the crossroads, the goddess as carrying a torch, covered by a veil or robe, a goddess who is a mistress of the wild, a goddess of love and erotic attraction, etc.—all are featured in this literature. One dominant prototype, directly established within the context of genealogy, is the goddess related to fertility and motherhood. While each named goddess of the epic poem or early hymn is associated with a specific set of attributes, fertility, nurturing, and virginity apply to several. Artemis is attached to the activities that have to do with the wild, hunting, and animals; Athena with wisdom and war; Hekate with the crossroads and the torch; and so on. Many of these characteristics are precursors to the decontextualized goddess figure of later history. Artemis's affinity to nature, for example, Gaia and Rhea's fertility, Persephone's relation to death and the seasonal return of life, all contribute to time-honored associations of the female deity with nature. Virginal, sexually active, and/or generative, she enduringly possesses traits connected to reproductive fecundity or erotic desire, as well, facilitating her role in later philosophical texts to perform a philosophical function as an assistant in the creation of the natural world.[2] Many of the identifying markers or rubrics that are attached to the formulaic sets of characteristics of the epic or hymn, in later chapters here, will be shown to contribute to the "memory" of these goddesses as they are transformed by later literature.

Not only particular functions, but also associated paraphernalia become part of the cultural memories of goddesses. A description of the Panathenaea festival in the *Iliad* (6.288-304), for example, describes the ritual whereby a priestess of Athena places a robe (*peplos*) at the knees of the goddess statue to petition her to save the city from harm.[3] Boethius (d. 584 CE) describes the robe of his "lady philosophy" which helps to connect her to the goddess Athena. As late as the nineteenth century, Isis's robe or veil appears in images of nature as concealed and in need of uncovering. Hekate's threefold persona can be found in the lasting association with triplicity in formulations such as the "maidenly" triad of the later Neoplatonists. The light-bearing function of many of the goddesses who bear torches creates a template for a wise goddess who provides spiritual guidance and enlightenment. Athena is a prototype for the female personification of wisdom found in a long progression of images in the cultural memory of the West. Although she is mostly mentioned as a leader of armies in Hesiod (Th. 925, for example) as Helleman points out, "Wisdom is one of the oldest personifications ... on the basis of allegorical exegesis of Homeric Athena."[4] Both Stoics and Platonists have based this personification on Athena.[5] The goddesses associated with earth mother, nature, and fertility in the contemporary popular "goddess movement" are a composite of several of these original types. The goddess as an icon of reproductive creation, or as wearing the robe that conceals the secrets of nature, or as a savior (particularly as related to the cult of Isis), and many other future appropriations of these mythical templates will appear in the extensive rhetorical use of goddess figures in later settings.

Gaia

In Hesiod's *Theogony* Gaia, whose name means earth, mysteriously emerges into being after her immediate predecessor, Chaos. Known for her reproductive fecundity, she is an ancient prototype for the clichéd expression "earth mother." A fertile goddess and the earth as the productive seat of growing vegetation are roughly analogous. Gaia mates with Ouranos (*Theogony* 130.3), whose name means the heavens. This originary pairing entails a binary composed of a lofty heaven associated with male gender and a lower earthly strata of existence associated with female gender. Earth and heaven as a dichotomy are found in the gold tablets from Crete and in the Baal (Ugarit) cycle (*arz zu shmin*), as well as in many other theogonies cross-culturally.[6] Interestingly, Plato is aware of the arbitrariness of this association, finding a more organic connection in the following etymological analysis: "The word *gê* (earth) shows the meaning better in the form *gaia*, for *gaia* is a correct word for 'mother', as Homer says, for he uses *gegaasin* to mean *gegenêsthai* (be born)" (*Crat.* 410B8-C4). Vernant describes Gaia as related to the "chthonic" (subterranean) deities and the earth qua geological entity:

> Gaia is a solid base that can be walked on, a firm support that can be leaned on; she has full, dense forms, mountain heights and subterranean depths. She is not only the floor upon which the edifice of the world is to be constructed, she is the mother, the ancestor who brought to birth all that exists in every form and in every place—with the sole exception of Chaos himself and his descendants who constitute a family of Powers, entirely separate from all others.[7]

In Hesiod's account, "Chaos was born first and after it came Gaia, the broad-breasted (*Gaia eurusternos*), the firm seat of all" (*Th.* 116).[8] The concept of an original source deity, notably, is not heaven and not the sea, but, of the three stipulated regions, the earth itself. In the canonical Greek myth, Gaia (earth) is the primogenitor of all the creatures that follow. She is preceded only by Chaos. At the same time, Eros also came into being. Vernant explains that Chaos, Earth, and Love constitute a triad of powers that precedes the entire cosmogonic organization. As she emerges from Chaos, Gaia produces the universe, first giving birth to the starry Ouranos (Sky); making him equal to herself. He, in turn, covers and envelops her on all sides. Gaia, mother of all the generations of gods, of monsters, and of created nature, is a complex character. She is capable of cosmic giving and cosmic betraying, producer of all that is beautiful in nature and mother of several monstrosities. Of the four primal elements that emerged at the beginning of creation, Gaia takes first place to water, fire, and air. In an odd twist, Gaia is the mother of the god Ouranos, the god of the heavens, as well as his mate. Their offspring include Zeus's parents Kronos and Rhea. Ouranos and Gaia also give birth to the Titans, six male and six female in Hesiod's account. Kirk points out, "Those Titans are a mysterious group, to suggest that they were originally nature gods is almost meaningless and the truth is that we have no idea where most of them came from."[9] Gaia's union with Pontos, a sea god, produces the sea gods, and mortal creatures are produced from her earthly flesh. It is she who opposes her husband Ouranos, who had imprisoned her sons in her womb, and it is she who assists Zeus in his overthrow of the

Titan Kronos. When she opposes Zeus for binding her Titan sons in the pit of Tartarus, she does so by producing the tribe of Gigantes through a liaison with Tartarus, and later the monster Typhon to dethrone him; both fail in the attempt.

Gaia worship appears to have been universal among the Greeks; she had temples or altars at Athens, Sparta, Delphi, Olympia, Bura, Tegea, and Phlyus, among other places, as recorded by Thucydides and Pausanias.[10] Although no statues of her survive, they have been mentioned in literature. At Patrae she was represented in a sitting attitude in the temple of Demeter (Paus. vii.21 §4), and there was a Gaia statue in Athens as well (Paus. i.24 §3). Her great importance may have to do with Athanassakis and Wolkow's description of her as a "quasi personified figure of the productive powers of the land, and often of procreation in general, a generic mother goddess with affinities to Rhea, mother of the gods, and Demeter." In the Homeric *Hymn to Gaia*, she is described as giving life and taking it away (30.5-7), and in an Orphic hymn she is described in just that way: "you nourish all, you give all, you bring all to fruition, you destroy all" (*OH* 26, 3-4).[11] She is known to have helped Rhea in the matter of Kronos in the swallowing of her children (*Th.* 453-500), but helps her grandson Zeus avoid being overthrown by his child with Metis. Metis is swallowed by Zeus and Athena is later born from his head (*Th.* 890-900; 924-26).

Gaia is the source for all the "earth mother" goddess associations of ancient and modern cultural imagination. Often romanticized and associated with what is allegedly women's essence, her darker side, clearly present in Hesiod and other literature, is ignored. In the *Theogony*, Ouranos and Gaia, as Lamberton tells us, represent the antithesis of the ideal of human society ruled by *dikê* (justice).

> They represent a vision of the fundamental state of the universe as an unstable tension between male lust and jealously hoarded power on the one hand, and on the other, ultimately triumphant female rage and resentment at subjection to that lust and power—a rage that finally destroys the sexuality and by the same stroke the anthropomorphic identity of the male partner.[12]

Gaia's own victimization and revenge, Lamberton says, are cosmic in scale. "Monstrous" Earth, nevertheless, is the archetypal mother of the *Theogony*. Fertile and productive, she produces some thirty offspring, some of them vague entities: "mountains," Furies, and Giants.[13] Monstrous or not, she is the mother of all the successive generations of Titans, and then of the Olympians. It is ironic that in modern "goddess spirituality" those followers who wish the first progenitor of all to be a goddess overlook Gaia's darker side.

Hesiod's Gaia was widely known to Greek literature. She is known, for example, in the *Iliad*, in Pausanias's *Description of Greece* (I.2.6), and in other places as mother of Erichthonios, a legendary early king of Athens (*Il.* 5.124ff.). She is also said to be the mother of humankind (as in the Orphic hymns, for example *To Earth*: "Divine Earth, mother of men and of the blessed gods," *OH* 26).[14] To Aeschylus she is known as both monstrous and a beloved nurse, documenting the fact that both roles were routinely ascribed to Gaia.[15]

Nyx

Nyx is a goddess figure who also embodies a dark side of female divinity. In Hesiod's *Theogony*, Chaos gives birth to two pairs of contrary entities, infernal darkness (Erebus) and black night (Nyx). Nyx mates with her brother Erebus and they in turn produce two children—Aither (ether) and Hemere (daylight) (*Th.* 123-25; *OH* 51). Nyx, often referred to in ancient literature as dark, produces parthenogenetically, in Athanassakis and Wolkow's words, "a brood of personified abstractions."[16] "Herself born of Chaos, Nyx gives birth to odious Death, gloomy Keres, Decease" (*Th.* 212).[17] *Thanatos* (Death) was first of all the daughter of Night to the Greeks. As Lamberton tells us, Nyx's offspring (*Th.* 211-32) account for the origins of negativity, of evil, and of oblivion, as her first children, Death, Sleep, and Dreams, are associated with the Fates and various manifestations of doom.[18] Nyx appears in Homer's *Iliad*, intervening in a scene where she averts Zeus's anger at Okeanos for putting Zeus to sleep against his will, and is described as having power over immortals and mortals and as one whom Zeus is hesitant to displease (*Il.* 14.256-61). Athanassakis and Wolkow suggest that this shows that Homer considered her to be a powerful figure. One of her female offspring, Eris (Strife), parthenogenetically produces a string of human ills: labor, famine, suffering, battles, murder, carnage, and lawlessness. In the Orphic theogonies, she is considered among the earliest divinities, and she gives Zeus oracular advice on how to reconstitute the world (Orphic fragment 241). She appears in Orphic rhapsodies, in one of which, as Protogonos' lover, she gives birth to Sky and Earth (Orphic fragment 149). Athanassakis and Wolkow mention that there are very few instances of cultic worship, one of which is Pausanias's mention of an oracle of Night on the acropolis of Megar, along with a temple to Dionysos, Zeus, and Aphrodite (*OH* 1.40.6).[19]

References to Nyx are quite numerous, particularly in the playwrights, where she is often mentioned in dark terms as black-winged (e.g., Aristophanes *Birds* 685ff.). Hesiod gives legend to this dark history, describing her as holding residence in the darkness of Hades (*Th.* 748). The primordial mother Nyx can be contrasted with the classical persona of Athena, sprung adult and fully armed from the forehead of Zeus and a symbol of intelligence, protection, and innovation. "Obscure, dark Night," as Liz Locke puts it in a somewhat Heideggerian interpretation, "hides something inside herself, something unrelentingly generative, the capacity to bestow both necessary powers of differentiation and the death sentence of Being-in-Time." Nyx contains within herself "the embodied world of changeable multiplicity, unfathomable, unknowable and so unknown."[20]

Rhea and Hera

Rhea, daughter of Gaia and mother of the Olympian gods in Homer, "lovely-haired Rhea" of Hesiod's *Theogony* (625, 633), is she who "succumbed to Kronos's love and bore him illustrious children" (Hestia, Aides, Demeter, Poseidon, Hera, and Zeus) (*Th.* 453). She is a Titan and both wife and sister of Kronos. Most notably, Rhea is Zeus's mother (*Th.* 453). In the *Theogony,* famously, she deceives Kronos, who has swallowed all her other children, by feeding him a stone, thus ensuring Zeus's safe childhood and the eventual dominance of the Olympian pantheon. She is later identified with Demeter, Kybele, and with the Mother of the Gods in Orphic hymn 14 and in Apollonius of Rhodes's *Argonautica* (first half of the third century BCE), where Rhea and the Phrygian Kybele are fused. Rhea, like her mother Gaia, was very much present and honored in relation to the eventual domination of Zeus over the other gods. Munn suggests that these matriarchs are the foundation of his sovereignty.[21] In the Homeric *Hymn to Demeter*, Rhea helps to reconcile her daughter Demeter to her place in Zeus's regime.

Rhea seems to be the singular source for the later "mother of the gods," Kybele, though, as M. L. West points out, the term "mother of the gods" or "great mother" appears in Akkadian Ugarit, Nabataean, and Carthaginian texts.[22] As Athanassakis and Wolkow point out, this was one of many equivalences that were made between a Greek goddess of fertility and the Phrygian goddess. In Orphic thought, they further point out, and as the Derveni papyrus documents in its quote from an early Orphic poem (Orphic fragment 87), Rhea changes herself into a snake to escape the advances of her son, which leads to the birth of Persephone. It is interesting to note that identifications between goddesses were made early. Here is a blending of Demeter, Persephone's traditional mother, and Rhea. The author of the Derveni papyrus quotes the following from a poem he attributes to Orpheus, "Earth, Meter, Rhea, Hera, Demeter, Hestia, and eio," suggesting a blending of identities. Rhea accrued more prominence when she was identified with Kybele, the great Phrygian mountain "mother of the gods" also known as Mother (*meter*).[23] Euripides associates Rhea with ecstatic elements related to Kybele's cult, the chorus of Bacchantes. The Phrygian drum of Rhea is mentioned in *Bacchae* by the chorus (58-59) for example.[24]

"Queenly Hera, the lady of Argos who walks with golden sandals," (*Th.* 11-12) is the wife and one of the three sisters of Zeus in the Olympian pantheon. Daughter of the Titans Rhea and Cronos, Hera's name is sometimes considered to derive from the Greek *hora* (season), though in Plutarch's *Isis and Osiris* the name is associated with air, reflecting another tradition. Hera is the goddess of women and marriage whose Roman counterpart is Juno, and she is identified with a number of mother goddesses along with Hestia in an Orphic verse cited in the Derveni papyrus. Hera is jealous and vengeful in Hesiod's and other accounts. It is notable, then, as with Gaia, that the generic "mother goddess" of popular lore today has only positive traits. Hera has a child parthenogenetically, Typhon, who represents all manner of destructive forces and is the enemy of Zeus. Homer mentions Hera's role with Athena and Poseidon in their attempted coup against Zeus (*Il.* 1.396-406).[25] In the Homeric *Hymn to Delian Apollo*, she detains Eileithyia, the goddess who assists in child-bearing, to prevent Leto from giving birth to Artemis and Apollo since Zeus, her consort, is their father. She wrathfully pursues Herakles and Dionysos, unleashing her fury on Zeus's lovers and illegitimate children. In the Orphic myth of Dionysos' death, Hera spurs on the Titans to kill the child (*OH* 37).[26]

The earliest known sanctuary to Hera, later replaced by the Heraion, is considered to date back to 800 BCE and is located in Samos. There was also a Heraion in Argos, dating from the eighth century BCE but destroyed by fire and replaced in 425 BCE. Apparently, Polykleitos's huge bronze statue of Hera was in the center of this sanctuary. Samos stood between the Mycenaean city-states of Argos and Mycenae. Sanctuaries dedicated to Hera had widespread presence in many areas of the ancient world. The shrine at Samos is mentioned by Apuleius, Strabo, and Pausanias, and the one in Plataia by Herodotus and Pausanias.[27] Hera's name appears with Zeus and Hermes in a Linear B inscription (*Tn* 316), attesting to the ancient omnipresence of Hera and her existence preceding Hesiod's poem.[28] The *Iliad* (4.50-54) describes her as "the ox-eyed queen of Heaven who loves the cities of Mycenae, Argos and Sparta," but tells Zeus that he may sack them though she will not be stopped in her intent to destroy Troy. In *Iliad* (5.711ff.), Hera "of the white arms" appeals to Athena in an attempt to support the Greeks in battle, and in *Iliad* (14.213-15.5) she seduces Zeus with the help of Aphrodite for a similar purpose. Plato uses this scenario in *Republic* (390B) as an example of how epic poetry portrays the gods in a shameful manner. The association with cattle, the Homeric epithet "cow-eyed" (*boôris*), is reminiscent of Hathor, the Egyptian goddess of motherhood and feminine love. Hera is sometimes associated with virginity as well. In Pausanias, for example, who wrote historical accounts of Greece in 110-180 CE, Hera revives her virginity annually, in rites that were unspoken (*arrhêton*) (Paus. 2.38.2-3). According to Burkert, Hera is everywhere worshiped as a goddess of weddings and marriage. In the wedding month Gamelion, sacrifices were made to her and Zeus, and in Olympia women celebrated a Hera festival every four years where she was presented with a newly woven robe (*peplos*).[29]

Joan O'Brien's book *The Transformation of Hera* sees the Hera at the shrines of Samos and Argos as related to the trifunctional Mycenaean Hera (renewer of life, protector of the citadel, and goddess of war),[30] and makes a case for the cultic myths and rites associated with both sites having Mycenaean antecedents going back to the Bronze Age iconography of a *potnia thêrôn*, a goddess accompanied by animals. O'Brien speculates that the enlargement of the shrine in the seventh century marked the assimilation of the local Hera cult to the Panhellenic Olympian religion. There is no connection with Zeus documented before the seventh century: she transforms from a fertility goddess pre-600 to wife and sister of Zeus post-600.[31] Ingrid Holmberg, in a review of O'Brien's thesis, remains skeptical of this as the evidence comes from much later authors such as Athenaeus and Pausanias. Certainly if such a thesis could be upheld, it would document the shift from cultic, votive worship of goddesses such as Hera after the impact of epic poets.[32] I think that this would be difficult to decide definitively but the general idea that ritual practice, statues, and shrines could be influenced by the epic poets' view of the deity in question is an interesting speculation. The widespread use of epic narratives in vase painting documents its influence on the culture at large. Holmberg suggests that O'Brien's most interesting interpretations concern the relationship between Hera, the season goddesses, and heroes. Hera, hero, and Horai (goddesses of the seasons) apparently have a common etymological Indo-European root of *ier, "year, spring." Hera thus means "of the year, spring" and hero "he who belongs to the goddess of the seasons." Hera controls or tames the seasons in their cycle as well as controlling the seasonal nature of the Greek hero through death, or less frequently, marriage. The paradigmatic example of a hero controlled by Hera is Herakles, whose birth and death are connected to her.[33] Hera, interestingly, in the Orphic hymn dedicated to her, is closely identified with the air and life-bringing rains. Plato etymologically relates her name and the word for air in *Cratylus* (404C), as do the Stoics.[34]

Rhea's identification with Kybele, the great Phrygian mountain mother of the gods, the equation in the Orphic hymns of Gaia and the Eleusinian Demeter (*OH* 40), the overlaps between Demeter and Rhea and the mother of the gods (*OH* 29, 27) and Earth (*OH* 26) are a few among many examples of how goddesses' names became fused in later accounts. In the second-century *Chaldean Oracles*, for example, Hekate is an aid in the transmission of noetic "life-giving substances," but the *Oracles* use the name Rhea to mean Hekate. "Rhea truly is the font and stream of the blessed noetic [substances]/ For she is the First of all power and having received in her marvelous womb/ She pours forth a whirling generation upon All" (fr. 56).[35] Johnston points out that Rhea means Hekate here, a view shared by Hans Lewy, who supports the idea that divinities of diverse systems were affiliated with one another.[36]

Athena: Goddess of Wisdom and War

The goddess prototype that survives the centuries transmutes with changing geopolitical and literary priorities, and does not fit the "earth mother" image is Athena, the most famous of all, the goddess of wisdom and war. She is the child of Zeus, who, after swallowing Metis, who was pregnant with her, and without recourse to any womb of his own, conceived Athena in his head, from which she sprung fully formed and armed after a blow from the liberating ax of Hephaestus. She is celebrated in a Homeric hymn (28) and Pindar's *Olympian Odes* (753-44), and the scenario is often depicted in vase painting.

> Then from his head he himself bore gray-eyed Athena,
> weariless leader of armies, dreaded and mighty goddess,
> who stirs men to battle and is thrilled by the clash of arms. (*Th*. 920-25)[37]

Athena is depicted in iconography as wearing a helmet and carrying a shield and at the same time showing evidence of her contemplative nature. She is the supreme virgin goddess, the Parthenos, and she presides over the *polis* of Athens. In the mythological tradition, she is known for her sagacity in war, her protection and instruction of artisans, her uncompromising virginity, and her general wisdom in all things. When it comes to archeological finds, Voyatzis finds diversity and differentiation in various regions and types, rather than consistent prototypes.[38] Athena's name appears in the Linear B tablets and many believe that she began as a Bronze Age goddess derived from the Minoan goddess with snakes, and later became associated with the Mycenaean palaces. Her function as protectress of the *polis* may be seen, Voyatzis suggests, as an extension of her Bronze Age function as protectress of the household. There is no evidence that she was armed in Minoan art, but the existence of an armed goddess in the Mycenaean period is possible, according to several scholars. A late sixth-century bronze figure of an armed Athena reflects the more traditional depiction of a warrior goddess.[39] Some argue she is an ancient indigenous goddess connected with weaving whom the Indo-European Greek-speaking peoples encountered when they came into the Greek peninsula. Her name came into prominence during the Mycenaean period in Athens. During the Panhellenic period, Athena's role as armed protectress of the city trumped her role as goddess of crafts, technology, wisdom, and fertility. In Athens her "masculine" traits are more dominant than the evidence from some sites, such as Tegea and Gortyn on Crete, indicates. There her role as fertility goddess and mistress of animals is more apparent and perhaps important to her female worshipers. Voyatzis suggests that a male image of the goddess was deliberately expressed in the sculptural program of the Parthenon in order to justify having a female as Athens's paramount deity, but perhaps this is an anachronistic idea.

Athena is a powerful female deity. Presiding over wars she is a challenge to any anachronistic reading of ancient epic poetry as strictly bifurcating male and female functions along traditional gender lines. Athena possesses powers that are not often attached to female divinity after the Roman Minerva, who absorbs her identity. Ares and Athena are the two divinities in Greece who rule over matters of war. Ares rapes and impregnates while Athena is endowed with *metis* (wisdom/cunning). Ares is hated by all the gods while Athena is admired. In the *Iliad*, Ares always loses in war while Athena wins and imposes her will in confrontation with Ares.[40] As the great goddess of the polis, she masters Ares, the raw force of war, and is political and industrious, a prototype of "just war." She rules over war to the extent that war is a function of the city as a whole, even helping in its defense by putting the technical skill of blacksmiths at the disposal of hoplite war. At the center of her shield is the hideous head of the dead Gorgon to petrify for all eternity anyone who dares look upon it. The aegis (a shield or breastplate connected with Athena and Zeus) guarantees Zeus' victory over the rebellious giants. She tames the forces of Ares and subdues the savage energies in the orbit of Poseidon. It is to be noted that in the frieze of the Siphnian Treasury (pre-525 BCE), Athena is depicted in the course of the battle of the gods with the giants.[41] Athena spears a giant who collapses onto his knees (Artemis and Hera are also involved in this battle and are depicted in these friezes). Athena's warlike nature is tempered by her wisdom, and this idea carried through to first-century CE literature where Heraclitus, a first-century philosopher whose epistles are considered early examples of Cynic philosophy, discusses Athena in relation to her contretemps with Ares. Ares and Athena are described by Homer, then, as respectively foolish and irrational versus intelligent and wise. Athena beats Ares, sending him sprawling to the ground (*Il.* 21.403-10).[42] Ares is "raving, a total evil, unpredictable" (*Il.* 5.831) while she is "famous among the gods for wisdom and shrewdness" (*Od.* 13.298-99).

Athena is one of the most often celebrated cult figures. She vied with Poseidon for the title of chief divinity of the *polis* later called Athens. Poseidon caused a salt spring to gush forth on the acropolis while Athena planted an olive tree and won.[43] The great festival in Athens, the Panathenaea, was celebrated every year in her honor. It is interesting that, at least in the Orphic *Hymn to Athene* (*OH* 26), she is called "male and female," "shrewd begetter of war." Athanassakis and Wolkow also mention that in Callimachus ("The Bath of Pallas," *Hymn* 5) she is one among a number of gods and goddesses who are addressed as androgynous, including Artemis and Dionysos.[44] Athena's reputation and fame survive the centuries. Proclus, the Neoplatonist who headed the Athenian school in the late fifth century CE, revered her and will serve here, in a later chapter, to illustrate how this myth takes on an elevated importance for the philosophical priorities of later Neoplatonism. Proclus comments on Athena's powers in his *Commentary on Timaeus* (*Tim.* 24D and 24B7-C3):

> they call her (Athena) **wisdom-loving** (*philosophos*), and **war-loving** (*philopolemos*). For she who embraces all the Father's wisdom is **wisdom-loving**, while she who has uniform authority over all rivalry could with good reason be called war-loving.
>
> (*In Tim.* I.166.17-21, trans. Harold Tarrant)

For Proclus, Athena possesses both creative intelligence and providential care, ruling over the polis and the universe by these powers (I.150.16-18). Proclus illustrates how the later Platonist philosophers construed a mythological character as a symbol. Athena's shield represents the invincible and unswerving character of reason, her spear cuts through matter and rids souls of demonic or fate-associated affections. Athena's wisdom, Proclus asserts, is displayed by her choice of Athens as the location for a polis that could produce mortal souls that resemble her (Plato *Tim.* 24C7-D3). When Proclus comments on Plato's *Timaeus* 24C4-5, he lauds Athena for imposing many structures (cosmos, learning geometry, astronomy, arithmetic, medicine, etc.) holding together the universe with proportion and with harmonious binding. Athenaic providence reigns supreme over the whole arrangement (*In Tim.* I.160.12-15).[45]

The military class of *Republic*, for Proclus, exemplifies the warlike nature of Athena. In the hierarchy of souls and their types (hieratic, guardians, military, hunters, etc.), they are led by their protector gods. Athena's warlike nature has, then, a cosmic function (*In Tim.* I.168.14-15). Like other Neoplatonists of late antiquity, Proclus finds metaphysical analogues for the functions of this revered goddess. An invincible and unyielding goddess, she "has uniform authority over all rivalry" (*In Tim.* I.168.1-2). She "manages the opposing columns in the All and presides over war in its totality, sets the whole of destiny in motion" (I.169.6-7). She bestows the gift of unity at the lowest of levels, wresting unity out of chaos, surrendering the Titanic to the Olympian, making that which is different similar. Proclus reminds the reader that one example is the dominance of mathematics over the physical world.

Athena is the patron of artisans as well, as the following descriptions, compiled by Nicole Loraux, demonstrate.[46] During the firing of a pot, the potter addresses his prayers to Athena, asking her to spread her hand over the kiln. A Corinthian table represents her in the form of a large owl perched on top of a potter's kiln, facing a phallic dwarf, the bearer of the evil eye. She presides especially over woodworking. Woodcutters, carpenters, chariot-builders, and shipbuilders require her protection. Hesiod in *Works and Days* attributes to the "servant of Athena" the capacity of attaching a piece of curved wood to the stock and fitting it to the shaft of a plow to make the plowman's tool (*WD* 430ff.). In the *Iliad* Athena states that "it is *metis* and not force that makes a good woodcutter" (*Il.* 15.412). The art of driving chariots and piloting ships also belongs to her, as does that of the artisans who work with wool and fabrics. She presides over and excels in spinning, weaving, and tapestry, making her own beautiful cloak and that of Hera.

In Greek drama, Athena assumes a role, as she did in the *Iliad*, of intervening in the affairs of humankind. She materializes suddenly in Euripides' *Iphigenia among the Taurians* (c. 413 BCE). Iphigenia, Orestes, and Pylades are trying to escape the land of the Taurians when adverse winds drive their ship close to the rocks. Athena intervenes and saves them. She implores the king of the Taurians to allow Orestes to carry the statue of Artemis to Athens as he intended. In *Ajax,* Sophocles' Athena advocates the Greek cause and is special protector of Odysseus against Ajax. In Euripides' *Trojan Women*, anger causes Athena to turn against the Greeks in the name of justice.[47] Athena is represented in Aeschylus's *Eumenides* as presiding over the trial of Orestes for the murder of his mother Clytemnestra (for killing Agamemnon because he sacrificed their daughter). Orestes, who has had a fear-filled escape from the Furies, appeals to Athena who intervenes and suggests the trial; then, as judge, she sides with Orestes. This may reflect the fact that she was born from her father Zeus and takes the "male" side of the conflict.

The most well-known and abiding characteristic of Athena is wisdom. This quality will take on an enormous future role in associating wisdom to goddesses. The ever-present Sophia appears in innumerable contexts in later literature. There is, however, another accessory characteristic of Athena that seems to take hold as a paradigmatic trait of goddesses in future contexts, and that is her *chiton* or *peplos* (a covering garment). The "veiled" goddess is one of the most widespread and persistent images of female deity. In the *Iliad* (14.166-68), Hera retires to a secret chamber and dresses herself in the garment which Athena made for her: "Then with a *krêdemnon* the bright goddess covered herself from the head down, a beautiful one, newly made: it was bright like the sun." Nagler focuses on the polarity of chastity and seduction and the metaphorical and literal use of the word *krêdemnon* as veil and as battlement and seal in Homer.[48]

The relation of the peplos to the imagery of the veiled goddess is documented by the aretalogies discovered in Egypt (reported by Plutarch). The phrase that appears is the well-known "I am all that is and that will be no one yet has lifted my veil." It alludes to the hidden and cryptic nature of the goddess and the ignorance of mortals as to her secrets. The veiled goddess imagery persists and gathers philosophical momentum with later philosophers. A second-century example of this is in Plutarch, who combines traits of earlier goddesses in the paradigmatic goddess of his time, Isis:

> As for the robes (*stolai*) those of Isis are variegated in their colors; for her power is concerned with matter which becomes everything and receives everything, light and darkness, day and night, fire and water, life and death, beginning and end. But the robe of Osiris has no shading or variety in its color, but only one single color like to light.
>
> (*De Iside* 382c-d)

Pierre Hadot, in his book *The Veil of Isis*, discussed here in Chapter 10, documents the persistence of the figure of Nature as a hidden cryptic essence that must remain "veiled" in order to protect the truths of the divine reality at its core. Athena, known for her peplum or chiton, and the later depictions of Isis and the forbidden lifting of her veil continue to feature in allegories of the unveiling of nature, as late as the seventeenth and eighteenth centuries.

Hekate

The earliest evidence for the cult of Hekate is a sixth-century BCE inscription on an altar in the temple of Apollo Delphinios at Miletus, where Hekate appeared with Apollo as the protector of entrances. She retained this role in the fifth-century triple statue of her as Hekate-Epipyrgidia near the entrance to the Athenian Acropolis on the site of the later temple of Nike (Pausanias 2.30.2), which has now been found in the agora.[49] The earliest known representation of Hekate depicts the goddess in single form. A terracotta statute from sixth-century Athens shows Hekate seated stiffly on a throne, wearing a long gown and headpiece.[50] The Hekate hymn in *Theogony* is located, as Lamberton points out, at the end of the rich proliferation of Titanic offspring, just before the children of Kronos and Rhea, the Olympians of the older generation.[51] Warr, in his 1895 essay "The Hesiodic Hekate," claims that Perses (Hekate's father) was the name of the sun god who was transformed into a hero when supplanted by the new cult of Helios (the sun).[52] It is notable and puzzling that in Hekate's debut in Greek literature in *Theogony* (411-52) she appears as elevated beyond all deities but Zeus. In the section of the *Theogony* referred to as the hymn to Hekate, she is the daughter of Perses and Asteria.

> Perses brought her (Asteria) to the great house, to be his dear wife
> There she conceived and bore Hekate, whom Zeus
> Honored above all others, he gave her dazzling gifts,
> a share of the earth and a share of the barren sea
> She was given a place of honor in the starry sky,
> and among the deathless gods her rank is high.
> For even now when a mortal propitiates the gods
> and, following custom, sacrifices well-chosen victims,
> he invokes Hekate, and if she receives his prayers
> with favor then honor goes to him with great ease
> and he is given blessings, because she has power
> and a share in all the rights once granted
> to the offspring born to Ouranos and Gaia.
>
> (*Th.* 410-22, trans. Athanassakis)

Scholars usually trace Hekate to Asia Minor. According to Athanassakis, it is possible to attribute Hesiod's obvious devotion to her to ancestral connections with the territory in which the goddess was strongly worshipped.[53] Hesiod's Hekate is an ethereal creature;

her role is unique and unprecedented in the *Theogony*. A Titan goddess, she survives the Olympian Titanic wars. She plays an important role in the Homeric *Hymn to Demeter* and later antique texts mainly in the *Chaldean Oracles*, described here in Chapter 3, an influential text for the Platonists of the centuries to follow. The Titans, defeated in the battle between the Titans and Olympians, seem to be followed by a succession of more reasonable deities. Still, mysteriously, Zeus honors Hekate above all others and names Hekate, of all the Titans, as the one to whom he gave "dazzling gifts" (*aglaa dôra*) (*Theogony* 412) and a share (*moira*) of earth and sea (413). Paradoxically, despite her unrefined genealogy as a Titan, she has an elevated status, yet in later literature she rises to the status of the celestial realm only as far as the moon. Zeus, of course, is the sky god and therefore transcends the sublunary sphere. Hekate, in this first appearance on the stage of Greek literature, rules over the sublunary world holding sway over all born after her, granting favors to humans and interceding in human endeavors.

Marquardt describes the functions of Hekate in the *Theogony* where she possesses an immediacy in the lives of men and a benevolent nature.[54] She provides the fostering presence that ensures man's success in courts and assemblies, battles and athletic contexts, and in horsemanship (*Th.* 429-39), as well as in more mundane affairs such as a good catch at sea and success in animal breeding (*Th.* 440-47). Her nurturing role is apparent as she is *kourotrophos* (nurse of the young), joining company with the Muses, who attend upon favored princes from the time of their birth (*Th.* 81-82). She is with Gaia, who raised the young Zeus on Crete (*Th.* 479-80). In Orphic hymn 1.8, Hekate was believed to be present at birth, marriage, and death. Hekate is well disposed to accept prayers and supplications. She was a politically important goddess and protector of Stratonicea, together with Zeus Panamaros.

Hekate's most enduring role is as a guide and intermediary between worlds. The Homeric *Hymn to Demeter* is the earliest clear allusion to Hekate's role as a guide at times and places of transition. At l. 24, she is one of two creatures who hear Persephone's cry as Hades snatches her away, and later at ll. 51-59 she discusses these events with Demeter. Hekate re-enters the story after Persephone re-ascends to the world of the living (l. 438) and embraces her mother. The hymn says that Queen Hekate was the *propolos* (preceeder) and the follower *opaon* (follower) of Persephone,[55] a role that Johnston claims is indicative of her protecting and guiding role as she accompanied Persephone on a physical journey to Hades and back. Vase paintings portray Hekate as accompanying Persephone as an escort across a very important boundary. In later literature, she regularly guides the dead back and forth across this line between life and death.[56] Hekate was also often placed as a guardian of entrances. According to Plutarch, these *hekataia* were very common at important city entrances. Most famously, Hekate Epipyrgidia stood at the entrance to the Athenian Acropolis.[57]

In the *Hymn to Demeter*, Hekate accompanying Persephone across the boundary between the underworld and the world of the living provides a template for commerce between worlds with a mediating guide in later literature.[58] In the more philosophically elevated accounts of later antiquity, Hekate and, in some cases, other goddesses serve a mediating function between levels of reality. Sarah Iles Johnston suggests that this role is an extension of her role as a goddess associated with the passage through crossroads, doors, and other liminal places. In some accounts, she is an important spiritual intermediary, acting as a guide to the aspirant to transcendence and assimilation to the beyond being or the One. Johnston reviews modern scholarship concerning Hekate's identification with the Chaldean Cosmic Soul in first and second-century CE literature and suggests that it springs from her connection with magic or from her syncretism with other goddesses by late antiquity.[59]

The fact that Hekate survives the centuries and becomes even more important in the Common Era is curious, considering that Athena is the most famous and important goddess of ancient Greece. Hekate is a Titan, after all, and the demise of the rest of the Titans is notorious. She is an anomaly. There is no mention of Hekate in Homer. Nevertheless, during the Middle Platonic period Hekate's role as a guide across liminal points took on new philosophical and mystical significance, most likely due to the influence of the *Chaldean Oracles*.[60] The original myth of Demeter and Persephone is a cultural and metaphysical iconography of multiple worlds and the necessity to traverse them. These images can be identified as a precursor to more abstract notions of worlds beyond this world and how they are negotiated. As late Platonic philosophy began to espouse the existence of a hierarchy of realms of being, mediation between worlds became a pressing issue. Hekate's mediating role, as Chapter 3 here will elaborate, is to intervene between worlds beyond being that are transcendent and detached, and the world of nature.

Artemis: Mistress of the Wild

Artemis
(not lightly do poets forget her)
we sing
who amuses herself on mountains
with archery and hare shoots
and wild circle dances.
When she was still just a slip of a goddess,
She sat on her father's knee and said:
"I want to be a virgin forever,
Papa, and I want to have as many names
as my brother Phoibos, and please Papa,
give me a bow and some arrows—please?—
not a big fancy set: the Cyclopês can make me
some slender arrows and a little, curved bow.
And let me be Light Bringer
and wear a tunic with a colored
border down to the knee, loose
for when I go hunting wild game.
And give me sixty dancing girls,
daughters of Ocean,
[t]o take care of my boots and tend my swift hounds,
when I'm done shooting lynx and stag, and

Give me all the mountains in the world, Papa,
and any old town, I don't care which one:
Artemis will hardly ever go down into town.
I will live in the mountains, and visit men's cities
Only when women, struck with fierce labor pains,
call on my name."[61]

Artemis provides one of the templates for the association of female deity with *physis* (nature). She is the daughter of Zeus and Leto, sister of Apollo, and like him, holder of the bow and the lyre. She runs in the woods, an archer who shoots wild animals and whose arrows, Vernant reports, when used among humans, can strike women unexpectedly to bring them sudden death.[62] An enduring goddess prototype, she is huntress, mistress of the wild and of animals. John Sallis tells us that her reign extended throughout Greece, from Ephesus, Miletus, and Samos to the Greek mainland and beyond to Magna Gracica.[63] In the *Iliad*, she comes to blows with Hera who strikes her on the ears with her quiver, causing her to go crying into the lap of her father Zeus (*Il.* 21.485-513). She is also the Maiden, a *parthenos*, dedicated to eternal virginity, who leads the chorus of girls known as the nymphs and graces in joyous dance and song. A virgin, according to the Homeric *Hymn to Aphrodite*, she, with Athena and Hestia, are the three maiden goddesses over whom Aphrodite has no power, "cannot persuade the hearts of or deceive" (Homeric hymns 5.7). Artemis yields a plethora of iconographical imagery to future literature, particularly the unusual association of animals and goddesses. Artemis and other goddesses as well have been depicted as surrounded by animals or between two wild beasts (particularly in Minoan art). Thus in the *Iliad*, we find Apollo's sister: Artemis of the wild, the lady of wild beasts, scolded him bitterly (*Il.* 21.470-71).

Artemis's pedigree has been thought to be Nordic, or Eastern—either Lydian or Aegean. Vernant points out that her imagery in the archaic period recalls the figure of a great Asiatic or Cretan goddess who was named "Mistress of the Animals" or "Lady of the Beasts," which is identical to the title attributed to her in the *Iliad* (above). Rangos points out that Artemis's role as one who presides over natural beasts has persisted in the literature even though the Homeric appellation was *Potnia Thêrôn*, which could also be translated "mistress of the wild." Artemis presides over the hunt, pursuing wild animals to kill them. Artemis is not wildness itself but sees to it that the boundaries between the wild and the civilized are permeable, as in hunting.[64] Rangos prefers "mistress of wildness" and does not think that the animal attribution should take priority over the other Mycenaean documents where she is called mistress of grain, of horses, of labyrinths, and so on. She is not, then, exclusively a divinity of the animal kingdom. There is also the sense of her authoritative surveillance and mastery over natural processes, such as birth, growth, and puberty.

Rangos cites the "Paris School," Vernant in particular, for whom Artemis' place is thought to be at the margins and borders of zones which are other than nature, suggesting that Artemis presides over marginal places where natural forces border on cultural and agricultural places.[65] This is clearly the approach taken by Paul Ellinger: "The sanctuaries of Artemis are generally at the end of cultivated territory. Already wild, adjoining the mountains or a part of them, bordering the sea, these regions bear the Greek name of *eschatai*: the extremities, the limits, and the land 'at the end.'" The boundaries between cultivated territory and wild country are transitional areas and the idea of *eschatiai* (ends) expresses "the complex relations between civilization and wilderness, between nature and cultivation."[66] Artemis, Jenny Strauss Clay tells us, has a realm that encompasses both the wilds (mountains and shadowy groves) and the city of just men. She is a goddess of open public spaces and the agora.[67]

Artemis has another set of traits in addition to goddess of the untamed world. She is considered a goddess of fertility who makes plants, animals, and humans grow. She is the *kourotrophos*, as Vernant points out, helping nurture and mature the young until they become fully adult. She helps young girls, for example, to cross over the threshold to fully socialized status when they enter marriage and motherhood, or young males to that of citizen-soldier. Vernant sees this as another example of the liminal position over which she presides where uncertain and equivocal boundaries separate the young from adulthood. Artemis also presides over childbirth and has a role in the conduct of war as a guide. "Artemis is mobilized when too much violence is used during a military engagement when warfare abandons the civilized codes through which the rules of marital struggle are maintained and moves brutality into the realm of savagery."[68] Vernant associates the philosophical concept of "alterity" or "otherness" to certain deities whose powers reflect the experience of the Greeks construction of the "other." He does not consider this approach anachronistic, as Plato himself opposes the categories of Same and Other.[69] The "other" of Greek culture can be the other of the civilized person, the male adult, the Greek, and the citizen. The idea of wild is associated with nature in its uncultivated state, lending itself to a symbolic sense of otherness. This may be one source for the fact that nature is treated as mysterious and alien in later literature, to be uncovered with trepidation.

In the play of the Greek playwrights, Artemis's association with nature is retained, but she also intervenes in human dramas. In Aeschylus's *Choephoroe*, for example, when Clytemnestra reminds Electra that Agamemnon sacrificed her sister to the gods to bring back the wife of his brother Menelaus, Electra insists that Artemis demanded the sacrifice because she was angry that Agamemnon had boasted of killing a stag in her sacred grove (575-76).[70] In the Chorus in *Agamemnon* the omen of the eagles and the hare was a sign to Agamemnon (explained by the seer Calchas) that Artemis was angry and demanded the sacrifice of Iphigeneia.[71] In Euripides' *Hippolytus*, Artemis represents chastity which is equivalent to *sôphrosunê*, as opposed to Aphrodite and the passions of love.

Demeter and Persephone

"Hail, great Earth Mother, lady of Grain!" says Callimachus in his hymn to Demeter, and goes on to exhort her to save his city:

> Keep it harmonious and prosperous ever,
> Bring good things home to us from the fields,
> Feed our cattle, bring us more flocks,

Bring the ears of gram, bring in the harvest!
And nourish peace, Goddess, so that he who plows
May also reap.[72]

Demeter's identity, grain goddess though she is, for all the rest of literary history is associated with her narrative in the Homeric *Hymn to Demeter*. In fact Demeter preexisted this poem, and as Jenny Strauss Clay points out, when each Greek community developed its own local cults and gods, she may have had diverse roles and descriptions. Strauss Clay gives the example of the Demeter of Eleusis and the black Demeter of Phigalia.[73] Around the eighth century "a strong centripetal force," as she calls the Panhellenic revolution, served to reorganize the more ancient traditions. The Homeric *Hymn to Demeter* becomes the core text that determines the narrative of Demeter and Persephone during these later periods. (Strauss Clay also gives us a list of the other important Greco-Roman versions of the Demeter myth, such as in Hesiod's *Theogony*, the Orphic hymns, Ovid's *Metamorphoses*, and others). According to Nicolas Richardson, it is impossible to overemphasize the influence of the *Hymn to Demeter*, partially due to its culmination in the building of Demeter's temple at Eleusis and the promise to teach her rites to the Eleusinians (293-304). These rites, said to be secret (473-82), have caused the hymns to be described as "the foundational myth of the 'Mysteries.'"[74]

The Greek goddess of grain, Demeter, and her daughter Kore or Persephone are the two goddesses that feature in the hymn, a story of mother-daughter love and separation. Persephone is abducted by Hades, god of the underworld, and Demeter struggles to get her daughter back after Zeus arranges for this marriage. Demeter, heartbroken, sojourns among mortals at Eleusis, during which she attempts and fails to immortalize a human child. The goddess brings about famine on earth and the gods, losing sacrifices, agree to return Persephone. Persephone, however, has eaten a pomegranate seed in the world below and so must return to Hades for part of the year. She can be with her mother in Olympus for only two-thirds of the year and becomes the powerful queen of the underworld at Hades' side for the rest of it. The poem closes with Demeter establishing the Eleusinian Mysteries. Demeter plays a minimal role in Hesiod or the Homeric epic but the *Hymn to Demeter*, composed 650–550 BCE, played an important part in the religious life of the polis.

Foley comments that in the *Hymn to Demeter*, Demeter and Persephone are represented in exclusively female company. Demeter adopts the disguise of a helpless old woman and lives in an entirely female environment while she is carrying out her design against Zeus. Demeter as a goddess of grain, and according to Foley, has a special symbolic relation to and power over nature. The myth is an oscillation between procreation and death, between nature giving and taking away its gifts. Persephone and Demeter live out their drama in the spaces of earth, Hades, and Olympus, and this role can be shown to be template for the idea that imaginary regions, here earth, Hades, and Olympus, will need negotiation and mediation. A very specific allusion to the "threshold," another liminal image, occurs when Demeter, disguised as a possible nursemaid to the infant son of the house of Keleos, reveals herself as a goddess while in the doorway.

They soon reached the house of god-cherished Keleos,
and went through the portico to the place where
the regal mother sat by the pillar of the close-fitted roof,
Holding in her lap the child, her young offshoot. To her
they raced. But the goddess stepped on the threshold. Her head
reached the roof and she filled the doorway with divine light.
Reverence, awe, and pale fear seized Metaneira.

(*Hymn to Demeter* 184-190, trans. Foley)[75]

Demeter and Persephone and their intense mother-daughter relationship have been given a psychoanalytic reading by Carl Jung and Kerényi concerning the archetypes of the Mother/Maiden and the Divine Child. Jung's use of this mythological material is an example of how time-worn myths are re-mythologized by a master narrative. Jung and his followers transmute prototypes that are found in ancient literature, into "archetypes" as will be discussed here in Chapter 11. The "reception" of this myth on the part of current scholars, as well, has used the mother-child relationship in this myth here as validation of female bonding in a male-dominated society.

Isis

The goddess Isis is a very good example of a "collective memory" across the centuries as Isis was known as far back as Egypt's Old Kingdom (*c.* 2686–2181 BCE) and her prominence continued through the New Kingdom (1550–712 BCE) as well. This ancient myth in which Isis resurrects her slain husband Osiris and gives birth and nurturing to a son Horus is documented in funerary practices and magical texts, such as the Pyramid Texts.[76] Herodotus, the Greek historian, deemed Isis an equivalent of a Greek goddess (*c.* 425 BCE).[77] In the Hellenistic period (323–30 BCE) and in the first century in Rome, the cult of Isis became popular in the Greco Roman world as well. As time goes on, Isis assimilated many of the characteristics of preceding Greek deities. Corrington tells us that the worship of Isis spread throughout the Mediterranean, beginning as early as the eighth century BCE, and was conflated with other nursing deities. Her attributes become combined with those of Demeter, the other divine regenerating mother.[78]

In the Oxyrhynchos Papyri dating from the second century CE, Isis is held to have many shapes and many names. She is one who "didst make the power of women equal to that of men" (*P. Oxy.* 11.1380).[79] Apuleius of Madauros (second century CE) describes her worship in the eleventh book of his *Metamorphoses*. Isis is Lucius's savior as he is turned into an ass; she aids his transformation back into a human being and he is assured of eternal life. In the Egyptian myth, later borrowed by Plutarch in *Isis and Osiris*, the second century CE, and discussed here in Chapter 3, Isis conquers death as she searches for the dismembered Osiris, her husband, who had been attacked by his brother, Seth or Typhon. She gathers the parts of his body and magically revives him, making a phallus out of saliva and mud and lighting upon it in the shape of a bird in order to gestate and give birth to Horus, whom she protects from death by hiding him in the rushes of the Nile.

The significance of the Isis myth, in general, stems from her role as the protector of rulers and sponsor of laws and cities—protector of men as mother, lover, sister, and spouse. She is the savior (*sospitatrix*) of all humanity, who saves in her role as mother. Assmann describes the Osiris mysteries which were celebrated at the end of the inundation of the Nile, when farmland once again emerged from the floods and was ready to receive new seed at the end of the month of Cholak. In the Late Period, these ceremonies were the supreme Egyptian festival that began with the finding and embalming of the scattered limbs of the murdered Osiris. The forty-two limbs of Osiris that were collected, joined together, and revived in the course of the ceremonies correspond to the forty-two provinces of the land, each of which was home to a particular member of Osiris's body as its central mystery and sacred object. This ritual and the elevating of Horus, his son and avenger, to the throne, confirm the political, cultural, and religious identity of Egypt. Egypt is exposed to all sorts of threats and centrifugal tendencies in the course of a year. Assmann attributes these festivals to the experience of centuries-long fragmentation of the monarchy of the pharaohs into minor kings and chieftains. After the Assyrian invasion, it was celebrated in all the temples of the land as well as during a period of subjugation to the Persians, Greeks, and Romans. Myths of fragmentation and reunification, Assmann suggests, arise from "threats of disintegration and oblivion which faced all the ancient high cultures in the Hellenistic period."[80] In these circumstances, the role of a savior goddess provides hope of salvation and unification. Isis' function of restoring wholes, as she rejoined the limbs of Osiris into a living body in Greco-Roman contexts, became a more general attribute contributing to her function as a savior and mother of Horus.

Kybele, like Isis, will assimilate many of the characteristics of earlier goddesses as "mother of the gods" and will be discussed in Chapter 7, which explores the intertranslatability of their names in later antiquity.[81] Aphrodite will be discussed in the chapter on goddesses as fertile mothers and erotic temptresses.

Conclusion

As I examined the various historical settings and diverse cultures in which goddesses appeared and reappeared and then looked at the relatively few ancient sources for the original prototypes, I was struck again by power of collective memory. The sets of descriptions of the gods and goddesses found in Archaic epic, Greek drama, and Homeric and Orphic hymns were never forgotten. No longer regional, no long embedded in hymn or in epic, they lived on in the imaginations of an ever-continuing series of interpretive communities. One thing that particularly occurred to me was the fact that, certainly in late Platonist, medieval, modern and contemporary usage, it is the more idealized characteristics that have survived: closeness to nature febrility wisdom, etc. This raised further food for thought regarding collective memory. It seems that it can be remarkably selective. Gaia arranges the castration of Uranus

(*Th.* 173-206) and takes the bloody drops to bear the potent furies (*Th* 160-85). Athena disguises herself as Hector's brother and then cheats him of his sword in the final battle to the death in the *Iliad* (*Il.* XXII. 225-230). Hera tries to prevent Leto from giving birth to Artemis and Apollo (*Homeric Hymn to Delian Apollo*), and Artemis contributes to the sacrifice of Iphigenia (Sophocles, *Electra* lines, 765-770). These and many other examples document a dark side to goddesses which seem to have been overlooked in the idealized versions, for example, of an all wise compassionate earth mother and other such constructions. The following chapter will discuss in more detail how these ancient and mythical figures were able to take on elevated roles in the conceptual fabrications of Platonist philosophers.

3

The Goddesses of Philosophy: The Literature of Later Antiquity

To make gods and goddesses personify the world soul or the intellect was not something that Plato would have practiced. It was, however, a move that first- and second-century Platonists did not hesitate to make. A challenging geopolitical situation can account, in many ways, for the necessity for a theologically enhanced Platonism. Celsus, in the second century CE, wrote a militantly anti-Christian polemic, foreshadowing the threat that Christianity was already beginning to pose to Hellenism in the Roman Empire. The *Contra Celsum* (Origen's refutation of Celsus in eight books, and our only source for Celsus's work) documents the concerns of this Platonist as he laments the possible denigration of revered Hellenic polytheism. As Frede points out, "we can only understand this attack if we see that Celsus thinks that Christianity poses a threat to Hellenism and thereby the Empire."[1] Frede asks why Celsus was so threatened in a time when all the different nations of the Empire were able to pursue their own traditional religions without undue interference. Celsus contended that the Christians had their own God and made it clear that it was their intention "to convert the whole Empire, including the emperor" (*Contra Celsum* 8.71).[2] It seems that the political danger that Christianity posed to other ideologies was known to Hellenists quite early in the Christian rise to power. An active reassertion of pagan theogonies on the part of philosophers may have been partially motivated to enhance Platonism and elevate it to a quasi-religious doctrine. To do so, they read Platonism through the lens of oriental and Egyptian theology. Hellenist and Roman hegemony had created a wider cultural milieu and forging some unique doctrines could compete with those of Christianity. The strange hybrid literature that resulted elevated the status of the ancient gods and goddesses changing them into actors in philosophical scenarios.

The expansionist conquests of Alexander the Great and the unbounded imperialism of the Roman emperors subjugated regional populations to overrule by imperial government. Gods and goddess were wrested from the sites of local worship to become universally known. In the world of the philosophers, Platonism prevailed over Stoicism and Epicureanism as the dominant philosophy; and in a strange marriage of ideas and myth, the gods and goddess were incorporated into its ideology. Goddesses, once separate in function and character, became less and less distinct, not unlike the fate of local cultures. According to Simon Swain, "[Part] of the reason why Platonism became dominant ... during the High Empire is surely its possession of core texts that were classics of Athenian literature and were therefore crucial means in the formation of Hellenic identities."[3] Swain suggests that Platonism (blended with Stoic ethics and Pythagorean mysticism) gradually dislodged alternative philosophical systems, emerging as the only intellectual alternative to Christianity. Greek classicizing both aggrandized the elite and could serve as a resistance of Greek culture to Rome.

Cosmopolitanism, the result of geopolitical appropriation of regional cultures, created an ecumenical atmosphere. Cultures once unknown to each other were now forced to interact. One of the practices that made the interaction work in the case of Hellenic expansion was the identification of Greek deities with those of a conquered region. Regional specificity was already changed through the literary generalizations achieved by the epic poets; now gods and goddesses could be further transformed and rationalized to fit philosophical doctrines. In the case of Platonist philosophy, the goddesses were upgraded to personify or deify the Platonic world soul, to be a mediator between higher hypostases and lower nature, and to be a third in ontological triads. Many examples of Hekate as a "life giving womb" analogous to the world soul of Plato's *Timaeus* are derived from the *Chaldean Oracles*, an important influence on the Platonist during this time. In Fragments 51 and 52, of the *Chaldean Oracles*, Hekate ensouls the cosmos. Later Proclus as well in his *Commentary on Cratylus* (*In Cr.* 8.1. 6-8) describes Rhea, who is an equivalent to Hekate, "having received into her marvelous womb .... Pours forth generation upon all."[4] The deployment of Hekate, sometimes called Rhea, in the role of world creating was also based on doctrines connected with theurgy and spiritual salvation. Goddesses were seen as mediating guides for the spiritual aspirant to unify with the divine. Ecumenical aspirations, in many instances, treated the names of goddesses from local sites, as intertranslatable: the functions of various individual goddesses fused as well. Given many names in aretalogies of these times, for the scholars of the first and second centuries CE, the goddesses of mythology became the goddesses of philosophy. This was facilitated by the increased use of allegory in the interpretation of mythology. While allegorizing mythology was a hermeneutical strategy as far back as Theagenes of Rhegium (525 BCE) and Metrodorus of Lampsacus (331–277 BCE), this strategy became a preferred genre of later antiquity.

Artemis, whose sanctuaries are at the end of cultivated territory and who roams natural places with her bow ready to strike, Gaia of earthly fecundity, Aphrodite who incites erotic passion in the most cerebral of gods and humans, and Rhea the eternal mother whose name means flow: all of these life-producing figures supply unique gifts to the universe. They represent nature in all its prolificacy, and it is to them that the Platonist philosophers of later antiquity looked to revitalize sterile philosophies and keep Hellenic culture alive. The lesser-known goddess Hekate achieved a new prominence and performed a mediating role within a complex Platonist ontology. Goddesses now were seen as the living agency that could convert the ethereal, intellectual, and formal structure of the transcendent blueprint for the universe into actual existence. Using them to perform these functions divinized philosophy meeting the need to make classical thought a vital theology.

The *Chaldean Oracles* and Gnostic literature, the two most dominant sources of esoteric mysticism to surface in the Common Era, were themselves heavily influenced by Platonic philosophy. Radically transforming Hesiodic and Homeric pantheons, the Platonic philosophers turned to the esoteric literature as an aid to divinizing philosophy. Abstract philosophical concepts and the epic figures of gods and goddesses fused within ever more complex ideologies. Deities that formerly held highly individual character traits were reincarnated as allegorical and symbolic exemplars of ontological categories. Hekate, who had been worshiped since the archaic period and Isis, since at least the Hellenistic period and, of course, long before in Egypt, had become known as common objects of worship and ritual in popular culture. Interestingly, they became prevalent in the documents of the philosophers as well. Athena's characteristic wisdom lent this attribute to the other more widely featured goddess figure of this time. Later Proclus, in his *Commentary on the Timaeus*, will devote many passages to Athena and particularly to her wisdom (see *In Tim.* 157.24-160.5). An equivalence between formerly regional goddesses, the renewed interest in Platonism and the fusion with "oriental" doctrines elevated the personae of ancient literary goddesses to philosophical icons.

Aretalogies

During the Common Era, a practice dating from Hellenistic times allowed the names and translations of the names of the gods to be used interchangeably. Isis, Persephone, Hekate, and other goddesses of Greek origin succumbed to a fused identity made up of shared character traits. In the more easily Hellenized parts of Egypt such as Alexandria and the Fayyum, religious syncretism was more prevalent. This was a two-way street; Egypt had an equal influence on Greece and, later, Rome.[5] As a result of this so-called "Egyptomania," Egyptian lore fused with Hellenism; gods and goddesses exchanged personae. Aretalogies of these times document the interchangeability of goddesses' names and traits. The Decree of Memphis (estimated date 218 BCE) is an inscribed sandstone stele, found in 1923, holding the second of the Ptolemaic Decrees issued by Ptolemy IV (the Ptolemy dynasty ruled Egypt from 305 to 30 BCE). It is trilingual in Egyptian hieroglyphics, Demotic, and Greek. A political document, it provides evidence for the ecumenical nature of Isis, as do many other aretalogies or encomia of these periods. The Memphis Stele shows Isis to be the epitome of the syncretism. In Chapter 7, the aretalogies that document that Isis became known as the goddess of many names will be described in detail. A very famous inscription discovered in 1925 at Cyme in Aeolia (*I.Cyme* 41) and discussed by Garth Fowden states that "these things were copied from the Stele in Memphis that stood near the temple of Hephaestus."[6]

> I am Isis, the ruler of all land. I separated earth from heaven. I showed the stars their path. I ordered the cause of the sun and the moon. I am mistress of sea faring. I make the navigable (seas) unnavigable, when I wish.

According to Fowden, fragments of similar texts exist in inscriptions from Thessalonica, Andros (dating from the first century BCE and discovered in 1838), Ios (a version dating from the third century CE), and Maroneia on the coast of Thrace (found in 1969 and dating to the Hellenistic period). Aretalogies are alluded to in Diodorus of Sicily's description of Egypt (Diod. Sic. I.22.2). Fowden tells us that Isis was often assimilated to the Eleusinian Demeter and to Aphrodite. The Greco-Egyptian Isis was the product of a fusion between nature, the Egyptian Isis, and a variety of Greek goddesses. She inspired an enormous devotional literature over all parts of the Greek-speaking world over a long period. The aretalogies that have been discovered are irrefutable evidence of this fact, but they also display an unquestioned interchangeability of goddess characteristics. Goddesses begin to function as a "metaform," an amalgam of goddesses' whose identities became blurred and which bordered on becoming a conceptual abstraction, "the goddess."

Middle Platonism

Theogonic myths, such as those found in Hesiod, detail the origins of the gods while cosmogonic myths, common to many archaic cultures, detail the origins of the universe. Another type of progression can be identified that is philosophical, one in which hypostatic levels of reality emanating from a transcendent source employ gods and goddesses to play facilitating roles. In its mythical form, earlier generations of gods and goddesses multiply and reproduce the later generations of divinities. In the Platonist accounts, their erotic couplings and reproductive fecundity facilitate higher transcendent levels of reality to descend from the intellectual to the psychical and material world. What was once a matter of mating and childbearing now becomes ontological rather than genealogical. In Archaic epic poetry, physical forces and substances became personified and were given the names and activities of gods and goddesses—now concepts became personified and given the names of gods and goddesses. Formal parameters, originating on higher levels (called hypostases in the literature), through the activities of gods and goddesses who mediate, infuse the lower world of material nature with "ideas."[7] Hekate, for example, becomes a mediating deity in allowing higher levels of reality to descend.

Unless the cultural milieu is considered, the way in which gods and goddesses became intertwined with philosophical concepts is counterintuitive and inexplicable. Oracular Literature such as the *Chaldean Oracles* has been a topic of interest for many scholars (such as Boys-Stones who provides a lengthy discussion of its possible influence on Numenius).[8] Other such literature as well contributed to Platonic philosophy. The first- and second-century philosophers created a multiplicity of ontological categories out of Plato's One and Many, discussed in his dialogue *Parmenides*, and his "One beyond Being" discussed in *Republic*. In later Platonism, this became level upon level of hypostases, the lower the level the more devalued and the more entangled with nature. The sterile intellectual "higher" levels split into an array of categories. These innovations were initiated by the earlier so-called Old Academy: Speusippus (407–339 BCE), for example, Plato's successor in the Academy, placed the One above Intellect, while Xenocrates (396–314 BCE), after him, identified the One as Intellect (*Nous*) and above both Monad and Dyad. The Dyad was responsible for multiplicity, a devalued but necessary category of existence responsible for the natural world. Xenocrates was said by his doxographer Aetius (first or second century BCE) to equate the Monad with Zeus and the Dyad with the mother of the gods.

> Xenocrates held as Gods the Monad and Dyad. The former as the male principle, has the role of Father, ruling in the heavens. This he terms Zeus and Odd (*peritous*) and Intellect, and it is for him the supreme God. The second is as it were the female principle in the role of the Mother of the Gods ruling over the realm beneath the heavens. This he makes the Soul of the Universe.[9]

The Middle Platonists, Eudorus of Alexandria (first century BCE), Philo of Alexandria (*c*. 25 BCE–50 CE), Moderatus of Gades (*c*. 50–100 CE), Plutarch of Chaeronea (*c*. 45–125 CE), and Numenius of Apamea (second century CE) and others, elaborated an even more multilayered ontology. In the Platonist milieu of the first and second centuries CE, a One beyond Being was considered to supersede the Monad and indefinite Dyad of the Old Academy and precede them in ontological importance and primordial causality. Number (higher in intellectual priority than geometric figures), soul itself (expressive in geometrical expansion), celestial and sublunary bodies, and ensouled beings (living creatures) formed a hierarchy wherein the latter categories were lower down on the scale of being. Things became even more complex as the first principle split into more than one category. While Eudorus of Alexandria posited a supreme principle above the One and Dyad, Moderatus of Gades (first century CE), whom Dillon describes as an aggressive Pythagorean, complicated matters even further by positing not the supreme One presiding over a Dyad, as in Eudorus, "but rather three Ones, arranged to form what one might be excused for calling a system of hypostases".[10] Simplicius preserves a passage attributed to Moderatus, for example, in which he asserted that Plato,

> following the Pythagoreans, declares that the first One is above Being and all essence, while the second One which is the truly existent (*ontos on*) and the object of intellection (*noeton*)—and he says is the Forms, the third which is the soul-realm (*psychikon*)—participates (*metechei*) in the One and the Forms, while the lowest nature which comes after it, that of the sense-realm, does not even participate, but receives order by reflection … from these others. Matter in the sense-realm being a shadow cast by Not-Being as it manifests itself primarily in Quantity, and which is of a degree inferior even to that.[11]

The First One is above Being, the Second One is noetic (having to do with intellect) and is the realm of the Ideas, the "paradigm" of the *Timaeus*, but subordinate to the supreme entity. Moderatus Second One, Eudorus' Second One, and Numenius's Second God all bifurcate the hypostases responsible for Intellect. As to how the material world comes into existence, Moderatus suggests a "third One" participating in the first two and an extension of the term One to embrace the Soul. In this three-level hierarchy, nature itself is forced into the place of a fourth level.[12] Numenius also goes beyond dualism, taking the mysterious "three kings" mentioned in Plato's *Second Letter* (probably spurious) as support for the triad of gods which he posits as first principles. The First God, simple, indivisible, and self-constituted, is the Good and is associated with the intellectual realm; the Second God is mind and is initially unified but divides in the process of coming into contact with persisting matter; and the Third God is roughly related to the World Soul. The Third God is a lower aspect of the Second God, not properly a World Soul but, as Dillon suggests, an aspect of the demiurge.[13] The First God is father of the demiurgic god. Albinus (*c.* 150 CE) also has a first god, an active intellect, a potential intellect, and a cosmic soul.[14] As the gods become more complex, the role of a goddess as mediator will meet the need to find agency for an interaction between levels of gods, intellect, and the world of nature.[15]

Gender

Ascribing goddesses to the categories of Platonic theology adds the attribution of gender to these philosophies. John Dillon has identified two sources of female personifications in this literature. The first is the logic of Greek grammar in which there may be no functional connection between the feminine gender and a feminine word, but it nevertheless helps to create the basic antithesis between reason or intellect (*nous*, masculine) and the sensible (*aesthêsis*, or soul, *psychê*, feminine). Philo, for example, following the logic of Greek grammar, allegorizes Adam as *nous* (intellect) and Eve as *aesthêsis* (the sensible).[16] The second source is what Dillon terms a "functional" connection. The origin of this is harder to pinpoint, but Dillon points to Plato's influence. Plato's Unlimited (*apeira*), for example in *Philebus* 16C, his womb of all being, the receptacle of *Timaeus*, and the World Soul in *Timaeus, Statesman,* and *Laws* X are all grammatically feminine. All of these are functional instances of female principles as well. Plato calls the receptacle in *Timaeus*, for example, a mother. Given these instances, the conflation of the feminine with Middle Platonist and Neopythagorean ideas, such as the Dyad as an unlimited or indeterminate entity, has the direct imprimatur of Plato.[17] Thus when Speusippus connects the primal multiplicity, the unlimited (the great and the small) with the receptacle of *Timaeus*, he uses the terms "fluid" (*hugra*) and "pliable" (*eupladai*) and links the Dyad with Soul and Matter. Only one further step will link these qualities to the female. Thus when Xenocrates theologizes principles, making the Monad Zeus and the Dyad "mother of the gods" (which Dillon understands as Rhea), it is not unprecedented.[18] In later antiquity, Plutarch fills the role of matter's evil aspect with the Egyptian Seth-Typhon while Isis takes on the less evil principles of matter. Isis is the female principle in nature and that which receives all procreation, by virtue of her identification with the receptacle (*De Iside* 372e). For Dillon, the Platonic underworld of this period of antiquity abounds with and proliferates female principles. He gives further examples (discussed below) of Sophia in Valentinian Gnosticism, and he mentions that in some versions of Gnosticism Sophia generates a lower projection of herself who serves as an immanent organizing principle of the physical world.

Gnostic, Orphic, and Oracular Literature

Some of the mystical literature, which was circulating in the first and second centuries, made mythology less alien to the philosophers of the first and second centuries. The *Rhapsodic Theogony* or *Sacred Discourse in Twenty Four Rhapsodies* attributed to Orpheus is a text that Martin West proposes was a Hellenistic first-century BCE creation, although Luc Brisson attributes it to the first or second century CE. In any case, it was of continuing interest in the Common Era right up to the later Platonic academies of the Empire.[19] In the fifth century CE, Proclus still followed the Orphic theogony.[20] The Orphic theogonies provided continuity with traditions that were presumed to go back as far as Pythagoras. Gnostic and Oracular literature also gained a considerable following. According to John Turner, the *Chaldean Oracles* are an influence and source for some of the Gnostic literature, and specifically may be a source of the metaphysical doctrine of the *Allogenes*, a Gnostic text dating from the first half of the third century CE. In the earlier Gnostic texts, for example, the *Apocryphon of John*, there is the doctrine of Barbelo, and in the *Oracles* the doctrines of Hekate. It may be, however, that both derive from a common source in Platonism. Some scholars have speculated that the oriental influence is responsible for transmuting Platonism, others that there is some sort of two-way street between the two forms of literature.

Plutarch of Chaeronea (most likely birth date 45 CE), author of *Isis and Osiris*, is a prime example of Hellenizing Egyptian myth. Plutarch is thought to have been a student of Ammonius in 66–67 CE and he probably died about 125 CE. He lived in Chaeronea and was a priest of the temple of Apollo at Delphi. A Platonist influenced by Pythagoreans, he produced many serious philosophical treatises and other literary writings. Under the spell of the ubiquitous Egyptomania of that time, his major late work *Isis and Osiris* was a widely circulated hybrid text.[21] This work is an intriguing example of the two-way street between the second-century fascination with Egypt and a steadfast Platonism. Fusing Platonism and Egyptian mythology, it recounts the well-known myth of Osiris and Isis. Using forced etymologies and other literary devices, Plutarch seems bent on providing Greek and Egyptian equivalents at all costs, as in the following passage:

> With these details, the Egyptian usages also agree [equivalence of Sarapis and Osiris]. For they often give **Isis** the name **Athena,** which has some such meaning as this: I come from myself, which indicates self-impelled movement.
>
> (Plut. *De Iside* 376a-b)

When Plutarch wrote *Isis and Osiris*, the myth had transmigrated and been a cultural anomaly for Hellenists for several centuries. Plutarch finds Platonic cosmogony everywhere in the Egyptian myth.[22] According to Daniel Richter, *Isis and Osiris* offers "some of the most sophisticated formulations of Middle Platonic metaphysics that have come down to us."[23] Richter notes that Plutarch chose the ostensibly Egyptian myth as a vehicle for his most mature and developed thoughts on the divine and the structure of the universe. He finds Platonic categories in the myth and sees the Egyptian gods and goddess as emblematic of primal pairs and triads wherein abstract concepts and gods and goddesses are equivalent. Richter theorizes that Plutarch's motive in doing so was his unwillingness to accept the culturally derivative status of Greece, implied by the assertion of an Egyptian origin of Greek wisdom. Plutarch, for example, claims a false etymology for Isis's name from the Greek verb *oida* (to know), evidence of his Hellenizing aspirations. Griffiths, recalling Herodotus's account, suggests that Plutarch's "false etymology" is an unexceptional example of sameness of Greek and Egyptian deities. Plutarch often etymologizes and gives examples of the various names that Greeks and Egyptians give to the same divine powers. The Egyptians call the power in charge of the sun's course "Horus," the Greeks call him "Apollo," etc. (*De Iside* 375e). When it comes to Isis, Plutarch says, "this goddess whom you worship is one who is exceptionally wise and a lover of wisdom, her name certainly seems to imply that, to her more than anyone, belongs knowing (*to eidenai*) and experiential knowledge (*gnôsis, oida, and epistêmê*)" (*De Iside* 2.352e). Plutarch fuses this Athena-like depiction with an Isis who loves and longs for the *logos* (which Osiris embodies) and is impregnated through this contact. She becomes the active principle that mediates the transcendent monadic intelligence and the dyadic and subordinates the infinitely active disorderly forces characterized by Typhon/Seth.

In order to transmute a goddess into a philosophical entity, the more graphic mythology had to be expunged from the traditional canon. One of the ways to ameliorate the negative aspects of myths (their violence and so on), something Plato had harshly repudiated, was to treat myth as allegorical, standing for more elevated ideas. Plutarch sanitizes the dismemberment of Horus and the decapitation of Isis in the original Egyptian myth, as *barbarous doxas* (barbarous opinions) and favors a metaphysical scheme. His main characters become transformed into "signifiers" for Platonist ontology. Plutarch reframes Egyptian myth into Hellenic tradition. Thus, there is an episode where Isis wanders, while searching for the body of Osiris, until she comes to Byblos where she sits down near a fountain and speaks to the queen's maids; they take her to the queen, who makes her the nurse of her child. Isis nurses the child by day, but by night burns away the mortal parts of his body in the fire and turns herself into a swallow, crying as she flies around the pillars of the great hall. The queen, hearing the lament, comes to see her child in flames, and her cry causes Isis to remove the child from the fire and deprive it of immortality. This story is identical to that of Demeter in the Homeric *Hymn to Demeter*, who, in the midst of her search for Persephone, sits by the fountain in Eleusis where she meets the daughters of Metaneira, becomes the nurse of the child Demophon, and burns away his moral parts until the panic of Metaneira causes her to stop.[24]

Apuleius's *Metamorphoses*, or *The Golden Ass*, is one of the most cited and researched documents of the second century. This novel narrates the story of a man, Lucius, who is transformed into an ass by practicing magic that goes awry, and who begs a goddess to turn him back into a human. As a consequence, he receives instruction in the rites necessary to achieve this end. Apuleius lived during the reigns of Hadrian and Marcus Aurelius when there was an intensification of interest in Egypt and its gods. The description of Isiac initiation in this book is most likely an account of how it might have been practiced in the imperial empire. It clearly regards Isis as the soteriological figure who can save the troubled soul and is testimony to the prevalent Egyptomania of the second century. The cult of Isis attracted members of all strata of Roman society, and Apuleius, who was a Platonist of sorts, has been considered by some scholars to have been himself an initiate of her cult. Solmsen questions whether Apuleius is a genuine Roman convert to the religion of Isis. He certainly documents the intense interest that persisted in Isiac worship in the Rome of his time.

In the eleventh book of *Metamorphoses*, there is a very famous aretalogy, an ecphrasis (vivid descriptive piece) written in Latin. Lucius, after an epiphanic moment when he claims he would rather die than be an ass, is enveloped by sleep, and Isis appears "the supreme goddess (*deam praepotentem*) who wields her power with exceeding majesty, the queen of heaven (*regina caeli*)." She announces:[25]

> I am the progenitor of nature, mistress of all elements, firstborn of generations... the peoples of where the rising sun shines its rays, both Aethiopians and the Aegyptians. Who gain strength by ancient doctrine worship me with the appropriate ceremonies, call me by my right name, queen Isis.
>
> (11.5-6)

Both Plutarch and Apuleius attest to the Isis phenomenon as well as to the fact that geopolitical ecumenism had reached scholars and authors of literature. In addition to the interest in Egypt, other sources of exotica influenced the late Platonists. The *Chaldean Oracles*, Hermetica, and Gnostic gospels provided mystagogic lore that could augment their arguments and theologize Hellenic philosophy with theurgy, soteriology, and cosmology.

The *Chaldean Oracles*[26]

The *Chaldean Oracles* is a collection of mystical verses purported to have been handed down to Julian the Chaldean and/or his son Julian the Theurgist, who flourished during the late second century CE in the time of Marcus Aurelius (reigned 161–180 CE). It is a work consisting of cosmological and soteriological gnomic statements. Psellus (1017–1078), a Byzantine Greek monk and philosopher/historian, who transmitted forty fragments of the *Oracles*, probably based on his reading of Proclus, reports that they were written in response to Julian's father, who obtained an archangelic soul for his son which he then put into contact with Plato. The result was that he produced utterances in hexameter verse that allegedly came from Plato himself. This legend persists and can be found in Iamblichus and the emperor Julian, and was reported by Proclus, the fifth-century Neoplatonist whose *Commentary on the Timaeus* preserves most of the extant fragments that we possess today.[27] Athanassiadi proposes that Psellus's account of the originators of the *Chaldean Oracles* is correct and that there were two Julians that lived somewhere in the eastern part of the Roman Empire, were father and son, and belonged to a sacred caste.[28] The son, in a state of possession, uttered hexameters (the work is written in dactylic hexameters) on metaphysical, moral, and scientific issues that his father wrote down as they emerged. Athanassiadi points out that by the late third century, if not before, the *Oracles* had attained their canonical status, and were recognized as a sacred text in certain circles. Porphyry was the first commentator on the *Oracles*, according to Marinus (*VP* 26, 622-3),[29] Proclus's biographer, and Iamblichus wrote a massive commentary on them. Athanassiadi thinks that they originated and emerged in the second century; other commentators believe the work was composed in the third century.

Oracular literature gives Hekate the prominence that impressed the first- and second-century Platonists. Hekate occurs in 5 of the 226 extent *Oracle* fragments and, according to Johnston, in perhaps 66 other fragments. She speaks in eleven fragments, some of which are of doubtful authenticity.[30] Kroll was the earliest modern editor and interpreter of the *Oracles* and he explains Hekate's prominence in the *Oracles* by the fact that in the second century she had become syncretized with other goddesses. These associations in the *Oracles* make the Chaldean theological system agree with the Orphic or Hermetic theological system. Luc Brisson explains how Platonic doctrine is represented in the *Chaldean Oracles*.[31] He points out that attempts to fuse soteriology and cosmology, Platonism and sacred texts were widespread in late antiquity. The *Chaldean Oracles*, in particular, were very much an active part of the textual syncretism that fused mysticism, theurgy, and Platonic theory. Athanassiadi proposes that this was not coincidental, or some sort of vague spirit of the times, but originated in the temples to the Babylonian god Bel found in Apamea. Confirming collateral evidence for this is the fact that Numenius, a second-century philosopher, produces fragments suggestive of similar concepts as those of the *Oracles*. He was from Apamea, and Amelius (246–290 CE, a leading figure of Plotinus's school) and Iamblichus chose to spend time there.[32]

The *Oracles* were regarded by late Neoplatonists from Porphyry (*c.* 232–303 CE) to Damascius (*c.* 462–537 CE) as authoritative, revelatory literature, the "bible of the Neoplatonists," as Cumont termed it.[33] In the *Oracles*, Hekate by means of her womb enacts a role related to the cosmic soul of Middle Platonism.[34] In the Chaldean system, as Majercik remarks, she is the "[d]ominant female principle operating at all levels and directly responsible for material creation as we know it."[35] Hans Lewy points out that, when it comes to the *Oracles*, Hekate is more the principal god than Aion. Queen of night and goddess of the crossroads in Greek mythology, she is identified in the *Oracles* as the "Ensouler of Light, of Fire, of the Ether and of the Worlds." The power of "ensouling," Hans Lewy says, is contained in Hekate; she is identical with the winding fire in the *Oracles* and is thought to be above the noetic region, situated beneath the Ideas, conforming to the doctrine of the Platonists as to the place of the Cosmic Soul.[36] Hekate is identified with the Chaldean personification of physics, according to Hans Lewy, and with *Zôê, Heimarmenê,* and *Anankê* (Life, Providence, and Fate). Johnston cites several fragments that do relate Hekate to the cosmic soul, but it is difficult to make a direct equation between the World Soul and Hekate. A recent article by John Finamore and Sarah Iles Johnston presents more nuanced position in regard to the *Chaldean Oracles* in which Rhea represents Life on a higher level, Hekate on a lower one. Hekate is "higher" than the World Soul as closer to the father within a triadic structure.

The precedents for an analogy of ontology and mating and reproduction as well as Neoplatonic emanation can also be found in the *Oracles*.[37] The forms or Ideas qua "noetic fire" enter Hekate's womb and create the physical world. In the *Chaldean Oracles*, the "Father" is self-generated (fr. 39), separated from all the rest, like the Good of the *Republic* and the One of the second part of the *Parmenides* (fr. 3; 84). The Father contains the forms inside himself while he himself is unknowable and ineffable and is associated with Intellect (fr. 7; 109), Principle (fr. 13), and Monad (fr. 11). The Father gives form to the Living Being, the eternal model of the sensible universe that is within time (while the Father is timeless). As Finamore and Johnston describe, the Intellect is the highest god since there is no transcendent One in the *Oracles* as there will be later in Neoplatonism. Below a triadic structure involving the Intellect (as Numenius proposes) are the World Soul, a host of gods and lesser divinities, individual souls, and nature. The highest god (fr. 3) is the Father dwelling in the intelligible or Empyrean world above the cosmos and is totally separate from the lower intelligibles. The triad is made up of the Father, a Power that emanates from him, and a Second Intellect that issues forth from the two (Simplicius fr. 6). The Power acts like a girdling membrane (*hypexôkôs hymên*) deriving the first from the second fire (intellect). It is the "girdling membrane" that can be associated with Hekate: an intelligible intermediary that separates the two intellects, thus closer to the father than the second Intellect. Furthermore, there is a second lower Hekate that separates the second Intellect from the lower realm, acting as a World Soul.[38]

The intricacies and complexity of Hekate's role in this literature are daunting but I think it is important to present it here to display its importance to the project of theologizing philosophy with goddess lore. Athanassiadi states, "The basic Platonic antithesis between paradigmatic and a created world becomes a trichotomy in the Chaldean system."[39] Triads, discussed here in Chapter 7, become very prevalent in later Neoplatonism. The *Oracles* contain an earlier account of the production of the sensible world entailing three factors. From the father, related to the First Intellect, come the forms (along with the heavenly fire, thunder). The Demiurge is related to the second Intellect associated with the Dyad and Dios (Zeus) and has a role in producing the sensible world, taking the Forms as his model (fr. 5). It, in turn, is accepted into the womb of Hekate. Her womb represents sensible things that are located in "hollows" that correspond to matter, the universal receptacle, and so on.[40] In this complex ontology, the Demiurge causes the intelligible fire, the source of which is the Father, to descend. Hekate is a third divine entity, between the two gods, the Father and the Demiurge. As intermediary at the center, she dissociates and associates, keeping the first and second Intellect as separate but also linking them together. She is called a "generative womb" and source of souls from her womb (fr. 28; 32.2; 35.2; 37.10; 56.2), in fr. 56 the goddess is Rhea. Hekate's womb is comparable to the receptacle of the *Timaeus* in which the Demiurge carries out the mixture from which all souls come. Brisson points out that though Hekate is identified with the World Soul, she is too high in the hierarchy to be the World Soul; however, the World Soul emanates from her. Since in the tradition Rhea is the spouse of Kronos and the mother of Zeus, there is some relation to Hekate since, according to Brisson; Hekate is the spouse-daughter of the first Father, and the mother-sister of the Demiurge (an Orphic notion).

Hekate, like Isis, is a good example of how a goddess could come to serve as a "metaform." Qua mediator, she is a paragon, a placeholder for the mysterious factor in creation of the material world out of ideas. The "highest" good is transcendent and "snatched away" (fr. 3) but nevertheless characterized as the father and paternal Intellect qua Monadic source. All the activity in the created universe is due to the intervention of Hekate. While the ensouling of the world and the animation of nature are important, it is not as highly valued as the transcendent origin of all being, visible and invisible, the One and its ambassador in being, the Intellect. There is an ambivalence toward nature in this and in all Platonist accounts. Nature is clearly subordinate and lower on the scale of ontological importance, and by association, female deity is as well. The later Neoplatonists associate the intellectual world with Providence and the world of nature with Fate, and it becomes a spiritual ideal to transcend the pull of fate and ally with Providence. Thus, Proclus in *Platonic Theology*, which is heavily engaged with the *Chaldean Oracles*, quotes fr. 102 of the *Oracles*: "Do not gaze at nature: her name is Fate (*heimarmenê*)" (*Plat. Theol.* V.32, 119, 12). Here in later chapters, the association of the goddess with nature will be shown to have a lasting influence on medieval and modern literature.

The Greek Magical Papyri and the Hermetica

The Magical Papyri, written in Greek, are part of a larger corpus that also includes texts written in Egyptian Demotic. They are a collection of magical spells, formulas, hymns, and rituals from Greco-Roman Egypt. The texts derive from earlier Egyptian religious and magical beliefs and the Demotic magical texts come from collections that Jean d'Anastasi gathered in the Theban area in 1827 and are now available to be researched in the *Thesaurus Linguae Graecae* databases. They were written between the second century BCE and fifth century CE in Greek, Coptic, and Demotic. In these writings, the goddess Artemis is identical with Selene, Hekate, and Persephone.[41] There is also frequent reference to "the goddess," without specifically naming her.

The *Hermetica* is a collection of texts from the second and third centuries CE, which includes the *Corpus Hermeticum* and the Latin *Asclepius*. Fowden locates the origin of the Hermetic literature in the fusion of Egyptian and Greek ways of thought that came about in the Nile valley during the Ptolemaic and Roman periods.[42] He considers them to have been in circulation in the first century BCE or earlier, and in wide circulation by the first century CE. They exemplify late Hellenistic gnosis, and they are a common source of revelatory lore and philosophy. They influenced Iamblichus, for one, who in his influential text, *De Mysteriis Aegyptorum*, impersonates a learned Egyptian priest. In general there is a long tradition of attributing the source of all wisdom, Greek included, to Egyptian origins. Most of the Hermetica claim to be the revelations of Hermes Trismegistus, who, according to Fowden, "was the cosmopolitan, Hellenistic Hermes, Egyptianized through his assimilation to Thoth (known throughout the Roman world as the Egyptian *par excellence*)."[43] Most of the texts are a dialogue between Hermes and one of three pupils, Tat, Asclepius, or Ammon. All three were considered to be sons or grandsons of Greek gods such as Hermes. The Hermetic texts are classic examples of late Hellenistic syncretism, combining allusions to magic, astrology, alchemy, Platonism, Stoicism, and the Mysteries, as well as Judaism and Gnostic thought.[44]

Hermetic literature was apparently well known to second- and third-century scholars, and around 200 CE, Clement of Alexandria mentions the "forty-two books of Hermes" which were used in the rituals of Egyptian priests. Hermes Trismegistus also appears in the Greek Magical Papyri as a syncretistic Hermes, a cosmic creator of heaven and earth and world ruler and has frequent association with the moon (Selene) and Hekate.

Hans Jonas points out that Hermetic writings that are composed in Greek are "purely pagan" and lack polemical reference to either Judaism or Christianity. The religion of Hermes Trismegistus originated in Hellenistic Egypt where Hermes was identified with Thoth. "The first treatise of the corpus, called Poimandres, is an outstanding document of Gnostic cosmogony and anthropogony independent of the speculations of the Christian Gnostics."[45] These are the Greek, as opposed to Demotic Hermetica, both of which, Copenhaver points out, come from a common environment. Garth Fowden, whom he cites, has argued that the Hermetica, whether practical or theoretical, magical or philosophical, are responses to the complex Greco-Egyptian culture of Ptolemaic, Roman, and early Christian times.[46] The *Poimandres* (a chapter in the *Corpus Hermeticum* and the most well-known text of the Hermetic literature) is a blend of theology, cosmogony, anthroponomy, ethics, soteriology, and eschatology. It centers on the divine figure of primal man and describes his sinking into nature as the dramatic climax of the revelation.

Festugière distinguished popular occultist writings attributed to Hermes from these more philosophical treatises, but the dissemination of both illustrates the *esprit de temps* that called for the resurgence of occult belief and philosophy. The following excerpts from book XI of the *Corpus Hermeticum*, translated by Copenhaver, illustrate the kind of split this popular wisdom makes between being and becoming, time and eternity.[47] They are included here as a prime example of the kind of dualistic paradigms and binary oppositions that appear in much Middle Platonist, Neoplatonist, and esoteric literature, which is important to note as it accrues to gender opposition in other contexts.

> God makes eternity; eternity makes the cosmos; the cosmos makes time; time makes becoming. The essence (so to speak) of god is [the good, the beautiful, happiness] wisdom; the essence of eternity is identity; of the cosmos, order, of time, change; of becoming, life and death. But the energy of god is mind and soul; the energy of eternity is permanence and immortality; of the cosmos, recurrence and counter-recurrence of time increase and decrease; of becoming, quality (and quantity). Eternity there is in god, the cosmos in eternity, time in the cosmos and becoming in time.
>
> (*Corpus Hermeticum* XI.2, trans. Copenhaver)

> The attracting and combining among things contrary and unlike became light shining down from the energy of the god who is father of all good, ruler and commander of the whole order of the seven worlds. Coursing ahead of them all is the moon, nature's instrument, transforming the matter below, and in the midst of the universe is the earth, the nurse who feeds terrestrial creatures.
>
> (*Corpus Hermeticum* XI.7, trans. Copenhaver)

In later chapters, the dualism sun/moon, god/goddess, permanence/motion and change will be seen to contribute to the genderized binary oppositions found in so many of the late antique texts.

The Gnostic Gospels

The Gnostic Gospels are a collection of about fifty-two ancient texts written between the second and fourth centuries CE. Elaine Pagels suggests that Gnosticism blends Christian doctrines with traditions originating in the East.[48] The Nag Hammadi Manuscripts containing these gospels were discovered in 1945 and have generated a vast amount of scholarly commentary and discussion. Turner notes the close doctrinal and terminological similarities between the Sethian Gnostic doctrines (the Sethians were a Gnostic sect during the Roman era who considered themselves enlightened by the divine wisdom revealed to Adam and Seth) and the *Chaldean Oracles*. The *Apocryphon of John*, a Sethian text, contains the doctrine of Barbelo, and the *Oracles* contain the doctrine of Hekate. In both the *Apocryphon of John* and *Zostrianos* (a second-century Sethian Gnostic text), Barbelo is the Dyad, the womb of the All, and then appears as Sophia who longs to unite with the Invisible Spirit. She wished to receive an image but declined downward because of her dyadic character and gave rise to precosmic matter from whose grasp she attempts to escape by her act of repentance.[49] In Valentinian Gnosticism, "The supreme God, the Forefather, procreates by himself an initial pair of entities, one male (Intellect—*Nous*) and one female (Truth—*Aletheia*) and through them a string of paired male and female entities called Aons, the most junior of which on the female side is Sophia."[50] Turner notes the parallel with the Triple Powered One of the Gnostic *Allogenes*. Barbelo in the Gnostic literature and Hekate in the *Oracles*, as well as Isis in Plutarch's account, are equivalent in the sense that they are the active, willing, womb-receiving and creating agents that actualize the active forces that can unleash the powers that reside in the cryptic unity at the source of all that is. The "goddess" serves to supply the "living" power and receiving site, then, within a Platonic two-world ontology where the source of all intellectual parameters is a static and transcendent unity but creation itself must proceed through motion and change.

Orphic, Gnostic, and Chaldean Lore and Platonism

In an atmosphere that John Dillon has termed the "Platonic underworld," a fusion of oriental mythology and Platonic philosophy upgrades the functions of all the gods. In the case of the goddess, her rebirth as a metaphysical category is aided and abetted by Orphic, Hermetic, and Chaldean lore. The classic daemoness is now a metaphysical entity with functions that complete an ever more complex Platonic ontology. The most ancient of goddesses acquires a triadic nature, a mediating function between higher and lower hypostases and a reproductive fecundity that becomes productive of the whole world of nature, and in some cases, of nature's mathematical underpinnings. Genest describes the systematic assumptions of the late Hellenistic age: "the Ptolemaic delineation of hierarchical cosmos under the rule of *heimarmenê* [fate or providence], the sympathetic parallel between macrocosm and microcosm, the attendant understanding of the consubstantial nature of all existent entities, the devoted or fallen feminine nature of reality, and the masculine redemptive possibility of cosmic and temporal reversal." Platonic syncretism is present in all of them.[51] The philosophical usage of a "goddess" resolves the troublesome separation between Mind and Nature that is omnipresent in Platonic thought. Static abstract principles cannot be active mediating agents nor living, productive "forces" that can actively insinuate themselves into the many-leveled production of the world but the goddesses, once known only to ancient mythology and pagan region, can assume that role. Hekate/Isis assumes mediating functions partly by possessing virtue. (In the *Chaldean Oracles* Soul gushes from the right flank of Hekate, whereas from her left flank springs Virtue). It should be noted here that virtue/wisdom is not the highest form of intellect and that, as will be discussed in later chapters, Nous (Intellect in the highest sense) is attributed to the gods and is eternally fixed and at rest: a goddess can assume the fluidity that can enact change associated with becoming.

Conclusion

Plato denigrates myth (*Republic* II.376E-398B; X.595A-608B) but nevertheless presents an ontology that is conducive to deification and personification. Plato's universe, as Mary Lenzi claims, is one of "polypsychic pantheism." His universe is imbued with life; the World Soul in *Timaeus* is animate while the individual soul is "self-moving."[52] Plato was a masterful artist, creating literary tropes that the Platonic literature of later centuries took literally. The close association between the esoteric texts (many of which are themselves "Platonized") and Middle Platonic philosophy was a crucial alliance enabling a rhetorical setting for the goddesses to be able to enter the conceptual nexus of Platonic ontology. On the one hand, most of the metaphysical structures found in Middle Platonism and Neoplatonism fall within the strict confines of the Platonic tradition. From that standpoint, the fusion with the more mystical content may seem to be window-dressing, political strategies to make Hellenic ideas more religious, or attempts to add popular appeal to philosophical doctrines. Still, it does seem that there is more to it than that. Theologizing philosophy is too complex and systematized to conclude it is mere window dressing. It remains, I believe, difficult to fully explain the unlikely marriage between the *Chaldean Oracles,* for example, a product of the second century, and the "theologizing Platonists." Scholars such as John Turner note the close relationship between Numenius (fr. 52) and the *Chaldean Oracles*, for example.[53] One can adopt two opposing viewpoints on the issue of the direction of the influence or see it as a two-way street.

In her edition of the *Chaldean Oracles,* Ruth Majercik comments that "in the 'underworld' of Platonism, abstract philosophical speculation gives way to mythic formulations and a complex proliferation of cosmic entities is introduced, with a dominant female principle, in each case, operating at all levels and directly responsible for material creation as we know it."[54] Philosophical systems consisting largely of abstract nouns cannot account for creation or how motion and change work in the universe. Placing specific deities in strategic positions adds a spiritual account of motion and causality to Platonic idealism. Plato's answer to this is Soul and its capacity for self-movement. Impersonal reifications such as Intellect are considered unities, so motion or change would entail division and multiplicity, destroying unity. With the addition of the activities of a goddess to this account, Soul can carry out specific functions that can be described in personified terms. The abstract nouns of metaphysical philosophy cannot be prayed to nor can they play a role in salvation and assimilation to the One. Plato had to conceive of a "Demiurge" (a craftsman) to account for the activity of creation. With the addition of personified spiritual agents, the cosmos can be imbued with soteriological activity and ensure that its purely physical aspect is under spiritual control. The fusion of Egyptian and Hellenic deities with Platonic ideas, as a theo-philosophical doctrine, serves a pragmatic function as well. Hellenism by these means is preserved in a milieu where Christianity was gaining increasing influence. The proof that these efforts can be enacted "on the ground" will come in the fourth century, when the Emperor Julian fuses Platonic ideas and mystical theologies in the service of the reassertion of pagan political hegemony in a Christianized Roman Empire.

4

Virgin, Erotic Temptress, Mother and Cosmic Womb

In the canonical Judeo-Christian account of creation, there is no reproductive imagery. God in seven days creates the world from nothing, or according to some interpretations, from a sort of pre-existing chaos.[1] The dominant creative force emanates from the word of God and the pronouns which refer to God are masculine; there is no womb or female partner. There are no divine couplings and no instances of heterosexual reproduction except by human beings created by God. In Hesiod's *Theogony*, on the other hand, a goddess emerges from (or simply after) pre-existing chaos and it is due to female fecundity that the rest of creatures, both divine and mortal, come forth. The idea of the female origin and female prototype for creation is restricted to pagan texts. In Genesis, God separates heaven and earth and, without the intervention of any other divine beings, creates all the flora and fauna of the universe. In the *Theogony* of Hesiod, there are both parthenogenesis (female-only creation) and endless coupling on the part of immortal divinities. Gods and goddesses lie with one another in erotic attraction, have love affairs with mortals, and produce all manner and kind of offspring. Some of these offspring are natural phenomena, others immortal gods and goddesses or demigods, some are monsters. One of the most powerful gender stereotypes in the history of Western literature stems from the association of the female gender with fertility. This association has led to the long-lasting identification of the concept "nature," with all its fecundity, as somehow female, and the elevation, in the minds of some contemporary spiritualists of a "divine feminine" as the creator of life. It is also a compelling contrast to the biblical story of male-only creation and has been exploited to counter this "bias." The subtle constellation of meanings around female reproductive fecundity found in myth has given impetus to gender essentialism, making its way into a long series of "acts of literature" and philosophy. A detailed examination of this aspect of early myth supports the premise that ancient mythologies have had their share in promulgating this lasting cultural memory.

Hesiod is not unique in making cosmogony a ruling organizing structure: it is characteristic of the mythology of early cultures throughout the world. The Platonist and Gnostic literature of later antiquity elevates cosmogony and makes it a template, not only for generating a theogony but for generating the very world itself. The philosophers of late antiquity reworked the ancient "gendered" account of the genesis of divine progeny and turned it into a philosophical account of the coming to be of the universe through binary oppositions. All cosmogonies exercise one or more of several alternatives to account for the generation of offspring. Reproductive copulation between male and female is the most common mythological paradigm, but there are several exceptions. Male divinity as the primal creator is one variety of creation myth, found in Hesiod, Orphism, Gnosticism. Parthenogenesis, female-only creation, is another. Chaos, the first progenitor in the Hesiod narrative and other Near and Far Eastern myths, is a gender-free origin of creation that has no precursor mother or father. In the case of the Orphic myths, an originary egg is the ruling prototype for creative production. The most common template is that of male and female progenitors, analogous to human mating. A primordial couple engenders everything that exists, not only the generations of the gods and goddesses, but also the physical flora and fauna of nature. The act of impregnation with seed (or "idea," as in Platonism) falls to the male, while reception, gestation, and birth fall to the female.

In later antiquity, Platonist philosophy updated the time-tested stories of the gods and the goddesses. With the passage of time and the interpretation of myth as allegory and then as inspired symbolism, the engineering of reproduction became transformed into a process wherein levels of reality interact to produce the universe. In the earliest myths, gods and goddesses create the generations of divinities. In later accounts, both Middle Platonic and Neoplatonic, they help to produce the world itself and sustain nature. To fully comprehend how these changes took place, I think it is important to be aware of the sweeping change that took place in the intellectual life of classical antiquity. After the advent of the Presocratic physicists and the Greek philosophers, Plato and Aristotle, as well as the Sophists, a different sort of discourse developed. It was one that supported abstract concepts and supplied overarching concepts like Soul, Mind, the Good, Form and Matter, etc. Bruno Snell's book *The Discovery of the Mind* encapsulates the idea that there were rhetorical developments with the advent of prose writing in Greek antiquity. In Hesiod, the practice of ascribing mythical names (proper nouns) to abstracts (Gaia, Ouranos, etc.) allowed for the practice of personifying nouns like earth and sky. The later Greek use of the participle and other grammatical innovations fostered the creation of philosophical abstractions that stood on their own as concepts. Snell suggests that "The article is capable of making a substantive out to an adjective or a verb and these substantivizations, in the field of philosophy and science, serve as the stable objects of our thinking."[2] "To Hesiod," Athanassakis points out, "Earth (Gaia), Sky (Ouranos) and Sea (Pontos) are not mere elements but gods. Likewise, positive and negative forces such as Justice and Peace or Injustice and War, are not merely conditions or abstract forces, but individual divinities or individualized divine powers."[3] This was personification in its most blatant form, a trope that was all but missing in the rhetorical prose of Plato Aristotle and the Physicist. Snell contends that Homer and Hesiod use the article in a different way than in later scientific usages. Plato, for example, speaks of "*the* just" (i.e., Justice) as opposed to Hesiod in *Works and Days* (226) who speaks of the just act (*dikaon*) or just things (*ta dikaia*), using the plural to indicate a series of individual just acts.[4] The use of the definite article allows a name to become substantial and fosters the innovations of science or philosophy. When water is thought of as *to hudôr* (the water), Thales can take it to be the primary principle of all things. Land, when owned, has boundaries, but when not owned is boundless (*apieron*). Anaximander used *to apieron* (the boundless) to identify the source of all that is in the universe. Anaxagoras could posit that Nous ruled all things, personifying the noun referring to mind, allowing the possibility that one could formulate the universal as a particular. Heraclitus pronounced the Logos as the source of all things ("Listening not to me but to the Logos, it is wise to agree that all things are one.")[5] Grammar itself, then, supplies the grounds for the possibility that names can be used as principles in cosmological accounts. Once "water" is formulated as "the water" (or "Water"), it can be an organizing principle. Plato theory of forms, and his coinage of many the abstract nouns that still feature in philosophical discourse, was followed by Platonists who, after Plato's death, formed the so-called "Old Academy." They espoused a Platonism built upon such Platonic and Aristotelian dichotomies as Monad and Dyad, One and Many, etc., but re-divinized some of these concepts (as will be described in Chapter 5 on dualism). Allegorizing concepts by associating them with the gods and goddesses of the epic poets created a precedent, one which came to full fruition in the Middle and Late Neoplatonists of the fourth and fifth centuries. In Chapters 5 and 6, this will be discussed more fully.

In epic poetry, then, abstractions such as Love and Strife, Mind and Justice were personified, and given the proper names of gods and goddesses. During the classical period in Greece, philosophical reasoning did not follow this practice. In later antiquity, the process was reversed again, and conceptual entities were treated as gods and goddesses. It is here that we find gods and goddesses once again operating in the cosmic scheme. While in the Archaic period their romantic liaisons produced both natural phenomena and divine descendants, in later accounts, they facilitate the ability of the world beyond being to interact with nature. The transcendent world beyond nature, pure and undefiled, intellectual and paradigmatic, is a province of male divinity. The gods bestow their intellectual gifts onto nature itself through amorous liaisons with female divinity. Time and change, motion and matter are associated with the activity of a life-producing female divinity as she longs for form and unity. Copulating activity becomes conflated with abstract principles and processes, and the acts of conjoining are analogous to human sexual union. Erotic reproductive coupling, through the alchemy of allegorical interpretation, becomes a philosophical account of emanation in the creation of the physical world. Once a mythological paradigm, it is now an account of how abstract entities such as form and matter, intellect and soul mix to produce the world.

There are several themes in cosmogonic myths that specifically fall to the role of a goddess. In these narratives, she is a mother and producer of offspring but also a protector of life, an iconic figure that reigns supreme in all functions that concern motherhood and fertility. As exemplar of fecundity, she extends her purview over all that is in need of nurture. Even the famed virgin goddesses, Athena, Artemis, and Hestia, known for resisting the sway of Aphrodite and never mating at all, contribute to the care and nursing of progeny that they did not themselves gestate. Artemis brings young girls to maturity and readiness for marriage. Athena nurtures and raises Erechtheus, the archaic king of Athens. Hestia is a personified hearth to all homes, thus a source of domestic protection. Karl Kerényi, an old school mythographer, who relies on Jung for his psychological approach to mythology, focuses attention on the fact that Athena is both virgin and mother. Susan Deacy mentions this aspect of Athena as well.[6] While this may have little to do with Jungian archetypes, it is nevertheless striking that, on the one hand, Athena is divine protectress and mother and, on the other, divine virgin and eternal maiden.[7] Rhea is a mother. Demeter is mother love. Demeter's nursing of Demophon in the *Hymn to Demeter* and her abortive attempt to immortalize him are a prototype for nurturing and mothering, apart from the role of gestating and giving birth. Gaia is the original primal mother of all that is created, coming forth, in some mysterious way, out of Chaos. All the gods and goddesses that follow are created as a result of her fecundity. Her first offspring are produced parthenogenetically. Aphrodite, famously the goddess of love, facilitates erotic attraction.

All of the several types of the role of the goddess in life-generating scenarios can be found in Hesiod, Homeric Hymns and earlier literature: (1) no role at all viz. male generativity; (2) life-bearing womb without any reception of male seed; (3) life-bearing womb as receptacle of male seed and later of male intellectual forms; (4) a goddess mating with a god, which involves heterosexual desire, impregnation, and birth; (5) birth of the world from an originating chaos. Hesiod's account of creation combines several of these and involves a series of couplings, pregnancies, and births.

> Tell me, O Muses who dwell on Olympus, and observe proper order
> for each thing as it first came into being.
> Chaos was born first and after it came Gaia
> the broad-breasted, the firm seat of all
> the immortals who hold the peaks of snowy Olympus,
> and the misty Tartarus in the depths of broad-pathed earth and Eros, the fairest
> of the deathless gods;
> he unstrings the limbs and subdues both mind
> and sensible thought in the breast of all gods and all men.
> Chaos gave birth to Erebos and black Night;
> then Erebos mated with Night and made her pregnant
> and she in turn gave birth to Ether and Day.
> Gaia now first gave birth to starry Ouranos,
> her match in size, to encompass all of her,
> and be the firm seat of all the blessed gods.
> She gave birth to the tall mountains, enchanting haunts
> of the divine nymphs who dwell in the woodlands;
> and then she bore Pontos, the barren sea with its raging well.
> All of these she bore without mating in sweet love. But then
> she did couple with Ouranos to bear deep-eddying Okeanos,
> Koros and Kreios, Hyperion and Iapetos,
> Thea and Rhea, Themis and Mnemosyne
> as well as gold-wreathed Phoebe and lovely Tethys,
> Kronos the sinuous-minded, was her last-born. (*Th.* 114-37).[8]

Pender suggests that misty Tartarus is the interior of Earth and that Chaos, Gaia, and Eros are primal while M.L. West suggests that it is conceived as a dark gaping space, located beneath the earth. The Titans in Tartarus are on the far side of it (Th. 814) and must have fallen through it.[9] Erotic coupling begins when Ouranos, in an evocative poetic imagery, sprawls over Gaia, covers her with his whole body, and pours himself into her ceaselessly, in an eternal night. Gaia and Ouranos produce a myriad of sons and even Cyclopes with one eye in the middle of their foreheads, and a hundred armed giants. Pontos lies with Gaia, Oceanus with Tethys, Thea with Hyperion, Styx with Pallas, Phoebe with Kios, giving birth to Leto. Asteria with Perses conceives the famous Hekate and, of course, Rhea with Kronos produces the Olympian gods.

Pathogenesis and Male-Only Creation

It is notable that a female deity, Gaia, is the most original source of all that follows, including her own infamous mate, Ouranos, giving legend to the idea of an "earth mother." Parthenogenesis on the part of a goddess, as the most originary source of life-producing powers, may have encouraged some modern-day advocates of an original matrilineal culture to suggest that goddess worship was primal. Although her progenitor status is a literary artifact, this myth supports theories like those of Marija Gimbutas, the archeologist who has made a study of the parthenogenic goddesses in Paleolithic and Neolithic eras of prehistory, suggesting they may mirror a matrilineal social structure. She asserts that the numerous archeological finds of female figurines are of a goddess that represents the continuity of life as a perpetual regenerator, protector, and nourisher.[10] The woman's body, she contends, was regarded as parthenogenetic, creating life out of itself. In fact the female figurines that have predominated in the excavation of Minoan and Paleolithic sites have been connected with fertility rites, which does not necessarily imply a ruling goddess or a matrilineal society

Aside from the unnatural birth of Athena from the head of Zeus, instances of male-only creation are few and far between. In the Derveni papyrus (340 BCE, discovered in a tomb in 1962 near Thessalonica in Northern Greece),[11] however, departing from Hesiod's *Theogony* and incorporating an Orphic cosmogony, the focus is on the creative role of Zeus in the cosmic ordering. In the Orphic Rhapsodies too, López-Ruiz points out, Zeus swallows Phanes/Protogonos and as a result there is a new beginning of the whole cosmos stemming from him:

> After retaining the strength of the first born (*prôtogonos*) Erikepaios, he (Zeus) contained the body of all things inside his empty stomach. Everything was formed again with him, inside of Zeus, the shining height of the wide aither and the sky, the abode of the barren sea and the glorious earth.
> (trans. López-Ruiz, 144–5)

In Hesiod's *Theogony*, Zeus comes to power through a series of struggles, and the final part of the poem is dedicated to his victory, while in the Derveni theogony Zeus is placed at the beginning and the center of the creation. In the so-called Hymn to Zeus, cited in later authors and in the Derveni papyrus, "Zeus is the head, Zeus the middle, from Zeus everything was created" (Cods. 17.2.18.1 and 19.8).[12] Male-only creation is a counterpart to the very peculiar and counter-intuitive idea of virgin birth and celibate motherhood.

Divine Coupling

Vernant gives us some background to Hesiod's account of the primordial divine couple. Gaia both produces and mates with Ouranos, giving birth to Okeanos. Okeanos presents a prime example of the equivocation between a natural force and a god. He is a circular river that encloses the world, related to renewal of vigor and youth and a "fountain of fertile production." Okeanos is mentioned in the capacity of an original "father" place "where the gods have risen," etc., in Homer (*Il.* 8.478; Il, 14.200) *Od.* 4.563, 19.511) and Hesiod (*Th.* 821.8).[13] Later the name will be a well-worn figure of speech for the origin of generation in the Neoplatonists. In Proclus' *Commentary on Timaeus*, for example, Okeanos is discussed in Book III from 178–187, given many epithets among which is "generation of the gods" and "producing cause of generative perfection" (III. 178). In the Orphic cosmogonies, on the other hand, Night as original source takes the place of Okeanos and Tethys.

In the *Theogony*, Earth (Gaia) and Sky (Ouranos) are the couple whose "marriage" produces a pantheon, an exotic collection of offspring. They emerge from, or exist following, an original singularity in the form of a vague and unorganized state of being, Chaos, which predates the two male and female progenitors. Vernant speculates that Chaos is a kind of darkness in which all things remain confused before emerging into light, or perhaps some sort of unformed state of being. Many ancient cultures begin their account of creation with an original chaos of some sort, out of which male and female principles emerge. Here in the *Theogony*, Chaos' two offspring, Erebos and Nyx (night), produce Ether and Day. Chaos, as an original deity, is a rare case in Hesiod of gender neutrality. Gaia is next mentioned as the mother of Ouranos with whom she later mates. Ouranos and Gaia give birth, in addition, to the Titans, six male and six female. Their offspring include Zeus's parents, Kronos and Rhea. The Titans are the first pantheon of Greek gods and goddesses, overthrown during the famous Titanomachy, a war that lasted ten years and was won by the Olympian gods. The twelve Titans are Okeanos, Hyperion, Koios, Kronus, Krios, and Iapetos, and the female Mnemosyne, Tethys, Thea, Phoebe, Rhea, and Themis. The second generations of Titans consist of Hyperion's children, among whom are Leto and Asteria, and Iapetos's children, among whom are Atlas, Prometheus, and Okeanos' daughter Metis (the goddess swallowed by Zeus prior to his giving birth, out of his head, to Athena).

The existence of some sort of actor or act that accounts for the ensuing separation of the primordial couple out of chaos or from each other is common to Indo—European accounts of creation. Here in *Theogony* Eris (strife) or Eros (love) intervenes. Cornford cites examples of other literature which report a similar arrangement. Apollonius Rhodius' (b. 295 BCE) uses an Orphic cosmogony, for example, "Orpheus sang how earth and sky and sea were at first joined together in one form, and then disparted [separated], each from each, by grievous strife." He cites a similar account in a hymn in the Rig-Veda (vii.86) which says of Varna, whom some scholars identify with Ouranos, that he "held asunder spacious Earth and Heaven."[14] Cornford raises the question why the dome of the sky, marked by unchanging stars, the most permanent and indeed eternal part of nature, would have been joined with Earth in the first place. With no clear answer, he does point out that this model seems a product of what he terms the "collective mind" as it appears in diverse cultural settings. While I find the term "collective mind" questionable, it does point in the direction of the fact that there are common features cross culturally, and raises issues concerning "reception" in the archaic period. M.L West comments that Gaia mating with Ouranos, Heaven and Earth mating as the primal couple, is common to Indo-European cultures. It features, for example, in Sumerian and Babylonian literature.[15] It is notable that many of the Presocratic philosophers as well as Aristotle discuss heterosexual reproduction wherein form is contributed by the male and matter by the female.[16]

Pender points out that "The polarities of one/many and male/female are at work in the first stages of the god's birth, ... "[17] In Middle Platonism and Neoplatonism, as discussed here in Chapters 5 and 6, these two types of polarities conflate as philosophical concepts fuse with god and goddess in a theologized ontology. As early as the Pythagorean table of opposites, however, the basic principles that govern the world are twofold and linked to gender. In fact, genderized dualism forever after impacts on Western rhetoric. Dualism seems to be embedded in Platonist accounts all the way to the last Neoplatonists for whom the One is the undifferentiated unity out of which emerge Limit and Unlimited, the two hypostases immediately below the One. It is notable that in Middle Platonist settings, when discussing the dichotomies such as form and matter, Numenius, Plutarch, and Moderatus present varying accounts of matter. Matter or the material universe in general is thought of as either an adversary or "the consort of god, the mother of the universe and even mother of 'the corporal and generated gods."[18] Matter continues to hold a somewhat devalued position in respect to form in the late Athenian school (Neoplatonic) and is associated with female gender. In Proclus, in the fifth century CE for example, on the supramundane level, Phanes is associated with the paternal and limit and Nyx with the female and unlimited. Ouranos and Gaia are below each of these on the sublunary level. Ouranos is the limited but perfect unity of the spherical heavens with their symmetrical oneness and Gaia the cause of the unlimited fecundity and multiplicity of nature. Multiplicity, characteristic of matter, is always second in value to unity but necessary for creation.

Gaia as a "Great Mother"

In the canonical Greek myth, Gaia (earth) is the most original progenitor (after Chaos) and produces the first male, as well as everything else that follows. Athanassakis points out that Zeus, eventually the ruling and chief god of classical antiquity, is thereby ultimately descended from Mother Earth. "[We] have here the record of an evolutionary process that takes us from the physical to the nonphysical and from feminine dominance to male dominance," which Hesiod equates with law and order.

In fact, Zeus's first children by his second wife Thetis are associated with rightful regularity and justice: Eunomia (Law), Dike (Justice), and Eirene (Peace).[19] After Gaia gives birth to Ouranos, this union with the god of the heavens produces the heavenly gods, while her union with Pontos produces the sea gods. Gigantes (giants) emerge from her mating with Tartarus (the pit of hell), and mortal creatures are produced from her earthly flesh. It is through the coupling with Ouranos that she produces the twelve male and female Titans, and in addition the three Cyclopes, and the *hecatoncheires* (three-hundred-handed). Kronos, the youngest of six boys, is the direct rival of Zeus in the battle for the kingdom of the sky. Rhea, the companion of Kronos, is similar to Gaia, a mother attached to her children and ready to defend them. Kronos mutilates Ouranos at Gaia's bidding and from his severed genitals Aphrodite, the goddess of amorous union, is born. Gaia has an active role in the power struggles of Olympus and opposes her husband Ouranos who had imprisoned her sons in her womb, and it is she who assists Zeus in his overthrow of the Titan, Kronos.

Chaos as Precedent for a Receptive Womb

Hesiod places Chaos before everything else: "Chaos was born first and after it came Gaia" (*Th*. 116). Chaos precedes the advent of gendered deities but possesses characteristics that will later accrue to female deity and female creativity. An original chaos is an undifferentiated and infinite state that is featured in many creation myths across cultures. "Chaos" in the *Theogony*, as well, is a kind of unity, undifferentiated and genderless, yet a precondition or precursor for the gendered deities that follow. Vernant points out that the term *chao* is etymologically connected with *chaskô, chandanô*: to gape, to yawn, to open, a cavity, void, or absence. Vernant claims it is more like an "abyss, a vertiginous whirlpool that swirls ever deeper without direction or orientation. Yet, as an "opening" ...."[20] Vernant points out that Aristotle saw chaos as the void, space as a pure vessel and the abstraction of the private place of a body (Aristotle, *Physics* 208b26-33). The Stoics describe it as a state of confusion, a mass in which all the *sunchusis stoicheion* (constituent elements) of the universe are mixed together without distinction connecting chaos with the verbal form *chesthai*: (to pour or spread). It is not the equivalent of air. Hesiod distinguishes air from Chaos (697–700): "and besides, Erebus and Nyx, who have more in common with Aer, are born of Chaos which is thus logically and chronologically anterior to them." While not identifiable with any of the elements, then, for Hesiod the Gaping Chasm which is born before anything else, has, in Vernant's description, an "absence of stability, the absence of form, the absence of density, the absence of fullness."

López-Ruiz compares the Hesiodic tradition with the Northwest Semitic one. In Hesiod's account, Chaos is the first step of his cosmogony followed by Gaia. Eros also plays a role in the mating of Gaia and Ouranos. Chaos, López-Ruiz points out, allows for existence itself, while Eros is a "sort of tension or motor of procreation."[21] In the Babylonian account, on the other hand, the primordial waters occupy the first place. This corresponds to Okeanos (in this case with Tethys as a primordial couple) in Homer's *Iliad* (14.201-302) and the watery elements of the Presocratic and

Orphic cosmogonies. The association with water goes back as far as Nippur. There the theogony asserts the reciprocity of the male (Heaven–An) and female (Earth–Ki), but the earlier tradition in the city of Erdu names the goddess Nammu, the personification of the subterranean waters. She is a prime element, the progenitor of all the deities, including An and Ki. She is a "goddess without a spouse, the self-procreating womb, the primal matter, and the inherently fertile and fertilizing waters."[22] It seems that in many ancient accounts, it is some sort of undifferentiated unity that is the most primordial entity. Whether chaos or primordial waters, these are a precursor to the receptive function in erotic male/female coupling and to the womb of the goddess in parthenogenesis. Both of these, closer to limitless, are a source or principle or prior condition for the emergence of duality, while Eros and Tartarus are intermediates for the copulating pair. In either case, action cannot go forward without the mediation of an additional factor that is neither male nor female. As presented in the Hebrew Bible, the creation of heaven and earth is preceded only by a state of chaos described as *tohu ba-wohu* (formlessness and void), but the source or first principle is God. In the opinion of some scholars, *Tohu va-wohu* is analogous to Chaos in Hesiod's *Theogony* (116). López-Ruiz also points to the fact that in the account of the first-century historian Philon of Byblos, who wrote a *Phoenician History* based on Phoenician texts to which he reportedly had access, a dark and gloomy air occupies the position of Chaos in the Hesiodic account. She associates this with the Hebrew narrative where the fine wind (*ruach*) passes over the waters (Gen. 1:2). Gaia, as opposed to the original Chaos which is amorphous and limitless, on the other hand, is the most primordial of female goddesses in the *Theogony*, and a stabilizer, generator, and organizer. Mysteriously, the original chaos somehow necessarily precedes her, but it is unclear whether it has any role in her coming to be. In later philosophical transformations of the goddess, the characteristics of these originary sources, Chaos and Gaia, conflate, allowing the possibility of associating the goddess with multiplicity, a kind of indeterminate unity, and, at the same time, a fecundity in the ability to generate life. The goddess, then, is the embodiment of a receptive womb. Plato's famous "receptacle" in his account of the creation of the physical world in *Timaeus* inherits this legacy.

Plato's Receptacle, the Womb of All Becoming

In 48E-49A of *Timaeus*, Plato proposes that a mixing bowl (*kratêr*) or "receptacle" (*hypodochê*), "a third thing, a form difficult and obscure" (49A4), must be added to the "*mythos logos*" (the likely story), he narrates, for the production of the world (there is Being and Becoming, and this "third thing"). Plato's "receptacle" (*chôra, krater*, or *hypodochê*) has engendered innumerable scholarly interpretations of the mysterious "third thing" that he identifies. This "mixing bowl" is a receptive but chaotic substrate that receives forms and elements to engender the universe. It is reminiscent of the mythical Chaos but also suggestive of a womb. He describes it as "the receptacle—as it were, the nurse—of all Becoming" (49A6-7). Plato's brilliant prose makes it difficult to separate trope from philosophical account, but it is clear that he associates the receptacle with the female and the mother. He claims: "We may fittingly compare the recipient to a mother (*mêtri*), the model to the father (*patri*) and the nature that arises between them to their offspring (*eiknonê*)" (50D2-14). At 51A, he calls it "mother (*mêtera*) and receptacle of the generated world," and at 51B he states that "in a baffling way" it "partakes of the intellective." While the gods and goddesses are absent in this account, the receptacle as an incubator and the "forms" or ideas or model is the spermatic contribution that injects form and order into the receptacle. Although the trace memory of the *Theogony* seems present here, the fact that there are conceptual entities at work here, not gods, makes Plato's account "godless" and largely philosophical. Plato refers to his account of creation "*eikos muthos*" (likely story) (*Tim.* 29D, 59C, 68D). His mysterious "mixing bowl" combines a receptive womb-like container, the mothering function, and the genderless primordial indeterminateness that is reminiscent of Chaos and Gaia in Hesiod's account. *Timaeus*, then, provides a paradigm within which a demiurge is the technician who constructs the world, receiving forms from the intelligible paradigm that is its "model," and the receptacle in which the forms are received. When Plutarch, writing in the second century CE, suggests that Plato's *hypodochê* (*chôra*) combined with the World Soul is represented under the image of Isis, the "receptacle" is no longer a figure of speech as it may have been for Plato. It is now a concrete reality, in fact, a goddess.[23]

Plato chooses to call the receptacle a mother and nurse. This may simply be a metaphorical usage that can supply a receptive space for forms while remaining an undifferentiated chaos that is also somehow generative. This allows Plato to bridge the "explanatory gap" between the paradigmatic Forms, "intelligible and always the same being" (48E5-6) and the copy of this paradigm, "generated and visible." The receptacle, qua nurse of all generation, supplies what is missing. Formal paradigms can mix with material reality and be generative but it has to be enacted in a medium which supplies materiality.[24] According to Kenneth Sayre, Plato deliberately avoided precise and technical language and his figurative discourse poses a difficult task for interpretation.[25] There is a sense of nurturing suggested by the *tithênên* (nurse, 49A7 and 52D5), and the words *mêtera* (mother, 51A5) and *trophon* (foster mother, 88D8), but the receptacle is also described as *hedran* (place, 52B1) and *chôra* (space, 52A8, D3). Sayre points out that the ambiguity between containment and nurture invokes not only the relationship between the Forms and the receiving element, but also the relationship between mother and father. For Plato, the forms interact directly with the elements in the receptacle to produce the natural universe. In many of the accounts that follow in later antiquity, logos/intellect/monad, etc., are regarded as the male principle of the universe, while the female principle is associated with matter, motion, and change. When this binary construction is given the names of gods and goddesses, and when these oppositions combine to produce the world as their offspring, the act is described in the language of erotic desire and mating.

Plato's receptacle (*chora* or *hypodochê* or *krater*) has held a great deal of significance for some feminist scholars. Emanuela Bianchi, for example, considers this "one of philosophy's founding gestures" when it comes to "relegation of the feminine to a position of a barely knowable, shifting, errant function in the production of a metaphysical system and world in which only men are able to be portrayed as fully agenetic reasoning beings."[26] Julia Kristeva deploys the notion of *chôra* or receptacle in the elaboration of her linguistic notion of the semiotic to describe the maternal body.[27] Luce Irigaray, Judith Butler, and others have also provided analyses along these lines.[28] While reading Plato will always be replete with polysemic possibilities for interpretation, it seems that the evocative receptacle that Plato identified survives the centuries. Chapter 11 here will take up these contemporary usages.

The Receptacle in Later Antiquity

In Gnostic literature of the second and third centuries CE, described here in Chapter 3, it is notable that the life-giving reproductive function is termed "Life" itself and is associated with the cosmic womb. Turner, discussing Hekate and the androgynous deity Barbelo, shows these connections as follows:

> The third of Barbelo's principal attributes is named Eternal Life. And in the case of Hekate, we have noted that the Chaldeans regarded her right side as the source of the primordial soul that animates the realms of light, divine fire, ether and the heavens (fr. 51 des Places). In this capacity, both Hekate and Barbelo are characterized as cosmic wombs. Of these two, only Barbelo is explicitly said to be androgynous, but it is clear that they were both conceived in predominantly feminine terms.[29]

Proclus in a later setting, the Athenian academy in the fifth century CE, associates the receptacle with female deity. Robert van den Berg asserts that the *Krater* is a real goddess for Proclus, who maintains that we need to practice the rites associated with her. The father is the demiurge or technician who constructs the world and the *Krater* corresponds to the life-producing goddess who receives the creation. In Proclus, the receptacle *is* the life-producing goddess and is equated to Rhea, who is located between the pure Intellect (Nous), also known as Kronos, and the demiurgic Intellect, that is, the Demiurge, properly speaking, also known as Zeus. Proclus claims that Rhea is the Orphic name of the deity whom the Chaldean theologians call Hekate.[30] In Proclus's account, Rhea *is* the receptacle.[31] There is nothing metaphorical at work; concept and deity are coded references to the same divine reality. Proclus's view that humankind is a microcosmic mirror of the universe at large, both subject to a life-producing goddess, can be seen in the following passage:

> Man is a microcosm and everything that is in the cosmos in a divine and complete way is in him too in a partial manner. For we have intellect in act and a rational soul that came forth from the same father and the same life-producing goddess as that of the universe.
>
> (Proclus *in Tim.* 1 5.11-17)

Erotic Coupling

As Athanassakis comments, "most of the *Theogony* is an account of birth that follows attraction and copulation. Eros is a silent partner to every fruitful union."[32] Plutarch is an exemplary second-century canonical Middle Platonist who adopts a model of heterosexual coupling to represent ontological creation. Fusing Gnostic, Chaldean, and Egyptian lore with Platonism, the paternal "intellect" becomes an impregnator and, together with a female goddess as a passive recipient, procreates reality. This model supplies a paradigm for dynamic interaction in the otherwise static universe of Platonic formal abstractions. Erotic attraction, or the intervention of the god Eros, makes desire the dynamic force that enables coupling. Isis's erotic attraction to Osiris brings about world creation. While she assumes fertility and a nurturing nature, as is her persona in Egyptian myth, she possesses a dyadic ability to multiply infinitely that is Platonist. Osiris is the unmixed and dispassionate Logos (54.323b) or the vertical of the most beautiful triangle (56.373f), and copulates with Isis as a creative principle.

> Plato [*Tim.* 50C-D] is wont to call what is spiritually intelligible the form and the pattern and the father, and the material he calls the mother, the nurse and the seat and place of creation, while the fruit of both he calls the offspring and creation. One might suppose that the Egyptians liken the nature of the universe especially to his supremely beautiful of the triangles which Plato also in the *Republic* [546B] seems to have used in devising his wedding figure. This triangle ... The vertical should be likened to the male, the base to the female, and the hypotenuse to their offspring; and one should similarly view Osiris as the origin [*archên*], Isis as the receptive element [*hypodochên*] and Horus as the perfected achievement.
> (Plutarch *De Is.* 56.373e7-374a5)

The specifically erotic nature of coupling involved in Isis's fecundity is evident in the following passage:

> Isis is the female principle in nature and that which receives all procreation and so she is called by Plato [*Tim.* 49A-51A] the Nurse and the All-receiving, while most people call her the Myriad-named because she is transformed by reason and receives all corporeal and spiritual forms. Imbued in her she has a love of the foremost and most sovereign thing of all, which is the same as the Good, and this she longs for ... she yearns ever of herself for what is better, offering herself to it for reproduction and for the fructifying in herself of effluxes and likenesses (*aporrias kai homoiotêtas*).
> (Plutarch *De Is.* 53.372e6-372f4)

In Plato's dialogue *Phaedo* (75AB), all becoming yearns for true being and strives to become united with it.[33] Jones tells us that the love of Isis for Osiris has as its background Aristotle's doctrine that god moves *hôs erômenon* (in an erotic manner) (*Metaphysics* 12, 1072b2). In Plutarch's essay *On the Face of the Moon*, desire and union both play a part in his quasi-scientific account. After he elaborates upon the physical properties of the moon, he includes a second part, which is a myth. It was common lore of the time to consider the moon to be the origin and destination of the soul after death. The soul's nature is associated with the moon's ether (*De Fac.* 943d) and the soul yearns to be joined to the sun, not as a heavenly body, but as Nous or Intellect, the supreme and ideal goal that reveals itself in the sun. The sun, in turn, is associated with the Good found in the *Republic* of Plato as the highest object of intellectual attainment, and with the First God found in Middle Platonism. The moon "is separated by love for the image in the sun through which shines forth manifest the desirable and fair and divine and blessed, toward which all nature in one way or another yearns" (*De Fac.* 944e).[34] Just as mortal souls that have died yearn to join with the sun/Nous, Isis too yearns for the sun.

> Isis is none other than the Moon; for this reason it is said that the statues of Isis that bear horns are imitations of the crescent moon, and in her dark garments are shown the concealments and the obscurations in which she in her yearning pursues the Sun. For this reason alone they call upon the Moon in love affairs.
> (*De Is.* 52.372d7-12)

The *Chaldean Oracles* account for creation with similar figurative images. The chaotic becoming that occurs in the receptacle of Plato accrues to the Greek goddess Hekate as she yields to reason. The paternal Intellect impregnates Hekate's womb.[35] The "Father" is self-generated (fr. 39), separated from all the rest like the Good of the *Republic* and the One (fr. 3; 84) is unknowable and ineffable and is associated with Intellect (fr. 7; 109), Principle (fr. 13), and Monad (fr. 11). The Demiurge, who is a skilled worker or craftsman of the fiery cosmos (fr. 33), taking the Forms as a model, produces the sensible world (fr. 5). The Demiurge, who has a somewhat confusing status, not quite a "god" but somehow a creator or technician, causes the intelligible fire, the source of which is the Father, to descend. It is initially received into the womb of Hekate, or into sensible things that are located in "hollows" that correspond to matter, the universal receptacle.[36] The goddess Rhea is assimilated to Hekate, who is the source of souls, for her "womb," as Brisson describes, is also assimilated to the mixing bowl in which the Demiurge carries out the mixture from which all souls come, including the World Soul:

> Truly Rhea is the source and stream of blessed intellectual (realities).
> For she, first in power receives the birth of all these in her
> inexpressible womb,
> And pours forth (this birth) on the All as it runs its course. (fr. 56, trans. Brisson)

Thus Rhea/Hekate receives that fire that is the Intelligible into her womb, whose source is the Father, and then the Demiurge uses this fire to fabricate all souls and sensible reality.

Hermetic and Gnostic Literature

Patterns similar to those discussed above are present in the Hermetic account. A male creator god is a first progenitor but does not act without first creating a female counterpart onto which he can project the plurality he needs for creation. In the *Poimandres* of Hermes Trismegistus, the world is engendered by the Demiurge, a purely masculine act. It describes the begetting of the Demiurge by the First God and then his fathering of the seven planetary powers and the spheres, the setting in motion of the system, and, as a consequence of this revolution, the production of the irrational animals out of the lower elements of nature. In addition, there is an account of how darkness originated out of light. After the first separate hypostasis of the supreme Nous, the logos issues from the divine light and "comes over the humid matter" (an intimate union). The logos' presence in the dark matter is the cause of the latter's separating into lighter and heavier elements. Logos performs a differentiating action upon chaotic matter. The cosmogonic function of the logos is to stay within nature as the principle of order. This occurs through the *Boulê* of god (god's will as a separate entity). Jonas describes what happens next: "As the humid nature, after the logos has 'come over Her,' separates into the elements, so the female Will of God, having 'received' into herself the Logos, organizes herself 'according to her own elements.'" He suggests that the *Boulê* is more of an independent agent than is the humid nature of the first vision and produces a "psychical" progeny. The female "Will of God" here is in an interchangeable position with the "humid nature" and the Logos has been received by the former.

Gnostic literature has many variations on these themes. In the Valentinian doxography from Hippolytus (an important third-century theologian of the Christian church in Rome who preserved this literature), Sophia wants to have a child by herself without a partner, in order to imitate (*mimesasthai*) the Father.[37] In the *Apocryphon of John* and *Zostrianus* (second-century Gnostic texts), the Dyad appears as Barbelo, the womb of the All, and then as Sophia who longs to unite with the invisible spirit. She wished to receive an image but declined downward because of her dyadic character and gave rise to precosmic matter from whose grasp she attempts to escape by her act of repentance.[38] The complexities of the Gnostic literature on these points go far beyond what can be covered here, but Barbelo, in the *Three Steles of Seth*, is a higher form of Sophia. In general, Gnostic texts treat Barbelo/Sophia in a manner similar to the way Hekate is treated in the *Chaldean Oracles*. In Middle Platonism, such as in Moderatus, there is the emergence of quantity from the second One, a self-production of the unitary source, as Turner describes, and the emergence of a receptacle of becoming which now forms a place for the discrete multiplicity. In the Gnostic literature concomitant to it, there is the emergence of Barbelo Aeon from the invisible spirit as a projection of shadow of the One (found in *Zostrianus* VIII 78, 6-8 and *Three Steles of Seth* VII 122, 1-34).[39]

> In the Sethian system, then, both Eve and Sophia are mother figures; Eve, of Seth, and Sophia of the demiurge who creates the physical world. In this sense, Sophia, the divine wisdom could, as mother, be considered as the consort of the supreme deity Man, but she is disqualified because she conceived the world creator alone, without a consort. Therefore, since Sophia is disqualified, the supreme deity is supplied with a higher, unfallen equivalent of Sophia as his consort, who in the Sethian system is Barbelo, the androgynous Mother-father of the All, in Valentinian Gnosticism.[40]

In Plotinus 204–270 CE, the Neoplatonist who precedes the later Athenian School, one can find erotic imagery commensurate with Gnostic influence. Zeke Mazur discusses the hyper-noetic union of the Intellect with the One in Plotinus, on analogy with erotic longing and notions. The love that arises in each Hypostasis leaves a trace of itself to its subordinates and reaches the soul, kindling in it a desire for its source.[41] Plotinus blends the mystical with reproductive imagery, for example, he describes the imprinting of indelible forms upon matter with phallic and ejaculatory images. At VI 9.9 of the *Enneads*, Plotinus interprets the Platonic division of Aphrodite into two distinct but related manifestations, one of which is "heavenly," representing the soul's love of God in the intelligible world (the other purely sexual). He suggests that all subordinate "Aphrodites" flow from and depend upon a universal Aphrodite. Mazur goes on to discuss the biological-reproductive model for procession. The sexual act of human lovers is mimesis of mystical union with the one. Mazur elaborates on the influence here of the notion in Stoicism of *spermatikoi logoi* and the possible influence of Gnosticism and the *Chaldean Oracles* which is replete with reproductive terminology.[42] The Father sows forms into Hekate's womb from which they are poured into the material cosmos (Mazur cites frr. 8, 30, 32, 35, for example).

Symbolic Interpretation: The "Mating" of Finite and Infinite

Proclus (412–485), the later Neoplatonist, actively and deliberately makes equivalences and analogies between gods and Platonic categories. For Proclus, giving the gods and goddesses important roles in the conceptual order stemmed from his firmly entrenched conviction that conceptual entities and divine beings were interchangeable. For Proclus, higher fundamental levels of reality interact and produce the world and the mythical prototypes for reproductive generation could be adapted to this process. The mating of god and goddess is related to the prime categories, Limit and Unlimited (the level of being immediately following the One): "we. find that everything that proceeds in any fashion into being is generated from both of them" (*in Tim*. I.47.5-8). When they mix together or combine it makes the creation of the world possible. The idea of mixing and the idea of copulation fuse; Limit and Unlimited enact creation through erotic desire. Proclus discusses Plato's allusion to the harmony of male and female as they share jobs and the economy in *Republic* (18C1-4). The opposition male and female represent a mediated harmony that takes place at high levels. Proclus says:

> Indeed everything that proceeds from the male is also brought to birth by the female, preserving its subordinate role. So Hera processes in company with Zeus, giving birth to all things together with the father, for which reason she is called "the equal accomplisher," and Rhea processes in company with Kronos, for the goddess is the recess that harbors all the power of Kronos, and Ge processes in company with Uranus, as Ge is mother of all that Uranus has fathered. And if we were to assume, prior to these basic divinities, limit and unlimited, which have been given the status of principle and cause in respect of them, we shall find

that everything that proceeds in any fashion into being is generated from both of them.

(*in Tim.* I.46.26-I.47.7, trans. Tarrant)

For Proclus in late antiquity, then, the goddess is the "god particle" whose life-producing and erotic longing supplies the agency in a static universe of forms and hypostatic ideas. Coupling now has a double signification: the coupling of Limit with Unlimited, and god with goddess. Specifically, the goddess contributes the life-giving fertility and fecundity that the unlimited represents.

Although Hekate is only mentioned once in Proclus's *Commentary on Timaeus* (III.131.26), as Harold Tarrant points out, the female life-giving power (described in relation to the *Krater*) that is associated with Hekate in the Chaldean literature comes to accrue to goddesses in general.[43] Robber van den Berg suggests that Rhea, Demeter, Hekate, and Kore, regardless of which name is used, represent the power of the female life-giving goddess, as she is named selectively in various Proclus texts.[44] When Zeus and the female life-producing goddess cohabit, this "mixing" is the source of generation by which the world is created. The solitary One, in the form of its ambassador in being, Intellect, must combine with motion and change for nature to be produced. The noetic (intellectual) "father" in combination with the infusion of life coming from the life-giving female goddess performs a complex generating process. The equivocation between logical and reproductive genealogy augments and transmutes theogony. This can be seen in the following passage in which Proclus is discussing earth (Gaia).

> She (Gaia) becomes manifest in the middle triads of the intellectual gods, together with Heaven, who connectedly contains the whole intellectual order. She proceeds analogous to the intelligible Earth, ... And as ranking in the life-generating orders (*en zôegonois taxesin*), she is assimilated to the first Infinity (*pros tên Apeirian tên prôtên*). She is the receiving womb (*kolpos*) of the generative deity of Heaven. unfolding into light his paternal definitive, measuring, and containing Providence, which prolifically extend to all things. She likewise generates all the sublunary infinity; just as Heaven who belongs to the co-ordination of limit introduces termination and end to secondary natures ... for there is much limit in all sublunary natures and much infinity.
>
> (*in Tim.* III.175.15-176.6)

In Proclus, causes are gods and goddesses, and reproductive figures of speech and personification work in tandem to enact active causality. Just as the gods generate offspring, concepts generate consequent premises. Both disseminate primary causes throughout secondary manifestations in hierarchical descending series. Gods and goddesses are primary causes and causes are interchangeable with conceptual levels of being. Goddesses operate on every level. Even the virgin goddesses for Proclus have a significant role as generative. Artemis, according to Proclus, is a virgin because she has procreative power to produce (*in Crat.* 105,18-107,11). Artemis and Athena, the two virgin goddesses, are integrally linked with Persephone who is both virgin (*korê*) and the mother of nine blue-eyed, flower-weaving daughters, as Orpheus says (*in Crat.* 106,819).

Robert Lamberton elaborates upon passages in which Proclus discusses the scenario in the *Iliad* on the deception of Zeus (*Il.* 14.153-351).[45] In this passage, Hera devises a plan to distract Zeus so that she can help the Achaeans win the war. She tricks Aphrodite into giving her an enchanted breast-band woven with the powers of Love and Longing which could drive any man insane with passion. She then visits Sleep and promises him one of her daughters in marriage, persuading him to lull Zeus to sleep. When Zeus sees Hera and the enchanted band he is seized with passion, makes love to her, and falls asleep, whereupon Hera calls to Poseidon who can now command the Achaean victory. Proclus divides the passages into five separate problems (*in Rep.* I.133.10-15), the first of which is divine copulation. Here he tells his reader that the copulation and mating among the gods evoke the Pythagorean polarities and columns of opposites, which are fundamental to the structure of the universe. Male and female are polar opposites and copulation is a figure that accounts for the mixing of such opposites to produce a third thing. Every level of divinity in the Proclean hierarchy reproduces those above it. Zeus and Hera represent, in a fragmented mythic form, an event on the level of Nous (Intellect). Zeus is the primal, self-sufficient, finite monad, resembling the "noetic finitude," and generates reality "into the order of the monad." Hera is the generative dyad, infinite and containing the generative principle of plurality without which the perfection of the One would be sterile and nothing could exist. Their "mating" produces the world. Lamberton describes "another etymological fantasy with a certain charm, but little power to convince." Proclus identifies the scene of the copulation, Mount Ida (*Idê*) with the realm of ideas and contrasts it with the bedroom made by Hephaestus. The bedroom is taken to be the physical universe. With this interpretation, the copulation takes on cosmic proportions. The representation of the generative dyad (Hera) invites the representative of the finite monad (Zeus). The monad is perfect, hence dominant, and draws the dyad up to it. In these passages, Lamberton points out, Proclus virtually ignores the "deception" of Zeus by Hera.

The Orphic Egg and the Cosmic Womb

The Orphic egg is a cosmic egg from which, in its original form, the primordial hermaphrodite Phanes/Protogonos (equated with Zeus, Man, Metis, and Eris, among others) emerges. Phanes creates the other gods. Sometimes the primordial chaos itself is described as the egg. The fact that Aristophanes elaborates on the cosmic egg shows its ubiquitous presence in Greek culture: The following was written in 414 BCE and comes from Aristophanes' play, *The Birds*:

> First of all was Chaos and Night and black Erebos and wide Tartaros, and neither Ge nor Aer nor Ouranos existed; in the boundless bosoms of Erebos black-winged Night begets, first, a wind-egg, from which in the fulfillment of the seasons ardent Eros burgeoned forth, his back gleaming with golden wings, like as he was to the whirling winds. Eros mingling with winged, gloomy Chaos in broad

Tartaros, hatched out our race and first brought it into the light. There was no race of immortals before Eros mingled all things together; but as one mingled with another Ouranos came into being, and Okeanos and Ge and the unfading race of all the lesser gods. Thus we are by far the oldest of the blessed ones. (*Birds* 693)[46]

Kirk, Raven, and Schofield point out that this is a parody of a traditional type of cosmogony clearly influenced by Hesiod, with the exception of the egg.

The later Neoplatonic tradition (fourth to sixth centuries CE), particularly Damascius, is a most prolific source for Orphic versions of the formation of the world. Phanes is the ultimate creator of the world, based on Orphic Rhapsodies, which are post-Hellenistic works. In Damascius (*De Principiis* 123), Kronos engenders Aither and Chaos who in turn engender the egg (*ôon*) which in turn engenders Phanes. Proclus, in the fifth century CE, presents us with a vision that arises from Orphic mythology illustrating the long-standing survival of the Orphic literature. In this compressed statement, one can see the complexity of the evolution of Proclus's metaphysical tropes:

For what difference is there between calling the hidden cause an egg and [calling] that which has issued (*ekphanein*) from it a living thing? What else but a living thing would emerge from an egg? And this egg was the offspring of Ether and Chaos, the former of which is situated at the limit of the Intelligibles, the latter in the [region of the] Unlimited; for the former is the root of all things, while for the latter 'there was no limit' (fr. 66 Kern). So if the first thing [to issue] from Limit and the Unlimited is primal (*prôtôs*) Being, Plato's Being and the Orphic egg will be the same thing. And if Phanes, who corresponds to Living-Thing-itself [issues] from this [egg], one must ask what it is in Orpheus that corresponds to Eternity, which falls in Plato between Living-Thing-itself and Being. (*in Tim.* I.428.2-12)[47]

In typical Proclean fashion, Mythology, Astronomy, Pythagoreanism, even Life, are all co-present in this image. Science (the astronomic heaven contains all the heavenly bodies and their orbits in synchronous arrangement), the dodecahedron (all the regular solids can be inscribed), ontology (the paradigm comprehends all intelligibles), Orphism (the egg contains all living creatures spermatically), Pythagorean Platonism (Limit and Unlimited), and in theogony, all conspire to produce this iconic form.[48] His treatment of the cosmic egg is a perfect example of the syncretism with which Proclus treats the Hellenic tradition.

Conclusion

Ancient cosmogonies talk about principles, gods, essences and forces in ways that call to mind galaxies, black holes, supernovae, and pulsars of modern day physical cosmologists. "There is a major difference, however, in that the descriptions of ... life generating new life ... in the archaic texts (they) are almost exclusively limited to biological and especially, sexual metaphors".[49] Although Plato does not have a role in creation for goddesses in his account of creation, the ingredients are present that would allow future philosophers to make use of these as placeholders for divinities. In later narratives, male divinity is associated with Plato's "paradigm" in imitation of which the demiurge constructs the world. An indeterminate receptacle as a pre-existing condition, like the more ancient concept of chaos, is ready to receive intellectual determination. In many of the accounts of later antiquity that follow, logos/intellect/monad, etc., are regarded as the male principles of the universe, and matter/soul/dyad as the female. The template, then, is that of male disseminating form which is received by a female or womb—like entity. The outcome is that the male gender, associated with eternal rest and intellectual stability, holds a more valued position in creation than the female, who is associated with fertility, motion, nature, indeterminacy, and change. This is common to both early and late antique accounts.

While the primary source of creation in monotheism is a singular and transcendent being, dualism is fundamental to most pagan accounts. These alternatives, male-only as the prime creator, and female/male desire and copulation, or parthenogenesis contribute to the root metaphors that survive the centuries. In the world of the Hebrews, the church fathers and philosophers such as Aquinas, creation, following Genesis, falls to the male creator alone. Traces of the power of female fecundity can be seen in Gnostic carryovers into early church imagery (see Chapter 9) and in medieval Kabbalist literature in the form of a Shekhinah (see Chapter 8). The attributes of the gender binaries that accompany reproductive imagery in the Archaic, Classical, and Platonist tradition found their way into Gnosticism and into almost everything else that followed. The male intellectual and unifying functions valued over the fecundity and life-giving potential of the female contribute to an ideology deeply ingrained in future cultural memory. It is one that preserves the persistent binary opposition that some feminist and structuralist contemporaries have seen as a distorted over-valuation of male characteristics. It also seems to determine the way in which some of them propose a re-valuation of the characteristics on the female side of this historical opposition while others dismiss the entire idea of a gendered essentialist binary.

5

Dualism and the Mediating Goddess

The Pre-Socratic philosopher Parmenides (floruit 475 BCE) posited an unchanging, eternal permanency as the basic principle of all things while Heraclitus (floruit 500 BCE) posited one of eternal change and motion. These two founding gestures represent a precedent for a dualism that survives the centuries. The eternal problem of the One and the Many finds its way into every discussion throughout the entire history of philosophy. As soon as philosophy became an articulate discipline, it began a ceaseless inquiry into "how," with the premise that the universe is a One Being, could Oneness result in the "many" that constitutes physical existence. Unity is beyond time, space, and causality. Multiplicity is not. How could it, then, emerge from Unity? Multiplicity and unity, one and many, all must be accounted for if there is to be a philosophy about this universe. Dualism, it seems, is inseparable from the very nature of metaphysical reasoning. Personifying dualities with gender, however, is not. When two fundamental dualisms—one and many, male and female—conflate, myth and philosophy coincide. Dualistic thinking, then, appears to be an entrenched characteristic of ontology: there is an irreducible difference between unity and being: unity is a transcendent singularity, being manifests in multiform existence. It is understandable that the biological dualism of male and female would lend itself to this rubric. Creation myths, universally and in particular in the Hellenic tradition, all begin with dualities. Male and female divinities couple and their intermingling produces the world, as was discussed in the preceding chapter. Earth copulated with Sky, with a third party set aside in order to bring them closer together in the name of Love (Hesiod *Th.* 200). Okeanos and Tethys are a primordial divine couple that are impressively fertile (*Th.* 337-70).[1] In Homer Okeanos is called the origin (or generating father) of the gods, and Tethys their mother (*Il.* 14.300ff.).[2] Rhea and Kronos, Zeus and Hera, separate in gender, are opposing figures that unite in love. In the first and second centuries CE, the abstract concepts of metaphysics not only became genderized, incorporating the legacy supplied by epic poetry, they became imbued with the functions and activities of the deities.

One of the earliest examples of philosophical dualities personified by gods and goddesses occurs in the practice of ascribing these deities to mathematical numbers.

Plato's so-called unwritten doctrine that there are two supreme and opposing principles, the One and the indefinite Dyad, was adopted in full force by Speusippus (438–339 BCE), Plato's first successor, and was a prominent doctrine in the early academy. Speusippus held that the fundamental duality, consisting of the One and the indefinite (or infinite) Dyad, (duality) generates so-called form numbers. Xenocrates, head of Plato's academy after Speusippus, continued this approach.[3] He associated Zeus with the Monad, the "odd," and Intellect, and the Dyad with the mother of the gods and the region of the sublunary world.

> The former as male holds the position of father and rules as king in heaven; he (Xenocrates) calls it Zeus and odd and *nous*, who is for him the first god; the Dyad as feminine, in the fashion of mother of the gods, governs the realm under the heavens; she is for Xenocrates the world soul.[4]

Chrysippus (279–206 BCE), a Stoic, allegorized Zeus and Hera in this sense as well. Apparently, this had become an accepted means of characterizing the numerical opposition of Monad and Dyad. In later Neoplatonist ontology, the Monad and Dyad as god and goddess reached a fully developed expression. The act of conception and the erotic nature of the coupling that is associated with theogonic reproduction, in these accounts, are comparable to mathematical operations. Mathematical operations "generate" further results. Mathematical formulas can reproduce multiplicities in a way that is still under the control of formal parameters and this is comparable to creating the diversity of nature under the rule of intellectual ideas. A removed and transcendent "one," the supreme One of the Neoplatonists, is considered to be an influence on the mathematical first number. Just as the transcendent One beyond being is behind the multiform world, the first number is behind the multiplicity that allows for the rest of the numbers to unfold, but not without the active mediation that will bring it about. This mythical/scientific fusion extends to sacred geometry as well. In Plutarch, for example, Osiris is the unmixed and dispassionate logos (*De Iside* 323b) or the vertical of the most beautiful triangle (373f) that copulates with Isis as a creative principle.

The *Theologoumena Arithmêtikês* (*Theology of Arithmetic*) by the second-century philosopher Nicomachus was an epoch-making work, as Charles Kahn describes it, relating the significance of numbers to cosmology and natural philosophy and to moral concepts such as justice and friendship, as well as to the pagan gods. Nicomachus identifies arithmetic as the first and highest form of knowledge, and number as the first and highest form of being.[5] Photius, a bishop who lived in the ninth century and who preserved the work of Nicomachus, calls it "heathen nonsense" and reports that Nicomachus assimilated various gods and goddesses to each of the first ten numbers.[6] Still, the theological interpretation of the numbers was a decisive influence on further Neopythagorean and Neoplatonic traditions. Iamblichus or Pseudo-Iamblichus wrote a commentary on it, and Proclus claimed himself to be a reincarnation of Nicomachus. Robin Waterfield has translated Iamblichus's *Theology of Arithmetic*, which consists of Nicomachus' *Theology of Arithmetic* and Iamblichus' *On the Decad*.[7] In this book, the Monad is said to resemble god and "every mode of opposition is potentially contained within it." Nicomachus compares it to "pure light, sun-like and governing, so that it may resemble god in each of these respects."[8] The One is considered as androgynous, a unity that contains all and produces the Dyad by dispersion. For this account and similar Pythagorean-influenced arithmologies, the Dyad has attributes of formlessness, a relation to nature, and generativity, and is conceived as the source of multiplicity and limitless productivity. As is stated in the *Theology of Arithmetic*,

> The Dyad is clearly formless, because the infinite sequence of polygons arises in actuality from triangularity and the triad, while as a result of the Monad everything is together in potential, and no rectilinear figure consists of two straight lines or two angles, so what is indefinite and familiar falls under the Dyad alone. The Dyad is also called '*Eroato*' for having attracted through Love the advance of the Monad as form, it generates the rest of the results, starting with the triad and tetrad.

Furthermore, Iamblichus states that Isis (both the Greek word for equal and the name of the goddess) is said to be the Dyad:

> and they call it 'Isis' not only because the product of its multiplication is equal to the sum of its addition, but also because it alone does not admit of division into unequal parts. The Dyad is also named Demeter 'the mother of Zeus' (they say that the Monad was Zeus) and 'Rhea' after its flux and extension, which are the properties both of the Dyad and of Nature.[9]

The associations articulated in the *Theology of Arithmetic* reflect Pythagorean and Neopythagorean ideas in circulation during early and late antiquity. The connections between theologized number and divinity are made explicitly in Plutarch's second-century *Obsolescence of the Oracles* (428e-f) and in his *Isis and Osiris* (373a-c). The Monad and indefinite Dyad are primal cosmic opposing principles. The Monad is opposed to the indefinite Dyad and is the element underling all formlessness and disorder. Gnostic literature performs this alchemy as well. In the *Apocryphon of John* and *Zostrianus*, the Dyad appears as Barbelo and the womb of the All, then as Sophia who longs to unite with the Invisible Spirit.[10] These associations became canonical for Platonism, persisting through time, and are known to the Athenian school in the fifth and sixth century CE, headed by Proclus. As Kahn puts it, "Nicomachus' systematic correlation between the first ten numbers and the Olympian gods provided Iamblichus and Proclus with this peculiar device, in their desperate effort to maintain the united front of Hellenic philosophy and Hellenic religion against the inroad of Christianity."[11] The association of the female deity with the Dyad is a very significant example of the "secondary and yet necessary powers" attributed to female deity. As goddess, the properties of the Dyad give her the dynamic principle of expansion (in mathematics and in nature). In the Pythagorean table of opposites, the Dyad is associated with the inferior side of the table of opposites while the Monad is at rest and contains or is a first principle. The Dyad represents the unfolding, active life of creation. Because it entails division, motion, and change, it violates perfect "Oneness" but at the very same time it is essential for the creation of the universe in all its multiplicity. It is devalued, however, when it comes to a spiritual scale of values since unity is valorized as primary truth.

Creation in time and space, which involves multiplicity and division, is a second-place project, though not an insignificant one, falling to the female.

Matter and Form

Matter and form are a duality, established during the classical period of Western philosophy and primarily associated with Aristotle. He is the source, as well, for documentation of the famous table of opposites attributed to the Pythagoreans and disseminated widely in ancient thought (*Metaphysics* 986a22). In it the following opposites are listed: Limit/Unlimited, Odd/Even, Unity/Plurality, Right/Left, Straight/Crooked, Light/Darkness, as are Good and Bad, Male and Female in separate columns. The Female designation comes out on the side of darkness, bad, etc., making it possible to make a normative evaluation of the table. Although the elements on both sides of the table are constitutive of the universe, while the earlier Pythagoreans may not have made value judgments, the later Platonist views suggest such practices.[12] The duality matter/form is an omnipresent pattern reflecting the fact that binary opposition is basic to the composition of the universe. The philosophers of the second century CE, in a revival of Pythagoreanism, adhered to the canonical Pythagorean scale of oppositions, which now add an elaborate divinization of monad and dyad, associating them respectively to gods and goddesses.

One claim here in *Goddesses in Myth and Cultural Memory* is that nature, matter, motion, and change, in short the "chthonic" attributes, devalued by religion and philosophy, remain associated with female gender even up to and including contemporary thought. Binary oppositions of gender are an abiding connective structure that has had a strong hold on cultural memory. E. R. Lloyd has done extensive work in his monograph *Polarity and Analogy*, providing an analysis of the use of opposites in Greek thought. He points out that some of this usage carries with it hierarchal distinctions in both primitive and Greek societies. He suggests that natural oppositions such as right/left, male/female, and light/darkness acquire powerful symbolic associations and stand for religious categories such as pure and impure.[13] The opposition between form and matter falls into this pattern. Jones suggests that Plato's receptacle in *Timaeus*, as it partners with forms and intelligence to create the physical world, facilitates the allegorizing of male and female deities as form and matter.[14] In Aristotle's *Physics* (192a23), matter is said to desire form. In later instances, the goddess is associated with the life-producing powers associated with material creation and the god is associated with form. In Plutarch's *Isis and Osiris*, the god (Osiris) sows in matter (Isis) *logoi* (forms or ideas) from himself (*De Iside* 372f). In another of Plutarch's works, *De Animae Procreatione in Timaeo* (1014b–1015f), there is form on the one hand and primal matter, disordered motion, and soul on the one hand.

> Himself (Osiris) is far removed from the earth, uncontaminated and unpolluted and pure from all matter that is subject to destruction and death … With this beauty, Isis, as the ancient story declares, is forever enamored and pursues it

and consorts with it and fills our earth there with all things fair and good that partake of generation.

(*De Iside* 382F2-383A5-8)

Clearly the male god is associated with the eternal and unmoving, unmixed principle while the female is associated with the devalued but necessary idea of movement which entails division, discontinuity, and disunity. The erotic nature of this arrangement depicts the dyadic as a dynamic principle that desires unity but falls short of it. In this rubric, Funk, Poirier, and Turner tell us, Plutarch, Ataurus, Atticus, Alcineus, Apuleius, Numenius, and the authors of the *Chaldean Oracles* all distinguish the realm of true being (*kosmos noêtos*) from the lower realm of change and becoming (*kosmos aisthêtos*). The figure of Hekate (Isis in Plutarch's account) is the mediator who functions both as the origin of all movement and multiplicity and on a lower level as the source of the Cosmic Soul that sheds life and animation in the cosmos. In Funk, Poirier, and Turner's words, in this configuration,

> the indefinite longs for the definite, sensibles long for forms, forms long for supreme unity and the Dyad longs for the One yet falls short of it, thus producing. defection, extension and declension.[15]

Thus while Plato describes the world of the forms and that of material existence solely in terms of abstract nouns and Aristotle does so with the notions of form and matter, in the later literature of Platonism the fundamental dualities become divinized and in addition take on the Pythagorean oppositions that are associated with gender. For Plutarch, Osiris and Isis are contrasted in terms of the fundamental philosophical distinction between matter and form, purity and contamination by generation into the physical universe. For Plutarch, the pure uncontaminated Osiris is so far removed from the earth that "there is no association with this god except in so far as they may attain to a dim vision of his presence by means of the apperception which philosophy affords" (*De Iside* 382F7-8). In Plutarch's revision of the *Timaeus* doctrine, the *hypodochê* (the receptacle) receives forms and combines them with matter to create the world. The World Soul that supervenes upon this creation is represented under the figure of Isis, associated with the indeterminate Dyad, plurality, indefiniteness, and so with matter. Jones points out that the fact that Plato's *hypodochê* and the World Soul are represented under the image of Isis can be inferred from the fact that matter is called *ouk apsuchos* (not without soul). Isis is said to be named from ascribing to her *autokinêtos phora* (self-moving motion), which is what is said of the World Soul.[16] Osiris's soul is eternal and indestructible; his body is torn asunder by Typhon (the indefinite Dyad) (373a-b). Isis becomes an intermediary force. In Plutarch' *Obsolescence of the Oracles* (428ff.), the Monad as opposed to the indefinite Dyad is the element underlying all formlessness and disorder. Typhon takes on the role of a disorderly principle, which acts on matter, in opposition to the Monad. Isis, when she becomes implanted with the logoi/sperm of Osiris, can create the world by bringing order and chaos together to form physical reality. Plutarch's allegorical treatment of myth exemplifies a practice that will become widespread in the later Neoplatonists of the Athenian school. He states that he relates Egyptian theology (*Aiguption theologian*) to Plato's *philosophia* (*De Iside* 371a). Iamblichus (242–327 CE), for example, influenced by this treatment of form and matter also associates Osiris with the stable and orderly and Isis with the ability to disseminate vivifying powers. Thus, he says in *De Mysteriis* (VI.7):

> The parts of the universe stay in order because the beneficent power of Osiris remains sacred and immaculate and is not mingled with the opposing confusion or disorder, and the life of all things remains pure and incorruptible, since the higher vivifying powers because of the reasoning principle of Isis do not descend into the apparent and visible body.[17]

Isis is not associated, *per se*, with matter as much as she is associated with the powers which are able to mediate between matter and form. Lamberton says that Plotinus provides "a point of departure for later attempts at reconciliation of myth and idealist cosmology."[18] The Neoplatonic association of metaphysical entities with divinity can also be traced to Iamblichus and Porphyry, who added further sophistication and refinement to the second-century literature.

Mind and Soul, Being and Becoming

In one form or another, metaphysics, even in its modern forms, inherits the being/becoming paradigm found in early and late Platonism. Plato's *Timaeus* adumbrates this distinction and relates being to truth and becoming to belief (29C3-4): (*hotiper pros genesin ousia, touto pros pistin alêtheia*). Remaining at the heart of Platonism, this paradigmatic bifurcation, in one form or another, characterizes metaphysics in the centuries that follow. In Plato the claim to truth rests solely upon reason. In idealist metaphysics in general, existence (material and in space and time) is separate from essence (being, intellectual form transcending space and time). Natural existence is "created" or is an emanation in temporal and spatial form or is deemed the "empirical" as opposed to the rational. Mind which is somehow a unified essence and natural chaotic, material, spatial and temporal, and bodily existence, also known as "nature," are worlds apart. For Platonists, "soul" is the intervening hypostasis which can span both the world of intellectual form and nature, being and becoming, and this is the point at which, in the theologized accounts, the goddess steps in. In the universe itself, the fundamental dichotomy of being and becoming has an analogue in ancient and late antique astronomy as well. The fixed stars in the outmost heavens, subject to perfect circular motion, are representatives of "Mind" and conveyers of Providence. They stand in for being. The erratic motion in the orbits of the planets and nature is associated with becoming. Gaia and Ouranos, as were seen in Hesiod's *Theogony* and Orphism, represent the opposing earth and heaven. The sun and the moon also pose, for Platonists, a fundamental dichotomy. Transcendental unity is associated with the sun, which represents mind, multiplicity is connected to the sublunary world, and the intervening conjoining factor is the moon. Chaldean, Orphic, and Platonic texts all share these views of the celestial hierarchy. When the heavenly bodies are fused with the personas of gods and goddesses, goddesses are intermediate between sun (being) and earth (becoming), consequently, associated with the moon. This distinction between the superlunary and sublunary worlds, associated respectively with male and female deities, is also a distinction between fixed heavenly bodies at rest and the moving elements in the sublunary world. Funk, Poirier, and Turner, discussing the Gnostic text *Marsanès* (4.6-7, r. 18-19, 22, 24-25), describe the goddesses' function as the origin of movement and multiplicity associated with the Cosmic Soul that bestows animation on the cosmos. In the *Chaldean Oracles*, the Dyadic principle functions at various ontological levels, but always in commerce with the realm of change and becoming. In Gnostic systems, the engine of motion and change is Ennoia or Sophia; in the Chaldean system, Dynamis or Hekate; in the Hermetica, Life or Nature.[19]

Mediation

In the ancient tradition, multiplicity and ceaseless motion and change as it is found in the sublunary world could be in danger of bordering on formlessness and nothingness. In order to more precisely understand the role of the goddess as an intermediary, it is necessary to understand the trepidation held by ancient philosophers concerning the possibility of formlessness. When a goddess intervenes, she "saves" the world of being from the ultimate irretrievable chaos of unmitigated becoming. The Platonic "vision of the whole" abhors infinity and chaos. The *Theology of Arithmetic* iterates this idea as follows: "the nature of inequality proceeds in an infinite sequence whose source is the Dyad, and they call it nature since it is movement *towards* being and, as it were, a sort of coming to be and extension from the seed principle."[20] Unmediated, nature would run to ultimate dissemination and formlessness. Limit, stemming from Intellect, is the stamp of transcendent unity upon existence. Without limit in number, for example, iterative seriality could potentially dissipate into nonbeing through ceaseless division or multiplication, as in Aristotle's definition of *apeiron* (limitlessness).[21] The more something is subdivided, a process that can continue without end, the closer it comes to featureless matter. Form could be lost to existent things were limits not able to intervene upon it.

From the earliest Pythagorean writings (of which a fragment of Philolaus [470–385 BCE] is still extant), limit (*peras*) and unlimited (*apeiron*) were considered fundamental dichotomies. Plato in *Philebus* stresses the importance of this dichotomy (24a-31a). The unlimited (apieron), "[d]oesnot permit the attainment of any end (24a-b)" and limit (peras) does not admit of the unlimited. Limit makes limit and unlimited commensurable when mixed (25a-27b). Theaetetus, a mathematician and contemporary of Plato, classified all line segments which could produce square numbers into those that are commensurable and those that are incommensurable. He showed that those of 3 or 5 or 17 feet are not commensurable in length with those of one foot. These are lines that have no common measure, thus the process of finding a least common measure can continue ad infinitum. The concept of lines that are without ratio goes back to a time before Plato. The Pre-Socratic philosopher Democritus, T. L. Heath claims, regarded these lines as divisible rather than indivisible.

He quotes Simplicius' view that Democritus claimed that even the atoms were, in a mathematical sense, divisible further and, in fact, divisible ad infinitum.[22] Limit stops all things that are potentially serial from dissipation. The outermost circumference of the universe (the fixed stars) is a limit, time conceived as a Monad is a limit, ratio imposed on a continuum is a limit, and so on. Limit (or boundary) which stems from "Mind" and "Intellect" contains nature and avoids deterioration toward formlessness by imposing form. Although they are of crucial importance in ensuring the stability of the universe, however, they can provide no agency in the world of physical reality as they are static and at rest. For Intellect to impose form on matter and interact with nature, a moving living agency is required. The philosophers of the second and third centuries CE saw the problem posed by a two-world ontology in terms of the need for active salvation. The irrational potential of nature's unlimited creativity could only be contained if the two worlds of being and becoming could be mediated with an active agency. Goddesses, able to have commerce with nature, receiving formal limits from higher up, can avert the dangers of unbounded expansion. Though not enjoying the elevated status attached to the intellectual parameters she receives, she, unlike male divinity who is exempt from worldly commerce, is able to impart them and save the world of nature from dissolution and formlessness.

Why Motion, Change, and Matter Are Irrational but Not "Evil"

Goddesses may be secondary in the ontological hierarchy, devalued by an engagement with the irrational forces in the cosmos, but this does not make them "evil" by association. Matter though secondary to form in value is not "evil" and is necessary for creation. Furthermore, the goddess is wise and ameliorates the irrational and out-of-control aspect of matter and so prevents irrational dissipation. Personifying the higher intellectual undisturbed principle, closest to the "source" of all being as male, and the assignment of commerce with changeability and disunity to the female deity, makes her responsible for ensuring that irrational forces in the universe can be subdued or controlled.[23] For Plutarch, Isis is depicted as subduing chaos and evil and identified as "Athenaic" when she does so. She embodies wisdom and at the same time is somehow identified with Plato's receptacle as nurse of becoming. She is a passive material principle who submits to Osiris and an active spiritual principle that attacks evil. As Jones explains, "The Isis of the myth, who is both the world-soul and matter, is co-original with Osiris and Typhon who typify the One or Monad and the indefinite Dyad."[24] According to *De Animae Procreatione in Timaeo* (1014b–1015f), there are primal matter, disordered motion, and soul. In the Isis-Typhon-Osiris myth, Osiris's soul is eternal and indestructible; his body is torn asunder by Typhon, the indefinite Dyad and hence the destructive force (at 373a-b). In his *Obsolescence of the Oracles* (428ff.), the Monad is opposed to the indefinite Dyad, the element underlying all formlessness and disorder. Typhon represents the unruliness of formlessness, a disorderly principle, which acts on matter in opposition to the Monad. Isis, when she becomes implanted with the logoi/sperm of Osiris, can bring order and chaos together to form physical reality. She repeatedly counters the forces of evil in her battle with

Typhon and in fact gathers and reunites the scattered and dismembered body parts of her brother/lover Osiris.

The discussion of matter as somehow bad or evil runs through late Platonist literature. The second-century Middle Platonist Numenius considered an important influence on Plotinus, in his *On the Revolution of the Academics against Plato* (fr. 24), labors to strengthen the link of Pythagorean philosophy to Plato and subsequent legitimate Platonists. He represents matter, following Plato's *Timaeus*, as a disorganized state identified with the Dyad giving "evil," a role in the necessary fecundity that allows Nature to come into being, provided it associates with higher realms of being. The goddess subdues irrational forces and keeps them from getting out of control. This does not insinuate that matter per se is evil but can have the propensity toward chaos. Proclus, in his *Commentary on Timaeus*, describes Athena as subduing chaos and resolving the struggle between matter and form by imposing order. Just as the Olympians triumph over the Titans, as creative intelligence Athena extends a providential concern over the universe (*In Tim*. I.150.16-18). She practices *sôphrosyne* (moderation and reason) and, according to Proclus, commenting on Plato's *Timaeus* (24C4-5), where Plato mentions the goddess' wisdom, says that she imposes order, learning, geometry, astronomy, arithmetic, medicine, etc., on the world and holds the universe together through proportion and with harmonious binding. Proclus calls this "Athenaic providence" (*In Tim*. I.160.12-15).

In Judeo-Christian theology, the soul struggles with moral evil and attempts to overcome sin. For St Augustine and Judeo-Christian thought in general, evil is thought to be a matter of human free choice and/or a punishment from God.[25] The "pagan" view of good and evil, one which appears in Gnostic literature but is also present in Middle Platonist and later Platonist doctrine, associates what is bad and less valued with the chaotic world of material nature, and good with the intellectual parameters that control it. The opposition of form and matter in Platonism, then, is not between good and evil as it is in theodicy, but between chaos and order. Just as Gaia and Ouranos are both necessary for generating the Greek pantheon, material fecundity and heavenly overrule are both necessary for generating the physical universe. Still, matter can be unruly and must be subordinated to form if creation is to remain a "cosmos" that is beautiful and good. In the pagan literature, evil is attributed to separate powers associated with the disorderly, chaotic, out-of-control aspects of nature or the human passions. Matter can be disruptive: physical events such as storms and earthquakes, irrational numbers which disturb geometricians, all must come under the control of order and providence if the universe is to be ruled by the good. Still matter is necessary to creation of a physical world. In an essay by Dennis O'Brian, "Plotinus on Matter and Evil," he discusses the fact that in this Neoplatonist account, Plotinus describes matter as "evil itself" (I.8.8.37:I.8.13. 7-14) and yet claims that it is derived from the One through the mediation of Soul (III.9. 37-16) (171).[26] O'Brian considers some of Plotinus arguments concerning the relation of matter to non-being as well as questioning how evil could derive from the One which is the sovereign good (187). Plotinus diverged from Numenius on this point, since he claimed that matter was not derived from the One. Plotinus discusses whether matter can be identified with privation (III.9.3. 14-16), and in his treatise *Against the Gnostics* disagrees with Gnostic dualism and describes matter illuminated by form. It is important to note, as did G. S. Kirk that *kakon,* the Greek for evil is in the Pythagorean column of opposites along with *apeiron* (unlimited) and accepted as a necessary component of the world.[27] The goddess, joining together the "irrational" aspect of matter with logical and limiting parameters, as the "Life" of the universe remediates this complex situation.

Life

I find it rather amazing here in the twenty-first century, after modernism's insistence on reason as a criterion for truth and especially after the turn toward positivism that has been taken by scholars in the twentieth century, that philosophy could have considered "soul" and "life" vital to philosophical thought. In Plato's *Timaeus,* ensouling the universe is the role of the Cosmic Soul, which provides the whole universe with its life.[28] The following fragment from Numenius (fr. 44), the second-century Platonist, is close to the *Chaldean Oracles,* expressing a similar view of the soul as responsible for unifying and organizing the natural world. Illustrating the synchronicity between Chaldean and Platonic literature, Numenius states:

> Since corporeal objects by their own nature are liable to alteration and disintegration and are completely dissolvable into infinity, they are in need of something holding them together and uniting them, and compressing and controlling them: this is what we call soul.[29]

The *Chaldean Oracles* state that from Hekate is derived the World Soul (fr. 51). In the Chaldean system, Hekate generates life from the right hip: "while the entity which springs from her right flank can be taken as Soul in its immanent aspect."[30] This trope has to do with the potency of the Cosmic Soul or its emanative property. Johnston explains this by an analogy with the sun as opposed to the illumination it provides: the Cosmic Soul and its powers are separate matters. Johnston discusses *Oracles* fr. 51, which portrays Hekate as responsible for ensouling (*empsychon*) the All, and cites Hans Lewy's expression, that Hekate is "the potency of the Cosmic Soul." Porphyry, in *Philosophy from the Oracles,* also discusses ensouling in terms of Hekate as a source, as do Psellus and others.[31] Proclus (*In Remp.* II.201.10) agrees with and quotes Oracle fr. 51 which describes Hekate as ensouling the All.[32] The father in the *Oracles* (fr. 20), on the other hand, is described as having within him the ability to think and is the noetic essence.

Johnston discusses the fact that this tradition is based on Plato's *Philebus,* wherein individual souls come from the soul of the cosmos. The equation of Hekate with Life follows a similar pattern. In the *Oracles,* Johnston points out, Soul (*Psyche*) is called "Mistress of Life" (fr. 96). In fr. 174 she provides life to others, rather than herself. Hekate is said to be a "life-giving" womb (fr. 32.2), etc., thus Hekate is associated with this aspect (life-giving) of the Soul. Proclus (*In Tim.* II.260.20) discusses Soul's "life-giving forces" and mentions Hekate by name. The life-giving function is also associated with Hekate as possessing a womb.[33] Life is a hypostatic category very particular to Neoplatonism, beginning with Plotinus:

Life, not the life of the One, but a trace of it, looking toward the One was boundless, but once having looked was bounded (without bounding its source). Life looks toward the One and, determined by it, takes on boundary, limit and form ... it must then have been determined (as the life of) a Unity (i.e. Intellect) that includes Multiplicity. Multiplicity because of Life, and Unity because of limit ... so Intellect is bounded Life

(*Enn.* VI.7.17, 13-26, trans. Armstrong[34])

One of the reasons that Proclus, throughout his *Commentary on Plato's Timaeus*, rejects the idea that the disjointing effect of motion is a source of evil, is because it is associated with Life. Life is a vital force in the universe, and motion has its roots in Life. Since Life for him is a hypostatic reality, even disorderly motion has a place in creation. Life associated with the intelligible is distinct from "that which moves in a discordant and disorderly fashion," and, in fact, is a necessary component of the basic infrastructure of reality. Disorderly motion may be a derivative of motion in general and other influences but is not totally divorced from the Good. Proclus's strategic move, in raising it to levels above the visible world, saves motion from being considered disruptive of the oneness of being and, therefore, an evil. It accounts for a core property of Nature and its creatures. Life is a higher and transcendent cause. The motion that is found in Nature is a consequence of Life, as a self-constituted cause that is able to give energizing power and activity to lower hypostases. This strategy pre-empts many of the *aporiae* that plagued classical philosophy, such as those in the *Parmenides* dialogue concerning the incompatibility of unity and motion. Proclus conflates Life with a goddess.[35] Goddesses are responsible both for the life of the universe and for exerting control over this life should it become overly exuberant. Life and wisdom, then, Athena and Hekate, are conflated in this usage. Providence is more divine than Intellect and Life a high and transcendent cause. Since the gods all possess providential energy, the goddess's life-giving function is vital to the completion of the universe and its escape from fate.

Topographic Regions

Dualism does not have only to do with the difference between the eternal and temporal, being and becoming, one and the many, but also extends to the distinctions between worlds. The ideas of a superlunary and sublunary world, earth and heaven, the bifurcation between the earthly realm and the underworld, are examples of some of the most powerful spatially conceived ideas. That there are two worlds rather than one world has a long cultural memory both in religion and in the history of thought and myth.[36] Reifying abstractions and making them function in ontology rely on spatial metaphor. The ancient Greek word for place is *topos,* and the creation of non-spatial regions in the archaic and classical texts can be seen as an analogue of personification. The "one beyond being" of Plato's *Republic* (509B) and the One of the Neoplatonists are signified by hypostatized abstract nouns. Hypostatization can only be discussed by using spatial metaphors, likening the hypostases to regions, albeit unseen. A "two-world ontology," in its concrete application, suggests that there are boundaries between worlds and difficulties in negotiating between them. Many theories of immortality of the soul rely on spatial metaphor to posit the transit of the soul beyond life. From Platonism's two-world ontology to the Freudian topography of conscious and unconscious regions of the mind, this construct persists. Mythology in ancient times is replete with imaginary worlds beyond the everyday world of human existence. In this context, there is an earthly world and an underworld, in Aristotle a sublunary and superlunary world, in later Platonists elaborate hypostases can only be described in quasi-spatial figures of speech. As Athanassiadi says of Proclus, for example, he "is compelled to follow his strong analytical and dialectic streak and to present metaphysics in terms of near spatiality."[37]

Early myths are full of topographic descriptions. Burkert cites the Akkadian *Atrahasis* text, which features the Babylonian pantheon: "They grasped the flask of lots by the neck, they cast the lots; the gods made the division: Anu went up to heaven." A second god, Enlil, took the earth, for his subjects, and "the bolts, the bar of the sea, were set for Enki the far-sighted."[38] Anu, Enlil, and Enki—the sky god, the wind god, and the water god—form a trinity. A different version, Tablet X, has Anu and Adad— sky god and wind god—for the heavens, Sin and Nergal—moon god and god of the underworld—for the earth. The realm of Enki, the Lord of the Deep, is fixed not as the salt sea but potable ground and spring waters. This is also the realm of Poseidon in Greek accounts. In Homer's *Iliad*, the world is divided among the appropriate Homeric gods: Poseidon receives the grey sea as his permanent abode; Hades draws the murky darkness; Zeus draws the wide sky of brightness and clouds. The earth is common to all, and spacious Olympus is the abode of the gods. In both texts, Burkert points out, there are three distinct areas of the cosmos—heaven, the depths of the earth, and the waters—and these three areas are assigned to the three highest gods of the pantheon, all of which are male. Burkert sees strong similarities between Homer and the Akkadian epic here.[39]

Many cosmogonic accounts begin with deities whose names carry a dual meaning as "regions." Tartarus, for example, in the *Theogony*, is the underworld. The underworld is an isolated and remote place (*Th.* 814), a "house" of the dead in Greek, Mesopotamian, and Canaanite-Hebrew traditions, and in some of these sources is characterized by darkness, silence, and forgetfulness.[40] In the *Iliad*, Zeus deposes or imprisons the great Kronos "in the depths that are under the earth and the sea" (*Il.* 14.203-4). In Hesiod's *Works and Days* (111), Kronos is known to be in exile in a paradise called the Isles of the Blessed.[41] López-Ruiz points out that Hesiod's view coincides with the Northwest Semitic traditions of Ugarit and Philon concerning the ancestral god El.[42] Parmenides' poem, while it can be interpreted as an allegory of epistemic enlightenment, is at the same time a topographically specific description of a mystical journey to the halls of Night. In Hesiod, the "horrible dwelling of dark Night" (*Th.* 744) is where the goddesses Night and Day alternately reside as the other traverses the sky above the Earth. Both Parmenides' and Hesiod's conceptions of this place have their precedent in the Babylonian mythology of the sun god's abode. This abode traditionally served as a place of judgment, and this fact tends to confirm that when Parmenides' goddess tells him that no ill fate has sent him ahead to this place (fr. 1.26-27a), she is indicating that he has reached the place to which travel the souls of the dead.[43]

A later influential example of the confluence of spatial and philosophical meanings can be found in the cryptic philosophical meaning that Porphyry finds in his *Cave of the Nymphs*.[44] Lamberton points that Porphyry's treatment of the cave (*Odyssey* 13) is our earliest surviving complete essay in the mode of allegorical commentary. Porphyry (233–305 CE) attributes a concealed meaning to the Homeric myth, contending that the very obscurity of certain passages is a signal that there is a hidden message at work. On the basis of just eleven lines of proof text, he writes twenty pages of commentary.[45] In the *Odyssey* (13.102-12) one of the gates leading to the cave is for men to descend and it is here that the Phaeacians deposit Odysseus when they return him to Ithaca. This is a good example of the use of symbolic topography. Odysseus descending into the cave, represents his descent into genesis. Struck points out that Porphyry surveys religious and philosophical traditions surrounding caves. They can be seen as microcosm of the sensible cosmos and of nature. Made of earthly matter, they have dark interiors and obscure boundaries yet are sacred to naiad nymphs. The second gate is an entrance for immortals. An olive tree sits adjacent to it. Porphyry identifies the goddess Athena with *phronêsis* (wisdom) along with the olive tree. It contains an eternal spring. Caves here and elsewhere can be seen as a microcosm of the sensible cosmos and phenomena of nature. In the use here it is the equivalent of a kind of birthing station where souls assume bodies and enter the material world.[46] Porphyry suggests that Odysseus represents the soul and the goal to which the poem leads him is union with Nous (Intellect) and away from the chaos of life. The mystical harbor of the soul is foretold by Tiresias's prediction that Odysseus will travel inland to a place where the sea is unknown (*Od.* 11.119-34).

Goddesses are not only mediators between formal intellectual stability and the ever-changing world of nature, they also mediate pseudo-geographical regions. The world of physical existence and a world that is somehow beyond this physical world, in these paradigms, both constitute reality. In the *Hymn to Demeter*, Persephone's commerce with the underworld and Hekate's guiding rescue are prototypes that are precursors of two-world ontologies. Persephone is a sojourner between worlds and Hekate is a guide allowing transit between liminal points. These mythical templates are premonitions of the kind of negotiation between hypostatic levels of reality that were conceived by later Platonists. Hekate, in the very well-known account of Demeter's descent to the underworld to find her abducted daughter Persephone, serves as a guide between worlds. In analogue to this myth, later Platonists also employ the persona of Hekate to connect the region known as the sublunary world with the highest levels of the superlunary world. Pseudo-geographic dualisms can be found in many ancient documents. The Orphic gold tablets that have been excavated over a wide geographical area are texts documenting the Orphic doctrine regarding the destiny of souls. They contain instructions for the journey to the underworld. *Katabasis* or descent to the underworld is undertaken by Orpheus in search of his deceased wife in Orphic literature in general. The template for transit between worlds can also be found as early as the Parmenides poem in which a nameless goddess guides the truth-seeker between worlds. This poem inaugurated the equivocation of an everyday world as opposed to the world of true being, one known to truth and the other to mere opinion, a mainstay of Platonism.

Persephone's descent to the underworld is predicated upon the existence of a world beyond that of everyday life, as is Orpheus's search for his Eurydice. In late antiquity, the proliferation of multiple worlds extends the earthly universe to a region where souls are judged after death (sometimes associated with the moon). The world of mundane nature is opposed to a world beyond being in all of Platonism. For the Neoplatonist, a hierarchy of hypostases results in elaborate philosophical speculation establishing substantive hypostatized "realms" that need mediation. The hierarchical hypostases inherit the bifurcation between worlds initiated by Plato, based on the separation of forms from nature and things. The bifurcation is basically between the world of nature, the created universe, and the world beyond being where intellectual truth prevails. The imperfections and divisions of the world of nature are ameliorated by intellectual parameters which originate "beyond being" in a world of unity and truth.

Philosophical coinage abducts earlier formulations. When Mind, Soul, Being, and the One are treated as though they are metaphysical "regions," these "philosophemes" reenact their mythological roots. To use Jacques Derrida's prescient expression, a "white mythology" of abstract nouns and hypostatized regions owes a debt to the colorful myths that they sublate. The debt is paid back with the reappearance of Hekate and her entourage. A hierarchy of hypostases, a removed One, and a panlogicism lead to the need for a causal account in the matter of mediation between hypostases. The bifurcation between the underworld and the world of the living, then, is a mainstay of earlier myth. Its most famous example is the Eleusinian mysteries. Only the guiding help of Hekate allows commerce between the two worlds. In the Neoplatonic hierarchy, as Sarah Iles Johnston so brilliantly explains, Hekate becomes the mediator between worlds in existence and the one beyond.

Conclusion

"The Greeks could predicate divinity of abstract notions in a way that cannot be done in Christianity and the secularized Occident without recourse to metaphoric language and homonymous usage. Already in Homer and Hesiod, the creators of Greek mythology, the tendency to hypostatize abstractions is well established and seems to have a long tradition behind it." "The ascription of divinity to what is perceived as a 'power' or force in the universe is in fact the recognition of its causal efficiency. The more operative and wide-ranging a force appears to be, and the greater the field of its causal power, the more divine is the cause."[47] Plato in the *Timaeus* posited a bifurcation, that of being (*to on*) and becoming (*to gignomenon*) and pronounced being to be more essential than coming to be (characteristic of nature). From the time of his immediate successor, Speusippus, to Xenocrates, to the first- and second-century CE Platonists, and the authors of the *Chaldean Oracles*, the problem of how the realm of intelligible true being (*kosmos noêtos*) could interact with the lower realm of change and becoming (*kosmos aisthêtos*) was an *aporia* to be solved. Only an agency that is capable of motion could bring this about. The realm of true being, Intellect, and Monadic Oneness are all associated with the male; the female alone is capable of movement and life can be associated with soul. The figure of Hekate, then, as the mediator (equivalent to Isis in Plutarch's account) functions both as the origin of all movement and multiplicity and on a lower level as the source of the Cosmic Soul that provides life and animation in the cosmos. She alone has access to the limits and boundaries that intellective paradigms can impose on nature. She is able to intervene in affairs of creation and can supply the intermediation, without incurring the danger that she will herself become dissipated by this contact. She is a goddess.

In the early modern era, there is Descartes's famous dualism of mind and body. In theology, there is heaven and earth. Duality can be found ubiquitously in the history of philosophy, religion, and rhetoric. It is found in discussions of matter and form, Monad and Dyad, subject and object, time and eternity, and in spatial depictions of ontological hierarchies. It is found in the Kabbalah with the distinction between the ineffable one source and the *sefirot*, which introduces multiplicity into the created universe. When Descartes posited his radical dualism consisting of mind and the physical world of the senses as two separate substances, the association with male and female was long out of the picture. Mind/Body, Intellect/Soul or Nature was an inviolate opposition, however, and the need for mediation opened up an "explanatory gap" that remains in contemporary philosophies of mind and consciousness. As will be discussed in Chapter 11, the "cultural memory" of gender opposition is seen by some to be cryptically embedded in the fundamental dualisms of philosophy from Plato and Aristotle to Descartes and beyond. Susan Bordo, a feminist epistemologist, and others make the connection directly between gender and Cartesianism.[48] Chapter 6, which follows, shows how dualism will lend itself ever more complex triadic formations as the role of the mediating goddess takes hold of Neoplatonic ontology. In Chapter 10, it is shown how these oppositions contribute to the persona of nature as female and how nature is personified as a goddess in medieval allegory.

6

"The Goddess of the Triple Ways": Triads and Trinities

Geopolitical change, specifically the anti-pagan developments in the post-Julian Roman Empire, certainly put Platonic pagan scholars on notice. Defending the Hellenic tradition through a Platonism augmented with theology gave mythology a new status. It seems that as the Christian Roman Empire became increasingly anti-pagan, after the demise of the Emperor Julian who briefly had restored pagan worship after the first Christian Emperor Constantine, the latter-day Platonic academy became more systematic. The Athenian School, which operated from the fourth to the early sixth century, elaborated a complex ontology, increased the output of commentaries on Plato and Aristotle, and theologized their texts. Examining the geopolitics of the times supports the idea that there was increased motivation to promulgate and reconfigure Platonic philosophy as "theology." The theoretical machinations of the late Platonic academies were dense, highly abstract, and baroquely complex. The names of the traditional gods and goddesses of Athens were embraced by a complex metaphysical ontology. The radical transcendence of the first principle in Platonism and the idea that the male god in his purity and static unity is exempt from actions in the cosmos led to the necessity for the co-presence of the very prototypical goddess that Julian had so venerated. Once again, the "cultural memory" of a goddesses with all its accrued meanings, some of them dating from the first and second centuries, only she, could enact a relationship between the created cosmos and its transcendent origins. This time however her roles expanded and proliferated along with the concepts she personified.

Edward Watts describes a very active intellectual and theological war between Christian and pagan ideas and figures during late antiquity.[1] Goddesses were attacked directly during these times, statues of pagan deities destroyed or removed and verbally condemned. The intellectual opposition between Christian and pagan doctrine had intensified during the reign of the emperor Julian, who disallowed Christian teaching and produced pagan philosophical texts of his own. Julian (361–363 CE) politzed the fusion between Platonism and mythology when he used this as a strategy in an attempt to restore pagan practices during his brief reign following that of the first Christian emperor, Constantine. Julian augmented his political program with platonic *paideia*, pagan ritual practice, and Eastern mysticism, even composing an encomium to "the mother of the gods."[2] Some of the same strategies that Julian had inaugurated continued in the late Athenian academy. A colorful example is the animation of statues, seriously believed to be an important practice by Proclus and his coreligionists. According to the fourth-century Sophist and historian Eunapius, Maximus, Julian's spiritual mentor, had made a statue of Hekate laugh and caused torches in her hands to light up (*Vitae Soph.*, c. 396 CE).[3] At the same time as Proclus adopted theurgic practices that would have been endorsed by Iamblichus, an important mentor for Julian's beloved spiritual advisor Maximus, he also infused Platonic philosophy with the presence of an array of gods and goddesses. Many of the goddesses put to philosophic use in his texts were the very ones that the Christians had expunged from the pagan shrines and cities. In order to do justice to their power and presence as agents of creation and mediation, he constructed elaborate triadic structures featuring Rhea, Demeter, Hekate, and Athena. A short review of the historical situation will establish just how serious the threat to pagan existence was in the late empire.

Constantine was proclaimed Augustus in 305 CE. In 312, he defeated Maxentius in the battle of the Milvian Bridge, and most historical accounts date his support of the Christian church to this date. He built a series of churches in Rome during the period 312–325 as well as later in Jerusalem (the Church of the Holy Sepulchre) and elsewhere. In 324, after eliminating Licinius (308–324 CE), who reigned over the East, he became sole master of the Empire. He founded Constantinople, a city destined to become largely Christian and one in which churches outnumbered temples, and actively condemned pagan practices. Bishops around the time of the Council of Nicaea (325) received increased recognition, and Christianity gradually eclipsed solar theology. In 321, for example, Sunday was designated as a day of rest: "the day of the Sun" became "the day of the Lord," the day Christ was resurrected. Dual reference was important when law prohibited pagan cults and their holidays. The calendar was Christianized as late as 325, coins were dedicated to "the Unconquerable Sun," while Christian symbols occasionally appeared on the reverse side. For Constantine, both Christ and Apollo served his political ends. Not only did he have himself portrayed on top of a porphyry column wearing a radiate crown of the Sun God, he also constructed a temple dedicated to the triad Jupiter-Juno-Minerva.[4] Christ was characterized as the Light of the World (*Lux Mundi*) in Latin and Sun of Justice (*Helios Dikaiosynes*) in Greek. Goddesses were not entirely left behind. Chuvin reports that, according to Zosimos, "Constantine took from Cyzicus a very ancient wooden statue of Kybele, said to have been consecrated by the Argonauts, and had it placed under a portico facing the figure of the Roman Tyche, so that she seemed to be gazing out and watching over the city."[5] On the other hand, he was said to have destroyed pagan altars, razed the temple of Aphrodite in Apheca (now Lebanon), and forbade pagan sacrifice. Very few pagan temples were closed by Constantine, and Cameron tells us that his social legislation did not particularly reflect Christian values. He deferred to the judgment of his bishops in such matters. Constantine intervened in ecclesiastical disputes and in the calling of church councils, particularly the ecumenical council held at Nicaea in 325 CE. Many bishops, including Eusebius of Caesarea, agreed with Arius, a priest of Alexandria, that the Son must be secondary to the Father, and the question was hotly disputed. Constantine contributed the crucial one-word definition *homoousios* (of one substance) to theology, which was accepted by the Council of Nicaea. It is notable that the Council was debating the composition and ontological status of the trinity at a time when "triads" became increasingly important to Neoplatonist doctrine. More immediately alarming to non-Christians than the political hegemony of Christianity was the developing atmosphere of intolerance. Cameron points out, "The Greek word *hairesis* ('choice'), originally simply meaning set of beliefs, now meant heresies or deviant beliefs as the church took on an increasingly authoritarian role." Disputes such as that at Nicaea played a central role in fourth-century history, and the doctrines officially approved there were regarded as universally binding.[6] Constantine was baptized by Eusebius (a bishop who enjoyed his favor) in 337 on his deathbed.

Eusebius and a number of other bishops during these and later times expressed deep fear and hostility toward Aphrodite. Eusebius claimed that Constantine had demolished temples of Aphrodite in Heliopolis and Apheca in Lebanon. While this has not been proven, there is direct evidence that a colossal marble statue of Aphrodite was bludgeoned and broken into chunks by pious Christians in Aphrodisias in Carian Asia Minor.[7] The site later became a Christian basilica. In 391, the temple of Artemis at Ephesus was sacked, and in 390, under the patriarch Theophilus, the library at Alexandria was burned. In 386, Bishop Marcellus had soldiers carry out the destruction of the temple of Zeus at Apamea in Syria. In 392, in Alexandria, Bishop Theophilus organized the siege and destruction of the famous Serapeum, the temple of the Egyptian god Serapis. Cynegius, praetorian prefect of the east at that time, was violently anti-pagan. The emperor Theodosius I (r. 379–395) passed edicts against pagan sacrifice and pagan cults in 391 and closed all the synagogues in Palestine. Temples were attached or destroyed at Petracea, Areopolis, Canopus, Heliopolis, Gaza, and elsewhere.[8] Notably, the last openly political rebellion during the reign of Theodosius I, carried out by Flavianus in 394, involved attempts to restore and rededicate temples, celebrate mystery cults, and so on.[9] Flavianus was involved in the cults of Vesta, Sol, Mithras, Hekate, Isis, Serapis, and others. The well-known incident in which the philosopher and mathematician Hypatia was attacked and murdered in Alexandria occurred in 415. By the middle of the fifth century, the academic life of pagans and other non-Christians was officially discredited. The Panathenaea ceased to be celebrated, and the Athenian temples were closed.[10] In 529, Justinian issued edicts forbidding teaching in the academy of Athens. As late as 600, the Parthenon of Athens was rededicated to Mary.

Constantine's reign after his dramatic conversion to Christianity had resulted in an expansion of Christian interests throughout the Roman empire. Athens, however, remained a stronghold of classical culture. During Constantine's reign, the Edict of Milan had promised religious tolerance for all religions, but things worsened for pagan practices after Theodosius I reign (379–395) when Christianity became the official religion of the Roman Empire. Athens was one of the last sites where pagan philosophers could freely pursue their interests.[11] There is a surviving letter Julian sent to the Athenians in which he describes Athens as the last stronghold and refuge of justice in a collapsing world (V.269b). Ephesus and Sardis were ancient centers of Hellenism, but the impression that Eunapius gives, according to Fowden, is that

Christianity had achieved a certain amount of hegemony in these cities while Athens seemed to remain a "living temple of Hellenism." For generations students, including Julian himself, had flocked there from all parts of the empire for education in rhetoric and philosophy. Pagan cults remained entrenched in the central area around the Acropolis, while in Sardis and Ephesus it became increasingly difficult to practice pagan religions.[12] At the end of his funeral oration for Julian, Libanius remarked that though he was buried near Tarsus, " a more appropriate resting place (was) Athens, so that he too might receive the honors paid to Plato by successive generations of students and teachers" (*Or.* xviii.306). Fowden points out that "Julian's spirit undoubtedly did make its abode in Athens" where devotees even adopted the practice of calculating the era from the date of Julian's accession.

The Athenian Academy, headed by Syrianus, Proclus, and later Damascius and Simplicius, regarded ancient texts by Homer, Hesiod, Orpheus, and Plato, and the *Chaldean Oracles* as sacred texts. Devotion to the traditional gods and goddesses was a priority. Potentiating philosophy with theology was genuine belief but also an influence on the sons of the senatorial class who attended Greek academies. Kristeller describes education in the late empire.[13] Future lawyers, administrators, and public officials in Athens, Alexandria, and perhaps in Antioch and other large cities of the East learned Greek and studied in Greece, or under Greek tutors, or at Hellenic-oriented academies. After the rise of Christianity, these schools remained under pagan auspices, as classical Greek education was still valued among the Roman upper class. The Athenian academy was untouched until the reign of Justinian (526–565) while the Alexandrian academy went through a major purge of pagan philosophers but remained in operation. The Academy in Athens was founded by Plutarch of Athens and organized by Syrianus, Proclus, and their followers. Proclus was born in 410 and his floruit coincides with the reign of Theodosius II (408–450), another staunchly anti-pagan emperor. The Athenian school promulgated Hellenic ideals and posed an alternative to Christian dogma. Upholding the pagan cause, Proclus's predecessors and his followers incorporated the oriental gods and theurgic practices into their studies of Plato, Aristotle, and Homer. The pantheon of gods and goddesses, fused with the oriental cult literature of the second century, made Platonism a theology and also in a clandestine manner fostered the political aspirations of pagan intellectuals.

With Julian as an inspiration, the pagan deities were once again able to inhabit Platonic philosophies. Maximus and Chrysantius, high priest of Lydia, had taught Julian the fundamentals of philosophy and theurgy, and then sent him to Nestorius the Hierophant of Eleusis for initiation into the Mysteries of the Great Mother. Nestorius was the father of Plutarch, the founder of the Athenian school. Proclus's gods and goddesses, his avid interest in the *Chaldean Oracles* and Orphism, a reverence for Julian and his militant anti-Christian program all came together in the late Athenian school. Julian, with his highly charged political agenda and the hope of restoring pagan theology, venerated the goddess. His encomium to "the mother of the gods" held that she was the "principle of all life." In the complex onto-theology of the Athenian school, the goddess becomes the powerful source of "life" in the Being-Life-Intellect triad inherited from Plotinus and the Gnostics. Julian's description of the goddess contains the standard constellation of characteristics attached to female deities, and is a one-fits-all goddess, as is apparent in the following:

> Who is the Mother of the gods? She is the source of the intellectual and creative gods, who in their turn guide the visible gods. She is both the mother and the spouse of mighty Zeus. She came into being next to and together with the great creator: she is in control of every form of life, and the cause of all generation. She easily brings to perfection all things that are made: without pain she brings together and with the father and creator of all things that are. She is the motherless maiden, enthroned at the side of Zeus, and in very truth is the Mother of the gods.[14]

Julian was a follower of Iamblichus (245–325) who wrote *De Mysteriis Aegyptiorum* (*On the Egyptian Mysteries*),[15] and a Neoplatonist who promoted theurgy as a means of worship. As mentioned above, knowledge of Chaldean theurgy was transmitted to the Neoplatonist Plutarch, founder of the Athenian school, by Nestorius, who was chief priest of Eleusis in 375.[16] Plutarch transmitted the Chaldean doctrines to his disciple Syrianus, Proclus's mentor, who authored the *Harmony of the Doctrines of Orpheus, Pythagoras and Plato with the Chaldean Oracles*, a programmatic text for the Athenians.

The Athenian school held to a doctrine that was not only as compelling as Christianity but was also politically contentious. Proclus worshipped openly in the temples that had been ordered closed fifty years before, according to Marinus' biography. Proclus uses the word *mokhthêrais* (corrupt) of Christians (as did Julian), and calls Christianity *paranomia* (transgressing the law).[17] Cameron tells us further that other Athenian figures, such as Proclus's immediate predecessor Hagias, aroused hostility by openly parading his paganism, although he came from a rich and noble Christian family in Athens. In the academic sphere, the use of pagan deities at every opportunity required that the older mythology be upgraded to be considered a true source of knowledge. Proclus wrote hymns appealing to and praising the goddesses he revered. He vivified goddesses by other means as well. They were invoked in theurgic rituals, in particular the peculiar practice of considering statues as animated. In philosophical texts, they served widely in complex triadic ontology as metaphysical agency. It might go too far to consider these far-ranging efforts to evoke goddesses as directly related to the very statues and temples of deities that were being destroyed, verbally castigated, and devalued by the Christians. Nevertheless it is evident that Athena, Aphrodite, Rhea, and others featured prominently in Christian efforts to destroy pagan religion. Athena, who according to Proclus functioned to moderate the strife that could destroy Athens, was in fact Proclus's protector deity. Marinus mentions the removal of the *agalma* (statue) of Athena from the Parthenon "by those who move what should not be moved" (*Vita Procli* 30). Van den Berg mentions that it was a common strategy in the ancient world to declare that one belonged to a deity and oblige that deity to protect one. According to Marinus, Proclus was born in Byzantium, a city dedicated to Athena. She appeared to him in a dream and called him to philosophy (*Vita Procli* 6).

Aphrodite was patron deity of Lycia, Proclus's fatherland. "Aphrodite," Proclus said, "is a goddess of divine love uniting and bring together opposite forces in nature

[but] also human society while engendering concord, harmony and peace" (*in Crat.* 109,22-111,20).[18] Proclus transformed Aphrodite, construing her as a facilitator of the soul's purification. This "theologized" transformation of the function of the very goddess (often depicted in statues that were nude) whom the Christians railed against as the epitome of sexual license is notable.[19] Two of the surviving hymns of Proclus are dedicated to Aphrodite, praising her as mother of the various *Erôtes*, an *Erototokos* (Love-bearer). Proclus invokes Aphrodite in quite a few of his texts; for example, in the 15th treatise of the *Commentary on the Republic*, he interprets the famous love affair between Aphrodite and Ares.[20] In this commentary (*In Remp.* I.109.1-3), Proclus links Aphrodite with the erotic madness that facilities the soul's purification through ascension toward divine beauty. Aphrodite features extensively in Proclus' triads. The twelve divinities in Proclus are divided into four triads. Aphrodite is the cause of beauty for the beings in the cosmos and the copy of the beautiful things in the noetic (intellective) triad. Following Plato's "lower" Aphrodite in *Symposium*, Aphrodite can be found on the level of hypercosmic-encosmic gods (a lower level of triads) as well. The last so-called uplifting triad is Hermes, Aphrodite, and Apollo. Souls ascend through this triad where Apollo (cult of the gods), Hermes (Philosophy), and Love (Aphrodite) are combined (*Plat. Theol.* VI.98, 18-21). Tuomo Lankila describes this: "Aphrodite acts as a primordial cause of loving inspiration, which permeates universally all things and orients uplifted lives toward primal Beauty (third triad of the first intelligible triad)."[21]

Proclus' Triads

Proclus treated myths as if they were philosophical arguments. Stoic, Epicurean, and Middle Platonist philosophers regarded allegory as the predominant mode of understanding earlier myth. Now, with the addition of a theurgic mysticism, and the fusion of Platonism and oracular and Gnostic literature, myth was regarded as a "real" account of the hidden divine world, transmitted by symbolic narratives. He considered Homeric and Hesiodic epic poetry as a lower but important source of truth about matters too transcendent to discuss by other means.[22] The gods and goddesses and their activities are signified and imaged by metaphysical concepts and they are the operating agents in the mechanics of triads. For Proclus, myth accomplishes a reading of philosophy as the truth about transcendent reality. His statement in his *Commentary on Cratylus* is telling for his concept of myth: "For in instituting everything the Fathers of everything (*ta hola*), sowed signs (*sunthemata*) and traces (*ikhne*) of their own triadic essence in everything."[23] The peculiar but quasi-logical use of triplicity to make a place for gods and goddesses on all levels of reality is testimony to the inventive contrivance of Neoplatonic philosophers: all of the gods and goddesses, embodied within triadic structures, operate within a cohesive ontology. Henotheism (*hen* is Greek for oneness) supersedes polytheism and gods and goddesses form a unity that transforms genealogical descent into ontological emanation. Originally, the pantheon was basically an extended family tree wherein all the gods and goddesses have separate roles. Zeus carries the sun across the sky, Poseidon rules the sea, Artemis is goddess of the wild, Hekate is goddess of the crossroads, and so on. By contrast, the late Neoplatonists conceived of a "golden chain" of divinities, an interlinked and forming sets or groups structured as trinities. Hekate, Artemis, and Selene form a single triadic identity, for example. The following section will examine the relation between this systematic ontology and the triads of goddesses. First, however, some comment on the curious fact that triplicity when it came to goddesses had a history of going back to the earliest times.

A Brief History of Triplicate Goddesses

Pausanias (second century CE) in his *Description of Greece* describes a sculpture of the triple Hekate by Alcamenes in the fifth-century BCE temple of winged Nike in Athens (II.30.2).[24] Apparently, triplicity was a cultural norm when it came to gods and goddesses, one found throughout the ancient world. In 110 BCE, for example, a temple of the triad "Spes, Fides, Fortuna" was built under Roman influence at Capua. Ovid refers to Hekate as "triple goddess" (*Metamorphoses* 7.22), while Virgil addresses her as *tergeminamque Hecaten* (Triform Hekate) (*Aeneid* 4.511). This is the goddess that is threefold; as Miller explains, she is called Luna in Heaven, Diana on Earth, and Hekate in Hades.[25] Horace calls Diana Diva Triformas (3. *Od*. 22.4). Hekate's triform nature (three heads, six arms) is well-known from the manner in which she is depicted in Greek sculpture. Hekate is also known as the guardian of forks in the road and is identified with the three phases of the moon. Hekate's threefold nature seems to persist even in the popular imagination of our own time, as attested by the many depictions of her as threefold. She appears in that form on the cover of Johnston's book *Hecate Soteria*, but also on innumerable websites in contemporary "pagan" spiritual revivals in cyberspace. Hekate's three-faced or even three-bodied iconography, as Athanassakis explains, "may in a way preserve her originally extensive powers, which encompassed land, sea and sky."[26] In Hesiod (*Theogony* 412-28), Hekate is awarded three cosmic spheres of influence (earth, sea, sky). In the Greek Magical Papyri, there is repeated reference to triplicity particularly as associated with the goddess Hekate, alternatively called Persephone and Selene and Artemis, and the old Babylonian goddess Ereschigal. The following passage is an example:

> Triple-voiced, triple-headed Selene
> Triple-pointed, triple-faced, triple-necked
> and goddess of the triple ways, she holds
> Untiring flaming fire in triple halters
> and you who oft frequent the triple way
> and rule the triple decades with three forms.[27]

In addition to ruling over three regions, Hekate, and the goddess in general, is very often related to the soul in Platonist accounts. In ancient Greek lore, the soul is judged at a place where three roads meet. One road led to the Elysian Fields, one to the Fields of Asphodel, and the third to Tartarus. Any crossroads where three roads meet might symbolize this place of judgment and be seen as a sacred place. Porphyry describes this relationship of soul and the three divisions of the soul as follows:

> The meeting of the three roads that are imagined as being among the shades in Hades is actually in this world, in the three divisions of the soul, the rational, the passionate, and the appetitive. We are no longer talking about a myth or a poem but about truth and a description of things as they are.[28]

In the *Hymn to Demeter*, there are triple worlds, as is the case with other mystery literature. There are three worlds that require mediation. There is the underworld to which Persephone descends (guided by Hekate), the world of earthlings and earthly things where Demeter can impose a famine, and the world of the gods on Olympus from which Demeter descends to protest at her daughter's abduction. Foley tells us that the tripartite division of the heavens, the sea, and the world below among the brothers Zeus, Poseidon, and Hades is first mentioned at *Iliad* (15.187-93). In the *Hymn to Demeter*, Persephone will have honors on earth, in heaven, and in the world below (365–69).[29]

Hesiod began the *Theogony* with a gender-neutral kind of substratum, Chaos. This can be found in many ancient cosmogonies. The beginning of the creation of the world is neither male nor female, not gendered, in fact quite abstract. When the male and female gods emerge, they are mediated by Strife, or Eros, etc. Hesiod's account, then, entails a third element out of which duality arises and another that facilitates coupling. There is a nascent awareness here that duality alone cannot be primordial and that the logic of a binary demands mediation: the continuity and unfolding of any progression from the combination of the two members of the binary require an agent catalyst. Philo's *Questions on Genesis* is a first-century CE source that documents an earlier use of triads in Platonism. He examines the Homeric division of the world into three parts (*Quest. in Gen.* II.15.189) and relates it to the Pythagoreans' assertion that the triad is the foundation of the being of the sublunary world (*Quest. in Gen.* 4.8).[30] The *Chaldean Oracles* (second century CE) are also responsible for the triadizing that becomes incorporated into later Platonist accounts. In the *Oracles*, between the two gods, the Father and the Demiurge, a third divine entity, a female divinity often identified with Hekate, is found. She is generated from the father, possesses the power of the father, and appears in the midst of the fathers as intermediary. In a double action, she dissociates and associates. Like a membrane (fr. 6), she keeps the First and Second Intellect separate and, as a generative womb, links father and Demiurge together: "Truly Rhea is the source and stream of blessed intellectual (realities). For She, first in power receives the birth of all these in her inexpressible womb and pours forth (this birth) on the all as it runs its course." (fr. 56).[31] She mediates creation. In *Chaldean Oracles*, there is a clear precedent for the triads found in the later Neoplatonic literature.[32]

Platonism's "two world ontology" is a binary (the transcendent world and the world of nature). A mediating third factor is required if there is to be any combination and subsequent production or creation of natural or spiritual phenomena. If the One, or the First Principle, is at rest and even Intellect is immobile and fixed in supreme and panoptic removal, for the world to come into being there needs to be an agency to enact the movement and change that can bring about the mixing of idea and material nature. Proclus, following Plato in *Timaeus*, puts forward the idea that soul is the boundary that stretches over all of creation. Soul touches both the universe/nature and the removed hypostases above nature. Soul is the "veil" cast over and around the world. Touching both Intellect and nature, it allows cosmic sympathy on all levels even to the far reaches of the universe. A modern philosopher might ask, why not leave it as Plato did, simply as "soul" and not invoke goddesses, letting this function remain abstract. Deification, a kind of personification, adds agented powers to conceptual abstraction. Hekate, associated with soul, and which is "self-moving," possesses such powers; abstractions do not. For Proclus,

> Since the cosmos has been exhibited to be an ensouled living thing possessive of intellect, there will be three things in it: body, soul and intellect. Now Intellect is entirely ungenerated, having been allotted both an eternal essence (*ousia*) and external activity (*energeia*). The world's body is entirely generated since it has been established as temporal through and through. Soul, however, has an essence of an intermediate nature.
>
> (*In Tim*. II.1.9-14 [on *Tim*. 30B6], trans. Baltzly)

Hekate's ancient role as goddess of the crossroads, and her position in the *Oracles* as the source of *Psyche* (Soul), qualifies her for the role of mediator. During the second and third centuries, triads and trinities became a widespread paradigm in both philosophy and religion. Some analogue to Soul was the middle of several of these triads, and the goddess was associated with Soul. Dillon mentions several precursors to the idea of triads in the Middle Platonists. Nicomachus conceived of a triadic division of the universe similar to Plutarch's threefold division of the universe, traceable back to Xenocrates (396–314 BCE) who was preoccupied with triadic distinctions.[33] At 54ff. in *Isis and Osiris,* Plutarch gives some prominence to Osiris, Isis, and Horus as a triad. They are compared to the parts of the most beautiful triangle Platonically conceived.[34] The Monad and Dyad and other dichotomies of earlier Middle Platonism fell short as the ultimate infrastructure that could carry out their elaborate ontology. The elaborate ontologies and baroquely complex metaphysical doctrines created by the late Neoplatonist philosophers were "dialectical." Dualisms, after all, are polar oppositions that required mediation. Reproductive coupling, the repeated omnipresent method of genesis in theogonies, is a mythical analogue to the mixture of opposites wherein form and matter, Monad and Dyad combine to produce the world. The dualist structure, however, does not account for causality in a world of multiplicity as a consequence of a single transcendent original source. How could the world begin as a twosome if it is, metaphysically, a One Being? For dyads to function and mix, there must be a third thing that supervenes upon the act of coupling that is beyond it. Strife and Eros are two examples in this older literature of a third element necessary for coupling. In the elaborate metaphysical triads devised by the Neoplatonists, a threesome, rather than independent divinities, demonstrates that all the elements interacting in world creation are ultimately the product of one unified divine cosmic sympathy.

Gnosticism, the *Oracles*, and the Proliferation of Triads

Both Gnostic and Chaldean literature actively created threesomes. The Existence, Life, and Intellect triad appears in the Platonizing Sethian Gnostic treatises from Nag Hammadi. In the *Zostrianos* and *Allogenes* as well as in the *Three Steles of Seth*, a triad Existence, Vitality, and Mentality is equated with a figure called the Triple Powered One. "The figure is a link between the Unknowable God or the Invisible Spirit and his first thought, or Intellect, called Barbelo, who is a higher form of Sophia, the divine wisdom."[35] Turner suggests that the author of *Allogenes* (a Sethian Gnostic text from the New Testament apocrypha), based on the author's interpretation of the figure of Barbelo in the *Apocryphon of John*, relates him/her to the triple powerful invisible spirit.[36] In the Gnostic doctrines, Barbelo is a masculinized female virginal figure who assumes the position of the mediating life-giving presence within a creation that emanates from a removed and transcendent origin. There is a parallel here to the role of Hekate in the *Oracles*. As with the Hekate of the *Oracles*, Barbelo is depicted as being (1) the transcendent World Soul who generates; (2) the immanent World Soul, from which in turn nature was derived; and (3) the world of nature. In later literature, Hekate is identified with the median term of the triad, Existence, Power, and Intellect, which triad characterized the supreme Father in Gnostic literature.[37] Turner mentions that, according to Damascius, the *Chaldean Oracles* also applied the Existence, Life, and Intelligence terminology to the principal transcendent entities of that system. (Between the highest principle, the Paternal Monad (equated with Existence), and the divine Intellect, they interposed a median principle they called Hekate.) Turner suggests that the author of *Allogenes* may have been familiar with the metaphysical system of the *Chaldean Oracles* and recognized a similarity between the triadic nature and function of Hekate and the triadic nature and function of Barbelo in the *Apocryphon of John*.[38] The *Allogenes* distinguishes three levels in the Aeon of Barbelo: Kalyptos (Hidden), Protophanes (First-appearing), and Autogenes (Self-begotten). There is a notable coincidence between these terms and the three forms of Hekate symbolizing the three phases of the moon, at first hidden, then appearing, and growing to fullness as a self-begotten being (as Turner notes). Turner further suggests that the emanative process by which Barbelo emerges from the Invisible Spirit via the Triple Powered One can be associated with the late first-century system of Moderatus of Gades, a Middle Platonist. In his account, a secondary One, or unitary Logos, functions as the divine Intellect which emanates from a first One beyond all being in three stages: Permanence (monê), Progression (propodismos), and a Return (anapodismos) upon its source.[39]

The intricacies of the Gnostic literature are beyond the scope of this discussion. Because of the relation of the Triple Powered One, however, to the later Neoplatonic hypostasis "Life," associated with goddesses, it is necessary to comment on this connection in Gnostic literature. In *Allogenes*, the Triple Powered One is identical with the Invisible spirit as Existence, but as Mind it is identical with Barbelo. As Vitality, however, the Triple Powered One can be regarded as discontinuous with both. "Thus the ontological status of the Triple Powered One is very close to that of the Life modality of the potential intellect in its procession from the One. In fact, *Allogenes*

(66.32-36) explicitly identifies the Triple Powered One with 'Eternal Life.'"[40] In terms of both emanative and intermediary functions, a common triplicity, and a strong association of both with Vitality and the source of Life and multiplicity. Turner notes that Chaldean Hekate and the Sethian Triple Powered One are parallel. In the Sethian *Apocryphon of John*, probably datable to the first quarter of the second century and excerpted already by Irenaeus (*Haer.* I.29) around 179 CE, one encounters the triadic intermediary goddess in the figure of Barbelo, the higher unfallen counterpart of Sophia, the fallen divine wisdom.

The bisexed Barbelo requested and was granted a triad of attributes: Foreknowledge (*prognôsis*), Imperishability (*aphtharsia*), and Eternal Life (*aiônia zôê*). These names, according to Turner, are conceptually close to the terms Existence or Being, Life or Vitality, and Mind or Mentality, applied to the Triple Powered One in *Allogenes*. Turner also mentions the prominent Sethian Father, Mother, Son triad. In the Sethian system, both Eve and Sophia are mother figures. A higher Father, Mother, Son triad consists of the Invisible Spirit, Barbelo, and Adamas or "Autogenes," the self-begotten son of Barbelo. Adamas, the Son figure, became the image according to which the demiurge fashioned the earthly Adam who begot Seth, whom the Sethians call the Triple Male Child. Barbelo, Sophia, and Eve here are counterparts of each other, and Barbelo is represented as triadic. The Triple Powered One, then, is, according to Turner, a transcendental duplication of the Sethian Father, Mother, and Son triad. The median term of the Sethian Triple Powered One is explicitly named Life or Vitality, and the third of Barbelo's principal attributes is named Eternal Life. Hekate in the *Oracles* and Barbelo are both cosmic wombs, and although Barbelo is said to be androgynous, both are depicted in predominantly feminine terms. Baroquely complex, these descriptions can be found in similar constellations in Neoplatonism, particularly when it comes to the equivalence of "Life," womb, and goddess. In fact, there is a notable similarity between Middle Platonism, *Chaldean Oracles*, Gnostic literature, and later Neoplatonism.[41]

Plotinus

The Sethian Gnostic treatises, *Allogenes* and *Zostrianos*, were known to Plotinus and his disciple Porphyry (*Vita Plotini* 16). According to John Turner, Plotinus uses Being, Life, and Mind to describe the three aspects of the second of his three hypostases, "Intellect." This highly paradigmatic triad is the prototype for all triads in one way or another. Damascius (458–550 CE), writing much later, points out that the *Chaldean Oracles* also applied the Existence, Life, and Intelligence terminology to the principal transcendent entities of that system. Between the highest principles, the Paternal Monad equated with Existence, and the divine intellect, they interposed the median principle Hekate equated with the processing power of the Paternal Monad. On a lower ontological level, they also identified it with the World Soul.[42] Plotinus used the Hesiodic succession myth, Lamberton suggests, as a mythic precedent for his breakdown of reality into the three "ruling hypostases" which he personified as Zeus, Kronos, and Ouranos (*Enn.* V.1.7-9). Lamberton points out that, here, Plotinus assimilates the Homer/Hesiodic account of the generations of the gods to his own triadic model of reality, setting a precedent for associating divinities with triadic entities, although the role of Rhea is limited to maternal nurturing.

> This, then, is the generation of his *nous,* and worthy of *nous* in all its purity: it came to be [in the first place] from the first principle (i.e. *to hen*), and when it had already come to be it produced all those things that truly are: all the beauty of forms, all the noetic gods. It is full of those things that it produced and, as if it had swallowed them up again, contains them in itself lest they spill into matter and be nursed by Rhea. Thus the mysteries and the myths about the gods say riddingly (*ainittontai,* usually translated as "hint at") that Kronos, the wisest of the gods, shuts up again within himself that which he produces before the birth of Zeus, so that he is filled full and is nous in its satiety (*en kopôi*). After this, they say that in its satiety, Nous produces Zeus, for Nous in its perfection produces *psychê*. (*Enn.* V.1.7, 27-38)[43]

Zeus represents Soul, the lowest hypostasis, spilling over into matter. Kronos is Mind and his grandfather Ouranos is implicitly the transcendent First Principle, as Lamberton explains. This is confirmed by Hadot in his article "Ouranos, Kronos and Zeus in Plotinus' Treatise against the Gnostics."[44] Plotinus's usage is clearly a precedent for aligning the Hesiodic theogony with an ontology that posits triads that are denuded of all the non-philosophical and nefarious activities of the gods and serve purely metaphysical functions. Plotinus nowhere refers to a goddess but does define the parameters of "Life" in a way that facilitates the later association and has derived his use of the triad, at least in part, from an argument in Plato's *Sophist* (248C-E). In that passage, Plato states emphatically that true being must have "life" as well as intelligence. Plotinus adopts this model and describes the generation of Intellect from the One:

> Life, not the life of the One, but a trace of it, looking toward the One was boundless, but once having looked was bounded (without bounding its source). Life looks toward the One and, determined by it, takes on boundary, limit and form ... it must then have been determined as (the life of) a Unity (i.e. Intellect) that includes Multiplicity ... multiplicity because of Life, and a Unity because of limit ... so Intellect is bounded Life. (Plotinus *Enn.*VI.7.17, 13-26)[45]

Turner suggests that the "rather static ontologies" that were typical of Middle Platonism gave way to dynamic emanations in Neoplatonism. Turner considers that it may have been the Gnostic doctrine of *Allogenes*, not just that of Numenius, that provoked Plotinus to place the triad Being, Life, and Mind in the Intellect rather than conjoining it with the One as the link between these two. The passage quoted above shows that Plotinus was certainly aware of the doctrine in his middle period (*c.* 263-269) during which Porphyry attended his seminars. "Life" becomes a key element in the universe of Neoplatonic ontology. In his multilayered highly complex system of triads, "Life" on every level will correspond, in the Neoplatonic triads, to a variety of goddesses.

Late Neoplatonic Triads

For the Neoplatonist, divinity operates on every level of the conceptual and natural order. All the gods have rationalized functions within a larger metaphysical picture. A golden chain of higher and lower divinities necessitates that the creation of triads reaches new levels of complexity. All the separate fundamental levels of being must interact to produce the world while the continuity of being must be preserved in a universe where unity stems from the One. The figures of gods and goddesses permeate spiritual and material creation, but continuity is maintained. As a consequence, every existing ontological structure is composed of triads that constitute derivative levels of divine presence. "Proclus," Rangos points out, "in all seriousness and without the slightest touch of irony, assigns to some traditional gods of Greek polytheism a definitive place in the structure of being."[46] To accomplish this, Proclus refines the practice of triadizing to a fine art. The Plotinian triad of Being, Life, and Intelligence; the Chaldean triad of Existence, Power, and Intelligence; the Aristotelian triad of Substance, Potentiality, and Actuality; Plato's *Philebus* triad of Limit, Unlimited, and the Mixture, all conspire to find a place. Polytheism is assimilated to henotheism as the divine figures that had featured in Hesiod's *Theogony*, the Orphic poems, and the *Chaldean Oracles* now allow all levels of being to dynamically and dialectically interact. Proclus expresses this as follows:

> All things are in all things but each according to its proper nature; for in Being there is life and intelligence; in Life being and intelligence, in Intelligence, being and life; but each of these exists upon one level intellectually, upon another vitally, and on the third existentially.[47]

The life-generating triad composed of all female goddesses described in Proclus' *Platonic Theology* will suffice here to illustrate the complex and baroque nature of this account.

> The life generating triad begins with Demeter who engenders the entire encosmic life, namely intellectual life, psychic life and the life that is inseparable from body; Hera who brings forth the birth of soul occupies the cohering middle position (for the intellectual goddess outpours from herself all the processions of the psychic kinds); finally, Artemis has been assigned to the end of the trinity because she activates all the natural formative principles and perfects the self-completeness of matter; it is for this reason, namely because she supervises natural development and natural birth, that the theologians and Socrates in the *Theaetetus* call her Lochia.
> (*Plat. Theol.* VI.22, 98, 3-13, trans. Rangos)

Corresponding to this is the passage that Rangos quotes from Proclus's *Commentary on the Republic* (I.95.2-7) in which Hera is the cause of the better souls and Artemis delivers and brings to light the less worthy souls.[48]

Luc Brisson tells us there are two major groups when it comes to the gods. The first group are those that are separate from the world and correspond to the first three levels in a Neoplatonic hierarchy: intelligible, intelligible-intellective, and intellective.[49] The gods of the world comprise the second group, corresponding to three levels: the hypercosmic, hypercosmic-encosmic, and encosmic. These comprise two basic levels of "gods" corresponding to the hypostases of Mind and Soul, and these entities permeate the complex triads that exist on each of the two levels. On the level of the soul, not only nature and fate but also archangels, angels, the companions of the gods known as demons, and heroes reside.[50] Luc Brisson's lucid though highly complex chart of all the levels of intelligible, intelligible-intellectual, and intellective gods is a good working model of these categories as they are treated in the Orphic rhapsodies and the *Chaldean Oracles*, and later in Proclus.[51] Jan Opsomer in his equally clear chart of Demiurgy explains that the transcendent and cosmic orders of divinities fall into three categories each: the "intelligible" gods (Being), the "intellectual" gods (Intellect), and a third intermediate class, the "intelligible-and-intellectual" gods (Life).[52] The cosmic deities are classified into the "hypercosmic" and the "encosmic," and an intermediary class which links the two, the "hypercosmic-and-encosmic." Each of the subcategories comprises three trinities (or triads) of individual gods. After the One come the transcendent gods and following them are the cosmic deities: each level has its own complexity. In Luc Brisson's chart, Being is First "Intelligible" Triad (consisting of limiting, unlimited, and intelligible being). A second intelligible triad in this series is Power (limiting/unlimited and intelligible life) and, third down in this series, Action (consisting of limiting-unlimited and intelligible Intellect). A second stratum, lower in the structure, consists of the Intelligible-intellective gods, and the third and final stratum consists of the Intellective gods. There are a multitude of triads under the umbrella of Intellective gods. The first intellective triad, "triad of the parents," consists of Kronos, Rhea, and Zeus (in the Orphic account) and First Intellect, Hekate, and Second Intellect (in the *Chaldean Oracles*). Next down is a triad of "immaculate" gods (Brisson) who maintain the preceding triad. These are Zeus, Poseidon, and Pluto (Hades). The second hypercosmic triad (triad of Kore) includes Athena, Kore, and Artemis. At the next level down, representing the impartible soul of the world, are the hypercosmic-encosmic gods, which include a first triad (demiurgic triad) made up of Zeus, Poseidon, and Hephaestus; another of Hestia, Athena, and Ares; and a lower "Vivifying" triad of Demeter, Hera, and Artemis. This level includes the "Uplifting" triad, mentioned earlier, of Hermes, Aphrodite, and Apollo. Triads in this complex system are conceptual and divine and derive, somehow, from the main triad of Being, Life, and Intellect, wherein Rhea is the middle and associated with Life. Rangos describes this further: One, Life, and Intellect are already encapsulated in Being. "Being is the opaque dynamism of existence which enables things to operate, i.e. to live and act out their activities."[53]

Spiritual motion, as Gersh has explained, must enable the unfolding of multiplicity from unity: an account must be made of mediation between timeless creation and the world of perpetual change.[54] Proclus's symphonic creation of a triadic superstructure addresses the fact that efficient causality cannot be ascribed to the transcendent Intellect, which must remain uncontaminated by encosmic realities. Goddesses alone possess the demiurgic power to engage with the encosmic world. Rangos tells us that in the tightly knit web of interconnected divine principles there is one Monad-trinity diptych that is called "life-generating" and is identified with Rhea who is the second member of the first trinity of intellectual deities. Rhea is the vivifying animating principle and as Proclus states, "the second life-generating principle" and is what Greek theology calls "maidenly" (*korikê*) (P.T., VI, II, 49, 20–30). All female divinities associating with her are life-generating within their own purviews. On the hypercosmic level, this principle becomes triple without losing its unity, hence there is room for other goddesses. The "maidenly," then, is a category of existence that includes all the goddesses and seems to be under the auspices of Rhea. In the *Platonic Theology*, Proclus, after calling the life-generating principle maidenly, states:

> The divine cause of divisible life has been united from all eternity with the entire life-generating source which the theologians call also "mother of the sovereign goddess" and to which Plato alludes since he always links Kore with Demeter. (*Plat. Theol.* VI.11, 49, 20-30)[55]

This is a reference to the Homeric hymn to Demeter.

It is through the "maidenly" that individual living beings are animated and perfected. The first member of one of the "maidenly" trinity is Artemis, the second Persephone, and the third Athena. This is the trinity through which this takes place. Artemis provides living beings with existence, Persephone bestows the precise form of life, and Athena imparts intellect. In another version of this, quoted by Rangos (*Plat. Theol.* VI.11, 51, 19-28), Artemis is equated with She-of-the-Distance (Hekate), Persephone with Soul (*Psyche*), and Athena with Virtue (*Arete*). Proclus adds that "amidst the barbarians the same deities are denoted by different names: they call the first Monad 'Hekate,' the second 'soul,' and the third 'virtue.'" Proclus is referring to the fact that as early as the fifth century Hekate was already an epithet of Artemis.[56] The maidenly triad corresponds to the well-known Neoplatonic tripartite model of metaphysical motion: *monê* (unity), *proodos* (procession), and *epistrophê* (return). Artemis is the *monê* of the Maidenly triad and provides beings with existential extremity. The ethical and intellectual perfection produced by Athena and the final coming back, or *nostos*, is attributed to Persephone (*Plat. Theol.* VI.11, 52, 14-23).

> "For these are the three life-generating Monads: Artemis, Persephone and Athena, our patron deity. Artemis, who makes the Monad come back to her is the extremity of the entire trinity, Persephone is the vivifying power of unties and Athena is the divine and uncontaminated intellect." Being, Life, and Intellect first appear on the level of the intelligible gods.

In another triad, Rangos tells us, Artemis has a secondary position in a trinity that includes Demeter and Hera (*Plat. Theol.* VII.22, 98, 3-13). The interweaving of deities within the levels of triads is complex and interactive. In Proclus, three goddesses appear bearing the name of Artemis: for example, the first is found at the hypercosmic level of reality in which we find the diptych of Rhea (or Demeter) and also a Maidenly triad. Rhea is the entire life-generating cause of everything, while the Maidenly triad is in fact a principle, which becomes triple without losing its unity. This is the triad discussed above that also includes Persephone and Athena. The second Artemis belongs to the worldly deities and has a place in the hypercosmic divine order together with Demeter and Hera, where she occupies the third position. Her responsibility is to animate natural beings in general. She deals with physical bodies that are the most elementary forms of life.[57] The third Artemis belongs to the encosmic level and is in fact one of the powers Persephone contains within herself in an indivisible and unified way.

It is difficult to catalog or sort out all the changes in goddesses' names that occur in these arrangements. Harold Tarrant points out that the female life-giving power (described in relation to the *Krater*, Plato's receptacle) can be associated with Hekate, but she is mentioned by name only once in Proclus's *Commentary on Timaeus*. It is helpful in grasping what is going on here to identify the function the goddess is serving at any given point, rather than the name. Tarrant suggests that Rhea, Demeter, Hekate, Kore, etc., whom van den Berg states are life-producing goddesses, actually can be considered not as individuals but as keys to identifying the power of the female life-giving goddess as a function within Proclus's larger scheme.[58] Proclus's prolific triadic structures are notable in the fact of the ubiquitous presence of powerful female deity. Many scholarly articles on the mechanics of Proclean metaphysics downplay the roles of gods and goddesses in the service of presenting a dialectical and philosophical account of his ontology. They do not, as Proclus did, consider how abstract entities without agency could *do* anything. In fact, the fusion of gods and concepts is a dominant explanatory framework for Proclus. Conceptual/theological fusions are more than just a way to keep the traditional pagan deities relevant. They fill an explanatory gap as conceptual parameters alone do not have creative force while gods and goddesses can cause motion and change. Just as the gods generate offspring resembling their own status in Hesiod's *Theogony*, in an ontological model, concepts generate consequent premises. Living agency intervenes to allow primary causes, transcendent and removed, to generate secondary manifestations. Nature can receive the gifts that are locked away in the furthest reaches of a removed hypostasis by the intervention of "lower" deities who can affect motion and change through the life-giving powers possessed by goddesses.

Conclusion

Living in the twenty-first century, one can only speculate about how and why triadic structures seem to proliferate in late antiquity in Gnostic, Chaldean, and Platonist literature. As further corroboration of Jan Assmann's idea that cultural memory can last centuries, triads consisting of abstract nouns, or in theology a trinity consisting of divine father, son and spirit, both mythological in their own way, appear in subsequent history of ideas. While there is no way to document any relation between the active preoccupation with the nature of the trinity in Christianity and the proliferation of deified triads in Neoplatonism, they do hold in common the idea that mediation is necessary.[59] J. Gwyn Griffiths, an Egyptologist well-known for his translation of and commentary on Isis and Osiris, has also written a book, *Triads and Trinity*, in which he makes some speculative generalizations. He points out that four centuries of Christian writers culminated in the Council of Constantinople in 381, when the Christian trinity was accepted absolutely. He traces possible origins for the trinity in the flourishing of triads in the second century. Griffiths suggests that the Graeco-Egyptian religious amalgam exercised a strong influence on early Christians, particularly in Alexandria. Triplicate structures, viz thesis, antithesis, and synthesis, can be found, famously, in Hegel (an admirer of Proclus). Carl Jung considered the arrangement of deities into triples an archetype in the history of religion.[60] The "cultural memory" of triadic oneness, a mainstay of Gnosticism, and Neoplatonism persists, with or without goddesses. It is an evocative structure. Perhaps the logographic necessity for triplicate structure is demanded by the dialectical nature of metaphysical reasoning. Though far removed from earlier settings, there persists an unsolvable "explanatory gap" in unmediated dualisms: between mind and body, the transcendent and the immanent, consciousness and perception that is often encountered in modern philosophies of mind. While once female divinity occupied the placeholder for mediation, scholars now still speculate about how one can fill the explanatory gaps that dualism entails and yet keep to the canons of positivism.

7

Naming the Goddess: Geopolitics and the Intertranslation of Names

Moshe Halbertal raises the following questions: is the identification of one god with another a matter of metaphysics or of politics?[1] Are those who make equivalences between the gods of diverse nations, expressing a metaphysical belief that they are really speaking about the same god under different names, or applying a convenient legal political convention? Several types of god-naming can be identified, all of which are characteristic of the world of polytheism; all attached to cultures that the monotheist could consider idolatrous. The first is the local and regional adherence to a particular named god or goddess native to that region and its peoples, thus differentiating that deity from its neighbors and enemies. Second is the articulation of a standardized pantheon for national adherence, as is found in the epic poets and Panhellenic festivals wherein the names of the gods and goddesses are identity markers accompanied by definite descriptions. Third, there is the political idea that names are intertranslatable and that the gods and goddesses are somehow universal and only differ in regional naming practices (cosmotheism). Geopolitical factors can expand the practice of naming gods to include making them inter-translatable. This can occur when regional affiliations become less important due to the priorities of ecumenical politics. In archaic Greece and Mesopotamia, there were regional gods; as mainland Greece attained hegemony over colonial outposts, the Hesiod/Homeric pantheon took hold, at times assimilating these gods and their names and epithets. In late antiquity, the inter-translatability of gods' and goddesses' names became generally accepted and the pantheon became one, not of names, but of functional descriptions. The Athenian school took this to the extreme, adding ontological reification to the unity of the gods and goddesses by adopting a principle that "everything is in everything, but each appropriately." Henotheism supervenes upon the differential qualities and deities that appear in the pantheon. Each god or goddess becomes part of a larger structure and the specific names become less important than the functions within the vision of the whole. This mirrors the "vision of the whole" of conquering and ruling emperors, and of Christianity, that there is "one world" over which there must somehow be one hegemonic divinity. In the case of polytheism, this means a single "set" of interrelated divinities.

For the polytheist, divine beings are agents, powers, and forces in the universe and beyond. They are not omniscient, infinite, and omnipresent. They limit one another, deceive one another, and fall victim to each other's lust, anger, and revenge. Gods and goddesses create in the same way as humans, through copulation, or in special cases through parthenogenesis, never by simply uttering a command as does the biblical God of Judeo-Christian monotheism. Gods and goddesses are subject to Fate. Even the god who is ascribed the greatest degree of hegemony, Zeus, is limited to intervening in the heavens and in human lives. In the absence of a creator god, Plato supplements the traditional account of his time by inventing a special "demiurge" to construct the universe. The gods and goddesses of archaic and classical mythology, then, are an aggregate of diverse powers. Organized in a pantheon in the epic poem, though holding distinct names, they are part of a larger schema of narrative interactions and sometimes bizarre genealogies. Often carrying the names of their cultic predecessors, they are not particularly similar in description to their pre-literary prototypes. This raises a question that has been of interest to the analytic philosophers of the twentieth century: do diverse descriptions denote the same referent? Gods and goddesses, as they are known to Western texts, receive their "definite descriptions" through the literary inventions of the epic poets and hymnists. Supernatural powers are projected onto these mythical figures to explain causality and sustainability in nature and to intervene in political, military, and personal life events. Although they are named with proper names, unlike their regional votive and cultic predecessors, their names represent constellations of meaning established by the textual context in which they are described. These divine figures, then, have names that are not, strictly speaking, "rigid designators," and in ecumenical geopolitical contexts their names can therefore be interchanged based on their descriptive attributes.[2]

The Presocratic philosophers inaugurated the practice of "naming" the first principle of the universe with the name of a natural element or abstract noun, Thales' "water," Anaximander's *apeiron* (boundless), for example. Anaxagoras's *Nous* ("mind") is a principle that acts to initiate a vortex out of which all things come to be out of originating "seeds" that contain the elements of all things in an undifferentiated form. *Nous*, the first principle, acts as an efficient cause rendering the undifferentiated material of nature into the objects of the world by setting in motion a rotating force (DK 58 B1, B12). No gender, of course, is possible in these accounts. The first principle is neither a natural force nor a personified deity but nonetheless seems to have an all pervading agency. Parmenides' "One Being" and Anaximander's "boundless" are not personified in any way but still cause reality. Plato's demiurge, the *archê*/technocrat, is unnamed, although some later interpretations would assert that Plato is referring to Zeus. In Anaxagoras, it is *Nous* which does the work of creation out of preexisting matter. In Porphyry, however, reflecting the changes that took place in later antiquity, Zeus is the demiurgic intellect, a tradition carried on by Proclus and others who equated *Nous* with Zeus and the first Intellect (Proclus *Plat. Theol.* V.15, 18-20).[3] Zeus, however, had never before been identified with creation, per se. The demiurge is analogous to a craftsman and is not the originator of the paradigm from which the demiurge works. In Plato's *Timaeus*, then, the source of the paradigm is not identified, nor does it claim divinity. The contrast between "naming" the first principle of the universe by affixing an abstract noun and giving proper names to gods and goddesses as originating sources is often taken as evidence that the Greeks were discarding mythology and embarking upon, as the title of Bruno Snell's book, *The Discovery of the Mind*.

The situation, however, is by far more nuanced than that and the interrelation between abstract nouns and the proper names of divinities complex. The Presocratic "naming" of an original source of all that is by means of an abstract noun has encouraged some scholars to advance a narrative that this practice initiates the advent of reason as opposed to mythology. It is not clear, however, that the Pre-Socratic philosophers were free of mythology; furthermore, the claim that abstract forces operate as agents in the universe is "mythical" in its own way. It relies on the trope prosopopoeia (personification of the inanimate). The fragments of their work that are extant may, in any case, be selective. What is distinctive about the Greek gods and goddesses, a feature that enables them to be conflated with gods of other regions and cultures, is the distinguishing of deities by name, shape, and function, as Assmann points out.[4] The assignment of a proper name, analogous to naming human beings, is a different enterprise from assigning conceptual names associated with nature (water, air, etc.) or philosophical ontology (boundless, *Nous*, etc.). The fact that, in Hesiod, the two are fused reflects a long mysterious history. Earth and sky seem to be the primordial god and goddess names in a variety of ancient cultures.

Chiara Bottici cites Vernant who recognized that there are similarities between the conceptual structure employed by the Ionic physicists and that employed by Hesiod's cosmogony. Hesiod presents the creation of the world by reference to Chaos, the Earth, the Sky as deities, although their names belong to a deity-free physics as well. Bottici points out that the Ionic philosophers and Hesiod correspond in the following details. The origin of the world is seen in terms of (1) chaos at the beginning, (2) the separations of pairs of opposites such as hot and cold, out of the primordial unity, and (3) the reunification and interaction between the opposites.[5] Where they do not correspond is in the naming of gods and goddesses. The goddesses that are the presumed objects of worship and appeal in the earlier cultures, to whom votive offerings were proffered and who were represented in temple art, were individually worshiped goddesses, known to the peoples of their regions. The goddesses of Homer, Hesiod, and the Derveni papyrus or the *Hymn to Demeter*, on the other hand, have been subject to the exigencies of the text in which they are found. In the case of the votive and cultic milieu, the name of a deity is idiolectic, in Kripke's words "a rigid designator." In the epic poem or hymn, the name is identified with a set of descriptions, which allows her to be identified with other goddesses that hold similar descriptions. Marquardt points out that the origins of Hekate, for example, appear to lie in the Near East, particularly Caria.[6] M. L. West remarks that in the Hymn to Hekate (Th. 211-4520 particulary at 411-52) the praise of Hekate has stylistic features of Babylonian and Assyrian hyns. Hesiod says that when people pray to Hekate or invoke her "great favors" are bestowed.[7] Here she is clearly referred to as a unique object of worship with very specific powers. Later when Hekate is de-regionalized and becomes a universally accessible deity, her functions supersede her name qua simple denotation. A similar process occurs in the case of Kybele and Isis. In these cases, all goddesses of a particular description can be equated with Isis or Kybele or Hekate based on similarity. In philosophical writings, such as Iamblichus's *De*

Mysteriis and the *Hermetica*, the divine names are considered to be sacred and unique presences that are not able to lend themselves to intercultural exchange. This is not the case though in much of the god-naming of Late Antiquity. The practice of conflating these names with philosophical functions is one far removed from original votive and cultic contexts. The practice done both in the service of ecumenical exchange and in philosophical texts reflects a development which facilitated matching the names of deities to philosophical concepts.

Interchangeability According to Political Priorities

Jan Assmann points out that polytheism is not something primitive and tribal. The polytheistic religions of the ancient New East and Ancient Egypt represent highly developed cultural achievements that are inseparably linked to the political organization of the early state. Polytheist cultures display a "general syncretistic tendency" to equate their own deities with those of other cultures based on the notion that all cultures worship the same deities but use names derived from their own heritage. The practice of inter-translating the names of deities for the purpose of intercultural exchange goes back to the Late Bronze Age (third millennium BCE). Assmann cites a few of the innumerable ancient glossaries equating Sumerian and Akkadian words in bilingual lists of gods. "The practice of forming these equivalences must be seen in the context of the general emergence of a common world with integrated networks of commercial, political and cultural communication." This common world extended from Egypt to the Near and Middle East and westward to the shores of the Atlantic. There is evidence of lists of gods giving the divine names in two or even three languages. Assmann describes one list which contains three columns, the first giving the Sumerian names, the second the Akkadian, and the third the functional definition of the deity (thus revealing the principle that operated in this practice). In the Kassite period of the Late Bronze Age, the lists extended to include languages spoken in Amorite, Hurritic, Elamite, and Kassite in addition to Sumerian and Akkadian. Assmann suggests that treaties that had to be sealed by solemn oaths and invoking the gods would have had to be recognized by both parties.[8] In later antiquity, the functional equivalence between gods and goddesses of diverse cultures was facilitated by the literature that imbued them with definitive descriptions, differentiated and personalized by name, shape, and function. Interchanging names, in Hellenistic and Roman times, ameliorated a regional conquest or made a treaty more palatable in the eyes of the local populace.[9]

The practice of creating equivalences between deities is specifically "pagan" in comparison with the Hebrew treatment of deity. From the earliest times, the name of God was considered to be unutterable and no equivalences to deities worshiped by surrounding cultures were thought to be possible. This name, whether known or unknown, is considered to be a "rigid designator" (a proper name that designates its object uniquely).[10] In Greece, on the other hand, as early as Herodotus, the intertranslatability of gods' names was recognized. In the *Timaeus*, Plato refers to this practice in passing: "in the Delta of Egypt, there is a certain district called the Saitic. The chief city in this district is Sais—the home of King Amesis—the founder of which, they say, is a goddess whose Egyptian name is Neith and in Greek, as they assert, Athena" (*Tim.* 21E1-7). During the Hellenistic and Roman eras, the practice proliferated, profoundly changing the nature and the identities of the gods. They are no longer singular and unique objects of worship and their respective functions no longer correspond to the god or goddess of epic poetry and ancient hymn. Singular identity is less important as the emphasis is on function; each goddess becomes less of an "existence" and more of an "essence" based on abstract characteristics. Some of the traits which become formulaic when it comes to goddesses accrue, in future usages, to gender per se.

The Isis Phenomenon

After Alexander's conquests and those of the Roman emperors, the need for a "universal" object of worship was very much in the air in a world where hegemonic rule relegated diverse cultures to subordinate positions. Aretalogies reflect a general *Weltanschauung* that appears in both ritual and votive practice and in the intellectual life of the times. This ecumenical spirit in some ways accounts for how a savior named Jesus came to be widely embraced in the first few centuries of the Roman Empire. Jan Assmann quotes several later Isis texts from Egypt that address the goddess invoking the names by which the various nations address her. The one from the first century BCE quoted on the bottom of this page not only attests to the political exigencies of the times, but also suggests that one dominant deity is the single entity to which all the names refer. The practice of stipulating a series of names referring to a single deity was particularly widespread the Greco-Roman Isis phenomena. In a papyrus from Oxyrhynchos,[11] for example, there is a long hymn to Isis:

> At Aphroditopolis in the Prosopite nome fleet-commanding, many-shaped Aphrodite; at the Delta giver of favors. at Nithine in the Gynaecopolite nome, Aphrodite; at Paphremis, Isis, queen, Hestia, mistress of every country. in the Saite Nome, Victorious Athena; in Sais, Hera, queen, full grown; in Iseum, Isis; in Sebennytos, intelligence, ruler, Hera, holy; in Hermupolis, Aphrodite, queen, holy; in Apis, Sophia; in Leuke Akte, Aphrodite, Mouchis, Eseremphis; at Cynopolis in the Busirite nome, Praxidike; at Busiris, Good Fortune. at Tanis, gracious in form, Hera.[12]

Assmann points out that after a long list correlating Egyptian towns with names of Isis, the list continues by naming places outside Egypt in Arabia (great goddess in Lycia, Cyrene, etc.), and that the list closes with that striking formula: "the beautiful essence of all the gods" (*theôn hapantôn to kalon zôon*).[13] The following aretalogy reflects the ecumenical nature of goddess naming as well:

> All mortals who live on the boundless earth,
> Thracians, Greeks and Barbarians,
> Express your fair name, a name greatly honored among all,

[But] each speaks in his own language, in his own land.
The Syrians call you: Astarte, Artemis, Nanaia,
The Lycian tribes call you: Leto, the lady,
The Thracians also name you as Mother of the gods,
And the Greeks [call you] Hera of the Great Throne, Aphrodite,
Hestia the goodly, Rhea and Demeter,
But the Egyptians call you Thiouis [because they know] that
you, being one, are all other goddesses invoked by the races of men.
(first century BCE hymn, trans. Assmann)[14]

Streete points out that as early as the fifth century BCE Herodotus described the worship of Isis in Egypt at Cyrene, Bubasis, Sais, and Memphis.[15] In his *Histories* Herodotus claims that "Isis is Demeter in the Greek language" (2.59.156). It is documented that in 333 BCE, Egyptians who traded with Greece installed Isis in Piraeus, with the consent of local authorities.[16] From the beginning of the second century BCE, Isis—with or without her associated deities—Sarapis, Horus, and Anubis, her jackal-headed assistant—was known through the Hellenistic world from Sicily to the shores of the Black Sea. Judging from the aretalogies to Isis found in the Mediterranean world from about the first century BCE, there also seems to have been a conscious attempt on the part of officials of her cult to win proselytes to the faith.[17] The earliest datable hymns, the aretalogies of Kyme in Asia Minor, Andros, and Maroneia in Thrace, emphasize Isis's sovereignty over "every land" and put forward her identification with goddesses like Artemis, Demeter, and the Roman Ceres. The Isis phenomenon, then, is a perfect illustration of the association between ecumenical efforts of geopolitical movements and the intertranslatability of the names of deities. It also suggests that in some senses she is regarded as one conceptual entity albeit with alternative names.

Isis attained a cross-cultural presence in the Hellenistic period and continued to do so in the Roman Empire. Egypt became a province of Rome in 30 BCE after Octavian defeated Mark Antony and deposed Cleopatra VII. Hellenizing had gone on since Alexander and the Greeks and Romans found Hellenic matches for the Egyptian deities (Thoth and Hermes, Imhotep and Asclepius, Zeus and Amon, etc.).[18] Syncretism was a political tool, the most famous instance being the cult of Serapis which came into precedence under Ptolemy I. Since Osiris was associated with death and rebirth, the dying bull of Apis became Osiris, yielding the amalgamated Osarapis or Serapis. Sculptors depicted Serapis with the head of Zeus. When Ptolemy took possession of Egypt and made Alexandria its capital, he legitimized himself by the word of Isis and his descendants adopted the indigenous religions of their own account.[19] Ptolemy wished to show Egyptians how their beliefs could blend with the Greeks'. Under the aegis of Ptolemy III, the Serapeum of Alexandria was one of the most prestigious in the ancient world.[20] This Serapeum, dedicated to the syncretic Hellenistic-Egyptian god Serapis, lasted until it was destroyed by a Christian band of Roman soldiers in 391 under the aegis of Theodosius I, who encouraged such assaults against major cult sites.

The Roman conquest of the Mediterranean, Turcan explains, had resulted in imported deities brought back by triumphant victors, altering the practices of Roman religion. Foreigners too, ladies' maids, etc., brought their native deities who sometimes supplanted those of the Romans in sheer popularity. The Egyptian gods reached Rome by way of Campania. A Serapeum located at Canopus in the Nile delta near Alexandria was dedicated to Isis and Serapis. Depictions of Isis between two sphinxes were discovered in the temple of the Palatine Apollo, which adjoined the residence of Augustus.[21] Pompeii had its Iseum and Pozzuoli its Serapeum. Despite resistance and attempts to destroy the Isiac temples on the part of Roman authorities, the popular nature of these cults resulted in one case, for example, of workman who refused to carry out the destruction. The Navigium Isidis, a yearly festival honoring Isis, continued to take place late in the Empire. It seems that Egyptian, Roman, and Greek religious usages easily flowed into each other.[22]

R. E. Witt discusses the Hellenizing of Isis. In Egypt, she had a distinct individual profile that dated back perhaps as far as 310 BCE. Originally she was an independent deity in pre-dynastic times at Sebenylos in the Nile delta. Her headdress was a throne and her name means "throne," a personification of the throne as the power of the pharaoh. During the Old Kingdom period, Isis was represented as the wife of Osiris. Her name appeared eighty times in the pharaohs' funeral texts (Pyramid Texts). She also was known to the Middle and New Kingdom periods. One myth has it that she was mother of the four sons of Horus, the four deities who protected the canopic jars containing the Pharaoh's internal organs. By the fifth dynasty, Isis had entered the pantheon of the city of Heliopolis and was considered to be married to Osiris. Her tale became the one known to Plutarch wherein Seth dismembers Osiris and she restores him to wholeness and gives birth to Horus. In Egypt, she came to have a certain individual profile: her love for her brother husband, her power to bring about the Nile flood, her knowledge of healing, and her control of the crops. Herodotus stated that Isis was the only goddess worshiped by all Egyptians.[23]

Isis took on the characteristic qualities of many of the Greek goddesses during Hellenization. She became known as "the goddess of many (or countless) names" (*myrionymos*). Witt points out that this title is found in inscriptions of the second century CE from Nubia, Upper Egypt, Cyrenaica, Italy, Dacia, Germany, and northern France. She is also a goddess whose characteristics make her amenable to philosophical usage. Plutarch associates her with the material substrate, which he discovers in the *Timaeus*, as well as the female principle of nature and, as such, the passive receptacle for every kind of shape and form (*De Iside* 372e). Witt terms this her "metaphysical depersonalization." The title *myrionymos* was significantly wider than *polynymous* "many named," Witt points out, which was borne by other members of the Greek pantheon—Aphrodite and Apollo, Helios and Hermes—and was a gift from Zeus by Artemis who held the title with the same special rights as Isis: queenly powers on earth, in the underworld, and in the sky. As Witt says, "Isis was the only divinity whose epiclesis marked that the number of her names was not merely large but even infinite." She alone claimed an infinity of divine titles and could be all things to all men (mother of nature, beginning of generations, and queen of the underworld), including the Roman goddess of war. Assimilation of Isis to Athena's Roman counterpart Minerva was easier than to Athena.[24]

Isis' universalism flourished at the same time as Christianity was moving the Roman populace toward a new form of monotheistic worship. In many of the towns, including the birthplace of Paul of Tarsus, and in most of the cities where he proselytized the newfound Christian gospel, Isis was an established and renowned object of worship. Cleopatra identified herself with Isis. Assmann, remarking on the cultural diversity in late Hellenistic mentality, notes that the names of the gods mattered little. Commercial interconnectedness and universalism were the ruling principle. Isis, in that universalist spirit, became known not by her traditional resume in Egypt, but in a syncretic form acquired in the Greco-Egyptian ecumenical fusion. Assmann cites the striking example in Apuleius's *Metamorphoses* (11.5.2-3) where the "queen of heaven" goes by different names among different people:

> I who am the mother of the universe, the mistress of all the elements, the first offspring of time, the highest of deities, the queen of the dead, foremost of heavenly beings, the single form that fuses all gods and goddesses; I who order by my will the starry heights of heaven ... my single godhead is adored by the whole world in varied forms, in differing rites and with many diverse names.
> Thus the Phrygians ... call me Pessinuntia; ... the Athenians ... call me Cecropeian Minerva; ... etc. But the Ethiopians, together with the Africans and the Egyptians who excel by having the original doctrine honor me with my distinctive rites and give me my true name of Queen Isis.[25]

Isis worship spread through the Greek-speaking colonies of outer Italy and eventually reached Rome. According to Apuleius, who lived in the second century CE and who may have been an initiate in the cult of Isis and Osiris, the cult was founded in the time of the dictatorship of the Roman general Sulla (*c.* 88 BCE). In early Rome, Isis did not achieve legal recognition by the senate and was distrusted as a new or foreign religion.[26] Her adherents were slaves, the lower class, or women. Josephus, in *Jewish Antiquities* (18.65-80), reports that Tiberius persecuted the worship of Isis in 19 CE. Corrington suggests that this seems to have been the result of the involvement of foreign and lower-class clergy and worshippers of Isis in the seduction of a matron of senatorial rank, Paullina, by a knight, Decius Mundus. Apparently, at least according to Josephus, she came to the temple of Isis in 19 CE to sleep with the god Anubis. Mundus bribed temple priests, disguised himself as Anubis, and seduced Paullina. Tiberius had the priests and their female accomplices crucified, exiled Mundus, and destroyed the temple of Isis. Other emperors embraced her with enthusiasm, as did the Flavian emperors, the Antonines, Commodus, and the Severan Caracalla. The cult gained momentum and the great Isis festival, the Navigium Isides, was still celebrated in Italy as late as 416 CE. It was not until the sixth century that the worship of Isis in Egypt was effectively suppressed.[27] Evidence for the ecumenical nature of Isis can be found largely in the aretalogies or encomia of Isis mentioned above.[28] Solmsen asks why Isis was so influential when other foreign deities were also present in Rome. He speculates that Demeter and Persephone, of great popular appeal, most closely approximated Isis, and Dionysus most approximated Osiris, and these facts aided this process. Furthermore, the maternal aspect of Isis made her appealing in terms of motherhood, fertility, and so on. Isis was more mobile than other goddesses who had restricted local roots. Solmsen claims further that Isis was "not too closely defined (so she could easily acquire new functions and enter into new partnerships). She was bound to appeal to different people for different reasons."[29]

Inter-Translation and God Naming

In the early empire, Augustus's religious policy was both traditionalist, involving restoration and renewal of traditional religion, and innovative, concerned with the foundation of the imperial cult.[30] During his reign, every attempt was made to absorb the culture of foreign nations. As mentioned above, although he banned Egyptian cults in 28 BCE after the conflict with Mark Antony and Cleopatra, terracotta plaques showing Isis between two sphinxes were to be found in the temple of Apollo Palatine that abutted on his residence. Assimilating Egyptian cultural icons was a process that began during the Hellenistic period and continued in the Roman Republic and Empire. Galinsky describes the Hellenizing of Rome, involving the assimilation of Greek language, manners, and beliefs, but also incorporating foreign conquests. As early as 211 BCE, starting with Marcellus's conquest of Syracuse, Roman generals hauled Greek art by the boatload to Rome and set it up in public places. Temples were constructed by a Greek architect, Herodotus of Salamis, who built the first marble temple in Rome. This temple was dedicated to Jupiter Stator. Surrounding it and the Temple of Juno Regina was a portico with a huge display of Greek sculpture. The Temple of Fortuna Huiusce Diei was a Greek round temple on a Roman podium and housed, among other Geek sculptures, an Athena by Phidias, as Pliny reports.[31] Galinsky, citing Erich Gruen, describes the Hellenizing project as "absorbing into the mainstream of Roman culture the traditions, literature, and the art of Hellas and employing them to draw out the distinctive features of Roman values." This endeavor was particularly evident when it came to the association of Roman success with "Greek" divinity. Eighty-two temples were restored, according to the *Res Gestae*, and importance was attached to certain gods and goddesses: Venus Genetrix, Apollo, Mars, and Vesta. The imperial cult used divinizing as a strategy to expand political power. In Horace's *Odes*, Augustus appears as a god descended to Earth. In around 2 BCE, the temple to Augustus and Rome at Pola and Tartacina was most likely dedicated to Augustus "son of the deity," as were many other similar temples. Augustus was deified by the Senate after his death in 14 CE and the house where he died was turned into a temple. Caligula in 40 BCE ordered a statue of himself in the guise of Jupiter to be installed in the temple in Jerusalem where a cult with an altar and possibly a priestly brotherhood was to be consecrated to his *numen*. Claudius recognized the worship of Kybele. Nero was associated with Apollo. Sun god theology began to underpin the political institution of absolute monarchy.

Isis was not the only goddess absorbed from a subjugated culture. The goddess Kybele is a good example of a regionally particular identity-turned universal icon. Kybele was originally an Anatolian mother goddess associated with mountains, hawks, and lions. In Greece, Kybele was assimilated to aspects of the Earth goddess Gaia and the Minoan equivalent Rhea and was associated with the harvest mother goddess Demeter. Kybele was associated with mountains, town and city walls, fertile nature. Around the fifth century BCE, Agorakritos created a fully Hellenized and influential image of Kybele to be set up in the Athenian agora with a lion attendant and a tympanon (hand drum).[32] Pindar calls Kybele "Meter" (the mother).[33] In Rome, Kybele was known as Magna Mater (Great Mother) and was adopted by the Roman State, especially after the Sibylline Oracle claimed her conscription after success against Carthage in the Punic wars (264–146 BCE). Roman mythographers construed her as a Trojan goddess, and thus an ancestral goddess of the Roman people. The Romans were frequently described as descendants of the Trojans, and Augustan ideology during the imperial era was particularly identified with Kybele for this reason,[34] as Augustus's family claimed Trojan origins. The Empress Livia, for example, identified with her, and the upper classes sponsored festivals to the Magna Mater. The Romanized form of Kybele cults spread throughout the Roman Empire.

Egypt held a fascination for the newly cosmopolitan Romans, as did Hellenic culture for the Egyptians. Plutarch, again, is a prime example of second-century syncretism in regard to the Hellenic gods, their Roman counterparts, and Egyptomania. His *Isis and Osiris* was widely circulated and displays the second-century fascination with Egypt. Plutarch's detailed account of Egyptian cultic lore is Hellenized at every turn. The gods and goddesses are, in addition, rendered as exemplars of abstract principles. Plutarch often etymologizes and gives examples of the various names that Greeks and Egyptians gave to the same divine powers, e.g., Isis's name from the Greek verb *oida* (to know) (*De Iside* 351e); "in the so-called book of Hermes, concerning the sacred names, that they call the power assigned to the revolutions of the sun Horus, but the Greeks call it Apollo" (*De Iside* 375f).[35]

Ramsey McMullan discusses the polynomial nature of god naming in these periods. Dio Chrysostom, a Greek orator, philosopher, and historian of the first century, notes this, reminding his listeners that "some people say Apollo, Helios and Dionysius are all one, and so you believe, and many people combine into one strength and power absolutely all the gods, so there is no difference in honoring one over another." McMullan cites similar statements later in time, such as from Maximus of Tyre (late second century), who said "that there is one god, kin and father of all things and many gods, sons of god."[36] Zeus, Helios, and Serapis, for example, are often found together. Similarly, the mother of the gods, Kybele, is depicted with characteristic articles so as to be portrayed as Bellona, or Astarte, or Ma of Phrygia, or her name is simply run together with that of some other female deity. Apuleius (123–170 CE) associates Hekate with Isis with Juno, Bellona, etc. (*Golden Ass* 11.47). In Apuleius's novel, the hero hesitates to say whether the goddess who saves him is Artemis or Persephone (Proserpina), but then he settles on her being Isis. McMullan gives an epigraphical example: a local goddess, Persia in Cilicia, was addressed in inscriptions as Selene, Artemis, Hekate, Aphrodite, or Demeter, all the same to the dedicant who thought to magnify her this way. The geographical connection between the assertions of political translatability is documented by the mention of places where the names are either used in their original form or changed but are equivalent. Assmann points out that after a long list correlating Egyptian towns with names of Isis, the list continues by naming places outside Egypt in Arabia (great goddess in Lycia, Cyrene, Sidon, etc.).[37]

Le Glay et al. point out that "The imperial cult and the Christian faith were born at much the same time, both witnesses to a 'spiritual revolution' in the Mediterranean world." They cite the great Italian historian Santo Mazzarino, who, employing "a modicum of rhetorical license," compares the "gospel of Augustus" with that of Jesus in order to underline the soteriological expectations that pervaded the ancient world in the first half of the first century.[38] Corrington in her book on female saviors and formative Christianity speculates that Isis as savior *(soteria)* was a precursor to Jesus in that same role, in the populace of the time who sought salvation.[39] Both Hellenist and Roman periods saw the rise of empire with its rule over regional areas, paralleled by the inter-translatability of deities formally possessing separate identities with regional specificity. Gods and goddesses now could enable cosmo-political hegemony and be universalized exemplars. The rise of Christianity was clearly a break from regional loyalties. Christians were devoted to their religion as a universal religion, over and above regional affiliations. When Celsus wrote his discourse against the Christians in the second century CE, one of his main objections to Christianity was the fact that he sensed that Christians had severed the traditional bond between religion and a "nation or people" (Origen *Against Celsus* 8.69). He claimed, "If everyone were to adopt the Christians' attitudes there would be no rule of law, legitimate authority would be abandoned, earthly things would return to chaos and come into the hands of the lawless and savage barbarians." He directly opposed exclusive god naming, stating, "It matters not a bit what one calls the supreme god or whether one uses Greek names or Indian names or names formed by the Egyptians."[40] "Cosmotheism," then, with its de-regionalized all-pervading deity, was one solution to the equalitarian ideals required by assimilation.

The increasing metaphysical usage of goddesses in allegorical and philosophical literature, as discussed in the preceding chapters, took place in this environment. Apuleius's Isis is, in Assmann's words, a "cosmotheistic deity." In Plutarch and later in Proclus, the goddesses of late antiquity are known for their functions; their names are secondary to their essential characteristics. Fertility on a cosmic level is far beyond the specificity of the genealogies stipulated for the named goddesses in Hesiod. The reproduction of generations of gods in theogony fuses with proliferations of superordinate and subordinate ontological levels in Neoplatonism. Proclus, one of the last spokespersons for a rapidly disappearing Hellenism in the late fifth century CE, has created the composite "goddess" of his texts (though not in his *Hymns*), perhaps partly as a consequence of the ease with which goddess identities could be fused in the late empire. For Proclus, Rhea, Demeter, Hekate, Kore, regardless of which name is used, represent the power of the female life-giving force. When the female life-producing goddess copulates, it is a mythological "place holder" for the function that is "mixing": the source of generation by which the world is created through the interaction of higher with lower levels of reality. The abstracting process that turns the traditional theogony into a panlogistic metaform could not be predicated upon a goddess whose name was a rigid designator.

Monotheism, Henotheism, Empire

The assumption that the names of gods and goddesses can be closely associated with their cross-cultural counterparts is based on the premise that there is a common universe of religion to which the names of the nations are subordinate. Furthermore, when there is a "highest" god, whether named Zeus, Serapis, Helios, or Iao (equals Yahweh), appellations like Hypistos (supreme) are attached to them, such as the oracle concerning Serapis:

> One Zeus, one Hades, one Helios is Serapis.
> One Zeus, one Hades, one Helios, one Dionysus,
> One god in all gods.[41]

Solar theology is another example of the tendency to unify the concept of gods into one force that Ramsey MacMillan describes as the "melding of several gods into one chief." "Zeus, Helios, the Great All-God Serapis" is an inscription on an altar from second-century Carthage.[42] Using the Sun as a metaform for the supremacy of the Zeusian deity was widespread. In Mithraism, the sun-Mithras is the supreme deity. In Egypt, magical papyri invoke the sun: "Lord god who grasps the whole, gives life to all, and rules the universe" (*PGM*) (7 line 529f). Similarly, in the Levant, a mosaic floor from Tiberius portrays Helios standing in his chariot wearing the commander's cloak like the Roman emperor, holding in his left hand the orb or globe of rule and raising his right hand in the typical gesture of benediction and mastery. The association of the sun god with the imperial cult is clear in the obvious example of Constantine's conversion from worship of the sun god to Christianity. When Dio Chrysostom in the first century stated that "some people say Apollo, Helios and Dionysus are all one and one strength and power," he identifies a nascent monotheism that is already in the air. The fact that descriptions and functions supersede names in late antiquity, then, like the change from genealogy to ontology, are indications of "henotheism." Hesiod provides the myths that allow the gods and goddesses to be extracted and arranged in a "family tree." In the third century CE, Porphyry forms a logical tree in his *Isagoge* to Aristotle's *Categories*. Here species is defined by genus and differentia and this logical process continues until the lowest species that can be defined is reached, from the highest (*summum*) genus to the lowest (*infima*) species. When this is mapped onto an ontology originating in a hierarchy of hypostases, gods and goddesses no longer possess primarily idiolectic names and are identified by their functions within the system. A genogram is now an "onto-gram" of abstract hypostases and their emanative separate levels of triads, as discussed in Chapters 5 and 6. In such an arrangement, there is separateness yet continuity as the levels of reality all process from a single unity at their origin. Individual naming of the gods is less important than their roles in the hierarchy. "Monotheism," in the sense of the oneness of all components of the onto-gram, changes the way polytheism works.

Negative Theology and the General Issue of Naming God

The Judeo-Christian tradition of regarding god naming as a denigration, as is the case with the Jewish Tetragrammaton, which is not allowed to be pronounced, can also be found in the Hermetic idea of God's anonymity, as Assmann points out. The inter-translatability of gods' names was not universally accepted by Neoplatonists. Iamblichus objected to it and Proclus devised an elaborate rationale for it, contending that the true names of gods were known only as a matter of revelation to qualified theurgists. Gregory Shaw points out that this was a much-debated topic in antiquity. He quotes Iamblichus:[43]

> If it were according to convention (*kata sunthêken*) that names were established it would make no difference whether some names were used instead of others. But if they are tied to the nature of reality those names which are more adapted to it would no doubt be more pleasing to the gods. Indeed, from this, as is reasonable, the languages of sacred races are preferred over those of other men. (*De Myst.* 257, 3-10, trans. Gregory Shaw)
>
> The translation of sacred names would be ineffectual for even if it were possible to translate them, they would no longer hold the same power. (*De Myst.* 257, 134-35, trans. Gregory Shaw)

One way to preserve the mystery and ultimate inaccessible divinity of the transcendent being or beings is to hold that the true names of the gods or God are known only through revelation. Assmann points out that the names which the deity is given by the various nations are not revealed but are culturally specific. In Apuleius, the *verum nomen* is exclusively revealed to the Egyptians and the Ethiopians.[44] A revealed name cannot be translated and is not known to believers of a lower level of initiation. The natural identity of the deity in question transcends all cultural differences. There is one doctrine among the Neoplatonists that supports the idea that goddess names could be interchangeable by virtue of the fact that they are not the "true" names anyway. Proclus explains this in the *Commentary on Timaeus*:

> Knowing therefore, that in the case of the cosmos this name pre-existed [before it came into being] and that there is a divine name differing from its apparent name, he left this name unspoken, but at the same time introduced it with the utmost caution as a symbolic name of the divine signature in it. For the words **whatever name** and **should receive** are a concealed hymn to the cosmic name as unpronounceable and the recipient of the divine essence, so that it would be coupled with the signifying name that he [Plato] gives it. (*In Tim.* I.274.10-17, trans. Runia and Share[45])

For Proclus there are names that are appropriate for every rank of the realities, divine names for the divinities, discursive names for discursive realities, opinable names for realities that are the object of opinion. Proclus cites Homer for giving different names for the same objects in the case of the gods and humankind and gives the example of "the bird which the gods call chalkis, but men call it kumindis" (*In Tim.* I.274.5). For Proclus, the names given by the gods reveal the entire essence of what is named and those given by humans only touch on them in a partial manner. Divine names of the cosmos have been handed down to the theurgists, both the ineffable names and those spoken among themselves.

> For just as the knowledge possessed by the gods and the particular souls differs, so do the names, those given by the gods revealing the entire essence of what is named, whereas the names given by humans only touch on them in a partial manner. (*In Tim.* I.274.6-10, trans. Runia and Share)

Proclus's mysterious and arcane view of the equivalence of statues (*agalmata*) and gods illuminates the idea that names may be the equivalent of statues of the gods. It is a well-known fact that statues were considered by Neoplatonists to be enlivened by the spirit of the god or goddess that they represented. In *Platonic Theology* I.29, Proclus writes:

> The productive activity of the Intellect makes by means of discourse similitudes of all the other realities and particularly of the gods themselves. Since then it produces the names in that way, our scientific knowledge presents them in the ultimate degree as images of divine beings; in fact, *it produces each name as a statue of the gods*, and just as Theurgy invokes the generous goodness of the gods with a view to the illumination of statues artificially constructed, so the intellective knowledge related to divine beings, by composition and divisions of articulated sounds, reveals the hidden being of the gods.[46]

Proclus goes on to propose the doctrine he espouses in his commentary on the *Cratylus*: that the soul makes copies and "by means of certain ineffable symbols makes the statues here below like the gods and ready to receive the divine illuminations, in the same way as the art of the regular formation of words, by that same power of assimilation, *brings into existence names like statues of their realities*." Saffrey documents that a similar view was held by Syrianus, Hierocles, and Damascus. He suggests that the reason why the Platonists of Athens developed the theory of divine names had to do with creating a spiritual substitute for the statues of the gods. These statues, at that time, were being removed from their temples. Proclus was an eyewitness to the removal of the statue of Athena from the Acropolis of Athens and he saw the goddess in a dream. She said to him, "Lady Athena intends to stay with you." Saffrey proposes: "It is only to the Platonists of the generations of Syrianus and of Proclus that one must attribute this devotion to the divine names as having taken the place of devotion to the statues of the gods."[47] For Proclus, the gods coincide with abstract metaphysical entities, they are inter-translatable, and names can activate the divinities they are connected with. He says:

> The fact that names are like statues is a great help. Our souls are incapable of grasping the metaphysical realities in an unmediated form, and it is only through images such as names that we can contemplate them. (*In Crat.* 9.3, 17-24).

An extensive discussion on this topic, the comparison of names of gods and statues, can be found in van den Berg's chapter in his book on Proclus's *Cratylus* commentary, "The Correctness of Names."[48] In this, Proclus roughly follows the idea of Iamblichus that the names of the gods are analogically effective *sunthemata* (material manifestations of divine presence) (*De Myst.* 1.12.42.5-13).[49]

Negative Theology

While there was a vocal and prevalent interest in the full pantheon of gods and goddesses, many of the philosophers of late antiquity, Proclus included, practiced an entirely different approach to attributing any attributes to the One. In the practice of negative theology, the transcendent One, first articulated in Plato's famous "One beyond Being" in *Republic*, is the final cause and primordial origin of all that is too infinite and unknowable to be named by mere mortals. Plotinus regarded the series of hypotheses of Plato's dialogue *Parmenides* concerning the One as a metaphysical teaching of profound importance (*Enn.* V.I.8-14). In that dialectic nothing, not even existence, can be predicated of the One (beyond Being), and by a reverse procedure, all predicates can be ascribed to the One (of Being or existing). By the time of the founders of the Athenian academy, Plutarch and Syrianus, the *Parmenides* passages were considered Plato's systematic theology. All names and attributions are negated, as affirmations predicating the One or God are anthropomorphic. Proclus, then, though he uses the names of the gods and goddesses at every turn, propounded a negative dialectic that he describes in the *Parmenides* commentary. Propositions can be posited which deny and affirm attributes to the One, and then these propositions can be negated since their object lies outside the parameters of these mutually exclusive premises.[50] Negative theology had a long history alongside polytheism in the Roman Empire, beginning with Philo. This development seems to coexist with polytheistic naming and is a byproduct, in many ways, of the fact that gods and goddesses are now known more by their attributes and functions than by their proper names. They can now fit into a schema wherein they are placed in secondary roles in an ascendency to the One. When Middle Platonists refer to a First God and the Neoplatonists design their ontology around a completely transcendent One, cause of all, the gods and goddesses can be considered as emanative functions of this first primordial source. Their names now become mere images, or as Proclus asserts, statues (*agalmata*) of the transcendent divine unity. Paradoxically, then, the names of the gods and goddesses so important and prevalent in Proclus's texts are reduced to symbolic effigies within the Proclean vision of the whole. At the same time, they are hymned individually as living beings and invoked with utmost devotion in theurgic rituals.

Conclusion

"Hebrew" ideology holds that the name of the true God is not to be pronounced by humankind: all worship and reverence toward named deities of alien cultures are idolatry. The Christian version of a triple monotheism of God the father, his son Jesus, and the Holy Spirit applies three nominations but considers them to apply to one "being." A third widely applied and indirect henotheism is that of negative theology, where the object of worship and source of creation are so removed and transcendent that names and attributes are unknown. In this context, in Derrida's expression, naming god by either proper name or ascribing attributes is "onto-theological idolatry."[51] Naming God is not practiced in the Jewish religion and it is considered to border on sacrilege to do so. The Hebrew practice and conviction are that the name of God must remain hidden and unpronounceable by humankind and is certainly not the equivalent of any other culturally embedded divine object of worship. To avoid pronouncing the name of god, the Hebrew God is referred to by the acronym "Ha Shem" (the name) even among contemporary religious Jews. In Western Judeo-Christian culture, in general, the word "God" is not exactly a proper name but a way to address the divine or speak about the divine being. It could be said that gods and goddesses who actually possessed names were a purely pagan phenomenon that disappeared after late antiquity. Hebrew religion is aniconic and does not allow visual image or symbol to represent the deity. In the pagan world, on the other hand, divine names are freely assigned and interchanged according to usage and geopolitical context. Celsus's complaint against Christianity and perhaps one of the sources of anti-Semitism based on the un-assimilability of the Jewish people was based on the fact that the Hebrew God was beyond regional ecumenical interchange.

Herodotus, the first known Greek historian, knew that the gods were named by the poets. "Homer and Hesiod lived four hundred years before my time. These are the ones who created a Theogony for the gods and gave the gods their names" (Herodotus 2.53). When the gods and goddesses become functionaries in ontological hierarchies, as occurred in late antique Neoplatonism, ideology comes closer to monotheism. The names of divine beings become powers and attributes of the totally transcendent and essentially unknowable One. In the medieval period, medieval philosophers become scholastic, preoccupied with essence and existence as it pertains to the godhead. Negative theory and scholastic semantic theologizing eclipse ontotheology, in Christian scholarly discourse. The goddess and her devoted followers seem to disappear from the stage of Western history. For a monotheist worshipping or directing one's devotion toward a god of the wrong name or being is idolatry. No such consideration enters the arena when the goddesses' names are conflated with each other and she becomes more of a principle than a separate function. For the Hebrew monotheist, the "I am who I am" (of biblical reference) "negates by its expression every referent, every *tertium comparatonis* and every translatability." "To translate Adonai into Zeus, would have meant apostasy."[52] It is notable that the caution taken by the monotheist, so careful to avoid the idolatry of naming, does not extend to attributing gender to deity. In the next two chapters, Hebrew and Christian treatment of female deity or its absence is examined, and in Chapter 10 goddesses will reappear as "literary" rather than theological presences, in medieval allegorical texts.

8

Asherah, Sophia, Shekhinah: Are They Hebrew Goddesses?

Rabbi Leah Novick's book *On the Wings of the Shekhinah: Judaism's Divine Feminine* is an example of the fact that the female presence that appeared in Kabbalist literature, the Shekhinah, has been appropriated by some contemporary devotional practices and imagination. The living nature of this experience is encapsulated in her opening statement:

> Wandering along the California coastline six years ago, I began to experience the Divine Feminine in the hills, the ocean and the landscape. A gigantic goddess was calling to me. (p. 1)[1]

Apparently Rabbi Novick has reactivated, perhaps metaphorically, a feminine principle and renders it as an active presence in her spiritual life. For many of those who follow this approach, the so-called divine feminine is associated with the Shekhinah. The beauty of nature prompts Novick to characterize the common aesthetic/spiritual experience of the awe one can experience in nature as an instance of gender-specific divinized presence. While Artemis is the Greek ancestress of the contemporary divine feminine that is experienced in nature, in this book, written by a rabbi, what is conflated with nature and her internal epiphany is primarily the Hebrew precursor to her divinization of nature: the Shekhinah. The age-old association of the female divinized or not, with nature, never seems to go away, either in Jerusalem or in Athens. From the possibilities suggested by female goddess figurines and inscriptions discovered in ancient Israel to allusions to female goddesses in the Prophets, to the Shekhinah imagery in the medieval Kabbalah, although female deity is not part of mainstream Hebrew doctrine, these instances encourage speculation about this issue. In addition to amending gender biases in traditional liturgy, modern scholars have taken renewed interest in the question of whether there was ever a Hebrew goddess. Furthermore, the "Shekinah" construed as a female presence within divinity has taken on new significance in some contemporary settings.

Rafael Patai, a cultural anthropologist, has taken a studied interest in this question. As he puts it: "No subsequent teaching about the aphysical , incomprehensible, or transcendental nature of the deity could eradicate the early mental image of the masculine god."[2] The very nature of most languages accounts for much of the genderizing of words and names. The descriptions, "King," "Master of the Universe," "father," expressions common in Talmudic literature, persist in contemporary liturgy. While none of these expressions are indicative of any doctrine concerning the masculinity of God, metaphorically, the dependence on God on the part of the Jewish people is generally stated as that of a child on a father. Is there any historical precedent for amending this practice? There is plausible evidence that in certain isolated instances, such as that of the Elephantine Jews (*c.* fifth century BCE), some sort of female consort of Yahweh (the Hebrew God) was worshipped. In biblical literature, particularly in the books of the Prophets, the worship of a female "goddess" is railed against and considered idolatrous. This is both proof that such a figure was worshiped in some ancient practices and an indication that it was not condoned. Isaiah rails against idol worshiping practices that were prevalent during his time, including an allusion to a female goddess figure (Isaiah 17:8, 27:9). In Jeremiah 7:18, Jeremiah laments, as he condemns worship of other gods, the worship of one who is clearly female. ("See how the women knead dough and make cakes to offer to the queen of heaven.") The Sages (a term used to denote the rabbis of the Oral Law who are mentioned in the Mishnah and Talmud of the Rabbinic period of late antiquity) also consistently disparaged any hint of idolatry.[3] The absence of any trace of the Canaanite female deity Asherah or Astarte (Phoenician, Canaanite, and Egyptian name for a goddess) in this literature supports the idea that she does not survive the early period. Karel van der Toorn, who has made a dispassionate assessment of the possibilities of a Hebrew goddess, cautions that, even if Asherah ever fulfilled a role in Israelite and Judean religion, it was never comparable to that of the national god Yahweh. The Hebrew goddess was never more than God's consort even when alluded to in inscriptions and texts. In any case, van der Toorn contends, "Scholars hoping for a religion in which men and women are equal will find little comfort in the fact that Yahweh had a consort. Her position vis-à-vis her divine companion was a fair reflection of the position of most women of the time regarding their husbands. The cult of these goddesses does not contain the seeds of women's liberation."[4]

Patai and others have made a case for the presence of a female deity in ancient Israel based on artifacts that have been excavated in archeological digs. The results are inconclusive if not negative. Several modern scholars have explored the possibility that the evidence for Asherah, a possible female divinity, suggests devotion to a female goddess in the Hebrew past, based on both archaeological sources and biblical references. Is there any precedent, other than the allusions mentioned above, for assuming that there was a goddess at any point in the history of Judaism? In several excavations conducted in the last few decades, mainly in parts of Israel/Palestine, a total of no less than 300 terracotta figurines and plaques depicting a nude female figure have been unearthed. In a recent article in *Ha'aretz*, an Israeli newspaper, Julia Friedman enumerates some of these more recent discoveries in settings such as Hazevah and Yaveh, or Tel Rehov's honey production site and Tel Hatif's industrial textile area.[5] The most recent findings were at Motza, just north of Jerusalem, where a cache of cultic items was found in an ancient temple. At Tel Rehov, nude female figurines were found embossing a horn-shaped altar, undoubtedly Canaanite. Tel Rehov is a 25-acre archeological site, located half-way up the Jordan Valley between the Dead Sea and the Sea of Galilee, that has yielded evidence of well-planned and densely built cities dating to the tenth and ninth centuries BCE. At the base of intact altars, nude female "goddesses," well-made with careful attention to detail, have been excavated.[6] In Israel's ancient Northern Kingdom, much of the population was Canaanite. Judges (1:27-28) documents the continuation of Canaanite populations in Beth-Shean and the Jezreel valley. Archeologists have puzzled over the cultic origins of these figures, which probably represent a popular cult of Asherah. Patai's book *The Hebrew Goddess* contains twenty-nine pages of photos of what he contends are goddess figurines. He claims that had there also been such figurines in wood they would not have survived, suggesting that they may have been even more numerous. Many of them were built like pegs to be stuck in the ground near a sacred shrine. Apparently, every major excavation in Palestine has unearthed these figures, known to date from 2000–1500 to early 900–600 BCE. Some of them go back as far as the first temple period or that of the early monarchy. Did the Chaldeans live in Palestine? If not, the figurines could have been made by the Jews and hence, Patai speculates, there was a Hebrew Goddess. He quotes James Pritchard, however, who cautions that it is still an open question whether they represented "the Goddess herself, a prostitute of the cult of the Goddess" or were fertility talismans.[7]

Asherah is a Canaanite goddess, one of the three prominent goddesses of Ugaritic origin known as the consort of El, the others being Anat and Astarte. M. L. West documents the fact that older forms of her name are found in fourteenth-century Amana texts as well as texts that are Ugarit and Hittite.[8] Some of the most intriguing finds, which have baffled archeologists, are those at the archeological site now called Kuntillet Ajrud in the northeastern portion of the Sinai Peninsula in what was Judean territory (end of the ninth/beginning of the eighth century BCE). The site was excavated by Ze'ev Meshel and a team from the Institute of Archaeology of Tel Aviv University in 1975–76. Several Hebrew inscriptions containing a reference to "Yahweh and his Asherah" were discovered there, and also at other sites. Asherah is well known from Ugaritic and other texts as the name of a West Semitic goddess. One inscription was found in 1967 at Khirbet et-Qôm in the Judean hill country midway between Hebron and Lachish. At the Kuntillet Ajrud site, two fragments of large storage jars are inscribed with texts that refer consistently to "Yahweh and his Asherah." Most of the pottery found there was of Judean origin, and some of the smaller pieces were from Israel (the Northern Kingdom at that time, as described in the Book of Kings). At this site, archeologists speculate, there may have been some sort of religious center, but not a Hebrew temple. Inscriptions have been found mentioning a variety of deities: YHWH, Baal, El, and Asherah (Ashrth). Much of the artwork at the site is Phoenician/Syrian. The scripts represented are those of Phoenician and/or Early Hebrew script descended from the Phoenician, and some scholars say that one cannot differentiate between the Phoenician and Early Hebrew, making the issue more complex.[9]

Inscriptions at Kuntillet have been translated "I bless you by YHWH and by Ashth [Asherah]," or "Bless you by YHWH of Teman and by Ashth [Asherah]."

These are inscribed above depictions of the Egyptian god Bes who is also found in Syria, Phoenicia, and islands in the Mediterranean. It remains uncertain whether the translation should be, as the popular version would have it, "YHWH and his Asherah" with the possessive, or simply "YHWH and Asherah."[10] There is a persisting uncertainty, then, as to whether the references to Asherah refer to a cultic installation that appeared at Israeli shrines (*bamot*) together with a cultic stele (*masaba*) or a goddess/wife. Tomb inscriptions in Khirget el-Qem (14 km west of Hebron) from the eighth century BCE are also uncertain evidence for some sort of goddess. These are "blessed by Uriah to Yahwah and his Asherah," and

> Uriyahu, the governor wrote it
> May Uriyahu be blessed by Yahwah
> My guardian and by [his Asherah]. [Save him]
> Save Uriyahu[11]

Whether or not the goddess mentioned in any of these inscriptions is a sacred grove, wooden pole, or goddess, Frymer-Kensky points out that it was actually Ba'al that was the dominant deity of the Canaanite religion contemporary with Israel.[12] A struggle to keep the allegiance of the people for YHWH vis-à-vis the competing male Canaanite gods may be reflected in these inscriptions. As far as Asherah goes, she points out, the blessing formula [at Kuntillet Ajrud] is by "YHWH and his/its (Samria's) asherah," but the asherah doesn't do anything. A third inscription from Kuntillet Ajrud mentions "by YHWH of the South and his/its Asherah," but continues with only YHWH as active, "may YHWH give him what his heart desires."[13] The biblical texts do not speak of Asherah as a consort, rather her connection is to trees and groves and her location at altars. According to Frymer-Kensky, this hints in some way that she is connected with the natural world and the powers of regeneration. The Asherah standing next to the alter was made out of wood, a tree-image, a pole, or an actual tree. According to Frymer-Kensky, these were part of the local worship that was referred to in Jeramiah as being "on every lofty hill and under every leafy tree." According to the historian who wrote the Book of Kings, the north continued with such worship until its destruction.

The Elephantine papyri are ancient Jewish manuscripts dating from the fifth century BCE from the Jewish community at Elephantine, an island in the Nile on the border of Nubia. Hundreds of these papyri have been retrieved, written in hieratic, Demotic, Egyptian, Aramaic, Greek, Latin, and Coptic, and they span 1,100 years. The largest numbers are written in Aramaic, the language most spoken in the Persian Empire.[14] The Jews of Elephantine had their own temple to Yahweh. The papyri state that the Jews were worshipping Anat-Yahu, either wife or sacred consort, or a hypostatized aspect of Yahweh. One of the Elephantine papyri recorded an oath in the name of Anat-Yahu. Van der Toorn suggests that evidence from the Elephantine papyri implies that Jewish migrants worshipped the goddess Anat. He asks if Anat is the so-called Queen of Heaven (of biblical mention) and claims that there is good reason to think that she is.[15] He contends that the Elephantine Jews were worshippers of Yahweh. The Elephantine temple is referred to as the temple of Yahu, and correspondence with the authorities in Jerusalem after the destruction of this temple by priests of the Egyptian god Khnum in the summer of 410 BCE shows that the sanctuary was acknowledged by Jewish authorities. In the Elephantine papyri, there are references to divine names other than Yahu and there is a specific goddess associated with him: Anat-Yahu, the official consort of the god of the temple of Yahu. Another account lists 128 persons who each contributed two shekels to the temple of Anat-Bethel, another name for the goddess. It seems, according to van der Toorn, that the "Queen of Heaven" is an epithet of Anat, who apparently could be associated with either Yahu or Bethel, or, what is more likely in Elephantine, Yahu and Bethel were identified with one another. Bethel means house of God and refers to a standing stone or stela. According to N. H. Walls in his book, *The Goddess Anat in Ugaritic Myth*, in the Ramesside period (*c.* 1300–1200 BCE) the cult of Anat spread southwards, and an Egyptian stela depicting Anat in a temple built by Ramses III found at Beth Shean in modern Israel calls her "Queen of Heaven, Mistress of all the gods." These titles echo her epithet "Lady of Heavens" in the Ugaritic text and foreshadow the appellation "Queen of Heaven" in Judah.[16] Noll suggests that the Elephantine Jews practiced a religion that stemmed from a common form of Judahite religion that existed prior to the Bible. He contends that they had more in common with the Iron Age Israel and Judah than the biblical Jews. This suggests that Yahu and Anat-Yahu were not isolated cultic figures in Elephantine but perhaps were widespread in early Judahite religion.[17]

In the Book of Jeremiah (seventh-century Judah), Jemimah complained that the people are worshiping "on every lofty hill and under every green tree."[18] Also in Jeremiah, "[t]hus says the Lord of Hosts…." "You and your wives have both spoken with your mouths and fulfilled with your hands, saying, 'We will surely perform our vows, to burn incense for the queen of heaven and to pour out drink offerings to her'" (Jeremiah 44:25-30),[19] while in Hosea (4:12, 13) "My people ask counsel from a piece of wood." It can be assumed from the finds at Kuntillet Ajrud, the Elephantine papyri, etc., that the goddess or her equivalent was an object of popular ritual if not worship, but that does not mean that this was an approved doctrine of "radical monotheism" (as Frymer-Kensky calls it). As far as the Bible goes, in Jeremiah (7:18) and 44:15-19, worshipers burned incense for the goddess, poured out drink offerings, and offered special cakes, in rituals in which the entire family was involved. These had the shape of the goddess as their symbol. Van der Toorn cannot directly associate these passages with Anat or the consort of Yahu, etc., of earlier lore. Mark Smith discusses the Jeremiah passages.[20] Jeremiah receives a divine oracle to be addressed to Judeans living in Egypt. The oracle declares that Yahweh's condemnation of the Judean worship of other gods is the reason for their punishment. The audience of this prophetic speech disagrees with his explanation and attributes the divine punishment to a reprisal from the Queen of Heaven (44:16-19). When offerings to the cult of the Queen of Heaven ceased, they were consumed by sword and famine. Jeremiah condemns this practice (the word for her cakes in 44:17-18 and 44:19 looks like an Akkadian loan word suggesting the cult of the goddess). Jeremiah responds by claiming that it was the devotion to the Queen of Heaven that led to Yahweh's punishment of Judah.

John Day has explored the relationship between the Ugaritic and Northwest Semitic texts, which he claims has revolutionized the understanding of the Bible. Asherah is not equated with Astarte, for example, a fact made clear since the discovery of Ugaritic texts. That there was a Canaanite goddess Asherah and she does appear in the Bible is the conclusion that Day reaches after a careful analysis of the data.[21] The earliest references to the goddess Asherah are in the Elba texts (*c.* 2350 BCE), Ugaritic texts from Ras Shamra on the Syrian coast, written in alphabetic cuneiform. This is the most important Northwest Semitic source for the goddess Asherah, and here she appears as the consort of the supreme god El. Scholarly debate concerns whether the mentions of Asherah in the Bible denote the name of a cult or refer to a wooden pole symbolizing the goddess Asherah or are the goddess's name itself. Asherah is mentioned in Exodus 34:13, Deuteronomy 16:21, Judges 6:26, 20, 30, and Kings 18:4, 23:14 among other places.[22] Van der Toorn points to evidence which can dispel the opinion of many scholars that the Jews in Elephantine and their "goddess" were an isolated phenomenon. It consisted of the worship by migrants and belonged to the popular religion of the time rather than to legitimate Israelite religion.[23] The consort of El in the Canaanite mythology is Asherah. Van der Toorn suggests that Yahweh inherited El's iconography and also his consort. He cites a hidden reference to Asherah in Deuteronomy (33:2): "When Yahweh came from Sinai, Asherah was at his right," although others would not translate the Hebrew word used here as anything but flaming ashes.[24]

The female figurines discovered in Israel from the biblical period (the Iron Age) pose another problem for interpretation. They are not "Canaanite" figurines (images of upright female figures with divine symbols, which were common in the Late Bronze Age during the Canaanite occupation), which disappear in Israelite times. In the eighth century, solid figures in the round with a "pillar" base, breasts, and molded head, sometimes with no arms, sometimes with arms holding breasts, and sometimes with arms raised, are found in two areas. Sixteen were found in the Jerusalem Cave, a manmade cave just outside the walls of the city, and others in Samaria (Locus E 207), perhaps associated with a large unused sealed tomb. Frymer-Kensky suggests that these instances may represent a "kind of tangible prayer for fertility and nourishment and may not represent goddesses."[25]

Frymer-Kensky contends that the essentially masculine God of Israel absorbed the attributes of various gods. She suggests that while some of the attributes of goddesses are also clearly absorbed by YHWH, others cannot be. She states that "the absence of goddesses causes major changes in the way the Bible—compared with the ancient texts—looks at humanity, culture, society, and nature." Monotheism, she contends, was a quantum leap and a fundamental change in paradigm wherein YHWH is the possessor of sole power over all functions in the universe. Thus in Exodus 23:25-27, God's mastery over the natural environment includes healing and procreation, contrasting with early Mesopotamian doctors who relied upon natural methods of healing and called upon the goddesses Gula and Minsinna. Divine control over pregnancy and childbirth in the enigmatic statement in Genesis 49:25, of God who bestows "Blessings of the deep that crouches below, blessings of breast and womb," she contends, reflects Yahweh's assimilation of this function. Many prayers and passages in Jewish liturgy refer to God's control over rain, fertility, and agricultural fecundity. In short, Frymer-Krensky suggests that all the functions of the goddess in surrounding cultures are eclipsed by a monotheistic Judaism. Yehezkel Kaufman holds to the more radical view that the Israelite religion did not pass through polytheist stages before reaching the level of biblical thought and monotheism.[26] Biblical figures of speech do not necessarily imply preexisting polytheism.

The Jewish Sophia

While there may not be any real evidence that mainstream Israelite religion ever held to a belief in a consort of Yahweh, or a female goddess in any form, the female personification of wisdom is present in Hebrew literature. From the canonical mention of a female form for the word "Wisdom" in Job and Proverbs, to the apocryphal books *Wisdom of Ben Sirach* and *Wisdom of Solomon*, all of this literature connects Wisdom (Hebrew *Hokhmah*; Greek *Sophia*) with creation and the structure of the created world.[27] Jane Webster suggests that links between the figures that archeologists have unearthed and the feminine figure of wisdom in literature is tenuous.[28] In the book of Proverbs, "Wisdom" takes on the personification that is suggested by the grammatical female gender that is attached to the abstract noun. It (Wisdom) becomes "she" in Proverbs 3:19-20. In Chapter 8 of Proverbs, Wisdom calls and cries aloud, standing beside the gates in front of the town (8:3). She proclaims divine origin:

> Lord created me at the beginning of his work, the first of his acts of old.
> Ages ago I was set up, at the first, before the beginning of the earth. (Proverbs 8:22-3)

As opposed to Job, where YHWH created the world through his "wisdom," in Proverbs wisdom is a personage having hands that hold long life, riches, and honor (3:13-18). The personification of wisdom is particularly prevalent, as Gail Corrington points out, in the wisdom literature of the Hellenistic period. The *Wisdom of Solomon* (written in Greek in the mid-first century BCE in Alexandria) and *Sirach* (also known as Book of Ecclesiasticus, 200-175 BCE), apocryphal texts, are the best known examples. Wisdom, a divine attribute in the Bible, is personified as female and takes on mythic dimensions that she shares with the pagan deities of the Mediterranean world. She descends and ascends; she is a mediator between the divine and human realms; she loves, protects, and saves humanity.[29] Wisdom is described as a cosmic principle too, for example, as "dwelling on the throne of glory next to God, and as knowing and designing all things" (Wisdom ix. 1, 4, 10).[30] Griffiths cites scholars who suggest that the Egyptian concept of Maat (the Egyptian goddess who personifies truth, order, balance, and justice and was an escort of the sun god Rê) had been influential through the medium of the Jewish settlement at Elephantine. Isis, as well, may stand behind the Sophia of the *Wisdom of Solomon*. Plutarch states that Isis was a goddess exceptionally wise and devoted to wisdom (*de Iside*. 2.35, 1e11-f2). An aretalogy from Andros, dated to the first century BCE, ascribes wisdom to Isis as well. A long record of Egyptian tradition precedes this evidence and the catalogue of the knowledge conferred by Sophia in the *Wisdom of Solomon*, according to Griffiths, is reminiscent of the praise of Isis.[31]

The apocryphal book of *Sirach* (200–175 BCE) is the largest wisdom book preserved from antiquity. It was written by the Jewish scribe Shimon ben Yeshua ben Eliezer ben Sira of Jerusalem, possibly in Egypt. In Egypt, it was translated into Greek by the author's grandson. Included in the canon of the Septuagint (the Greek translation of the Hebrew Scriptures) in the second century BCE, it was considered canonical by the Catholic Church. In it, Wisdom is personified as instructor and indictor of the way to God and source of life. She is the robe and crown that adorns priests and kings and even elevates slaves (*Sirach* 6:31; 7:21).[32] She is a heavenly mediator between the divine and the human realm and has descended to earth because of love and compassion for humanity. As Corrington tells us, in the pseudo-epigraphical book of *Enoch* Wisdom descends from her heavenly home specifically to make her home in Israel (I Enoch 42:2). In the apocryphal book of *Baruch* in the Septuagint, Wisdom is sent down to Israel by YHWH and is identified with the Torah (*Baruch* 4:1).

Burton Mack, like Griffiths, finds many parallels between this mythology of Wisdom and that of Isis. Wisdom, like Isis, is concerned with justice and teaches the arts of civilization to humanity, and protects kings and rulers.[33] John Kloppenborg claims that the saving aspect of the Jewish Sophia has much in common with Isis and that "The author of the *Wisdom of Solomon* 're-mythologized' the figure of Sophia in order to maintain [Judaism] as a saving religion" in response to the needs of Hellenized Jews living in Egypt "and to rival Isis as a central figure of salvation."[34] There is no doubt, however, that the precedent for Sophia (*Hokhmah* in Hebrew) is biblical. Patai cites the Book of Proverbs, which asserts that Wisdom was the earliest creation of God and has been God's playmate (8:22-31). He also finds allusions to Wisdom in Job (28:13ff), but it is not clear that this is an instance of personification, as he seems to claim. Patai also discusses the role of Wisdom in the Apocrypha, for example, in the *Wisdom of Solomon*.[35] Philo (a Hellenized Jewish philosopher of the first century CE in Alexandria) states that God is the husband of Wisdom. Wisdom becomes important in Jewish Gnosticism.[36]

Kabbalah

Gershom Scholem tells us that Jewish tradition, as a religion of monotheistic revelation, excludes mythology or takes it in a purely metaphorical sense.[37] The Rabbinical tradition was concerned with the purity of the concept of God and this canonical literature is largely devoid of myth with certain exceptions.[38] Scholem suggests, "The more the philosophers and theologians strove to formulate a unity which negates and eliminates all symbols, the greater became the danger of a counterattack in favor of the living God, who, like all living forces, speaks in symbols." He suggests that the attraction to Kabbalah (Kabbalah literature includes the *Bahir* and the *Zohar*, two books of mystical wisdom that were known to the late medieval period) was a "reaction" of popular religion responding to a need for this sort of expression. Reaching its fullest development in twelfth-century France and in thirteenth-century Spain, it spread and found a plethora of followers. In fact, it still is finding a following, as current postmodern, popular, and scholarly interest in Kabbalah attests.

The book *Bahir* (*Sefer ha-Bahir*) was written perhaps a century or more before its publication around 1150 or 1180. It is the earliest known Kabbalist document, and it appeared in southern France.[39] Scholem claims that no one knows exactly where it came from. It displays what could easily be seen as a frankly "mythical" statement describing, for example, a tree of God or of Life and a series of *sefirot* (emanations of the attributes of God—wisdom, mercy, beauty, etc.). The Tree of Life is a visual representation of these ten *sefirot* and each one corresponds to a stage in creation and a character from the Bible. It is also the body of the primordial Adam. The crown, for example, is associated with the head, the penis with the foundation or source of man, etc. At the lowest level of the "tree" is the last of the ten emanations, Shekhinah, the purely female aspect of the divine, is said to dwell among the children of Israel who are good and righteous. "The sefirotic process thus leads to the great union of the nine sefirot above, through *Yesod*, with the female *Shekhinah*. She becomes filled and impregnated with the fullness of divine energy and in turn gives birth to the lower worlds, including both angelic beings and human souls."[40] (Arthur Green commenting on the *Zohar*, the best known book of Kabbalah.)

These conceptualizations seem unrelated to the traditional concepts of Jewish theology. Its doctrine of divine attributes mapped out in this fashion leads Scholem to contend that "we are no longer dealing with mythical vestiges employed poetically or allegorically, but with the reappearance of a stratum of myth within Judaism itself."[41] It also seems to have a similar structure, with descending levels of being, to that found in Gnostic and Neoplatonic literature.

According to Scholem, the Kabbalah was first produced in Provence, in Languedoc. From there it was transplanted, in the first quarter of the thirteenth century, to Aragon and Castile in Spain, where most of the classical development took place.[42] Southern France between 1150 and 1220 was not a backwater when it came to intellectual and cultural matters. It was a center of Talmud study, medieval culture, troubadour poetry, and so on. Kabbalist literature is a full-blown systematic mystical approach to classical Judaism and is difficult to account for by means of an examination of previous Jewish texts. The *Bahir*, or *Sefer ha-Bahir* (Book of Brightness), the earliest of the Kabbalah literature, is attributed to a first-century sage, Nehunya ben Hakahha. It includes symbols and appellations for this or that *sefirot* (emanations or attributes through which the Infinite reveals himself and creates the world) similar to the processes by which the Gnostics designated their Aons. The Gnostics "liked to adopt as names of Aons, abstract terms such as thought, wisdom, penitence, truth, grace, greatness, silence, or images such as father, mother, abyss, etc.," and Scholem finds that the *Bahir* has a similar practice, correlating these categories with biblical verses or aggadic dicta of the rabbis.[43] The Book of Splendor, or the *Zohar*, was written *c*. 1286 by Moses de Leon (*c*. 1240–1305) in Castile, Spain (a center for Jewish mysticism), who attributed it to Shimon ben Yohai, a famous second-century Palestinian teacher revered by Talmud scholars throughout history. After the expulsion of the Jews from Spain in 1492, Spanish Kabbalists immigrated to the town of Safed in Galilee, which became the new center of Kabbalah.

In Kabbalah, although all the rest of the nine levels of emanation are knowable, it is not possible to know anything of the divine life of the infinite unknowable "root of all roots" or "cause of all causes, the highest level of the *sefirot*." As Lawrence Fine explains, only with the second *sefirah*, *Hokhmah* (Wisdom), does the first truly discernable aspect of the Godhead become evident and it is an active masculine principle within God that is known as the "Upper Father."[44] It is said to impregnate the third *sefirah* termed *Binah* (intelligence). *Binah* is the female counterpart to *Hokhmah* and is the "Upper Mother," the "Womb" from which all the rest of life will emerge. The union of the parents *Hokhmah* and *Binah* results in the birth of the lower seven *sefirot*. *Binah* is a divine Mother, also described as the flow of a stream of water from Eden (*Hokhmah*) into a river (*Binah*). *Din* (judgment) and *Hesed* (Mercy) are the fourth and fifth *sefirot*. *Tiferet* (Beauty) is the sixth *sefirah* which stands in the middle of the divine structure and is a harmonizing principle which binds the forces of *Hesed* and *Din*. *Tiferet* is the son of *Hokhmah* and *Binah*. The seventh and eighth *sefirot* symbolically express two aspects of divine kingship, *Hod* (compassionate rule) and *Nezah* (regal king). The ninth *sefirah*, again in the middle of the structure, is *Yesod* (Foundation). It is symbolized as "phallus" and is the vehicle through which the procreative vitality of the divine flows downward. Finally, *Malchut*, the last *sefirah*, is the receptive female called by the name *Shekhinah*.[45] She is filled with divine abundance and goes by many names: Daughter, Lower Mother, Princess, Queen, Bride, Matrona, Rachel, Earth, and Moon. She is *Tiferet*'s lover. The *Zohar* makes clear symbolic imagery associating the *sefirot* with Abraham, Isaac, and so on (Moses and Aron represent *Nezah* and *Hod*; Joseph *Yesod*; *Malchut* is sometimes symbolized by David, more commonly by mother Rachel). This elaborate hierarchical structure is reminiscent of Neoplatonic emanation and Gnostic ontology, and that resemblance has allowed scholars to speculate about non-Judaic influences. Certainly the ontological hierarchy so endemic to Neoplatonic ontology mapped onto Porphyrian trees organizing local taxonomies is common to both worlds. Gnostic and Neoplatonic patrimony or, conversely, a more ancient Jewish connection with Gnosticism as influence on Neoplatonism is an issue best left to scholars in these areas to explore.

Shekhinah: The Feminine Gendered Aspect of God

Peter Schafer points out that the idea of God's femininity is not found in the Jewish tradition preceding the Kabbalah literature. The biblical Wisdom literature, Philo, the Rabbinical (Talmudic) Shekhinah, which refers it to the personification of God's divine presence in the world,[46] and other medieval Jewish philosophy show no evidence of a precedent for the *Bahir*'s concept of a life of God that includes "a female potency through which he reaches down to earth."[47] Arthur Green suggests that there are parallels with contemporaneous Christian interpretations of the Song of Songs and the ubiquitous "Mariology" of the twelfth and thirteenth centuries.[48] Scholem, discussing the *Zohar*, contends that the feminine potencies in God that attain their fullest expression in the tenth and last *sefirah* are "a representation of myth that seems utterly incongruous in Jewish thinking."[49] The ninth *sefirah*, *Yesod*, is the male potency, described with phallic symbolism as the foundation of all life, which guarantees and consummates the holy union of male and female powers. These are radical departures from the old rabbinical conception. While in the Bible, God's face is his Shekhinah, in the Talmudic literature, the Shekhinah, literally "indwelling," is the indwelling of God in the world. It is used as a term denoting the presence and activity of God in the world and in Israel particularly. The Shekhinah, in this traditional literature, is not a special hypostasis distinguished from God as a whole. The earliest references to Shekhinah are as a Hebrew abstract noun derived from the biblical verb *shakhan,* which Patai points out means literally "the act of dwelling." The verbal root letters with the added *–ah* suffix have the feminine gender, but so do many words in languages which have gendered words. In actual usage, the term "Shekhinah" refers to the more physical manifestation of deity and is not overtly referring to a female deity.[50] Patai points out that Shekhinah is the frequently used Talmudic term denoting the visible and audible manifestation of God's presence on earth, whereas in late Midrash literature, as well as Kabbalah, "the *Shekhinah* concept stood for an independent, feminine divine entity prompted by her compassionate nature to argue with God in defense of man."[51] Patai contends that Shekhinah is a direct heir to the ancient Hebrew goddesses of Canaanite origin, Asherah and Anath, but does not really make enough of a case for this possibility.

According to Scholem, "The discovery of a feminine element in God, which the Kabbalists tried to justify by Gnostic exegesis, is of course one of the most significant steps they took."[52] The usage in the Kabbalah is very different from that in the Bible and Talmud. The third *sefirah* is the Upper Mother, or upper Shekhinah, which is also the demiurgic potency. Of the seven potencies that emanate from it, the first six are symbolized as parts of the primordial man's body and epitomized in the phallic "foundation" (*Yesod*) which is the symbolic representation of the righteous one (*Zaddik*), the god who maintains the powers of generation within its legitimate bonds. The tenth *sefirah* is a complement to the universally human and masculine principle, the feminine, seen at once as mother, as wife and as daughter, manifest in their respective ways. Scholem points out that while this feminine element in God is eschewed by the rabbinical tradition, the feminine principle of the Shekhinah was enormously popular among the masses of the Jewish people, and had a second coming in the Christian Kabbalists who equated Shekhinah with Mary, and has a latter-day revival in modern spiritual feminism.[53] In view of the unlikelihood of a Hebrew goddess in any part of canonical Jewish texts, the apocryphal nature of most allusions to Wisdom as female, and the mostly masculinized allusions to God in the major texts of Hebrew literature, it is surprising that a literature that holds to a definitive female principle could arise. Since Hebrew liturgy generally eschews all images and personification, Kabbalah takes a radical turn when it identifies a female mediating element that plays a part in the ontology of world-making. The revealed manifestations of the life of God unfold in mostly male potencies, but the one that is called alternatively Malchut or Shekhinah (dwelling) is clearly female. In Kabbalah, disseminated divinity and divine powers are consequential to a primary source, which erupts into the multiplicity of the *sefirot*.

Halbertal points out that in Kabbalah the fact that God has a multiplicity of aspects and powers raises the issue of idolatry. He claims that this structure can be seen as blurring the distinction between polytheism and pure monotheism.[54] Scholars who have devised apologies for this possibly unholy polytheistic multiplicity have contended that the *sefirot* are manifestations of God who remains one being but has levels of active powers. Still, a figure like the Shekhinah lends itself to personification and to reification apart from being a mere emanation. In both the *Bahir* and the *Zohar*, the sphere of the Shekhinah is also the dwelling place of the soul. The soul has its origin in the feminine dimension of God himself. This soul of the people in exile, too, is a female aspect of God. In eighteenth-century Hasidism, for example, Shekhinah seems to break away from her encapsulation in the larger structure in several homiletical works where she is personified as "homeless." The Shekhinah, representing the Jewish people in exile, and God can become separated. Wolfson gives many examples of later usage, for example, "the Shekhinah was in flames about them."[55]

Eliot Wolfson focuses on one of the more overtly innovative features of Kabbalistic symbolism, this ready utilization of masculine and feminine images to depict aspects of the divine reality that takes the form of androgyny.[56] In his chapter, "Crossing Gender Boundaries," he has a section on "Ontic Containment of the Feminine in the Masculine." The ontic inclusion of the feminine in the masculine is a recurring and fundamental motif in Kabbalah, he suggests, which has an androgynous aspect. Wolfson cites many passages that corroborate an androgynous vision of the whole. He contends that although pregnancy and childbirth are ordinarily associated with the female, in Kabbalist literature they are valorized as positive masculine traits. In the *Zohar* text he quotes, "When a woman brings forth seed and bears a male" (Lev. 12:2) means that the intention of a woman is to bear a male child which has the effect of masculinizing her, so she produces seed like a man and gives birth to a boy. Wolfson contends that the idea of motherhood in Kabbalistic symbolism is decidedly masculine, for the womb that gives birth is valorized as an erectile and elongated phallus. It would not be possible to critically examine this aspect of the Zohar here, clearly; however, the motherly aspect of the Shekinah as "lower mother" can be documented. "From this Female are united all those that are below, they are sustained from her and to her they return, and she is called the mother of them all (Zohar3: 296a)." Wolfson also quotes the following passage: "[w]hen the Shekhinah receives the influx form the upper masculine divine potencies she is transformed from an empty cistern (*bor*) that has nothing of its own into a well (be'er) that is full and overflows to every side" (Zohar1: 60a).[57] According to Scholem, there are two aspects of femininity, that corresponding to the upper and lower Shekhinah, the active energy and creative power, on the one hand, and the passive receptivity on the other. The former is the image of the "upper mother," the female gradation of *Malchut*. *Malchut* is the tenth and final *sefirah*, which contains two contradictory qualities—exaltedness and humility. It receives all that it has from the other *sefirot* and is described as having nothing of its own. The *Zohar* compares this to the moon which has no light of its own. It is a receiver and the consummation of receiving.[58]

Kabbalah, Gnosticism, and Neoplatonism

In the Jewish religion, the prohibition against idol worship limits tropic "figures" that have divinity attached to them and are not fully human. Jan Assmann asserts that the prohibition arose from a reaction to Egypt's most conspicuous practice, the worship of images. This came to be regarded as the greatest sin, and the Ten Commandments, a law code for all times, condemned idolatry. The second commandment is a commentary on the first: "Thou shall not make unto thee any graven image." The patriarchs and matriarchs who are remembered at all points in prayer and in Torah study are fully human and do not fit the patterns of myths as they are being examined here. Biblical tales are not myths about God but are homiletic tales deeply ingrained in Jewish cultural memory, concerning God given laws and narratives of ancestral figures and their lives. It is certainly an anomaly that the Kabbalists have envisioned a feminine principle, and further that it is relegated to the last *sefirah*, the one that can be cut off, the one related to the world. With the premise that the female iconography associated with the lowest *sefirot* cannot have come from normative Judaic sources, there is the possibility that it has Gnostic and Neoplatonic sources. Scholem suggests Gnostic sources, while Wolfson takes a more cautious and nuanced approach.[59] Although there is admittedly no direct historical evidence of transmission of Gnostic sources to the *Bahir*, there are, as Peter Schaefer points out, "illuminating structural or phenomenological similarities." Schaefer and Arthur Green both advance the idea that in the Christian context of twelfth-century France, the Mariology prevalent at this time, wherein the Virgin Mary became a popular topic, influenced the *Bahir* and its successor texts. When it comes to the issue of androgyny, there are striking analogies between Gnostic and Kabbalist texts. Pagels, examining the *Trimorphic Protennoia*, one of the Nag Hammadi Gnostic texts, quotes the following aretalogy:

> [I] am Protennoia the thought that [dwells] in [the Light] ... [she who exists] before the All ... I move in every creature ... I am the invisible One within the All ...
>
> I am androgynous [I am both Mother and] Father, since [I copulate] with myself ... [and with those who love] me ... I am the Womb [that gives shape] to the All.[60]

The metaphor of love-making and giving birth, used as a language for cosmogony as it is in many Hellenic sources, is particularly notable in Gnostic texts. Patricia Cox Miller points to salient examples in the Gnostic text known as "On the Origins of the World," which features Eve, Psyche, Zoe, Sophia, and Eros in scenarios for cosmogonic creation. Love-making and giving birth in particular are used to describe the inner dynamics of the divine world, as they are in Plotinus's erotic imagery (discussed here in Chapter 3).[61] Peter Schäfer seems ambivalent about ascribing Gnostic roots to the *Bahir* but does admit "stunning and unexpected similarities." He is put off, however, by the fact that there is nothing in the *Bahir* that resembles the role of the lower Sophia in emanation of the material world. She is crucial in redeeming Israel but has nothing to do with creation. By the time of the *Zohar*, however, the lower Sophia is clearly involved with creation and the parallels with Neoplatonism (and Gnosticism) are more evident. Irenaeus's version of the Valentinian form of Gnosis situates two Aons, both called Sophia. The upper Sophia sits above the Pleroma; the other is the lower, the "fall of the lower *Sophia*." Here Schaefer cites the analogy between Gnostic Sophia and the *Bahir* Sophia, both in exile in the lower world. Sophia wants to return to the father and be part of his universal and undivided essence.[62] In the Gnostic *Apocryphon of John*, Barbelo is Second Principle and first emanation of the father, but Sophia/Barbelo is the last of the divine Aons between the spiritual and material world. The lower Sophia acts without a partner and is thus considered disruptive and independent. He suggests that Scholem wavers on the issue of positing Valentinian Gnosticism as a source. Valentinian Gnosis cannot be documented to have a direct connection to the sudden and unexplained emergence of Kabbalah in the thirteenth century. Schaefer admits that there is a phenomenological and structural similarity, most salient with regard to the concepts of Sophia and Shekhinah.[63] Establishing historical textual connections remains an open field, and books such as Birger Pearson's *Gnosticism, Judaism and Egyptian Christianity* are a good entry to the vast subject of, for example, Alexandrian Judaism and Jewish precursors to Gnosticism.

One more example will suffice to suggest some sort of synchronicity between Gnostic texts, Neoplatonism, and Kabbalah even if the direction of influence cannot be established. In the Gnostic *Marsanès*, the cosmic hierarchy, similar to that in *Zostrianos* and to a lesser extent *Allogenes*, which is made up of thirteen levels, has a similar structure to Kabbalah. The highest level in the thirteen-level hierarchy in *Marsanès* is the unknown as Silent One, while at the bottom are the corporeal, physical, and sublunary realms. In *Marsanès* there is a visionary ascent to the highest realm and concomitantly a descent of "Autogenes," a middle structure, through the instrumentality of Sophia. Other Sethian treatises also mention the instrumentality of Sophia facilitating descent into the lower world.[64] The Hebrew Shekhinah seems to have nothing to do with the elusive Asherah of early biblical reference and a somewhat obscure connection to Sophia/*Hokhma* of Hebrew texts. Kabbalah, it seems, is discontinuous with earlier biblical, Mishnaic, or Talmudic literature, and its personifications, erotic and reproductive analogies, do suggest some affinity with Gnostic or Neoplatonic structures, regardless of which direction the influence works.

Mythologizing, Genderizing

Halbertal and Margalit discuss Gershom Scholem's remarks concerning Kabbalah and a return of myth into the monotheistic tradition. The presumption that God has an inner life which can be diagrammed and reified conceptually, and the idea of a feminine presence within God's kingdom of levels, can be seen as mythology. There were Kabbalists who were sensitive to the possibility of polytheism in considering the *sefirot* as objects of worship, or as introducing multiplicity into a unified divinity. Some Kabbalists considered the *sefirot* as creating vessels or instruments of divine action, putting less weight on myth. Some perceived a complete unity within divinity itself while the *sefirot* were seen as existing outside God as intermediaries between God and the world. Other approaches to this problem also existed. Abulafia, a thirteenth-century Kabbalist, took the view of Maimonides concerning the internal unity of God and rejected the idea of the organic unity of the *sefirot* as a theosophy of polytheism.[65]

It is surprising that Kabbalah literature has gained widespread currency in recent times. Kabbalah, which resembles the structure of the Neoplatonic treatment of creation, does not seem especially suited to the modern mind. Kabbalah does not fit into the category of allegory, mythology, or symbolism. It is more a doctrinal set of ontological commitments that the creators of the Kabbalah articulate by name and posit as fundamental entities. According to its devotees and interpreters, the doctrine does not diminish the unity of the Godhead, but articulates the manifestations of divinity in creation. The mythology that Kabbalah does espouse, however, is that of gender: the higher more lofty functions are male, and the lower ones are female. The erotic and reproductive analogies are reminiscent of Hellenic myth. Kabbalah, in the most general terms, seems to present God as manifest in both male and female form. The masculine refers to transcendent infinite terrain of the Sefirot, while the feminine describes how God manifests within Creation or Nature. In a paradigm, then, that is very similar to Greco-Roman Platonism, the Kabbalah teaches that God manifests in a male form that refers to the higher realms of divine manifestation and is close to the infinite source of being; the feminine is associated with how the divine manifests within creation/nature. Wolfson recognizing the explicit and repeated use of gender symbolism contends that "gender identity is engendered by cultural assumptions concerning maleness and femaleness that interpret the body."[66] He makes a strong case for the Kabbalist theosophy as reflecting the androcentric and patriarchic norms of medieval society and more particularly in rabbinic culture. In these contexts, wholeness is predicated on a "reconstituted male androgyne" and "ontologically there is only one gender in Kabbalistic theosophy." The sexual coupling of male and female is indicative of an androgynous unity that has been fractured. In the ideal state, gender differentiation is neutralized and the female is absorbed back into the male. "The task of the *homo religiosus* is to restore the feminine to the masculine, to unite the two in a bond that overcomes gender differentia by establishing the complete male who embodies masculine and feminine."[67] The female then is part of the male, reflecting the original creation story of genesis in which the male androgyne is the origin of the division of sexes.

Conclusion

Every Hebrew-speaking individual and almost every Jewish worshipper, in nearly every language in the world and every time in Jewish history, with the exception of modern reform and conservative Judaism and their newly minted politically correct prayer book, addresses all references to God using a masculine pronoun. In this chapter, I have provided a number of possible historical precedents for considering the question of whether there are reasons to believe there is a female presence within the Hebrew tradition. Perhaps the most legitimate argument that can be made for this possibility can be found in the Bible itself, wherein God is described in female terms. In Deuteronomy, for example (52.18), God says to the Israelites that he is "The rock that bore you ... the God who gave birth." Or Isiah (49:15) where God likens himself to a nursing mother. Elizabeth Johnson reminds us of passages to this effect.

The Scriptures depict God as mother, with all that this entails pregnant with a child in her womb, crying out in labor, giving birth, nursing, carrying and cradling her child, comforting and having womb love (tender mercy and compassion) for her child. Given the frequency with which mention of God's merciful compassion occurs throughout Scripture and the liturgy and given the root of this word in the Hebrew word for womb (*rhm*), such female imagery is far from peripheral in the tradition, although until recently unnoticed.[68]

9

Did Christianity Make the Goddess Disappear?

Goddesses are virtually absent, in fact exiled from Christian theology and it is only in some contemporary practices that female gender is attributed to God. As Helen Foley points out, the dominant myth of Christianity and the dominant myth of the Greco-Roman past present a remarkable parallel. Gender in the Eleusinian mysteries is based on the myth of the mother and the daughter while Christianity is grounded in the theology of father and son.[1] In order to better understand the demise of the goddess as a philosophical or theological entity, it is important to look at Christology, Mariology, and Christian theology. From the time of the earliest church fathers, the trinity is, by and large, masculine, and divinity itself, except for gender attribution, is not anthropomorphized. While traces of goddess mythology appear at the margins of Christian doctrine, in late antiquity developing Christian theology was instrumental in absenting them from their central role in Greco-Roman culture and worship. Goddesses were anathema to the increasingly powerful church. As Barbara Newman explains, in her book *God and the Goddesses*, after the advent of Christianity the names of pagan gods and goddesses survived in the names of planets and days of the week, festivals, etc., but their status as divinities did not survive the centuries. The Christian "pantheon" (God in three persons, mother of God, saints) and the pagan pantheon will come to hold a totally divergent status. The former will henceforth belong to the realm of belief, the latter to "make believe."[2]

Bertrand Russell points out that at its outset, Christianity was preached by Jews to Jews as a reformed Judaism. Paul (*c*. 5–67 CE), the first major organizer and proselytizer of Christianity, facilitated conversion by removing two obstacles that stood in the way of enabling the Hebrew religion to become universal. Men who wished to convert to a monotheistic religion did not want to be subjected to circumcision or conform to the Mosaic laws with their cumbersome dietary restrictions.[3] Paul was born in Cecilia, a province that attributed its power to Isis *Myrionymos* (many-named Isis). The essential doctrine that he promulgated was that Christ was the power (*dynamis*) and wisdom (*sophia*) of God.[4] He preached salvation as a means of religious piety as opposed to following a set of laws. Tarsus, like a dozen other cities of Asia Minor that Paul visited during his missionary efforts, was well acquainted with Isis worship. Witt emphasizes the fact that Paul's journeys through Cyprus, Asia Minor, the Aegean, Macedonia, and Achaia, in the middle of the first century, took place in venues, as well, where Isiacism was on the ascendance. The last chapters of Acts, for example, list places that Paul visited before his departure for Iran. Samos, Chios, Cnidus, Crete, Myra in Lycia, and many others cultivated the faith of Isis at the time when Paul preached. Witt suggests that there are analogies between Isiacism and Pauline doctrine and gives the example of Paul referring to the god of peace while Isis was referred to as queen of peace. This comparison is somewhat simplistic, since the similarity in figures of speech does not indicate similarities in doctrine.[5] Interestingly, Clement's *Hymn to Christ* contains parallels to the Isis Oxyrhynchos litany during a later period.[6]

An overt and antagonistic encounter between the "mother of the gods" and the early Christians is well documented and recorded in incidents and statements made by Christian authorities. Augustine recorded his reaction to the procession that carried the mother of the gods through the streets of Carthage in his youth. The goddess, who was named Berecynthia, was received by large crowds in what Augustine refers to as "shameful rites" and "repugnant ceremonies." In the martyrdom of St Symphorian (c. 179 CE), the martyr refused to participate as a Christian and was executed. According to Gregory of Tours, Bishop Simplicius (d. 418) eventually ended the cult of Berecynthia and built a church on the site of St Symphorian's tomb. Apparently, Simplicius had prayed that the people around him would see the light and give up these practices. In Autun (St Symphorian's town), they still had great processions to Berecynthia. In the dramatic scene, described her in Chapter 1, the bishop threw the image of Berecynthia, an idol carried in this procession, to the ground. When she was unable to be reerected despite all efforts of prayer and sacrifice, the people began to doubt her power and all the onlookers converted on the spot to the Catholic Church. These incidents document the long struggle between Christianity and the Roman Magna Meter as an object of veneration.[7] The Carthage temple of Celestas, for example, according to an eyewitness account by Quodvultdeus (fifth century, taught by Augustine, later bishop of Carthage), was condemned, littered with garbage and overgrown with brambles. It was taken over by a throng of Christians led by Bishop Aurelius and consecrated to the One God. The bishop seated himself on the empty throne of the deposed goddess and announced that the building was now a cathedral.[8] It was subsequently demolished; however, this example is paradigmatic. Goddesses were literally overthrown, their statues removed from shrines, their legacies relegated to obscurity. Marinus, in his life of Proclus, documents the fact that sometime after 450, Proclus, founder of the Athenian school in Athens, witnessed the removal of Athena's statue from the Parthenon, after which the goddess appeared to him in his dreams. He alludes to the transgression "by those who move what should not be moved," a coded reference to Christians.[9] Witt documents the history of the destruction of temples on the part of Christians who often used the remains to construct churches. A geographically wide range of churches numbering nearly fifty retained inscriptions in honor of Egyptian gods. The West Coptic church of St Mary, for example, stands close to the temenos wall of the Great Iseum. Isis "bringer of the crops" is an inscription in the Church of Ara Coeli in Rome, and these are but a few examples that Witt cites.[10]

As Christianly gained hegemony in the Roman Empire, female deity, already placed in jeopardy by the fact that the gospels largely followed the Hebrew Bible, accrued extra condemnation. After the conversion of Constantine, the Edict of Milan, issued in 313, called for religious toleration for all religions, including Christianity. In 380 CE, Christianity became the official religion of the state. The power of bishops in great cities increased and coincided with a more centralized state presence for Christianity. Bishops were given judicial and administrative functions. The decade from about 392 to 402, Chuvin tells us, saw an outpouring of anti-pagan laws, some of which were later preserved in the Theodosian Code. The removal and desecration of statues of goddesses and the anti-pagan legislation are concrete examples of an anti-paganism that took place on a conceptual level as well. The life-giving presence ascribed to goddesses in triads and trinities devised by Neoplatonists found a Christian counterpart in the mediating figure of the Holy Spirit. This gender-neutral presence within an essentially masculine trinity included a Christ who acted in the same manner as Sophia, although all traces of goddesses have vanished.

The fact that pagan intellectual Platonism was assimilated to Christian doctrine makes it clear that there is not an absolute disconnect between the two traditions. The academies of the late Roman Empire in Athens and Alexandria educated a mixed population of students, both Christian and pagan, during the fourth and fifth centuries. The education received at these institutions preserved and taught Hellenic traditional texts. The pagan nature of some of the teachings and methods, however, came under increasing disapproval. There had already been a history of violent confrontation in the late Empire between pagan and Christian. The murder of the pagan teacher and philosopher Hypatia (415 CE) had been preceded by a sweeping attack on pagans in 391–394, resulting in the suicide of the opposition leaders Arbogast and Flavianus. The phrase "prevailing circumstances," mentioned unfavorably in the writings of the late antique Neoplatonists Proclus, Demarcus, Simplicius, and Olympiodorus, alludes to the Christian threat felt by pagan academics. Proclus himself was harassed by "giant birds of prey," as his biographer describes it (Marinus *Vita Procli* 55). Apparently, he had to depart for a year from Athens following the closure of the temple to Asclepius, under politically dangerous circumstances. The schools at Athens and Alexandria, where Platonic philosophy and Hellenic studies were taught, were attended by sons of the senatorial class, both Christian and pagan. These schools were left untouched until the fifth century, when violent eruption broke out in Alexandra in an anti-pagan operation that began with the destruction of the sacred shrine of Isis. It was followed by anti-pagan speeches, derision of the priest of Isis, the burning of idols at a public feast, and the torture, death and/or exile of professional teachers. This took place in the mid-480s. Damascius, in his fiercely anti-Christian *Philosophical History*, provides a vivid description of the persecution of pagan philosophers.[11] This history is significant for understanding the relation between Christian and Platonist ideas. Political pressure to change to a Christian mode of expression was fostered and sometimes adopted in order to preserve pedagogical positions in the Christian Empire. Ammonias of the Alexandrian school, for example, was spared persecution by compromising with Peter Mongus, patriarch of the city, who had organized the attack on the Alexandrian school. He was allowed to continue teaching by agreeing to change doctrine, no longer use the *Chaldean Oracles* or Orphic texts, and teach Plato and Aristotle in a non-theological manner.[12] The way was thus cleared for Platonic and Aristotelian ideas to pass on to the medieval and Renaissance eras, as long as they were given a Christian "misreading." Pagan doctrines were not entirely given up but accommodated to a Christian setting.

There are certainly pagan philosophical roots of Christian doctrine in the writings of Paul and of the church fathers, theologians who were educated in the Roman period and who were familiar with Hellenic literature. According to Hyam Maccoby, Paul synthesized Judaism, Gnosticism, and Stoicism, as well as Hebrew thought, to create Christianity. Stoicism, it seems, was the dominant philosophy in Tarsus, his birthplace, and he probably received a Greek classic education. He uses Stoic terms, and Platonic abstract nouns, in creating philosophical support for Christian dogma. During the time of Origen (185–254 CE), Greek philosophy and Hebrew scripture became organized into a syncretic amalgam. Gnosticism was also widely disseminated during these times. Origen is a good example of a Christian figure who was educated in the same manner as the pagan Middle Platonists of the second century and was possibly schooled, as was Plotinus, by Ammonius Saccas (he was taught by an Ammonius who might possibly be the same Ammonius Saccas). There remains controversy as to whether Origen the colleague of Plotinus is the same as Origen the Christian.[13] Scholars still debate who Ammonius was, as well, a Christian, as Eusebius contends, or a pagan, as is more likely. Scholars have done considerable work on the role of Platonism and its subterranean influence on Christianity, a topic that is still a subject of debate.[14] When it comes to the Gospels, Matthew, Mark, and Luke are less imbued with philosophy, but in John, Christ is identified with the Platonic-Stoic Logos. During this time of doctrinal proliferation, all traces of female gender are absented from Christian liturgy. The following quotes illustrate the fact that there are similar constructions in pagan and Christian literature, however, even if not officially acknowledged.

> I (Sophia) call forth from the mouth of the most high, the firstborn before all creation (Ecclesiasticus 245)
>
> He (Christ) is the image of the invisible God, the firstborn of all creation. (Colossians 1:15)

Barbara Newman, in contrasting these two quotes, cites Ecclesiasticus, or Sirach, or Wisdom of Joshua ben Eleazar ben Sirach, a book written in Hebrew after 190 BCE but before 175 BCE and translated into Greek after 117 BCE (not the canonical Ecclesiastes). According to Newman, the sage ben Sirach wrote Ecclesiasticus in part to stem the assimilation of Diaspora Jews, so the alluring Sophia could compete with the popular Hellenistic cult of Isis. Colossians are Pauline letters that seemingly ascribe the attributes of Sophia to Christ. The issue of similarities and differences between pagan and Christian doctrine is even more complex, as will be discussed below, with the church's struggle concerning the use of a triadic formulation in the doctrine of the Trinity.[15]

Ramsey McMullan points out that paganism had its origins in particular localities and its fate corresponded with the fortunes of these localities. "Athena and Jupiter were great because they were the deities of conquering peoples; Artemis and Saturn guarded great cities."[16] The demise of a political association between gods and goddesses and political entities changes with the hegemony of empire. With the addition of Christian theocracies instituted by Constantine, a new age was ushered in. The state cult becomes free of the imprimatur of any pagan deity, although in some areas paganism retained its hold. In Athens, for example, the Asclepius cult still thrived, although in Syria, in the great city Antioch, the inhabitants were largely Christian by 375. In Egypt in the mid-fourth century, an army commander had in his charge plenty of Christians, including priests. Christian theology gained increasing political hegemony and ruled the Roman Empire after Constantine, with only a brief respite during the reign of the emperor Julian. One way to gain entrée into the complex subject of the disappearance of female divinity, then, lies in Christianity's historical success in the late Roman Empire. Salvation was a widespread source of attraction for those who, in Corrington's words, had the need for freedom from the constraints of "Roman economic determinism" and the "rigid social structure." The explanation for the popularity of conversion to Christianity is often attributed to its ability to restore a sense of "class mobility and group acceptance" together with a sense of identity related to a universal ideology.[17] Corrington points out that a universal religion of salvation dissolved old class and regional limitations during a time when the concept of a savior or savior-ess was very much in the air. The terms *soter* and *soteria* were being used for the deities of the mystery religions by the beginning of the first century. The saving deity as a mediator between the divine and human realm offered the worshipper safety, health, and security.[18] The fact that the cult of Isis was so popular offered salvation and an all-purpose divinity, a desirable object of worship during difficult geopolitical times. Thus, there was a preexistent readiness to receive comparable notions of salvation with open arms.

The goddess, Corrington points out, in the culture contemporaneous with the rise of Christianity, holds the roles of wife, sister, and mother, and, as both Isis and Sophia, represents wisdom. In addition, she was a savior. In Apuleius's *Metamorphoses*, her role as savior reflects her role in the culture of that time. Isis aretalogies proclaiming her "ruler of every land" and "holy and eternal savior of the human race" reflected a change from regional specificity. The worship of Isis was potentially open to all nationalities and was found throughout the Empire in the early Common Era. Isis religion had been initially regarded as subversive by the Roman senatorial class, which banned worship of Isis in Rome a number of times during the Republic and early Empire.[19] Isis prevailed. Mother and wife, giver and sustainer of life, Isis is the throne of the pharaoh, the nursing mother who imparts the milk of salvation to the king, conqueror of death and giver of life. Some scholars suggest that these roles accrued to Mary as mother of Jesus. One epithet for Isis in Apuleius's *Metamorphoses* is "Queen of Heaven" (11.5 2-3), notably the epithet used for Mary in a long history of the Catholic Church beginning with Revelation (12:1-2). In several respects, then, Christianity was configured like the Isis cult. It had a growing universal appeal as opposed to regional specificity, and it offered salvation to its followers. The earliest writers of Christianity, however, are absent of any female principle and posit male creation and sustenance as well as male salvation. One can speculate that the missing ingredient in Isis worship in a society that was patriarchal in all respects was the idea that salvation was supplied by a male savior. More likely is the bureaucratic and well-organized efforts of the church to promulgate Christianity and gain political power.

Mary

Gerard Manley Hopkins (d. 1889), the Jesuit priest-turned poet, either consciously or in the grip of a less than deliberate evocation of the mythic past, calls Mary "great as no goddess is" in a poem he titled "The Blessed Virgin Compared to the Air We Breathe" (Gerard Manley Hopkins, 1923). In doing so, he invoked what had long become part of Western literary history, the long gone but nevertheless still "present" past. First, an Orphic hymn to Hera:

> You lodge yourself in dark hollows,
> and your form is airy,
> O Hera, blessed queen of all
> consort of Zeus,
> The soft breezes you send to mortals,
> nourish the soul
> O mother of rains, mother of winds
> you give birth to all,
> Life does not exist without you,
> You are everything
> even in the air we venerate
> You are queen,
> You toss and turn
> When the rushing wind tosses and turns. (Orphic Hymn 16[20])

Hopkins's poem ("Wild air, world mothering air, Nestling me everywhere. This needful, never spent, And nursing element," etc.), written in the nineteenth century, is comparable to its Orphic predecessor, documenting the persistence of cultural memory. Marianic theology is from the outset a striking example of feminine presence woven into the all-male theology of the Christian church. While there is a questionable analogy between Mary and any female goddess, many scholars have found analogies and equate the Virgin Mary with the goddesses of mythology. Certainly the statues of mother and child are quite similar to those of Isis and Horus, and one could make inferences from this fact alone. Immaculate conception seems sufficiently analogous to virgin birth, the parthenogenesis that features in the resumes of several goddesses. Many scholars speculate that there is more than an accidental connection. The fact that the official church itself resisted the possibility of developing a cult of Mary can be considered proof, in and of itself, that the connection was plausible. This fear is evident in the proceedings of the Council of Ephesus (431) where Mary was defined as the *Theotokos* ("genetrix of god"). The fear was that according a divine status to the Virgin Mary could associate her with the ancient Mother of the Gods. Borgeaud points out that in Ephesus, Nestorius would have preferred, contra Cyril of Alexandria, that Mary be designated *Christotokos* rather than *Theotokos* for fear that people would make the Virgin into a goddess. Borgeaud gives other instances. In the seventh century, John of Damascus (*c.* 675) wrote in his *Homilies on the Dormition of the Virgin* about guarding against possible confusions along these lines. He specified that the Christian festival of the Mother of God be without flutes and corybantes of the "Mother of pseudonymous gods" (ritual practices associated with Kybele).[21]

Sarah Jane Boss, director of the Center of Marian studies at the University of Wales, explores these issues in her edited volume *Mary: The Complete Resource*. Marianism apparently asserted itself at various times in history. The twelfth century, for example, revived Marianism as the prolific iconography of those times attests. Boss considers the fact that conversion of local populations was aided by synchronizing holy days and pagan celebrations, constructing churches on the very sites where temples once stood, and installing Mary, rather than any pagan goddess, as a protectress of cities.[22] Arthur Green extensively discusses the Marian revival in twelfth-century France, represented for example by commentaries on the Song of Songs on the part of Christian devotees. In this literature, Mary is extolled and her glories and virtues proclaimed, falling short of attributing divinity to her.[23] Public Marian piety was very prevalent in twelfth-century France, at times reaching cult status. Mary was venerated in street processions, sacred drama, town squares, festivals, and music, and was depicted in art as Queen of Heaven. The need to find equivalence between pagan goddesses and Mary persists into the twentieth century among scholars and in popular culture. In books such as that by Rudolph Steiner, *Isis Mary Sophia*, Sophia is equated to the Holy Spirit and Mary to Sophia, and all to the so-called "divine feminine." Today, innumerable websites and popular books focus on equating Mary and Isis.[24] Corrington suggests that "evidence might support the thesis that Mary existed in popular piety because of a need for female deity or at least some female aspect to the deity that seemed so exclusively male."[25]

John van den Hengel, a scholar specializing in Christology, suggests that the mother goddess/Mary connection has been an object of intense research because Roman Catholics have been put on the defensive by reformation Protestants who accuse them of making excessive connections between Greco-Roman practices and Christianity.[26] Cases have been made for both a strong connection and none at all. Michael Carroll, for example, contends that the "facile" identification of Mary with the great virgin mother goddesses of the ancient Near East, Canaanite Astarte, Asheroth, and the Akkadian goddess Istar or the Sumerian Inana must be differentiated from Mary's uniqueness as a perpetual virgin. These goddesses, he contends, as well as Athena, Artemis, and other Greek virgin goddesses, provide no basis for portraying them as mother goddesses in the same sense as Mary is a mother of Christ. He uses the argument that their promiscuity, especially in the case of Isis, where a stronger connection might be posited, precludes the analogy.[27]

Stephen Benko provides a scholarly appraisal of this literature, citing a critique by the Jesuit scholar Karl Prümm. Examining similarities between the ancient goddess and Mary, he concludes that a syncretism between Marianic doctrine and its pagan precedents does not hold up. Based on the premise of the full humanity of Jesus and, hence, his fully human mother, the analogy with female divinity is questionable.[28] Benko contends that, although Isis left many marks on the cult of Mary, Mariology was more substantially determined by the theology of the Great Mother (Kybele). Benko cites Phyllis Treble and Andrew M. Greely, among others, who have contributed to the extensive literature on the possible connection of Mary with the goddess. Greely, for example, describes Mary as the symbol of the feminine counterpart of god. "God is both masculine and feminine and may well have been thought of as a woman long before she/he was ever thought of as male."[29] Mary should be rendered as the "symbol of the feminine component of the deity."[30] Rosemary Ruether, author of many books on feminist theology (*Gaia and God*, *Sexism and God Talk*, for example), claims that masses of people came into the Christian church bringing with them their former devotion to the mother goddess, especially Isis whose iconography was borrowed and applied to Mary. Speculation on both sides of this issue is clearly motivated by a vested interest in the outcome (Christians denying the analogy and secularists relishing it). Kilian McDonnell gives a complete evaluation of the good and the bad in Mariology and a critical review of Mariology literature.[31] The early church did not emphasize the role of Mary, either in theology or in the account of the life of Jesus. The role of Mary is minimal in the Gospel of Mark; the Gospel of Luke emphasizes Mary's virginity, while Paul did not attach any importance to the biological birth from a woman.[32] The very issue of Mary's "purity" and virginity and the fact of biological birth, as opposed to spiritual birth, shows that Mary is regarded fundamentally as human. It is not the intention of the present study to take up these particular issues, more appropriate to the wider domain of the sociology of religions. It could be said, however, that although the direct connection between Greco-Roman goddesses cannot be established, an indirect influence in terms of attributions may be a matter of "cultural memory" as it impinges on Mariology.

Christian Theology: Pneumatology

Benko points out that the image of God that emerges from Judaism is of a God that is solely male and in Christianity the Holy Spirit is referred to as male. He points out that *spiritus* in Latin is a masculine noun, while in Greek the word which designates something similar to spirit, at least in Stoic thought, is neuter (*pneuma*), and in Hebrew it is feminine (*ruach*).[33] The Latin equivalent is probably *anima*, a term picked up by the Jungians to refer to the feminine. While technically *anima* is related to the soul, the word *spiritus* is closer to the sense of a breath-like spiritual entity. One of the defining doctrines of monotheistic religion is the hegemony of a single deity. Since grammatical considerations dictate the use of gender pronouns, and there are no neutral ones when it comes to animate being, it is unavoidable that a choice of gender be male. Beyond the grammatical difficulties of a neuter pronoun for deity, the male character of divinity has been strongly promulgated by the Judeo-Christian religions. The Christian Church fathers, Clement and Origen, as well as theologians such as St Thomas Aquinas and the early Christian philosopher, Augustine, all reinforce the masculine nature of deity.

J. Gwyn Griffiths, a classicist and Egyptologist, in his book *Triads and Trinity* attempts to establish the original sources of the Christian Trinity in Greek, Latin, Egyptian, Coptic, and Hebrew triads. A far-ranging account, it has been criticized as having too wide a sweep. The parallels between Neoplatonic triads such as "One, Intellect, Soul" and the Christian trinity do have some functional parallels. Pneumatology within Christian theology is a very complex issue. There is a common idea in both Platonic and Christian accounts that a "third" factor is necessary in mediating the relation between the divine and the world. In pagan theology, a female presence or goddess could serve that function, while in Christianity the Holy Spirit, though soul-like, is usually designated by a male pronoun. The eclipse of the female presence as mediator between god, the universe, and humankind is not due solely to patriarchal/societal factors. The real problematic may be the necessity to adhere to the Athanasian doctrine of the singular substance of the divine triad (Athanasius of Alexandria used the language of *homoiousia* (one-substance) that was ratified by the Nicene Council). If the Father and Son are one substance, the Holy Spirit must be "masculine" in some sense as well, as a presence within a *homoiousia*.

As Christian theology developed, it brought with it an increasing concern with the trinity and with establishing an official creed. It is interesting to speculate why this, of all issues, dominated the attention of those who debated church doctrine. Randall Collins and many other commentators have suggested that pagan concepts were the impetus for heresy disputes. The Christian doctrine of the trinity which emerged after 150 CE may have been influenced by Middle Platonist and Neopythagorean triadic hypostases.[34] Faced with the fact that Christ was a second divine figure and the Holy Spirit a third, the question of how three entities could be one was a concern that had to be resolved in the service of maintaining monotheism. The church had to ensure that Christ attained an ontological status fitting to his divinity, but it could not be through any structure that could be seen as polytheistic. The ontological status of the Father, Son, and Holy Spirit, a seeming multiplicity in a trinity that was present in a monotheistic religion, became a heated and controversial topic. The issue of female gender never even entered what was already cause for argument and condemnation.

During the doctrinal debate at the Council of Nicaea (325), Arius (*c.* 250–336), an Alexandrian priest, had asserted that the Son of God was subordinate to God the Father. He maintained that the Son is not the equal of the Father but created by him. Most fourth-century theologians rejected this, and the view that finally prevailed was that the Father and Son were equal and of the same substance (*homoiousia*) but were distinct persons. The Council of Nicaea condemned the Arians by an overwhelming majority. The Emperor Constantine ordered Arius's book *Thalia* to be burned. In 381 and in other councils that followed (such as the second Ecumenical Council), the Nicene Creed, which is accepted by the Catholic Church today, was approved. Constantinople and Asia inclined to Arianism; the West adhered to the decrees of the Council of Nicaea. By the time of the Council of Chalcedon (451), the more conventional Trinitarian Christological doctrine was the established doctrine of the Catholic Church. It holds that the Godhead and the manhood of Christ are one substance. The non-Trinitarian doctrine of Arianism retains the "dualism" of Platonism regarding, according to some interpretations, Christ as the Logos. The Father created the Son and the Son created the world. Arius had also taught that Christ was sent to earth for the salvation of mankind, but the Father, infinitely primordial, was beyond that. The Holy Spirit is the giver of life and the Son is not consubstantial with either Father or Holy Spirit. The kind of triadic and dualist thinking that is analogous to Gnosticism and Neoplatonism had to be rejected and the life-producing functions ascribed to the Holy Spirit considered homogeneous with Father and Son. The Holy Spirit is referred to as He (John 14:16 and 16:7 and Acts 8:16, for example) and as a giver of supernatural life (2 Corinthians 3:8). He is also described, as were the Shekinah and the Platonist goddess, as immanent, at least in the sense of dwelling in the church and soul of individuals. These attributes could make the Trinitarian doctrine dangerously close to pagan Platonism. A closer look at Arius's poem *Thalia* reveals that he thought through the problem of the Trinitarian nature of the godhead with reasoning reminiscent of Greek philosophical thought. Excerpts from the *Thalia* make it evident why the unity of God, a central tenet of monotheism, was violated by Arian doctrine. God himself is unbegotten while the son is the beginning of created things. "He [the son] has none of the distinct characteristics of God's own being (*kath' hypostasin*). For he is not equal to, nor is he of the same being (*homoousios*) as him." "Understand that the Monad [eternally] was, but the Dyad was not before it came into existence. It immediately follows that, although the son did not exist, the Father was still God."[35] The paradigm for this last statement is similar to the pagan idea that the One (Monad) and the Dyad are separate beings and both factors in creation (as was discussed in Chapter 5). The argument to counter dualism was to consider the components of the trinity an equal hypostases within monadic oneness: both one essence. The bishops of the Council of Nicaea, then, focused on the eternal nature of the godhead, and treated God and Christ as substantially monadic and essentially one. On these grounds alone Christ or the Holy Spirit cannot be analogous to the feminine mediating principle of Platonism. Central to the idea of essential oneness is that all components be of a single gender (or at least neuter), rendering any possibility of a "female" presence logically impossible.

The Cappadocian Fathers, Basil of Caesarea (330–379), Gregory of Nyssa (335–394), and Gregory of Nazianzus (329–390) finalized these doctrines. They clarified the Trinitarian principle: mediatorship of the Son and the Spirit in creation and redemption was not a matter of their separate *ousia* (being or substance) but their separate *hypostases* (levels of being) ultimately in unity or "consubstantial" with the Father.[36] The Cappadocians were well steeped in Neoplatonism. Gregory of Nyssa titles his letter on this subject "An Answer to Ablabius: That We Should Not Think of Saying There Are Three Gods," illustrating that the danger of polytheism was one of the issues at stake in the machinations regarding consubstantiality. Any hint of female presence would be anathema to consubstantiality. While there are many reasons for the eventual eclipse of the goddesses of pagan texts, Christian theology certainly plays a role.

Origen, Clement, and the Association with Gnosticism and Neoplatonism

The church fathers, earlier than the Cappadocians, were both knowledgeable and dismissive of Gnosticism and Platonism. Titus Flavius Clemens (*c.* 150–215) was a Christian theologian influenced by his pagan origins and Hellenistic philosophy, and Origen (185–254) was his pupil; they are both regarded as church fathers (although in Origen's case this epithet is disputed due to some of his doctrines). Clement of Alexandria, as he is known, knew of "forty-two books of Hermes considered indispensable for the rituals of Egyptian priests."[37] In one of Clement's major texts,

Protrepticus, he displays knowledge of Greek mythology and the mystery religions. Origen was a staunch critic of pagan philosophy and reviled Gnosticism. He adopted a Middle Platonism that he construed along Christian lines and responded in detail to Celsus's attack on Christianity. In his own *On First Principles*, however, he conceived of a holy trinity based on standard Middle Platonist paradigms. Triadic emanation, the pre-existence and fall of souls, multiple ages, the migration of souls, and restoration of all souls to a state of perfection and godhead in an apocatastasis of time were all doctrines that found their way into his texts.

There is no doubt that close ties existed between Gnostic literature and Christian philosophy in the second and third centuries. Major differences exist, however, certainly in regard to the presence of any feminine goddess or powers in Christian doctrine. Like his contemporary Plotinus, Origen may have been a pupil of Ammonius Saccas, the founder of Neoplatonism. It was during Origen's time that Greek philosophy and Hebrew scripture became organized into a syncretic amalgam. Russell points out that Origen's doctrines as set forth in *De Principiis* have much affinity to those of Plotinus.[38] Origen claims there is nothing incorporeal except God—Father, Son, and Holy Ghost. He preserves the Platonic distinction between Nous and soul, as did Plotinus. Both Origen and Plotinus adhere to the idea that when Nous (Intellect) falls away, it becomes soul; soul when virtuous becomes Nous. In Gnosticism, Nous qua male principle and the soul qua female goddess follow similar patterns. Soul becoming virtuous, in Plotinus, longs to be reunited with the god, also known as Nous. According to Origen, the soul in its fallen state is "akin to being set aflame with the fire of divine love" (*De Principiis* I.I.6). The soul wishes to be reunited with the divine logos in whose image it was created. For Plotinus, Nous is transcendent and intelligible, and the soul is attracted or desires to become Nous. This is canonical Platonism viz the soul desires to assimilate to Nous. The erotic longing of goddess for god, or, as in Plutarch, the desire of Isis for Osiris, construed in terms of the soul desiring Nous, reflects a Platonist version of this doctrine. In Gnosticism as well, there is the desire for the fallen soul or earthly goddess to reunite with her source.

Triads such as in those found in Plotinus with his partition of Intellect into Being, Life, Intellect, or in the Sethian Gnostic treatises with their Being, Vitality, Mentality (*Allogenes* XI.49.28-38), discussed here in Chapter 6, are associated with the goddess in pagan Platonist doctrine. In the *Chaldean Oracles*, the middle term is associated specifically with Hekate; in the Sethian Gnostic texts with Barbelo/Sophia. She is roughly associated with the spiritual, moving, and living aspects of being.[39] The manner in which Clement construes the trinity shows the close relationship between him and the Platonist Gnostics although Clement held firmly to the belief that there was equality of substance and that the Son was one with the Father, eternal and uncreated. The Christian trinity confines its members to the Father, Son, and Holy Spirit, the last being somehow the movable breathable life of the trinity. Origen describes these principles using Platonic language. The "Father" is a perfect unity, complete unto himself, and associated with mind. God the Father exercises his intellectual aspect in Christ the Son, the Logos, or Wisdom (*Sophia*) of God, the first emanation of the Father. The third and last principle of the divine triad is the Holy Spirit, who "proceeds from the Son and is related to Him as the Son is related to the Father."[40] Here is Origen explaining the status of the Holy Spirit, in a passage preserved in the original Greek:

> So that in this way the power of the Father is greater than that of the Son and of the Holy Spirit, and that of the Son is more than that of the Holy Spirit, and in turn, the power of the Holy Spirit exceeds that of every other holy being.[41]

The Father's power is universal, but the Son's corresponds only to rational creatures, while the Spirit's power corresponds strictly to the "saints" or those who have achieved salvation. The structure of divine influence on the created realm is found much later in the system of the Neoplatonic philosopher Proclus.[42] The hierarchical structure, then, adopted as a way to explain triplicity in unity in Christian accounts, parallels its pagan Neoplatonic and Gnostic counterparts except as related to feminine presence as a living power and third member of the triad/trinity. The Gnostic version of Christianity, on the other hand, preserves feminine divinity and alternatively the hermaphroditic nature of divinity. The absence of female gender in Christian Platonism is not the absence of comparable functions as those in Gnostic and Platonist contexts. Arius Victorinus, who was born in Africa between 281 and 291, and who converted to Christianity, puts forth the same argument that is promulgated by second- and third-century Neoplatonism (as Mary Clark describes, citing Pierre Hadot).[43] While the theological Platonist would have the goddess intervene in bringing higher hypostases into nature, Victorinus taught that Christ was eternal life, bringing a higher life and knowledge into the intelligible world and the sensible world (to lead people to God). The mystery, for Victorinus, includes the descent of Divine Life through the son into the world and the ascent of thought through the Spirit to the Father.[44] The bifurcation between the father as actual existence, and the son as existential act, is reminiscent of the bifurcation in Platonism between being and life, only in the latter case it is the female divinity, not Christ, that is associated with living activity.

Cornelio Fabro's study of Thomas Aquinas further supports the idea that Christian theology holds ideas in common with Neoplatonic/pagan philosophy. Aquinas, however, "overcomes" the Neoplatonic-type triad and ultimately opts for a First Cause which renders the "second" factor an act of the first, rather than a separate hypostasis. For Aquinas, there is an efficient cause as the second cause after the First Cause. The First Cause proceeds in activity; the second cause is material and efficient causality. Aquinas cites Proclus's term "production" to express the causality of an efficient cause. "The First Cause of all things is compared to the whole of nature, just as nature is compared to art. Hence, that which first subsists in all of nature is from the First Cause of all things and is particularized in each individual by the work of second causes."[45] Fabro goes on to show that Aquinas reduces the second cause to the First Cause:

> And so through his radical reflection on principle taken as act, Aquinas has overcome the static and circular dialectic of the Platonic triad: Being, Life, Intellect (*On, Zoê, Nous*), in such fashion as to make *esse ipsum* emerge as the constitutive metaphysic of God and also to make participated *esse* (*actus essendi*) emerge as the act of all acts and perfection of all perfection.[46]

Aquinas's theology, then, takes a step toward reducing the triadic to the omnipotent causality of God and reduces the role of a mediating principle in his theology. The First Cause becomes the "very substance of the second cause, because the operative power itself of the second cause originates from the First Cause."[47] While the masculine rhetoric concerning the First Cause identified as God persists, with the demise of the secondary cause as a principle, in favor of acts, the placeholder for a second divinity, such as was female divinity in the Gnostic and Neoplatonic system, gives way though the structure remains.

Negative Theology

The disappearance of the goddess in Christianity and in Western thought is related to the larger issue of the unknowability yet monothetic nature of God as well. Theologians and some Neoplatonists in the effort to avoid personalizing or anthropomorphizing divinity resorted to negative theology to achieve that end. Different from Judaism's imageless monotheism, this practice claimed that attribution of any characteristics at all to God diminishes God's infinity and unity. In the middle ages, this becomes a central issue for Christian philosophers. This theology claims that applying superlatives to God reduces God to human descriptions and applies limitations to God. In medieval scholasticism, increasing and prevalent use of abstract nouns and concerns about the real existence of universals, and a focus on logical propositions and their role in philosophical and theological reasoning, made discourse about God problematic. Negative theology is an exercise in avoiding predicating God with any earthly excellences or attributes for fear of denigrating God by imposing a limit on God's perfections. One is allowed to use positive terms about God as freely as negative, provided that one prefix something to indicate their inadequacy. One can state what God is in the affirmative, negate that affirmation, and then negate the negation, a refinement of negative theology termed "double negative theology." In other words, one can say God is not omnipotent but neither is he not not omnipotent. The so-called apophatic tradition originated with Philo (20 BCE–50 CE) and Clement of Alexandria (150–215) and appears in Gregory of Nyssa (335–395) and others, but most famously in Thomas Aquinas and Maimonides. Negative theology is an outgrowth of increasing emphasis on the "logical" aspect of philosophy. With the rise of universities and the revival of Aristotelianism, scholastics emphasized a correspondence theory of truth. Propositions are required to truly reflect reality; their predicates should correspond to referents that can be empirically identified. Radical double negative theology allows one to avoid reducing God to human categories when God in fact has no intelligible content.[48] A divine object as a subject of a proposition could not be characterized the same way as an empirically verifiable proposition. Armstrong contends that expressions of traditional religion, by this premise, become mythical or iconic, as do the Neoplatonic inventions. "The most abstract and logically constructed treatments of the Henads or the Trinity can only function for us mythically, if they function at all."[49] In this atmosphere, there is no room for female divinity if only by virtue of the unknowability of God by any attribution.

Elizabeth A. Johnson, in her book *She Who Is*, uses the idea of an apophatic theology to approach the subject of gender and theology. The book, and her article in *Theological Studies*, highlights the Patristic and Thomistic understanding of God and the Trinity. She bases her arguments on the ultimate unthinkability of God and on divine incomprehensibility as the most reverent position to hold. "No human concept, word or image, all of which originate in experiences of created reality, can circumscribe the divine reality."[50] On this basis, she rejects all attempts to envision God exclusively through association with the male human being. There is a vast Christian literature to this effect, which she cites in a footnote that is partly reproduced here.[51] Carrying this to a logical conclusion, the Christian analogy of God with spirit, mind, reason, and act, and the female reality with body, instinct, and passive material principle, are essentially Greek in origin. The androcentricity that results in ascribing the aggrandized traits to male divinity, within the Christian writings, is based on the Greek history, originally, of a Pythagorean set of opposites. On the basis of these latter characteristics, the female is absented from divinity and relegated to nature and earthly existence. Taking the approach stipulated by negative theology however would, carried to its conclusion, preclude all gender attributions to Divinity.

Conclusion

Although the female as a divinized presence has disappeared entirely from Christian liturgy and philosophy, she can still be found in the metaphorical language of church doctrine, once again illustrating the power of cultural memory. Thus, Clement of Alexandria in "The Rich Man's Salvation" uses the imagery of suckling the infant to describe the love of the mother god: "God, in his very self is love. And while the unspeakable part of Him is Father, the part that has sympathy with us is Mother." Augustine also refers to the "Suckling infant, our Lord, in order to convert his wisdom into milk."[52] Medieval iconography is replete with mother and child imagery expressing divinity only in the ever-present nimbus around the Madonna's head and the ethereal lighting that surrounds her. Although the early church fathers definitively relegated the female to the "earthly" realm, females of great holiness could be elevated to sainthood. While this does not elevate them to goddess status, neither is it purely earthly. In the following chapter, some of the medieval allegorical deployment of goddess lore will illustrate the continued survival of interest in goddesses after the delegitimizing of female divinity in Christian theology. Barbara Newman contends that medieval Christendom is the "father of only one son but many daughters." She treats the numerous allegorical poems, theological fictions, and the visions of holy women as evidence of the continued presence of the goddesses in medieval ideas. These creations, she contends, are not mere personifications and poetic figures but distinctive creations of the Christian imagination: emanations of the divine, mediators between God and the cosmos, even embodied universals.[53] She is determined not to reduce them to personifications or ideological constructs or iconography. Assmann's concept of cultural memory, again, applies here. Goddesses did not disappear from the stage of literary and philosophical history, but in fact retained a considerable presence in the early medieval period in the genre of allêgoria poetry. Not at all forgotten, they were transformed and became iconographical and literary phenomenon, rather than objects of worship or philosophical doctrine. There is much that is alive in the world of nature and mind that finds its voice through poetry, iconography, allegory, and symbolism: tropic genres which have some legitimacy as a different kind of truth. "Natura" and "Sophia," the goddesses of medieval literature, allow the forces of nature and the transcendent causes that lie beyond nature to take the form of allegories of world creation, while avoiding any commitments to theological or philosophical truth.

10

Personifying Nature and Wisdom: The Medieval and Early Modern Goddess

Nature

Alfred North Whitehead asking, "What do we mean by nature?" responds, "Nature is that which we observe in perception through the senses. In this sense-perception, we are aware of something which is not thought, and which is self-contained for thought, and which is impenetrable by thought."[1] The idea of "nature" as a unified force or entity is a cultural construct.[2] Nature, from the ancient world to the twentieth century, is considered as the "other," alien to thought, though amenable to mechanical explanation; mathematical, chemical, and biological scientific study; and practical exploitation. From the Presocratic philosophers who titled their works *Peri Physeôs* (*On Nature*), to our current usage, nature has been portrayed as a self-contained region of existence differentiated from the world of mind and the supernatural world of theology. The very idea of the supernatural is predicated upon the idea that nature is a non-spiritual realm of materiality. Aristotle, or one of his followers, coined the term "metaphysics" to refer to matters that came after (*meta*) the book he wrote on *Physics*. First causes, soul, and intellect were beyond nature. Hesiod's *Theogony* is a noteworthy cultural precedent for the association of goddesses and nature. Artemis is goddess of the wild, Gaia is earth, and Rhea is a mother. All of them personify nature's fecundity. Aphrodite has to do with erotic activity and attraction, the forces through which all of creation comes to be. Persephone, the queen of the underworld, suggests a dark side to the goddess while her mother Demeter is associated with nature's bounty and harvest. The concept "nature" embodies all of these traits, and the goddesses who personify them, over time, become iconic figures who encompass all aspects of nature. This includes a perceived danger should one engage with her as Proclus expressed in the following quote: "Do not gaze at nature: her name is destiny (*heimarmenon*)" (Proclus *Plat. Theol.* V.32, 119.12).

The goddess as "veiled," whose garment must be removed to reveal nature's secrets, is an additional theme stemming from classical ritual practice and myth. Athena was known for her *peplum* or *chiton*, Isis for the famous aretalogy and the forbidden lifting of her veil, and these images lent themselves to the later allegories of the unveiling of nature. In the literature of the seventeenth and eighteenth centuries, Nature as a veiled goddess can be understood only by lifting her veil One can only approach her, however, with trepidation. There is a more troublesome side to nature as well. In this regard, she may trace her heritage to the original mother Nyx or to Gaia's darker side. Nature is associated with fate, not the higher Providence. She is nearer to "matter" (dark and unknowable) as opposed to form, thus inaccessible to the enlightened intellect. Matter and darkness are always somewhat resistant to form; thus, the female deity as Nature has the double attribution of being wildly out of control but also responsible for all the fecundity and unlimited production that is granted to the material world. Pierre Hadot, in a detailed study of the history of the idea of nature and its relation to the goddess Isis, tells us that nature was often conceived, beginning in the first century BCE, as a goddess or mysterious female presence. Macrobius, in the early fifth century, for example says the following:

> Nature has concealed the knowledge of her being from mankind's coarse senses by hiding beneath the vestments and envelopes of things; likewise, she has wished that sages should discuss her mysteries only under the veil of mythic narratives. (Macrobius *Commentary on Scipio's Dream* I, 2, 17, 8[3])

For the ancient world, nature was thought to be a cycle between renewal and perishing, as in the cycle of the seasons. The Demeter-Persephone myth can be interpreted as an allegory for nature, winter being associated with the time of the year when Persephone is in the underworld. The Pythagorean Hippodamus (498–408 BCE) describes nature as follows:

> All mortal things, by necessity of Nature, revolve in a wheel of changes. When they are born they grow, and when they are grown they reach their height and after that they grow old and at last perish. At one time Nature causes them to come to their goal in her region of darkness, and then again out of the darkness they come back into mortal form, by alternation of birth and repayment of death in the cycle where Nature returns upon herself.[4]

Hadot points out that "*physis* (nature) originally designated the action expressed by the verb *phuesthai*—to be born, to increase, to grow—or its result the springing forth of things but came to signify a kind of personified ideal."[5] Plato's association between the creation of the universe, characterized as "coming to be" in *Timaeus*, adds temporality and fecundity to the idea of nature while his "receptacle" adds receptivity and chaos as the underlying substratum of the natural world. The goddesses of the epic poets easily personify these ideas and the association of female gender to nature has perennially capitalized on these ancient associations. The first association of nature and the female deity is evident in how the classical gods and goddesses are named. Rhea for flow, Ge for earth, and Hera for air already invoke the four elements and associate three of them with female deity. While the Presocratic philosophers seem to treat nature as purely physical in matter and process, Plato, in *Laws,* articulates the idea that nature is not merely a spontaneous advent of growth and creation, but is "animate," powered by soul. The soul is the movement that moves itself (892–96), and nature is moved by psychic force. Still, for Plato, "nature" is the lesser realm of being than Mind, Soul lower in status as well. In the binary opposites, eternity/time, rest/movement, intellect/soul, Plato prioritizes the "higher" first term. In the beginning of *Timaeus* when the question is raised as to whether the world is eternal or whether it has come to be (*poteron ên aei, geneseôs arkhên ekhôn oudemian, ê gegonen, ap'arkhês tinos arxamenos*), the answer is it has come to be (*gegonen*) (*Tim.* 28B7-8). Some interpreters have considered this an allusion to continuous creation and others to creation in time. Nature is never complete, never arrested in the eternal now of being, but always in time, always "coming to be." For Plato, eternal forms and Ideas, on the other hand, do not "come to be," but are permanent and unchanging and account for the possibility of stable knowledge. Nature can only be known by opinion, is always in movement and flux, while Being is a realm of reality where things do not come to be and grow, change, and move; but are the object of true knowledge. Plato, then, is a prime source for the idea, so fixed in the collective memory of the West, that the physical world is secondary in the hierarchy of being. Plato's metaphysical account, having nothing to do with gender politics, nevertheless created a bifurcation that valorizes the transcendent world and devalues the world of nature. The Platonist ontology, coupled with the Parmenidean devaluation of sense perception and belief, as opposed to certain and stable knowledge, conspires to render nature a derivative and inferior instantiation of transcendent principles. Knowing nature, for Plato, is secondary to knowing forms, as the famous divided line in Book VII of *Republic* illustrates. As many scholars have noted, then, Platonism provides the groundwork for a "devaluation" of female characteristics, based on the assumption of an affinity of female gender and nature.

Aristotle in *Physics* furthered the Platonic association of nature and movement as follows: "Nature is the source of the movement of natural objects, being present in them, either potentially, or in complete reality" (*Physics* 1015a15). Peters points out that Aristotle *physis* takes over many of the functions of the Platonic *psyche*: notably it has a *telos* (purpose) and is the source of its own natural movement.[6] The Middle Platonists and Neoplatonists ascribed the "movement and change" apparent in nature to causes beyond nature and these causes, in turn, were able to be personified by deification identifying them with gods. Nature continues to be devalued compared to Mind (*Nous*) and its intellectual qualities but still important to creation. For Plotinus, nature is bound up with Soul, but a lower aspect of it. The contemplative aspect of the soul is *phronêsis* (wisdom), but the lower aspect of soul is *physis*, forever turned away from Nous (*Enn.* IV.4.13). Both are beneath *Nous*, the highest form of intelligence. Higher realms of being and intellect are associated with permanence and stability. Intermediation between the physical world and the world of Mind requires intervention on the part of an agency capable of movement and commerce with both permanent ideas and nature. Goddesses, as explained in the preceding chapters here, enable nature to receive the gifts that intellect can bestow upon the material world. At the same time, however, the association with nature brings along with it the idea of its "materiality." In the second century CE, Numenius typifies the treatment of matter in Platonism. Matter is not "evil": it is generative and fecund, albeit secondary to intellectual and formal parameters. Numenius cites Heraclitus approvingly and asserts that if the bad were eliminated so too would be the world, as it is necessary to creation (fr. 52). Kirk rightly points out that to translate or interpret *kakos*, in its usage either in Pythagorean tables of opposites or in Heraclitus's fragments, as "evil" is anachronistic. Thus when Numenius asserts that "The world, then, has been fashioned from God and matter," he calls matter the world's mother and, in a following discussion on Providence and necessity, claims both to be at work (fr. 52). Nature, then, is secondary, but a necessary aspect of reality, one to be subdued and designed by reason. This becomes a time-honored convention, one to be so interwoven in cultural memory, that it is assumed, with or without conscious intention, by future generations of scholars and popular culture alike. In what follows, it can be seen that in medieval allegory, goddesses personify nature, possessing a certain obscurity but giving a forceful life to the intellectually designed and controlling paradigms, personified in turn, by gods. The fact that goddesses morphed into "witches" in some medieval contexts might be based on the presumed darker side of matter and nature as opposed to the more valued spiritual and intellectual realities.

Natura: The Personification of Nature in Medieval Texts

Christianity contributed to the demise of a female deity but did not succeed in entirely eliminating this age-old cultural icon. The consistent personification of nature as a goddess, Natura, in medieval literature demonstrates that the connection between female deity and nature persists. In an Orphic Hymn, Nature was hymned as the mother goddess of all things, and as a fecund queen who "tames all but who is never tamed."[7] Christianity's recycling of this image is a notable example of how the goddess as a metaform and a cultural connective survives the centuries. A ubiquitous literary figure, her continued existence was assured when her status changed from a theological and philosophical entity to an allegorical presence. Barbara Newman bases her book *God and the Goddesses* on the premise that goddesses occupy a spacious domain in medieval religious thought. Natura and Sophia are personifications of nature and of wisdom featuring in medieval literature. They abound in poetic creations, theological writings of clerics, and the revelations of holy women. Newman catalogues the complex and interlocking histories of the medieval goddess, Hildegard of Bingen's Caritas, Alan of Lille's Natura, Christine de Pizan's Lady Reason, Boethius's Lady Philosophy, Hadewijch's Minne, Suso's Eternal Wisdom, and the high Mariology of the late middle ages, all fall under the compass of Natura, Sophia, and Sapientia[8] (Lady Wisdom is "called Hagia Sophia in Byzantium, Sapientia and Philosophia in Latin Christendom"). Newman traces the source of these personifications to the Sophia of Proverbs, Ecclesiasticus, and the Wisdom of Solomon, and describes this figure as becoming "progressively more universal, ethereal and goddess-like" in the later literature.[9]

Claudian (370–404 CE) provides an early example of what will become a widespread hermeneutic practice. He deploys a goddess, Natura, as a poetic figure, anticipating later medieval usages. A court poet to Christian emperors, Claudian wrote hexameter verse in the silver age of Latin poetry. In his panegyric to Stilicho, he describes Natura as at once-aged and youthfully beautiful (*De Consulate Stilichonis* II, 431). In this poem, Natura parts the ancient strife of the elements, is a powerful goddess who appoints gods to serve the young Zeus, is a marriage-maker (*pronuba*), and is a cosmic power standing between Zeus and the gods. Curtius remarks, in his book on literature in the Latin middle ages, that Claudian, in these attributions, is close to late antique theology, and gives the example of the Orphic hymns of the third and fourth centuries, of which the tenth hymn is dedicated to *Physis* (nature). In the hymn, she is described as Mother of All, all wise, all bestower, etc. Curtius claims, "She is not the personification of an intellectual concept in the Orphic hymn but part of religious experience of late paganism." Claudian's usage, Curtius claims, is the "link in the golden chain which connects late paganism with the Renaissance of the twelfth century."[10] Natura as a true allegorical personification, then, is a tradition stretching from Claudian in the fourth century to Chaucer in the fourteenth and beyond. For Claudian, who Economou tells us is the last poet of classical Rome, Natura speaks, acts, and has a powerful role in creation. In Claudian's *De Raptu Proserpinae*, Proserpina, left in Sicily for safekeeping by her mother, sews a tapestry on which she embroiders the plan of the universe and depicts "how Mother Nature ordered the elemental chaos" and "how the first principles of things sprang apart each to his proper place" (I.248-51).[11] In another passage, Natura describes herself as the mother of all living things (*genetrix mortalibus*) (III.33-40). Claudian is a good example of a transitional usage of personification that equivocates between theology and poetic rhetoric. When Chaucer, in the late fourteenth century, uses Natura as a literary device in the *Parlement of Foules*, where Natura presides over a debate of birds on love and marriage, all traces of the metaphysical/Orphic theology are absent and the goddess is encapsulated in a purely allegorical narrative.

Edgar Knowlton gives a detailed account of the medieval literature on Natura and asserts that Plato's characterization of nature is the most important influence on the later allegorical figure.[12] George Economou's study, *The Goddess Natura in Medieval Literature*, documents the instances of the personification of nature that had become a common literary artifact in medieval literature. The *De Mundi Universitate* or *Cosmographia* of Bernard Silvestris, the *Anticlaudianus* and *De Planctu Naturae* of Alan of Lille, the *Roman de la Rose* of Jean de Meun, and Chaucer's *Parlement of Foules* all contain a general concept of the goddess Natura as the *Mater generationis*, the intermediary, subordinate, or vicar of God in the universe.[13] In the *Anticlaudianus* of Alan of Lille, Nature comes to the realization of its failure to produce a perfect man, only a soulless body. In Jean de Meun's *Rose*, Lady Reason and Natura are personified characters. Knowlton discusses these and other instances, such as Jean de Hauteville (1185) and Chaucer who 200 years later refers to the works of Bernard Silvestris as though they were familiar to scholars and literati of his day.[14] Natura assumes a central position in the mid-twelfth century within the intellectual setting of the school of Chartres in the works of Bernard Silvestris and Alan of Lille. Economou describes the Christian vision of the universe as based on the conviction that the natural and moral order of the universe as a harmonious whole participates in divine reality and is a microcosm. In the later Christian medieval contexts, Natura retains a role as *pronuba* of earthly marriages and in Alan of Lille's *De Planctu Naturae* and Chaucer's *Parlement of Foules* she appears an intermediary between man and God. *De Planctu*

Naturae and *Anticlaudianus*, Economou points out, are the seminal works in which the goddess Natura receives her essential characterization within a Christian context. Economou also points out that the concept of nature was threatening to Christians who "took measures to place definite limitations on the potency of nature which they accomplished largely through making nature the creation and servant of god." Bernard's poem influenced subsequent Natura poems of Alan, Jean de Meun, Chaucer, and even Spenser.[15] Although most of the medieval literature does not allow Natura the activity of ordering chaos, since that is a role for the *mens Dei* alone, in Bernard Silvestris's *De Mundi Universitate*, Noys (nous, intellect) pleads with Natura to give the chaotic state of matter the shape of order.[16]

The *Cosmographia* or *De Mundi Universitate* was composed between 1145 and 1156. John Whitman calls it "one of the most spectacular cosmic narratives."[17] Scholars have debated whether Bernard's concept of Natura in this work is essentially pagan or Christian. It is clearly influenced by Neoplatonist theories of emanation and the astronomical view of nature as a celestial generative principle.[18] Etienne Gilson complains that it espoused a dualism of God and matter, but Silverstein insists that Bernard does not believe in the eternity of matter (Bernard does not refer to *creatio ex nihilo*).[19] Silvestris's figure of Natura follows the template seen before in Neoplatonist accounts. As Knowlton describes it, there is God removed, Nous as divine intelligence, a primeval chaos, and Natura (the goddess) as the principle of life presiding over matter and awaiting the application of order before proceeding with the material creation.

The *Cosmographia* opens before the beginning of time when Natura appeals to Noys, (divine providence), on behalf of Silva, the material of created life, which yearns to come into existence. Noys then creates the earth, fills it with its flora and fauna, and charges Natura with the task of invoking Urania, who imparts celestial reason, and Physis, the principles of physical life, to the lesser universe, charging Natura with the task of joining body and soul to create mankind (I.iv.32).[20] Natura acts as an intermediary between the world, soul, being, and becoming. In the second book, Natura joins the body formed by Physis to the soul provided by Urania, connecting the earthly with the heavenly, the divine with the material.[21] Economou points out that the major figures, Noys, Natura, Urania, and Physis, are all personified abstractions but limited to prosopopoeia (the attribution of speech). Their physical presence is the logical extension of the ability to speak and move. There is no description of Natura's looks. In this sense, these might be limited to personifications and allegorical literary devices, rather than providing a new mythology per se. It is interesting to note that Silva or *hyle* (matter) is described in Natura's opening speech as a mass discordant with itself (*sibi disonia massa*), formless (*informa chaos*), turbulent (*turbida*), and "longing" for form and cultivation.[22]

Chaucer's use of Natura in the *Parlement of Foules* does not have the metaphysical implications of the usages mentioned above but illustrates that the goddess had become a figurative presence and a matter of common usage in scholarly and literary circles.[23] Hadot, whose work on the veil of Isis will be discussed below, identifies the many depictions of Artemis/Isis in the allegorical iconography of Nature in later centuries.

The Veil of Isis

Athena was known for her *peplos* (a tubular draping body-length garment that fell in folds and was typical attire for women in ancient Greece during the classical period). During the Panathenaea, an annual festival of great importance, a new robe was woven for the cult statue of Athena and she was presented with a new *peplos* of saffron-yellow during a procession of great pomp and circumstance. Homer (*Od.* 15.250) and Hesiod (*Th.* 381) describe goddesses as "saffron-robed."[24] Lamberton points out that Athena's garments symbolize both her transcendent activity (the *peplos* of *Iliad* 5.734) and her providential activity (the *chiton* of *Iliad* 8.385).[25] Book 6 of the *Iliad* alludes to the festival where Athena is given cloth for her *peplos*. Traditionally, it was related to the battle of the gods with the giants, while later, in Proclus, it was related to the rivalry in the cosmos between matter and form. Athena's *peplos* becomes symbolic when associated with concealment, the secrets of nature. When the Presocratic Heraclitus states that nature loves to hide, he calls upon lovers of the logos to uncover her secrets. This famous phrase invites the future scientist to raise the curtain hiding nature and expose her secrets by mathematics or science. In the more mystical traditions, this is considered to be a dangerous mission. Salvation must be in line with Providence, not Fate, since fate is associated with blind and passionate nature. Nature can lead one to dissipate and turn away from spiritual purification. The goddess who hides her "body" behind a veil or garment, then, is shielding the spiritual seeker from direct exposure.

Pierre Hadot's *The Veil of Isis: An Essay on the History of the Idea of Nature* supplies a history of this connection. From its roots in Heraclitus' famous statement ("Nature loves to Hide") to the metaphor of veiling and unveiling, the idea of nature as a woman to be undressed has persisted. The veiled image of nature as Isis or Artemis appears across a range of 2,500 years of philosophy and literature and in all genres from the late antique Isis aretalogies to the German Romantics. In the eighteenth to early nineteenth century, for example, nature as many-breasted Artemis, veiled or unveiled, appears in engravings, in the work of figures such as Karl Leonard Reinhold, in Viennese freemasonry, Schiller's poetry, and so on. Ralph Cudworth, an eighteenth-century Cambridge Platonist, interprets the veil that covers the goddess as a symbol of the distinction between outer and inner, "something Exterior and Visible" covering "something Hidden and Recondite, Invisible and Incomprehensible to Mortals." He compares it to the description that God makes of himself to Moses in the Bible (Moses will only be able to see his back parts, but never his face).[26]

Plutarch reports that at Sais, the seated statue of Athena, whom they identified with Isis, bears this inscription: "I am all that has been, that is, and that shall be, no mortal has yet raised my veil (*peplos*)" (*De Iside* 354c). Proclus's version of this, commenting on *Timaeus* 21E, is "That which is, that which shall be, that which was, I am that. No one has raised my tunic (*chiton*). The fruit I have engendered is the sun [Horus]." Hadot tells us that, in Plutarch's view, Isis is the feminine aspect of nature for the Logos leads her to receive all forms and all figures.[27] The veil of Isis is an enactment of the hidden secrets of nature and has a relation to the general issue of esotericism and to the genres of allegorical interpretation and inspired symbolism. The preservation of classical mythology through these methods is predicated upon the conviction that the transcendent world is inaccessible to mortals and can only be accessed by myth. Theurgy and prayer, hymns and votive offerings are direct ways to access the hidden world of divinity. Interpreting texts as though they were "veils" that conceal their true meaning is another avenue to hidden truth. The Platonic tradition, for the most part, valorizes "reason" and logos as the highest level of thought. For the later Platonists, the idea that there is a cryptic and hidden reality, which is inaccessible and even forbidden for mortal minds, is a different matter. It comes to be represented by the figure of a veiled female deity. Porphyry's cautionary tale of the philosopher Numenius, who unveiled the mysteries of Eleusis by interpreting them rationally, illustrates this idea. He dreamt that the goddesses Demeter and Kore, or in Latin, Ceres and Proserpina, were prostituting themselves dressed as courtesans, in front of a house of ill repute. When he asked them what happened, they replied that this occurred because they had been torn violently from the sanctuary of their modesty and delivered over to all who passed by. This scenario encapsulates an enduring image of how rational discourse can violate the secrets of nature. In the eyes of the philosophers, the mysteries of Eleusis contained secret teachings on Nature.[28] Hadot points out that Neoplatonism also treated the hidden or veiled idea of nature as an inferior form of being which has to wrap itself up in corporeal forms.

Isis survives the medieval age of allegory and the demise of female deity in Christian theology and makes a reappearance in the Enlightenment, as nature whose veil represents all the mysteries that nature holds. Hadot tells us that at the beginning of the sixteenth century, there appears a type of allegory in which nature is represented in conformity with the ancient model of Artemis of Ephesus but can also be linked to Isis. The figure is of a female whose head bears a crown and a veil. She possesses numerous breasts and a lower body that is enclosed in a tight sheath on which one sees representations of various animals. Raphael's 1508 fresco of the Stanza della Segnatura in the Vatican places Nature as Artemis on the two supports of the throne of philosophy. Niccolo Tribilo in 1529, in the Chateau de Fontainebleau, depicted various animals nursing at Nature's breasts. Hadot suggests that the influence on these depictions was the discovery of Nero's famous Domus Aurea, decorated with Artemis of Ephesus. Hadot gives many other examples of the identification of Nature with Artemis of Ephesus in collections of drawings in emblem books of the time depicting Artemis of Ephesus similarly, and relates this to the fusion of Artemis and Isis as a result of the common imagery.[29] The notion of concealment, related to a goddess, plays over and over in the history of ideas. It can be found in the enlightenment philosopher Kant in his *Critique of Judgment* where he says, "One has perhaps never said anything more sublime or expressed a thought in a more sublime fashion than in the inscription on the temple of Isis (Mother Nature): 'I am all that is, that was, and that will be, and no man has lifted my veil.'"[30] Hadot claims that the unveiling of Artemis comes to a close at the end of the nineteenth/early twentieth century when unveiling loses its meaning as the revelation of nature's secrets. According to Hadot, a reading of the gods of mythology, for the medieval, was metaphorical. In the Renaissance, these depictions represented the incorporeal forces that animate the universe. Following this into modern philosophy, Hadot later finds it possible to equate the secrets of nature to the mystery of being.

Esotericism has to do with the figure of concealment and revelation, and the *peplos* of the goddess is a trope transposable to religion. Halbertal rightly points out, "Our ontology and epistemology is, so to speak, in a grip of the 'depth metaphor.'" We discover or uncover the underlying assumption. Esotericism is a radical version of this construction and privileges the secret and the hidden existentially and ontologically. Heidegger's conception of truth (*alêtheia*) as an emergence from obscurity is an exemplary case of the centrality of disclosure and the privileged position of the hidden in a metaphysical setting. Heidegger's "mystery of being" may inherit the tropic essence of the idea of secrets of nature. Jan Assmann also discusses Leonhard Rheinhold, a Kantian, taught at Jena and Kiel from 1787 to 1823 and published a Masonic treatise. He espoused the Egyptian origin of Mosaic Law and was an Egyptophile. Interestingly, he equates a Hebrew source, the Torah's "I am who am" with the inscription on the veiled statue at Sais in service of his thesis regarding the hidden name Jehovah.[31]

Nature and the Divine Female

The above histories show once again that a deeply ingrained relation to ancient myth, to Platonism, and to Pythagorean oppositions pervades Western culture. These sources contribute to the deeply entrenched practice of referring to nature as feminine and the feminine as nature. One outcome of this deeply embedded cultural practice is the dichotomy between nature and reason, mature and culture as gendered. The conflating of nature/female, reason/male constitutes one of the prevalent binary oppositions that has led, in the case of some feminist literature, to a plethora of theory and writing. The goddess revival on the part of popular goddess movements, as well, has relied on this bifurcation, associating the male with removed and unresponsive "reason" and female with the warmer earthly qualities associated with nature. In the service of reversing the valuation of reason as "male" and superior, and to award equality if not primacy to the allegedly "female" qualities, this approach preserves the same mythology that it seeks to undercut. The ideology held by those who promulgate this reversed binary holds to the idea that there should be value related to embodiment and to nature in opposition to the presumed detached and otherworldly values held by philosophy and theology.

Paul Reid-Bowen raises this generalization to the level of metaphysics in his doctoral thesis, now book, *Goddess as Nature: Towards a Philosophical Thealogy*. Femaleness is seen as inseparable from the natural world and nature is conceived as sacred. In Chapter 3 of Reid-Bowen's book, he presents a the*a*logy in which the goddess is seen as nature. All processes in nature are related to female embodiment and female functions, such as generativity and ontological transformation. In goddess feminism, he claims, the "processes of emergence, generativity and transformation are used to originate, organize and relate to the whole of nature." He examines feminist models of the cave, the cauldron, and the cosmogonic womb, brought in to support the orgiastic and pantheistic concept of the goddess as Nature. He relates this to cycles and processes in the life of nature and even death as a return to earth. Cycles of birth-death and rebirth are important in his view, as are the wildness, fecundity, and generativity of the goddess.[32] Nature in this model is divine. This, he claims, leads to ecofeminist practices which regard nature as out of the limits of patriarchal control and hence politically subject to feminine respect, preservation, and a sound ethical ecological philosophy. Kune Biezeveld, in a review of Reid-Bowen's book, remarks on the author's assumption of a self-evident link between femaleness and nature, as if it were not to be questioned. He asks, "Does this link, at the end, not confirm the binary oppositions we so eagerly want to leave behind?"[33] The revival of Natura in her contemporary posture as an ecofeminist super-heroine incorporates the gender binary and exploits very time-worn myths. Activist politics and informed political agendas that support sustainability and other ecological important ideals and programs can stand on their own without gender essentialist concepts of nature. An association with nature and with the goddesses is exemplified in the following quote from Charlene Spretnak, who cites several ecofeminist classics of the 1970s and '80s.[34]

> Sophia is the wisdom of a body and mind joined in sensitive response to and dance with the wisdom of Gaia, the earth. Both Sophia and Gaia are Greek words of feminine gender. They link us to the goddess figures of the ancient Middle East, Europe, China and South Asia as well as the Americas. That the earth has traditionally been imaged as feminine provides a clue to the connection between the oppression of the earth and the oppression of women that began in earnest with the rise of patriarchal religion and culture some six to seven thousand years ago.

The fact that Gaia was capable of arranging for the castration of Ouranos, or gave birth to monsters, and other unnatural occurrences, apparently does not distract, here, from her earth mother persona. In fact, the ramifications of sticking to female/nature essentialism denigrate reason and nature at the same time. The binary opposition nature/reason itself is biased not only toward reason but toward nature itself. In its symmetries, chemistry, biology, and physical laws, nature displays an intelligence and beauty that are not simply a matter of reproductive fecundity, but must be associated with intelligence. Its majesty, free of gender, does not seek personification by Sophia, Zeus, Natura, or any other mythological gender-specific association.

Wisdom

Sophia is one of the most powerful and intractable images of the goddess to appear in literature. Athena, the goddess of wisdom in the earliest Greek texts, and Sophia in the wisdom literature of Ancient Judaism, Gnosticism, and many other places conflate in what is a persistent perennial icon of theological and rhetorical history, right up to the present day. Sophia can be found in Hellenistic Platonism, Neoplatonism, Gnosticism, and Orthodox and Esoteric Christianity. She is the Gnostic goddess of wisdom still adumbrated by modern Neopaganism, new age groups, and those that promulgate goddess spirituality. She has inspired architecture, as in the famous church of Hagia Sophia. She was the cosmic figure admired by the twelfth-century St Hildegard of Bingen in her writings, and the mystic figure featured in Jacob Boehme's sixteenth-century German Christian mysticism. Russian Sophrology in the work of Vladimir Solovyov (1853–1900), Nikolai Berdyaev (1874–1948), and Sergei Bulgakov (1871–1944) makes Sophia central to their writings. The Eastern Orthodox Church makes Holy Wisdom equivalent to the divine Logos who became incarnate in Jesus Christ. Feminist concerns in religious, biblical, sociocultural, and literary studies are responsible for a renewed attention to a feminine figure personifying philosophy and wisdom.

Athena, the goddess of wisdom, personifies the kind of wisdom that uses reason wisely in the affairs of the polis and the universe. Traditionally, *sophos*, used by Plato in the *Symposium* as well as other places, is only one among several terms connected with intelligence and reason (*nous* is the highest form of intuitive knowing and *epistêmê* is a form of understanding connected with science and learned knowledge). *Sophos* is closer to *sôphrosunê* (prudence) and not exactly in the same sort of radical opposition to nature as the higher forms of intellect. Wisdom is a virtue in most classic sources and not a transcendent intellectual entity. If there is any "political" issue here, it concerns the personification of wisdom qua female, as possibly secondary to the philosophical "truth," which resides in an inaccessible and transcendent domain. In the Hebrew wisdom literature and the Bible, *Sophia* is an attribute of the divine but not the highest aspect of divinity. Generally, the female personification Sophia, or a Sophia-type figure, is an ambassador or deliverer of truth, or wisdom, to creatures of this earthly realm, but she is not reason itself. In this sense, she has inherited the second-century two-world ontology: the source of wisdom is transcendent and male; the messenger and disseminator or practitioner is female. A similar pattern is to be found in the signifier "Shekhinah," the Gnostic Sophia and other personified divinities designated female and secondary to the primary source of being.

Louise Derksen, in her preface to Wendy Hellerman's book *The Feminine Personification of Wisdom,* suggests that feminists ask to what extent the allegoric descriptions of women as Sophia are an affirmation of the strength and power of women and to what extent this portrayal means that women are objectified and made passive objects of the male desire for the virtues that they represent.[35] Barbara Newman raises the issue of the ontological status appropriate to allegorical feminine personifications. Are they to be thought of as angels? Objects of vision or epiphany? Deities? Human? Or just a literary construct?[36] Newman's thesis is that the interlocking history of the medieval goddess, as she is characterized in the imaginative theology of the middle ages, was a significant phenomenon that should be studied in detail. She cites Hildegard of Bingen's Caritas, Alan of Lille's Natura, Christine de Pizan's Lady Reason, Boethius's Lady Philosophy, and the high Mariology of the late middle ages, as mentioned above.[37] Newman suggests that these figures possess an ontological status that goes beyond rhetorical tropes, personifications, or allegorical figures and prefers to call them "goddesses." Some may be treated simply as allegorical but others, she points out, add an "irreducible dimension to the spiritual universe" that is beyond personification or allegory. They are not survivals from paganism nor versions of the Great Goddess but utilized as "emanations of the Divine, mediators between God and the cosmos." She suggests further that they "deepened Christendom's concept of God."[38]

Hellerman studies four famous literary images: Penelope (Homer), Marcina (Gregory of Nyssa), Lady Philosophy (Boethius), and Beatrice (Dante): all personify *Sophia*. Although the texts that Hellerman chooses vary in character and genre, she unites all of them by an underlying theme of reason opposing the passions.[39] The status of a figure of speech like personification, as Newman suggests, seems to go beyond that of literary trope in some theological contexts. When *Sophia* is seen as the wisdom of Christ or God, it is a usage that is not purely textual embellishment but the use of allegory in the service of theology. Hellerman mentions Whitman's and Paxson's valuable work on allegory and personification to present a nuanced picture of these rhetorical figures.[40] Hellerman asks to what extent authors appeal to well-known social realities, aspects of feminine life, or the female body, in presenting Lady Philosophy as feminine. How does the feminine personification of philosophy relate to the role of women in Greek culture, or in the schools of philosophy? Her book provides ample evidence that the figure of Sophia, a successor to the omnipresent goddess of wisdom of antiquity, is alive and well in the cultural memory of succeeding centuries. As a literary icon, she lost the powers of a goddess but gained a persistent presence in the history of literature and ideas. Hellerman herself believes that Boethius's Lady Philosophy, for example, possesses "goddess status" in the powers she displays but reverts to philosophy when she argues logic, physics, and ethics.

Hellerman describes the symbolic use of Penelope, on the part of Stoic interpreters, to represent philosophy and enhance its status as a pursuit.[41] She turns to Bion of Borysthenes (*c.* 325–255 BCE), Aristippus of Cyrene (*c.* 435–350 BCE), founder of the Cyrenaic school of philosophy, and Ariston of Chios (fl. *c.* 250 BCE) who was influenced by the Stoic Zeno. These interpreters claim that the fact that in the *Odyssey* Penelope's suitors take advantage of willing servant girls, instead of the unattainable Penelope, is an allegory for students who do not give priority to the study of philosophy, but waste their time on less worthy studies like music or mathematics. Penelope represents philosophy itself and is the true object of desire. The Stoics, according to Hellerman, did not value, as did Plato, a study of music and mathematics as preparation for abstract thought. They prioritized First Philosophy. In a second allegorizing account, the focus is on Penelope's weaving, the main source being Eustathius's scholia on the *Odyssey*, in the twelfth century, which preserve an older allegory of weaving as a symbol of logic. Hellerman, then, finds the cultural memory of the goddess-like Sophia already in Homer's *Odyssey*, in Penelope qua Sophia and in her interpreters.

Helleman's choice of a figure like Macrina, a dedicated ascetic Catholic, as an exemplar of Sophia is another example of a larger-than-life embodiment of the wisdom figure in Christian literature. In *Vita S. Macrinae* and *De Anima et Resurrectione*, Gregory of Nyssa eulogizes his ascetic sister Macrina as an exemplar of Virtue (*aretê*). Here the status of this female figure is aggrandized and, for Hellerman, reminiscent of Sophia as an archetypical figure. She rose above nature and "beyond patience and courage" by not giving vent to "base womanish" lamentation. She is "reasoned" even when hearing of her brother's death. Her life was one of philosophical combat, her enemy being the passions and nature, raising herself to the heights of virtue through philosophy. Virtue as a unifying theme in other biographical writings of late antiquity can be compared for similar themes of martyrdom and asceticism (such as in the lives of Pythagoras by Iamblichus and Diogenes Laertius and Christian ascetic literature). Gregory, in this encomium to his sister, uses terminology characteristic of Stoicized Platonism. *Sôphrosunê* (self-control), for example, was one of the four key virtues for Zeno. For Plato, it meant subjecting lower parts of the soul to the higher rational part (*Rep.* 430E-32A, 442C).[42] Like Porphyry's Marcella, Eunapius' Sosipater, and Hypatia, Macrina was connected with aristocratic circles. Porphyry's *Letter to Marcella*, in which he advises her to "Flee all that is womanish in the soul, as though you had a man's body about you. Let reason direct all your impulses," expresses a similar zeitgeist. Macrina, as logos personified, conflates key ideas of Epicureans and Platonists, but they are now given a scriptural imprimatur related to the cosmic battle of good and evil in Christ's life. Hellerman relates the theme of the triumph of logos over pathos to an evocation of Christ's redemption on the cross. For Hellerman, Macrina is yet one among many memorialized Sophia figures here put in the service of Christian piety.

Hellerman confines her discussion of Boethius's *Consolation of Philosophy* to the opening sections, emphasizing the Neoplatonic context.[43] Lady Philosophy appears to Boethius in the gloomy dark of his prisoner's cell, where he was imprisoned in 525 for treason and astrology, or magic, and condemned to death. At times, she appears to be so tall that her head reaches right up to the heavens (1.pr1.2 [8-13]). Her garment, of the finest of threads, she wove herself in one indivisible piece. Commentators use this to associate her with Athena, goddess of wisdom, also said to have woven her own robe (*Iliad* 5.74). Hellerman provides a review of the scholarship surrounding the *Consolation*. While some scholars suggest the dialogue between the poet and the Lady is Menippean satire, a genre loosely connected with Cynic philosophy, she thinks that this does not do justice to the seriousness of the philosophical discussion of problems of providence, fate, and philosophical consolation for the experience of evil and injustice.

Dante created one of the most celebrated women in all of literature, Beatrice, in the fourteenth century. Like her predecessor Macrina of the fourth century, she is an advocate of "reason against passion." Unlike Macrina, she is an object of desire, pointing not to herself but to God as the ultimate source of wisdom. In the *Divine Comedy*, she is also a personification of Love, in which she differs from the other three figures treated in Helleman's book. In the service of the poet's quest, she discourses on many philosophical issues: the order of the universe, divine prudence, etc. Her role, as object of Dante's love and desire, guides him to "understand the divine cosmic love that moves the sun, the stars and planets and all human life."[44]

Hellerman reviews an extensive literature on Beatrice. She cites Charles Singleton, who associates Beatrice with Christ as "wisdom of God" (1 Cor. 1 and 2), using the advent sermons of Bernard of Clairvaux (who speaks of wisdom as the link between Christ and Grace).[45] Hellerman argues that Beatrice can also be understood as an analogy with Mary. Popular devotion to Mary, in hymnology and liturgy, statuary, and centers of worship in Dante's own time, supports this claim. Hellerman contends that "it is hard to avoid the conclusion that Dante would have considered Mary as the quintessential Lady Wisdom." The four figures that Hellerman treats in her book embody reason, as linked to virtue and nobility of character. This reinforces the idea that *Sophia* is a virtue rather than connected with theoretical reasoning. Macrina uses her *sôphrosunê* as a kind of prudence or temperance to keep passion under control and exercise reason, and Lady Philosophy is a messenger delivering insight into philosophical truths, while Beatrice is an intermediary and guide to the love of God. Hellerman links Lady Wisdom with Christological Logos theology.[46] Helleman's use of larger-than-life figures who are not goddesses emphasizes the continued presence of an aggrandized *sophia* as the inarticulate back story that influences literature but is unacknowledged. The idea of an "unknown known" as a rhetorical influence is applicable to these examples: a cultural memory can operate outside the direct awareness of a literary author.

John Meyendorff traces the history of *sophia* in the Byzantine church. He points out that the frequent usage of *sophia* in this tradition, in the names of churches, in iconography, and in liturgy, is roughly based on the concept that *sophia* is the wisdom of Christ. The complexity of the usage, he suggests, is a combination of the philosophical wisdom of antiquity and the wisdom literature of the Jews fulfilled in Christ, "including even the former image of Athena, goddess of wisdom and protectoress of Athens and Constantinople."[47] Sophia became the permanent symbol of Christian truth in the Orthodox East. Justinian's well-known church, Hagia Sophia, and St. Sophia in Kiev are examples, as are the many icons that Meyendorff cites. In Greek patristic thought, the wisdom of ancient philosophy is fulfilled in Christ. The derivation from the canonical book of Proverbs, apocryphal and deuterocanonical books of wisdom, and Sirach also contributes to this usage. While the iconography is usually a feminine figure or angel, the theology is of a divine attribute, or energy, that is the perfect wisdom of God. Philotheos, for example, the patriarch of Constantinople (1353–54 and 1364–76), describes *sophia* as the "energy of the one and consubstantial trinity." The Paleologan Renaissance (the rule of the Byzantine empire by a family known as the Paleologoi, from 1260 to 1678) is a period in which wall paintings depicting Sophia proliferate. Meyendorff gives an example of the Novgorodian School where the female figure of wisdom is depicted with the inscription "Power and Wisdom of God" (the title of Christ in 1 Cor. 1:24).

Barbara Newman describes the liturgical identification of wisdom with Mary, with extensive citation of the literature, in her chapter (5) on "The Goddess Incarnate." Sapientia Mariology capitulates a tension between official dogmas in which Mary is the mother of God, but not divine, and epithets that suggest divinity without naming it as such. The entire vast subject of Sapientia Mariology, generally speaking, is the study of the figure of Mary which incorporates the epithets of the Sapiential books of the Bible and applies them to her. The church doctrine of *sedes sapientiae* is still today a branch of Catholic theology which elaborates on the idea of Mary as the "seat of wisdom." Newman points out that in the liturgical and exegetical tradition of the Catholic church, the term Sapientia vacillates between the manifestation of Christ's wisdom and identification with Mary, a "feminization of Christ" and/or a "divinization of Mary." "If Christ qua Sapientia is androgynous, Mary qua Sapientia is amphibious, with one foot in the official church and the other in more dangerous ground."[48] Newman mentions that there are countless allegorical poems and iconographic programs which deploy Sapientia. Romanesque frescoes and illuminated manuscripts also depict Mary as the seat of wisdom.[49]

Sophianic themes, interestingly, found a voice in the seventeenth century in the work of a German Christian mystic, Jacob Boehme (1575–1624). The Russian religious philosopher Nikolai Berdyaev has written a great deal about Boehme's "sophology." Boehme, a German Christian mystic, was a Lutheran Protestant with strong Catholic elements in his theology, akin to the Eastern Orthodox. He was influenced by Neoplatonism and was, in turn, a great influence on mystical movements of all sorts: Marianism, Christian theology, German Romantic philosophy, and on William Blake. He also influenced the poetry renaissance in Russia in the early twentieth century, particularly its Sophianic themes. Boehme, in many citations, made mention of the virgin Sophia as the pure, virginal, chasteness of man and the image and likeness of God in man. In a context which, Berdyaev points out, is based on the androgyny and bisexual male/female nature of man, the innate spiritual essence of man is the Virgin Sophia. The loss of Sophia, through sin, places man in eternal quest for her. Often quoted from Boehme's work is the phrase "the wisdom of God is an eternal Virgin" (*Die Weisheit Gottes ist eine ewige Jungfrau*).[50]

Boehme emphasizes androgyny as an aspect of Christ: "He was neither man nor woman, but rather a manlike Virgin (*er weder Mann nicht Werb war, sondern eine männliche Jungfrau*)" (*Mysterium Magnum* vol. V: 464). The virgin Sophia returns to earth in Mary, the Mother of God. Mary creates her immaculate virginity from the heavenly virgin, however, not from Eve or any earthly source. "The Virgin as a Godly power, is in Heaven" (vol. III: 119). The descent of the Heavenly Virgin into Mary is the waking of the Holy Spirit (vol. VI: 697). Berdyaev points out that this differs from Kabbalah where the second *sefirah*, *Chochma*, is Wisdom as theoretical reason, which is masculine, while the feminine element is *Binah*, practical wisdom. Boehme also influenced John Pordrage, the English mystic and theosophist of the seventeenth century, who wrote a book titled *Sophia*. Virgin wisdom, according to him, is an all-pervasive divine energy and mother of the soul. Earthly beauty, which he associated with Aphrodite, is the beauty of the cosmos, which has a feminine nature and is related to Sophia.

Vladimir Solovyov, a Russian philosopher, poet, and theologian influenced by Boehme, also emphasized Sophianic themes in his work. He had a widespread influence on the spiritual reawakening of early twentieth-century Russia.[51]

Conclusion

That the image of a goddess should survive the centuries, become entwined with Christian imagery, become an icon for nature during medieval and enlightenment eras, and feature in both academic and poetic discourse on nature and wisdom in almost every century once again, must be attributed to the power of cultural memory. Certainly the personification cum deification of nature and wisdom confirms the confluence, rather than the polarity, of *mythos* and *logos* and allows an appreciation of allegory as a means of conveying knowledge. Traces of the ancient goddesses, it seems, can be found in the "tropics" of every genre of discourse. In the following chapter, the full force of the connection between nature and gender will be shown to be fully exploited by twenty- and twenty-first-century texts. From Freud's description of the female as a "dark continent" to early feminist literature valorizing the female gender as somehow embodying nature, to the more sophisticated feminist literature that dismantles the nature/gender confluence, the reader will be brought into the present. He or she will discover that collective memory very often unacknowledged as such continues to play a role in our current world views.

11

New Mythologies of Gender: Feminists, Psychoanalysts, Epistemologists

Qualities such as movement, change, fluidity, reproductive fecundity, affinity to nature, and multiplicity constitute a "cultural code" that has been associated with female gender. These qualities in many contexts were elected to hold secondary status to the rest, intellectual attributes and unity associated with male gender. Given a mythological imprimatur by Hesiod's *Theogony,* this code was reinforced by the Pythagorean table of opposites and influenced Middle and late Platonism, medieval allegory, and the later history of ideas. There is an explanatory gap between biological essentialism (male and female physical differences) and cultural constructions. Recognizing that binary opposition in regard to gender is "mythic," itself a cultural construction, is enhanced by the examples that have been discussed here. Going back to ancient literature and philosophy has presented an opportunity to fill in the explanatory gap between biology and culture. It has shown how deeply entrenched in our reception history of ancient mythology, this opposition lies. Admittedly, ancient accounts of gender are complex and do not fall easily into binary oppositions, as Brooke Holmes has discussed in her book *Gender: Antiquity and Its Legacy*. Strong assertive women like Antigone and Athena, while outside of the norms for the culture, however, do not mitigate the mythology of binary opposition, especially since they are considered exceptions to the rule. The cultural code of binary oppositions in regard to gender has been ubiquitously present in the history of ideas and is operative even when it is not deliberately invoked. Understanding and acknowledging its omnipresence can help to identify the persistent myths that, as unexamined cultural memories, have permeated literature and scholarship. This "cultural code" has also contributed to the devaluation and oppression of women in society. In the service of changing the unjust overvaluation of presumed male attributes, current discussions have reversed this code to revalue female natural, fecund, intuitive sensitivities as antidotes to cultural biases toward rigid rationality, or have deconstructed the essentialist binary altogether.

The idea of the eternal female as a dark force of nature in the modern novel is further evidence that these binaries are a cultural code and connective. Thomas Mann, as Jan Assmann points out, discussed Magna Mater and the Queen of Heaven in an essay; Mann, Pär Lagerkvist, Nikos Kazantzakis, and Jacques Roumain are all modern novelists who exploit this mythology. Assmann comments, "Before Mary there is Isis, Ishtar, Inanna and ultimately all distinctions are blurred in the eternal feminine."[1] What is worthy of some attention as well is the fact that a twentieth-century discipline aspiring to be "scientific," namely psychology, could, without question, assume the oppositional gender binaries of ancient and medieval literature. Sigmund Freud, Carl Jung, and Jacques Lacan created powerful "myths" of psychological development for the twentieth century. Similarly, some feminist epistemologists holding to the highest standards of scholarship still aggrandize essentialist female attributes such as nature, caring, and the maternal body, claiming they are alternative ways of knowing that were disparaged in Western thought. A closer examination of gender binaries can show that they operate like other mythological paradigms and support ideologies which may, or may not, be shared by a universal community of scholars. Here I will focus on the legacy that gender binaries have contributed to twentieth-century psychoanalysts and feminist scholars, and also comment on how that is changing with the more current focus on decoding gender essentialism.

Psychoanalysis: A Mythology for the Twentieth Century

Sigmund Freud, Carl Jung, and Jacques Lacan supplied the twentieth century with rhetorical ideologies concerning psychological development that have been embraced enthusiastically in many quarters. With the proviso that mythology is unverifiable discourse, neither falsifiable nor affirmable, viewing the theories of psychoanalysis as mythical does not necessarily relegate them to the realm of fantasy. Myths can, as Plato realized, give us the ability to talk about matters inaccessible to prosaic discourse. What may be objectionable, however, is the credence given by these analysts to the "mythical" binary oppositions of gender as though they were scientifically verifiable truth rather than cultural constructions. Psychoanalytic theories have perpetuated gender oppositions, along with claims to veracity, that have insinuated themselves into the thought of many followers and critics. Sigmund Freud's inventive psychology provides very good examples of constructs that do not meet the criteria of scientific veracity but still claim attention. His terminology is a product of a creative innovation that has far surpassed, in expressivity, the abilities of his followers to interpret it other than literally. Freud was sophisticated enough to realize the fact that his own constructions were mythical, many of his coinages reified abstract nouns and some incorporated powerful Greek cultural myths, used uncritically in his creative efforts to develop a vocabulary for psychoanalysis. For Freud, ancient mythology captured a certain kind of truth and contained foundational narratives that could serve as allegories of unconscious memories and desires. Wittgenstein spoke of his theories as "Freud's fanciful pseudo-explanations" and characterized psychoanalysis as "powerful mythology."[2] He quoted Freud's well-known statement: "The theory of instincts is, so to say, our mythology." The Ego, Superego, Id (a Freudian triad), and the Unconscious are all "fictional" entities, structured in topographical figures of speech. These inventions are still in play for Freudians, who consider them to be heuristic as explanatory models for human behavior.

Christine Downing identifies what she calls Freud's "implicit polytheism" based on the fact that he finds it necessary to speak of *Eros* and *Thanatos*, of *Logos* and *Ananke*, and to use the names of the gods in order to identify certain categories of experience.[3] In his theories of civilization and culture, for example, he elevates the interplay between the gods Eros and Thanatos to one between cosmic principles that operate both in concert and in opposition. Freud was an artist in his own right and used literary contrivances in a sensitive and creative fashion. He needed to address features of the human psyche and behavior that no one else had identified. He was fascinated by the mythical figures of all ancient cultures, and his collection of figurines, including ones of Artemis, Athena, and Demeter, attests to his fascination with symbolic meaning. Athena was the sole piece that he smuggled out of Austria when he immigrated to England; in Vienna, it had been in the center of his desk. He commented on the sexual symbolism of the decapitated Medusa on Athena's shield as a symbol of female genitals (with the association of castration), the "terrifying genitals of the mother."[4] Freud's literary genius is evident in his large palette: he drew upon dreams, art, ancient myths, and ancient drama to augment theory. The ancient names of gods, for Freud, became signifiers for the elusive "forces" that he suggests are operating in civilization and in the human psyche.

Freud's narrative of female psychosexual development poses a mythical narrative all of its own. Penis envy, it claims, is an inevitable and universal factor in the female psyche and her renunciation of it is superseded by accepting the substitute of a child, which serves to resolve its impact. When viewed in the twenty-first century, this seems incredibly reductive, negating the primacy of the female desire for parenthood as a central source of psychological identity (as it could be for males as well). It is interesting that in the 1970s a feminist scholar, Marilyn Arthur, would interpret the *Hymn to Demeter* along these lines, ascribing to the narrative of psychoanalysis a hegemonic discourse in which Demeter's attitude toward Demophon (she wanted to immortalize him through fire) can be interpreted as a manifestation of penis envy.[5]

Christine Downing suggests that Freud knew that his project had a mythical quality. She quotes his 1932 letter to Einstein: "It may perhaps seem to you as though our theories are a kind of mythology. But does not every science come, in the end, to a kind of mythology like this? Cannot the same be said today of your physics?"[6] Freud, a master of linguistic coinage, easily gives names from mythology or literature to psychic structures and psychological complexes, as Downing points out. He uses mythical allusion unabashedly ("In the unconscious, as in the realm of the gods, nothing ever dies"). A topographic model, (creating pseudo-"regions" out of abstract nouns), a feature of myth, is exemplified by his tripartite construction: conscious, preconscious, and unconscious realms of experience. As discussed in Chapter 5, heaven and hell, or in the case of Greek mythology the earthly realm as opposed to the underworld, are indicative of mythical thinking. In a broad sense, the unconscious, preconscious, and conscious levels Freud posits are based on spatial metaphors. Freud evokes a female goddess in only one context, the imagery of a mother earth, who receives the male as if she were his lover, in death. He concludes: "It is in vain that the old man yearns after the love of a women as he once had it from his mother, the third of the Fates alone, the silent goddess of death, will take him into her arms."[7] Downing suggests, "Without the father, the masculine, the power of the mother goddess seems overwhelming." Longing for the feminine is associated with castration, passivity, and death. The Mother means the pull to the Id, the undifferentiated, to pantheism, not polytheism, to the chaotic and the undifferentiated indeterminate pre-phallic receptacle.

The idea of the female as possessing a castrated organ, a lack, an absence, similarly characterizes the feminine in terms of nothingness, structural breakdown, and diffusion. The myth of the longing for and envy of a penis, on the part of the desiring female, becomes the desire to possess the mythical absent organizer, the phallus. This is reminiscent of the mythical longing that was seen in Plutarch, the Gnostics, and other early literature, wherein the female goddess possesses the desire to unite with the higher male hypostases. Female goddess figures in this history desired to possess the male and transcend to a higher level of being and of intellectual structure, uniting soul to intellect. Penis envy, in line with this template, posits that the female desire is to possess phallic unity instead of female disruption, absence, and lack. Both the myth of the longing for a penis and the Platonic goddesses' wish to become one with the god are based on the devalued, secondary, less differentiated state of female being. Freud's narratives of desire and death, it seems, operate with the same gender opposition that associated goddesses with undifferentiated chaos and unbridled desire and the male before this seduction by death, associated with a more organized (phallic) distinctiveness. Freud admits that he does not know where to place female deities in the evolution of religion but acknowledges that at one time there may have been a "mother goddess" who preceded male deity: "I cannot suggest at what point ... a place is to be found for the great mother-goddesses, who may perhaps may have preceded the father-gods" (SE 13, 149).[8] Freud's assertion of the unknowability of women, calling woman a "dark continent," and his treatment of the female body as somehow formless or destroyed (castrated) are remarkably reminiscent of the cultural code of female indeterminacy, etc., that has held its grip on cultural memory.[9]

Carl Jung famously alleges a binary opposition associated with male and female that has assumed veracity among his followers as a universally present archetype, housed in the human psyche. The "anima," a principle that he confabulated and hypostatized, is central to his theory. This signifier has, in some contexts, been linked to the presumed Great Goddess of prehistory. Like Freud, Jung regards female deity as some sort of primordial, dark destiny, and warns: "It happens too easily that there is no returning from the realm of the mothers."[10] Archeologists, feminists, and psychotherapists who are influenced by Jung celebrate the "feminine principle" linked to elements such as the moon, mothering, and intuition, and selectively support these views with findings from archeology and anthropology. Jung's "collective unconscious" is widely known and an example of a "topography" which, unlike the Freudian model for the unconscious, takes on cultural and universal significance and is conceived to exert influence on psychic life. This region is the "site" of archetypes such as the 'Great Mother'. Adherents to the so-called goddess movement inspired by Maria Gimbutas follow Jung in claiming an original Great Mother goddess in early matriarchal societies based on this archetype. Anima and animus are operative archetypes that are repressed according to gender. The animus, or male archetype, is found in the unconscious of the female, while the anima is found in that of the male. The anima consists of the feminine psychological qualities that a male may possess, appears in dreams, and influences men in their interactions with females. Jung proposed that there are four types of anima development: Eve, Helen, Mary, and Sophia. Mythology plays a large role, according to Jung, in creating a man's anima, as it is an inherited albeit unconscious collective image of a woman. Eve has to do with the male awakening to the female as an object of desire, with intuition, creativity, spirituality, and emotionality. The Mary archetype has to do with virtue on the part of the perceiving male. Sophia allows the fully developed personification of wisdom, the female as an object that possesses both positive and negative qualities. Demeter and Persephone, for Jung, are representative of the archetypes of mother and maiden, figures that operate in the unconscious of societies and individuals, dreams and myths.[11] A male will obtain psychological health if he gets in touch with his anima. In relationships, a man may project his anima onto a given woman, in the alluring form of a Circe, or a Calypso, etc.[12] Jung creates his own "modern" mythology conflated with the ancient prototypes of early literature. The archetypes encapsulate the meanings that had been supplied by the very ancient myths capitulated in Hesiod and Homer. A Jungian might interpret ancient myths themselves as manifestations of anima and animus, by way of circular reasoning, the mythical figures are emblematic of anima and animus. For Jung's followers, anima and animus are a hegemonic engine of interpretation.

Object relations theory, a revisionist psychoanalytic theory, as opposed to Freud and his Oedipal period of development, focuses on earlier mother-child relations and is also a well-worn interpretive framework for some contemporary scholars. Nancy Chodorow, combining object relations theory with sociology and cross-cultural anthropology, interprets the *Hymn to Demeter* as a narrative of gender identity in the pre-Oedipal phase of development. While the child is in a symbiotic state with the mother, separation from the mother represents the first phase of individuation. Genders differ in how they negotiate this phase of development. Male identity requires separation from the mother at the "phallic" stage, whereas mature female selfhood requires continued identity with the mother. The adult female, consequently, has more fluid ego boundaries than the adult male and her identity is more fundamentally structured by intimate relations with others. Of course, as Helen Foley acknowledges in her discussion of Chodorow's essay, one must "beware of inappropriately imposing anachronistic readings on ancient texts."[13] Nevertheless, she too finds object relations theory illuminating as it involves an exploration of the psychology of mother-daughter relations, as opposed to the mother-son focus in Freudianism. Demeter/Persephone, and their bond and forced separation, constitutes an especially notable myth in a traditional society such as that of archaic Greece. Luce Irigaray has discussed the Demeter/Persephone relationship and argued that patriarchy (Zeus as enabler and Hades as abductor) functions to separate women from each other and to suppress the transmission of maternal genealogy.[14] Symbiotic mother-daughter bonds, such as are mythologized in the *Hymn*, are essential to women's autonomy and identity. Chodorow's suggestion that the "fluid" nature of female ego boundaries that goes along with this symbiosis recalls the indeterminate, chaotic, "watery" connotations associated with certain ancient goddesses and later binaries.[15] (Fluidity, interestingly, has become a term that appears in feminist discourse since Luce Irigaray's essay "The Mechanics of Fluid.")

Lacanian thought has entered the discourse of literary studies, feminist literature, film studies, and social theory, to name a few of the academic disciplines it impacted. It is a psychanalytic theory that blatantly demonstrates the survival of binary opposition according to gender. Lacan posits the idea that the unconscious is structured like a language and the relationship between the Symbolic and the Subject supplies a framework for understanding the play of unconscious desire. Masculine and feminine are not biological essences but instead symbolic positions. The narrative of development that he advances posits that the Symbolic is the pre-established world of culture, law, and language into which a child is born. It is equivalent in some way to patriarchy and the "phallic signifier." This phallic signifier, within the familial context, becomes the first point of social differentiation and hence also the first point of sexual difference and identity.[16] The figure of the Father, referred to as "the Name of the Father," delivers the child from the realm of the Imaginary to that of the Symbolic. It is the first imposition of law, against incest, and disrupts the symbiotic bond with the mother as an object of desire. The desire for the mother, who herself holds the phallus of the father as her object of desire, catapults the child from the desire for the mother to the Name of the Father as a substitution.[17] Lacan's theory proposes a normative narrative of psychological development. The child assumes that the father satisfies the mother's desire and possesses the phallus and as such is an object of desire. Again, reminiscent of its archaic prototype, the desire of the female is to unite with the male to achieve a higher status. An unexamined assumption is that the female or child is powerless without attaining an identification with the male. The desire for the mother that is an essential piece of the Freudian Oedipal complex is reworked by Lacan to involve an element of substitution of one signifier, the desire of the mother, for another, the Name of the Father. When the children achieve this latter state, they enter the symbolic order. Through the Name of the Father, the phallus is installed as a critical organizer and signifier: theory, a reified "sign" of principal significance. (There was an Egyptian festival where the phallus was carried around, and Lacan's revival of its primacy in his conceptual apparatus somehow evokes this association.) Lacan has his own triad: the Imaginary, the Symbolic, and the Real. The father with whom the child identifies in the mirror stage of development integrates the Real and the Imaginary. With the Symbolic stage, the child now enters a phase of development also known as the Name of the Father or the Law of the Father (we can recall here Zeus as father of deities symbolizing law and order!). This presumes that the feminine order is commensurate with the pre-phallic child, is less differentiated, and is superseded by a more organized stage of development. The Lacanian narrative is an allegory of the development of the human psyche and its cultural equivalents. It embodies gender essentialism of a cultural memory that has survived the centuries. The mythical phallic/paternal order is the social, symbolic, and rational in human culture, and the mother signifies a shadowy realm of pre-phallic undifferentiated desire. It is curious that so many feminist scholars have seen it as a less pejorative way of making distinctions pertaining to psychological development than Freud's. There is no intrinsic necessity for the "Symbolic" to be associated with the male in these ideas, any more than it was so for nature to be associated with the goddess, or logic with the male, in ancient thought. As Derek Hook explains:

> The notion of the phallic signifier has, without doubt, been a profound and challenging theoretical contribution of Lacanian psychoanalysis. It has been one that a number of feminists have been at the forefront of advancing as a means of understanding sexual difference in symbolic and non-biological terms, apart from the dubious trappings of the idea of "penis envy."[18]

Some feminists are less than enthusiastic concerning whether Lacanian theory is really an advance over Freudian psychology. Luce Irigaray, for example, addresses the Lacanian constellation in *The Sex Which Is Not One*, arguing that Lacan's historical master-signifier of the symbolic order—the phallus—is a projection of the male body. Elizabeth Grosz is concerned that by elevating the phallus to the privileged position that Lacan accords it, the patriarchal gestures of Freud have simply been repeated at a higher level; that a sign of masculine privilege has come to be over-valued such that male dominance is implicitly naturalized.[19] Hook raises the problem of the phallus as a "privileged signifier" and asks whether psychoanalysis simply extends patriarchy or whether it diagnoses and explains it.[20] The implicit assumption of Lacan's account is that the "phallus" somehow signifies something more organized and advanced in the staging of human development while earlier stages are less differentiated, more "primitive" and unstructured. Even if these stages are a reality of some sort, there does not seem to be any intrinsic reason for the more advanced, symbolic stage to be male.

Julia Kristeva, adopting Lacanian discourse, equates the feminine with the semiotic, or the pre-Oedipal, as opposed to the symbolic. The father of personal prehistory or pre-Oedipal father understood as the mother's desire for the phallus intervenes at a crucial time of a child's life (fourth month) in order to effectuate the first preliminary split within the void of primary narcissism. Maternity as the power of life is on the margins of the symbolic order and trapped in the semiotic *chôra*/receptacle. For Kristeva, the notion of Plato's *chôra* evokes the space connected to the maternal body which is the origin of the semiotic. She describes the semiotic as "a *distinctiveness* admitting of an uncertain and indeterminate articulation … [which] does not yet refer to a signified object." *Chôra* is "anterior to naming, to the One, to the father and consequently maternally connoted." "The symbolic, as opposed to the semiotic, is the inevitable attribute of meaning, sign, and the signified object for the consciousness of Husserl's transcendental ego." (By this, she means an object for a judging, objectifying subject.) Poetic semiotic language, on the other hand, is related to the body as self, to the maternal and thus to a semiotic subject, one that would be "a subject-in-process." Science, she suggests, tries to reduce the semiotic component as much as possible. The semiotic, on the other hand, allows wandering or fuzziness into language and hence is potentially creative.[21] These two orders lead to two types of writing: masculine writing, which is linear, rational, and objective, governed by rules of syntax, and feminine writing, which emphasizes rhythm, sound, color, and so on.[22] In language, Kristeva "semiotic" order subverts the symbolic order of discourse. In the semiotic space, men and women would both have access to a pre-symbolic experience of maternal functions. (We are reminded here of the Orphic egg, Plato's *chôra*, Pythagorean indeterminateness, as incubators of later developments.) Kristeva's work is complex and does not, strictly speaking, preserve a binary opposition according to gender. The bifurcation, however, between the symbolic and semiotic does suggest traces of this gender code. The semiotic is tied to the pre-Oedipal mother-oriented developmental state, while the symbolic is still associated with more organized male attributes.

In her book *Powers of Horror: An Essay on Abjection*, Kristeva gives the example of bodily fluids as representing non-objects that are banished in the course of ego development. Non-objects are related to the maternal body which needs to be excluded so that self and other can establish a true dyadic relationship as opposed to the undifferentiated material space of the semiotic chora. In her book *Black Sun*, abjection and melancholia are related to semiotic drives and rhythms related to early maternal object relations. Being in touch with this dimension results in negative states such as abjection and melancholia which are the source of semiotic creativity. Kristeva differs from Hélène Cixous and Luce Irigaray in that she ascribes these differences only in relation to language and meaning and not to essentialist feminine identity. As Toril Moi puts it in her introduction to *The Kristeva Reader*, for Kristeva the feminine is only thinkable within the symbolic and therefore is necessarily subject to the law.[23] Kristeva's search for the origins for another kind of discourse that is not subject to the masculine symbolic rational language characteristic of Western thought, however, takes her to mother and infant symbiosis prior to law and language and dependent on a bodily maternal phase of developmental prehistory. Suk Oh points out further that "Kristeva's theory supports the notion that the material body is a site for dissolution of Western dualism."[24] Kristeva's distinction between the symbolic and semiotic, ascribing the former to the masculine and phallocentric and the latter to the maternal and female body, then, does fall under the compass of the cultural "code" of gender binaries discussed here.[25] The following quote certainly documents the binary opposition connected to gender implicit in the Kristeva narrative:

> Phallo-logocentric thought is founded on a repression of the semiotic and maternal body, whereas the semiotic order is cyclical and eternal, the symbolic order represents linear and sequential time.[26]

The Recurrence of the Same: Materialism and the Feminine

The goddess Nammu, in the earliest stories of creation, the Babylonian-Assyrian theogonies, is a personification of the subterranean waters. Hesiod's goddesses have similar epithets. Artemis, goddess of the wild and nature, was worshipped near swamps and lagoons. According to a Stoic interpretation, even the primordial Hesiodic Chaos was meant to signify an aboriginal liquid substance. It is notable that the first "earth mother," Gaia, somehow follows immediately upon a mysterious, preexisting chaos. In Chapter 4, it was noted that contemporary feminist scholars have focused on Plato's *hypodochê,* or *chôra,* considering it one of philosophy's rare invocations of a female gender-related construct. In this coinage, the Hesiodic legacy of a mythical Chaos conflates with Gaia and other goddesses' maternal fecundity, providing a probable influence on Plato's coinage of a world-producing, life-producing receptacle characterized by him as a mother or nurse of becoming. It also provides early documentation that what is female is associated with fluidity, womblike receptivity, as opposed to what is male being associated with law, order, and unity. One can be impressed anew by the power of cultural memory, then, and its hypnotic hold on the history of ideas, when we encounter some contemporary feminist theory that incorporates a terminology reminiscent of these binaries. Brooke Holmes has specifically examined ancient sources in relation to the sex/gender binary and has focused on the question of nature and the material in ancient thought. She discusses Judith Butler's work where the identification of female and the material is re-examined, relating its source to metaphysics.[27] Butler, she says, objects to the "[l]egitimacy of the material body as the bedrock of gender identity." Holmes also points out how for Marilyn Arthur and Helen Foley, and others, who have taken up the myth of Demeter and Persephone, there "[i]s a universal female subject who is allied with fertility, nature and other women against an aggressive sexually invasive and destructive male force." She mentions that "[t]he very presupposition of such a subject has been sharply challenged within feminism and gender studies." While it is not possible to take up the vast literature on these discussions here, the so-called "new materialism" described by Elizabeth Stephens in her article "Feminism and New Materialism: The Matter of Fluidity" documents the continued interest, for and against, in relating materialism, fluidity, bodily existence to feminist concerns. Luce Irigaray's article "The Mechanics of Fluids" is an influential essay in the emergence of feminist new materialism.[28] This prototype is not always negative via reducing the feminine to the indeterminate but is also used as a positive life-giving counter-image to the rigid logic that has been associated with masculine being.

Emanuela Bianchi's nuanced and complex study of *hypodochê/chôra* as the "errant feminine" in Plato is an example of the use to which it has been put in relation to sexual difference. Bianchi sees Plato's account of the receptacle as a positive contribution to better articulate feminine existence. As opposed to men portrayed as fully reasoning beings, she suggests the receptacle can be understood "not merely as a violent abstraction and expropriation of feminine corporality, but also critically reapproached as offering a fecund and generative philosophical terrain in which a feminist rethinking of corporality, spatiality, figurality, temporality, and life may take (its) place."[29] She claims that *chora* "[i]nvites us to think through what it may mean to be in space, to be there as a woman, to the role, place, shape, and construction of the feminine within sexual difference."[30] Bianchi invokes Irigaray's "liminality," bordering between inside and outside, topological, carnal (in terms of Irigaray's "two lips" as a metaphor for vaginal lips/mouth and their meaning on a symbolic level as opposed to rigid phallus and its associations), as particularly feminine and analogous to Plato's receptacle. Bianchi elaborates a view of *hypodochê/chôra* relating it to a space (*chôra*), based on its capacity for separating, defining, and differentiating (as is indicated by the relation of *chôra* to *chorizô*, the Greek verb "to separate"), and at the same time to its "indeterminate incalculable movement, a ceaseless receiving/giving without arrival, without possession property or ownership, erasing and eluding our attempts to determine the truth." Bianchi relates *chôra* to the shaking oscillating motion linked to women's labor of winnowing grain, and at the same time to Kristeva's view of *chôra* as a site of ordering, an "extremely provisional articulation constituted by movements and their ephemeral states."[31] Bianchi sees value in the traits that are *chora* related and goes on to explore its ethical implications. Calling upon Emmanuel Levinas, in *Otherwise Than Being or beyond Essence*, she relates them to his concept of "ethical alterity," "a chiasmatic relation to the other that is abyssal, mobile, that both gives and receives, that articulates self and other, that discloses other in self, sans an exterior vantage point." Presumably this associates female interior space, with its potential to make the boundaries between self and other fluid, to Levinas's emphasis on the "other" in his theories concerning the primacy of ethical relatedness. Drawing on the work of Drucilla Cornell, she valorizes the indeterminacy and mobile generality of the receptacle/*chôra* as "a zone of creativity where dwelling, living being as becoming, is always already taking place" and which is presumably resistant to the law of the polis.[32] While for Plato, the formless receptacle must be subdued by intellectual parameters for the creation of the physical world to take place; for Bianchi, this is ameliorated by her idea that *hypodochê*, as opposed to *chôra*, carries with it a sense of structure.

The Proliferation of Gender Vocabulary

While the term "phallocentrism" was originally coined by Ernest Jones to refer to Freud's phallic stage of development, this term has been picked up by some scholars to characterize Western culture as biased toward masculine traits, presumably reason and a rigid discursive logic. Western thought, by this reasoning, excludes or marginalizes the feminine, as Rudavsky describes, and thus can be characterized as both "phallocentric" and "anti-female."[33] The term attaches to the privileging of logos and signifies a patriarchal agenda that is thought to exert a power over Western thought and determine culture as rigidly rationalistic. In his essay "Plato's Pharmacy," Derrida expands the term "phallocentric" to phallo-logo-centric, making it an explicit code word that came to be widely deployed. "Phallologocentricity" henceforth refers to male-gendered Western thought in which a determinate logic prevails. Its opposing category is one version or another of a feminine and more indeterminate mode of truth, which somehow emerges from embodiment. French feminists who utilize this opposition suggest that phallologocentric thought is founded on a repression of the semiotic in discourse and the maternal body. Thus, Hélène Cixous, Luce Irigaray, and Julia Kristeva claim that thinking takes place with the body and embodied thinking must not be ignored as a valuable source of knowledge. The appropriation of the male body part for a philosophical terminology is a form of personification (if only of a biological human anatomical part), a trope characteristic of myth. It becomes attached to any concept that privileges "logos" and becomes the signifier for a patriarchal agenda.

Derrida uses this term as a means to oppose a "feminine" and more indeterminate mode of truth to a determinate one. Is there, in fact, any such real referent or phenomenon as phallologocentricity? It seems to be a portmanteau term coined as a prelude to valorizing a less determinately rational agenda, and to overcome cultural bias toward the over-valuation of rigidly rationalistic thinking. The gender binaries of the mythical past, in this construction, and a conviction, based on true societal realities, that women are marginalized, conflate. Derrida and others, further, appropriate the legitimate bifurcation that exists between writing and speech, indetermination and polysemy versus logical, symbolic, and determinate discursive meaning, to be deployed to advance the narrative of injustice toward marginalization of women. This narrative stamps a legitimate bifurcation (logical discursive reasoning/creative semiotic and poetic discourse) with a presumed gender essentialism along these lines.

Jacques Derrida has taken on the substantivized abstract nouns of Western metaphysics, considering much of its terminology "white mythology." It is, therefore, remarkable that Derrida would adopt a strategy in his own work that makes use of a construction like "phallologocentrism." While it serves to characterize a legitimate distinction between symbolic logical linear discursive reasoning and semiotic poetic discourse, it adds a gender binary to the mix. Similarly, Derrida's comments on the feminine seem to be in clear contrast to his claim "Il n'y pas une femme"—there is no truth in sexual difference in itself[34] since his characterization of women as aligned with his famous neologism *differance* seems to contradict that claim. *Spurs* has been widely both attacked and admired by feminists. In this work, discussing Nietzsche's view of women, Derrida uses the term *differance* (his neologism for the eliding nature of meaning in discourse), something he claims supersedes the assumption of a one-to-one correspondence between a signifier and its meaning. Differance is one of his main deconstructive tools for dismantling metaphysics in favor of elided disseminated meaning. He claims that *differnace* is woman's truth. Critics, such as John Caputo, recognize the allegorical nature of the construction. As Caputo writes, referring to *Spurs*,

> In Derrida's "allegory" of gender, the hard upright, canonical Knight of Truth is spun around, to mean a rigid dogmatic, phallogocentric essentialist and philosopher of identity, while the beguiling deceptive temptress woman becomes an allegory of difference.[35]

Derrida's *differance*, a term that is omnipresent in his early writing, is a philosopheme and closer to the "truth," for him, than any metaphysical signifier, as it incorporates the reality that temporality and eliding meaning can never be arrested in the now of pure presence. Associating this term with gender, however, suggests that he is operating with the binary code which he does not seem to recognize as such, despite his analytical astuteness in other matters. Derrida plays in the field of trope and his thinking is fluid and difficult to pin down. When reading Derrida, the law of non-contradiction is not necessarily a criterion for intelligibility. When logocentrism becomes phallocentric, patriarchal, and masculinist, there is a confluence of meanings that seem to fuse without critical examination.

Feminist Readings of Philosophers

Plato, Aristotle, and Descartes, in the eyes of certain feminist scholars, are perpetuators of essentialist rubrics. Charlotte Witt, for example, extensively discusses feminist readings of Aristotle's distinction between form and matter along the line of a gender binary. This association is discussed in detail by Holmes. Aristotle's *prote hyle* (prime matter) and his views of the female contribution to human reproduction as spatial and material are taken up extensively by Irigaray, for example, who considers remembering the past by examining Greek texts crucial to feminist and gender studies.[36] Irigaray, Holmes suggests, is notable for having put Greek texts in the foreground of feminist theory. Holmes traces the gendering of "matter" in early Greek philosophy, as well, suggesting that "[A]lcemanon, Parmenides, Empedocles and Democrates," Presocratic philosopher/physicists, believed that "[t]he female contributes generative matter to reproduction" (as did Aristotle). Holmes discusses Irigaray's view of philosophy, particularly as she refigures the famous allegory of the cave in *Republic*, to suggest that the body of the mother is left behind in the emergence from the cave in this allegory of enlightenment. Aristotle can be considered to have had a predecessor in Plato's *Timaeus*, in its descriptive account of the receptacle (*chora*) as well, in so far as Aristotle's associating the feminine with prime matter.[37] These arguments cannot be adequately covered here except to note the ever-persistent binary they incorporate. Plato, for example, becomes the antihero who canonized the dichotomy between reason and irrational ways of knowing, such as poetic myth. In fact Plato, in banning poetry from the ideal polis, is not subscribing to any male hegemonic agenda but differentiating *mythos* from *logos* in the service of establishing a truth-seeking discourse for philosophy. He valorizes abstract nouns and their abstract predicates over gods and goddesses and their outlandish activities. The hegemony of the abstract noun and substantive, the valorizing of reason and dialectic that Plato supports, may have a negative impact in determining a bias in what Western thought values as truth. It is an added step to conflate this with gender. Emanuela Bianchi discusses a number of topics related to feminism and Aristotle, and Susan Bordo, in her *Feminist Interpretations of René Descartes*, provides a collection of feminist essays on Descartes.[38] The Cartesian valorization of mind over matter and the assumption of the superiority of spirituality over nature have been given unjust preeminence to presumed male intellectual qualities. Irigaray in *Speculum of the Other Woman* has an extensive analysis of Kant's transcendental subject, along these lines, as an unembodied entity that sublates the feminine. Green describes her position as one which renders nature or the empirical world comparable to the body of the mother. The otherness of the empirical world is an element in the construction of the Kantian subject.[39]

Feminist Epistemology

Donna Wilshire's article in Alison Jaggar and Susan Bordo's collection of essays on feminist epistemology can serve to exemplify the kind of argument that feminist epistemologists put forward in the 1980s. Positions of later feminist epistemologists are more nuanced and complex, but this particular piece is a good example, writ large, of a prevalent type of formulation which uses the gender binaries to expose gender discrimination in epistemology. Wilshire incorporates the Pythagorean table of opposites, constructing two columns juxtaposing attributes associated with female gender to those associated with the male gender in order to highlight what she terms "hierarchical dualisms." Wilshire considers the binaries: linear/cyclical, permanence/change, independent/dependent, rational/irrational, objective/subjective, as constituting meaningful oppositions. In the table she produces reason juxtaposed to emotion, order to chaos, public to private spheres, and Apollo as sky-sun to Sophia as earth-cave-moon.[40] Wilshire loads these oppositions with attributes that pit every cliché and myth concerning the more "earthly" qualities associated with the female gender against the more intellectual and spiritual qualities associated with the male. She does this in order to "redeem" the attributes connected to the female and make them equal in value to those of the male. Included in her project is the admonition that it is important to re-value the idea of the body as "knowing." A feminist version of knowledge, she claims, must not continue a dualistic either/or pattern, particularly in so far as associating the female negatively valued qualities which she claims is a cultural bias.

For Wilshire, Aristotle epitomizes the limitations of Western philosophy; furthermore, he calls women "mutilated males" (in *GA* II 3-737a), emotional and passive. She finds this a devaluing of earth and body, and female-associated ways of knowing, that continues in the modern period with Descartes.[41] She suggests that during the scientific revolution, Soul and Mind were still thought to be fulfilled only in males, still experienced as striving to conquer the body. Descartes associated Mind with divinity, she claims, while the body was dissociated from God by calling it nature. "Determined to remove himself, as much as possible, from the lowliness of his body and its matter," Descartes is characterized as having labored in his mind "to give birth to himself out of his own Reason-head." (Wilshire here makes an analogy to Zeus, who bypassed the mother goddess Metis and gave birth to Athena from his own head.) She contends that "the philosophical tradition *continues* to extol things culturally perceived as male (e.g., knowledge in the mind) and to demean and suppress things culturally perceived as female (e.g., knowing in the body)." Wilshire would like to refigure this hierarchical dualism, redeem all things on the right column of her own table of opposites, and reclaim things associated with the female that were "anciently, unfairly relegated to lowly status." "I suggest," she says, "we mine the warmth of women's experience and way of knowing (dark, inferior, female wisdom) as well as the cool, higher enlightenment of public, male Apollo/Logos."[42] Descartes continued the classical attempt to extricate knowledge and reason from any bodily contamination, from the Mother Earth, and all things female, and to free logos from Sophia, and her mind from nature. Wilshire goes on to invoke Kore/Persephone as seed/child of the earth, born and reborn from Earth Mother's womb, and suggests reclaiming the power inherent in the goddess. She calls for a new ideology out of the myths of the distant past "to support earth, nature, time, women and woman's bodies in the service of ecology." With allusions to Gimbutas, she re-envisions knowledge as entailing revivifying the goddess and the notion of "female as primordial creature." The feminist quest is to validate the highest human values, social bonding community experiences, and to claim the second place column as a vital positive force.

Feminist epistemologists after Wilshire are more sophisticated and nuanced. Wilshire produces an ideology quite typical of some feminist accounts of the 1980s. The idea that "semiotic," poetic, and non-discursive ways of knowing are valuable, and that Western philosophy has been biased toward the discursive, logical, and symbolic modes of linear thinking, is a defensible point. It is one that has been remedied by a growing appreciation of semiosis, poetics, allegory, and myth as alternate and legitimate ways of knowing. Following the premise that all binary oppositions are the material for mythology, Descartes can certainly be read as creating his own myth concerning the primacy of Mind and Mind/Body dualism. Critiques concerning bias in the history of ideas toward symbolic, discursive thinking are well founded. To associate these forms of thought with gender, however, is only one among other more conventional counter-arguments to Cartesian rationalism by empiricists and phenomenologists. Tamar Rudavsky points out that the hegemony of reason has been dealt many blows from non-gendered arguments. Husserl, for example, dealt a blow to Cartesian solipsism by emphasizing the intentionality of consciousness. There can be no subject (*noesis*) without a corresponding object (*noema*); consciousness is always consciousness of something.[43] Rudavsky quotes Daniel Boyarin's argument concerning the fact that rabbinic Judaism invested significance in the body ("for Hellenistic Jews and Christians, the essence of a human being is a soul housed in a body").[44] For Spinoza, body and monad are one entity; mind is the consciousness of the body, thus providing an alternative to Descartes' substance dualism. Spinoza's monistic materialism overcomes the radical alternatives represented by Platonism and Aristotelianism. Rudavsky recognizes that the metaphysical basis for gender associations in dualism can be traced back to Pythagoras's table of opposites. The Cartesian notion of the solitary ego and privileging of the mental over the physical—if associated with this table of opposites where the female is associated with negative characteristics—unlimited, plurality, left, movement, darkness, and evil, Cartesian dualism—too can be seen as denigrating the female. Cartesian dualism does bifurcate the world in a way that creates an insoluble explanatory gap for scholars of mind, self, and consciousness to account for the world of nature. To project gender-based binary oppositions into readings of Plato, Aristotle, or Descartes, however, is anachronistic and serves the feminist narrative of injustice, ideational, and otherwise.[45] Judith Grant, in her article "I Feel, Therefore I Am," argues that the general idea of this kind of criticism of reason is axiomatic and unconvincing. Woman's experience, as a basis for feminist epistemology, perpetuates the issue of a stereotypical female and fosters essentialist theories.[46]

The vast literature on feminist epistemology now appreciates the intersectional and social understanding of knowledge production and no longer isolates gender per se from race ethnicity, sexuality, and other forms of oppression aside from gender. Standpoint knowing, for example, examines epistemology from the standpoint of marginalized groups, empowerment, and the social nature of knowledge production. It asks who the subject of knowledge is. Books such as Alcoff and Potter's (2013) *Feminist Epistemologies* and Sandra G. Harding's *The Feminist Standpoint Theory*

Reader (2004) exemplify the "standpoint" approach. In Harding's words, "standpoint epistemology calls for stronger standards that can deter and eliminate sexist and androcentric assumptions."[47] Patricia Hill Collins, for example, writes about the black feminist standpoint, while Sandra Harding and Elizabeth Anderson continue to re-evaluate its many nuances and controversies. This takes a perspectival approach to knowing and emphasizes the interaction between epistemology and sociopolitical positions. As Alcoff and Potter state, "gender as an abstract universal is not a useful analytic category … feminist epistemology is emerging as a research program with multiple dimensions."[48]

The Persistence of Gender Essentialism and Greek Myth

One final example from the field of ancient studies illustrates the persistence of binary assumptions in contemporary scholarship. Adriana Cavarero describes her project in *In Spite of Plato* as "Freeing female figures from ancient patriarchal discourses."[49] She advocates the foregrounding of natality: an originary, fecund, generative, feminine plentitude beyond the reach of the polis and its laws. Cavarero claims that maternal power is precisely that boundless mode of generation extending between two infinities—infinite origin and infinite perpetuation: "Both infinities, past and future, origin and perpetuation, always exist through the feminine." This formulation associates the feminine with a sort of limitless fecundity, reminiscent of the second- and third-century CE association of the female with limitless multiplicity and fecundity so powerful that a goddess can mediate the creation of nature itself. Cavarero argues that the philosophical project, throughout its history, is a masculine project fixated on death and on its universalizing impulse, as opposed to life-giving natality.[50] Philosophy is the practice of death. Bianchi emphasizes that in antiquity the first flourishing of philosophical maximization—the rise of *to hen* (the One)—took place in a site where there had been "a prior disavowal, literally performed in annual festivals, of feminine corporeal generativity." The feminine (and Dionysian) became subsumed within the *polis* and came to be governed by laws of patriarchal kinship. Stuart Gardner, a reviewer of Cavarero's *In Spite of Plato*, remarks that Cavarero is out to "challenge the whole symbolic axiom of Western thought which prioritizes the masculine order."[51] She alludes to the "patriarchal order" as the enemy of female genealogy and strikes a political note in her assertion that reproductive capacities are (wrongly) "[r]egulated by the patriarchal order in a society that determines the ethical and legal order of maternal gestation."[52] Citing Irigaray in *Sexes and Genealogies*, Cavarero analyzes the myth of Demeter along these lines. She asserts that there is "an interruption in a feminine genealogy that is caused by its being violently overpowered by the patriarchal order (Hades and Zeus in collaboration) which is oblivious to birth and emphasizes death." Maternity, she asserts, is "the matrix of the arrival of humans in the world." Their arrival is rooted in nature, or *physis* (from the Greek *phyein*, to be fecund, generating). The maternal, then, is a continuum "infinite, past and future: origin and perpetuation always exist through the feminine." By continuum, she means that there is a "feminine root of every human being, generation to generation." This misreading of biology of course excludes the male contribution to this "infinite" process and is replete with traces of gender essentialism. Women's sociopolitical position vis-à-vis reward for achievement and professional success has not been valued in the past, not necessarily reproductive fecundity, not generativity, but philosophical, professional, and political contributions.

Bianchi focuses on Reiner Schürmann's discussion of Iphigenia's sacrifice in Aeschylus's famous drama, supporting Cavarero's claims. The tragic fates of both Iphigenia and Antigone represent the violent founding of the law of the city and of unadulterated patriarchal rule. In the case of Iphigeneia, a daughter's "[i]nescapable death at the behest of the father's law becomes the symbolic precondition for the nomological and political community from which the feminine is effectively banished." The family, the household, and the woman are subsumed in the universality of the state. Agamemnon's jubilant and passionate affirmation of this sacrifice with its "singularizing undertow of mortality" and the "tragic denial of the counter-law of the family in favor of establishing the law of the state" confirm this formulation. A hierarchical regime secures and even encrypts the household and the place of women within the purview and limit of the polis. Here "tragic denial [is] the impetus for hegemonic maximization."[53] In *Antigone*, similarly, "the daughter, the family, the *oikos* (home), are sacrificed in the name of the law of the city, the law of the father." Bianchi sees these instances as passages into patriarchy: the tragic subsumption in the Greek city-state of a feminine order of corporeity, but also of fecundity and natality. Classic oppositions such as the Apollonian/Dionysian distinction (discussed by Nietzsche), logos/mythos (originally in Plato), or *oikos/polis* (as in *Antigone* in the conflict of traditional religions/rule of the state) are also ways to interpret these classic works. Seeing them through the lens of gender politics is certainly of interest. In the case of *Antigone*, the scale of the tragedies and the conflict between the law of the gods and archaic tradition versus the laws of the polis suggest larger universal issues, as well, of which gender specificity is only one aspect.

Conclusion

> Discourses of gender are among the explanatory cultural frameworks which have been interpreted by some cultural semioticians as myths or mythologies (Daniel Chandler[54]).

The second-century Platonists associated key metaphysical concepts with gods and goddess. While this may seem bizarre to the modern mind, a closer look at some of the rather idiosyncratic coinages of the twentieth century, and the narratives that accompany them, shows them to be fanciful as well. Jung's anima and animus, Derrida's phallologocentricity, Lacan's "Law of the Father" consist of aggrandized abstract nouns that somehow are gender related and that are regarded by their inventors as foundational and operative in the psyche and in society. They embody a cultural code that can also be found in ancient myths, embedded in cultural memory and literary history.

Recourse to gender essentialism is not useful as theories of society or psychosexual development or when used to foreground presumed valued female attributes. Social justice needs no more support than an assertion of human rights for all people and appropriate social action to bring about change. Activism through global networks that address women's rights and push for better legislation and political equality in social and business settings is best equipped to bring about an ethical egalitarianism. Political activism does not need rhetorical ideology based on an outworn cultural code to combat androcentricity and solve the problems of a disrespect for nature that has led to ecological disasters, violence toward women, or the internalized self-identifications of both men and woman. Important feminist work has been done on the social and normative construction of gender, resulting in a deconstruction of the dimorphic subject in favor of the possibility of true multiplicity.[55] Racial and ethnic diversity, for example, can override dimorphic assumptions. These efforts can be enhanced by a recognition of the past and present harm caused by the now-devalued binaries, not by considering them a scientific, psychological, political, or social reality.

12

The Goddess Interpreted

Hesiod might not have considered his *Theogony* to be an account that could be held up to a standard of truth: the phantasmagoric theogonic narrative he was about to present could be both real and unreal. He gave responsibility for that possibility to the muses, quoting their bold assertion, "We know how to tell many lies that pass for truth. And when we wish, we know how to tell the truth itself" (*Th*. 27-28). As one travels back and forward in time, it is apparent that the gods and goddesses were considered both real and unreal. In some milieus, they were transcendent divinities, in others merely literary artifacts. The narratives recounting their activities have been considered place-holders for the highest categories of philosophical truth, or examples of shameful behavior that needed to be sanitized and reformulated as allegory. The lovely goddesses of "golden sandals" and "dazzling gifts" were considered forbidden idols for the Hebrews but were named "mother of the gods" by the Romans. For the Christians of late antiquity, goddesses were the object of disparagement and dismissal, especially the blatantly sexual Aphrodite, while Christians of the middle ages made widespread use of pagan myths as allegories for Christian ideas. Aphrodite, disobeying her detractors, appears over and over in poetry from the medieval period through the twentieth century.[1] Russian Christian mystics adored Sophia and Kabbalists gave an ontological status to the Shekhinah whose right to exist within a monotheistic framework is still a matter of debate. Some considered this figure a violation of the organic unity of the godhead others regarded her as an emanation of the highest *sefirot*. What were idols for the Hebrews and abominations for the Christians, for late antique Platonists were figures representing Platonic concepts in disguise. For the eighteenth century, a quest for the secrets of nature and the mystery of being held the goddess to be a figure of concealment and revelation, while for spiritual feminists of the twentieth century she was an antidote to the masculine image of deity. Psychoanalytic theorists reached into this archive to name concepts that otherwise had no known designation, and in almost every century, goddesses personified nature and wisdom. Denied a sacramental reading in some contexts, they were given awe-filled piety and abject devotion in others. Even the names of goddesses refuse oblivion. For the ancients, a goddess's name was a way to name natural phenomena such as earth and sky, for contemporary star-gazers a way to name newly discovered astronomical bodies. It seems that goddesses are still figures that are seriously considered worthy of devotion. Aside from neo-pagan goddess worship and spiritual feminism, several recent articles suggest that in Greece there are now followers of Hellenism who wish to return to their cultural roots through worship of the ancient gods.[2] All these instances exemplify the power of cultural memory.

Jan Assmann, building upon the work of the French sociologist Maurice Halbwachs on the social frame of collective memory, suggests that "[t]he past only comes into being as far as we refer to it."[3] He identifies several categories of "forgetting," as well, "the traumatic kind as in the German memories of the Holocaust, the implicit kind where the knowledge is too self-evident to become explicit in communicating, and the marginalized kind, a form of latency" which can be restored when a new discovery or interest revives the cultural memory.[4] Fulfilling the last criterion, *Goddesses in Myth and Cultural Memory* has documented how goddesses could be dismissed in settings that are disenchanted by mythical creatures but welcomed when and where it was acceptable to deploy them. The goddess always found a new important job to do. In the *Iliad*, she intervened on the battlefield, and in Greek drama she intervened in human affairs. In Late Platonism, she saved concepts from being lifeless abstractions, allowing Platonic super-nouns to become divinized and pagan Platonism to become a competing theology to Christianity. She served as an actor in allegories in the middle ages and a concealer of the secrets of nature in later centuries. In the contemporary world, she has served to counter the imbalance of the Judeo-Christian practice of regarding divinity as male and to personify desirable attributes alleged to be characteristic of female gender.

According to Slavof Žižek in his path-breaking book *Event,* "unknown knowns" are those things so well-known they are forgotten, but this does not mean they are not operative. Lamberton suggests, using Harold Bloom's concept of "misreading": "At any given moment, in any given interpretative community, a range of (mis-)readings of any text is possible."[5] The unknown knowns, as concealed influences, must be considered when we make sense out of any transformations of archaic literary martials when they fall into the hands of interpretative communities. These communities render the tautegorical (that which only represents itself), such as Hesiod's *Theogony*, into the allegorical, the symbolic, the philosophical. While Lamberton was referring to the Neoplatonists' reading of Homer, this applies across the board to the uses to which goddess mythology has been put throughout history. After Plato, to avoid the embarrassment of treating the phantasmagoric as real knowledge, especially in terms of what he regarded as its shameful barbarism, myth was treated as allegorical and thought to stand in for philosophical truths. Proclus took this further and claimed that myths were philosophical arguments. In every new geopolitical context, myths that were tautegorical and irreducible received new interpretations and were transformed and augmented. The "unknown knowns" that persisted, however, were the binary oppositions of gender along very specific lines: nature, fecundity, and indeterminateness were associated with goddesses and aloof, intellectual organizing principles with gods. This code, based on an essentialist rendition of gender, became the culturally implicit "unknown known" that made countless appearances of the stage of literary history and social practice.

Katya Silverman describes a cultural code as a conceptual system which is organized around key oppositions and one in which a term like "woman" is defined in opposition to a term like "man," and each term is "aligned with a cluster of symbolic attributes."[6] Binary oppositions are cognitive and logical ways of organizing and structuring experience, but the framework that is applied to them or the knowledge they embody can become intransigent, turning them into a mythology in their own right. Only in the twentieth century did feminist scholars scrutinize these oppositions and see them as a product of the cultural history and context within which gender attributes were formed. The primal dichotomy between the indeterminate and the determinate, unlimited and limited, nature and culture, fluid and rigid, with the former member of each of these pairs a secondary or even denigrated form of existence, when fused with gender, has been a ubiquitous source of ideologies as well as a widespread source of discrimination and bias. Current research on sexual difference has shown that dimorphism can no longer be held to rigid determinations.[7] The trend to deconstruct the essentialist binaries of gender itself documents their insidious survival as cultural codes that require critical examination.

"The" Goddess

"To Hesiod," Athanassakis points out, "Earth (Gaia), Sky (Ouranos) and Sea (Pontos) are not mere elements but gods. Positive and negative forces such as Justice and Peace or Injustice and War, are not merely conditions or abstract forces, but individual divinities or individualized divine powers."[8] This was personification in its most blatant form. The close relationship between the concrete and the abstract and the ease with which they conflate prepared the ground for the advent of the metaform "the goddess." Hekate becomes Isis, and Hekate/Isis, Demeter etc. in the literature of the Common Era: whichever the name was not as important as her role as a placeholder for a mediating function. The *Chaldean Oracles* conspired with Middle Platonism to construe this now-somewhat abstract figure as the active "god particle" in world making. The Platonic World Soul, thought to incorporate reason from above, acts to apply it to nature, and the goddess, personifying this process, can connect nature and reason and also can bypass the possibility that the highest forms of intellect would be contaminated by nature. "The goddess" is able to have commerce with the world's body. A goddess, whoever she may have been originally, is now a formal entity able to operate in venues where concepts interact with reality. In an increasingly text-oriented culture, the old tales could not compete, with the testaments of the gospels and church fathers. Plutarch in the second century repackaged Isis in a way that elevated the Egyptian cult, via Platonic exegesis, "to the level of holy mystery."[9] He was able to do this as he could now operate with a "philosophical" goddess. The goddess could now be incorporated into philosophical ontology as a formal entity whose set of descriptions mirrored a cultural code that allowed her, qua female, to intermediate between nature and intellectual higher hypostases. In Proclus, in the throes of a latter-day Hellenic revival, given fuel by the brief reign of Julian, this elevation of Platonic theology became an elaborate, though short-lived, competing ideology to Christianity. The creation of a conceptual goddess allowed her wide range in future contexts as well. In the developing rhetoric of early Christianity, the trinity became a doctrine that retained the structure of the Gnostic, or Platonic triad, where a goddess was a model for an instance where mediation was required. Christianity could make that work by discarding the "female gender" attribution in favor of pure spirit. In the medieval period "the" goddess, now a literary icon, reemerged in the form of Natura and Sophia. Figures that were once an assembly of goddesses acting diverse roles in mythological epic narrative are overruled by their symbolic substitutes. The simulacrum of the goddess, then, found in the persona of nature and wisdom in medieval and eighteenth- and nineteenth-century literature and art is a generic "every goddess." She is a larger-than-life figure whose memory as a symbol of wisdom appears as Beatrice in Dante, St. Macrina in the eulogy of Gregory of Nyssa for his sister, even as Helen of Troy in Homer. As exemplar she is now able, as well, to transform into the desired object of a hoped for female deity in the twentieth century and even become a newly minted object of worship. One principle of interpretation that can be applied to all texts and cultural contexts is "the impossibility of settling down in the 'now.'" Something new, a re-assemblage, is always an open possibility.[10]

Politics and Rhetoric: A Challenge to Divinity as Male?

The movement to challenge divinity as male, reenacting the binary oppositions of gender to reinvent divinity as female, a gentler more mothering version of the godhead, is a good example of the political at work in theology. Carol Christ and Judith Plaskow are the coauthors of two anthologies on women and religion, both of which endorse the view that many feminists across religious boundaries challenge the images of God as male.[11] According to Christ, familiar images of God as Lord, King, Absolute Ruler, and Father are masculine and hierarchical depictions of divine power based on "ancient and feudal notions of kingship." They are patriarchal, racist, dualistic, and judgmental. In one of the articles in the Christ and Plaskow anthology *Womanspirit Rising*, "Why Women Need the Goddess," Persephone and Demeter are evoked in support of Christ's thesis that goddess revival is of the essence in a much-needed change in theology.[12] In another article along these lines, "Reflections on the Meaning of Herstory," Sheila Collins claims that feminist artists, writers, psychologists, and theologians are returning to a pre-Judeo-Christian understanding of ancient myth, symbol, and archetype and resurrecting the ancient mother goddess's powers to create an equivalence to the Christian Christ.[13] Nikki Bado-Fralick reviews Carol Christ's book, *She Who Changes: Re-imagining the Divine in the World*.[14] She suggests that Christ views the situation in literal and simplistic terms not appropriate to actual theologians of today. While Christ rejects the cultural binary that connects women with nature and with the transient body and men with immortality and rationality, she still affirms "change and embodiment, touch and relationships, power with, not power over"[15] as desirable templates attached to the female. To compensate for Western biases, Christ refers to the divine as "Goddess/God." The reviewer terms this view "feminist process pantheism."

Perhaps the attempt to genderize divinity is prompted in the words of Elizabeth Johnson, by "The ultimate unknowability of God."[16] Genderizing divinity as female may be a springboard to understanding and connection with divinity; however, there is a clandestine political motive at work here as well. When Hekate is reborn, in contemporary revivals, as a goddess embodying the "divine feminine" or when archeologists searched for evidence of a great goddess who once reigned supreme, they wishfully promote a dominant female object of worship who still "lives" and has not succumbed to male domination in the spiritual realm. Scholars such as Sir Arthur Evans and Axel Persson wrote about a Great Minoan Nature Goddess, discarding the fact that female divinities in early cities and in all Near Eastern and Egyptian religions were numerous and coupled with gods. The Minoan and Mycenaean cultures were, after all, polytheistic. In any case, the possibility has not been ruled out that these figurines, which support these views, were personal charms, dolls, spirit figures, initiation objects, and vehicles for sympathetic magic.[17] The "master narrative" that followers of Jung/Gimbutas put forward may not have been a deliberate political act. Many similar narratives incorporate a deeply embedded cultural "code," of gender essentialism that colludes with these efforts. Along with a desire for female hegemony in a male-dominated culture, the literary artifact that is Hesiod's *Theogony* is reactivated as a chronicle of archaic actual goddesses. Stripped of their darker characteristics, imagined as figures of archaic regional history, they now can serve an identity marker for a marginalized group. While Gaia, in the *Theogony*, is the mother of all, the evidence for a regional goddess occupying that role is questionable. As Lefkowitz asks: "how could a religion that so precisely met the needs of the twentieth century CE have existed in the twentieth century BCE? Certainly not in the form that Gimbutas, Campbell, or any of their predecessors imagined it."[18] With this as a cautionary tale, and along with the idea that cultural memory is as immortal as the figures it holds dear, it is evident that political motivations can collude with unrecognized "unknown knowns" and influence the historiography of interpretation.

Hesiod and Homer, the Homeric Hymns and other ancient texts can be left intact, as we appreciate the fact that interpretation itself is the mythology of every period. Jean-Pierre Vernant tells us we cannot read philosophical systems into Hesiod. We cannot imbue ancient artifacts with contemporary meaning. To do so would entail using a conceptual vocabulary alien to Hesiod, which "follows a different logic from that of philosophy."[19] Hesiod's *Theogony*, much like the figurines unearthed by archeologists, is a unique cultural artifact. It is "tautegorical," referring only it itself. Like a dream, it is full of imagery so vivid that it wards off discursive exegesis. One cannot put an elephant through the eye of a needle. Allegoresis and symbolic metaphysical readings of myth are interpretive readings and thus can create new myths. The fact that the goddess transforms through time is a comment upon the incredible changeability of historiography and first and foremost evidence of the power of cultural memory. It serves to remind us, as well that political agendas can enable scholars to apply predetermined templates that are sometimes out of their awareness. The foregrounding of natality, or of the rhythmic and process nature of female experience, in order to make what was considered a lower order higher, all embody the same intransigent code. We recall the fluid Rhea, fecund Gaia, and the Sethian Gnostic Dyad/womb of the All, or the Chaldean womb of Hekate, and must be impressed by the persistent survival of these cultural prototypes as they assume new forms.

Conclusion

> Max Müller's view of mythology as a "disease of language" can be abandoned without regret. Mythology is not a disease at all, though it may like all human things become diseased. You might as well say that thinking is a disease of the mind. It would be more near the truth to say that languages, especially modern European languages, are a disease of Mythology. (J. R. R. Tolkien[20])

Personified mythical figures with their own names and specifications, gods and goddesses codified and poeticized by Homer and Hesiod, are gone. Scientific method and a positivist approach to propositional assertions have administered an Occam's razor so powerful that all creatures of imagination and unproven rhetoric are relegated to the literary and the fictitious. The space that was once occupied by personified mythical figures has disappeared or known only to the popular domain of film, fantasy, and to wishful thinking. The strict bifurcation between *mythos* and *logos* that some scholars thought constituted an advancement over an earlier stage of less logical and scientific discourse, however, is not a reality on the ground. Greek rationalism has not superseded all other forms of discourse as a means to access truth. As I have discussed in a recent article, scholars traditionally approached mythmaking as though a change occurred in the history of ideas and Hesiod came at a point of transition from mythopoetic to rational modes of thought. A greater sophistication and appreciation of "semiotics" have changed that perception and texts can now be considered polysemic and subject to a wider range of possibilities for hermeneutic practice. Hesiod's *Theogony* is, after all, a literary creation, not subject to being regarded as mythology, nor is the mythos/logos distinction one that can be upheld and that has to be subject to standard of what Luc Brisson considers either "falsifiable" or "nonfalsifiable" discourse.[21] In recent years, semioticians acknowledged the mythical nature of all sorts of discourse. The theological issues of centuries ago, such as the location of heaven and hell, are rendered meaningless by modern cosmology and our improved understanding of the nature of space and time.[22] This does not stop spatial metaphors from persisting in theology, creating worlds beyond this world or psychology, envisioning regions like the so-called unconscious as constitutive of mind. The history of metaphysics is replete with abstract nouns, capitalized and treated in a personified or deified manner as though they have causal efficacy. Now Plato's famous "Good," Neoplatonism's Soul, Life, and Mind are the flora and fauna of the literature of late Antiquity. Hegel's Absolute Spirit is long gone from the ranks of acceptable continental philosophy while Heidegger's "Being" is a signifier that still makes sense to his latter-day followers but not to the majority of philosophers. It seems that all reified abstract nouns posited in these arcane ontologies are now considered to be fossils of a way of thinking that has been happily deconstructed for the twenty-first century. This metaphysical cleansing, however, does not seem to extend to discussions in terms of the binary oppositions of gender. We must ask, then, what is the power of this cultural code, what makes it so intransigent that it does not yield fully to scholarly deconstruction? Bifurcations such as that between the female as semiotic, womb, creative, chorological source, and the male as phallic, symbolic, intellectual (in a negative sense), etc., instantiate a mythical dimension and essentialism to meaningful discussions of gender. It is clearly an outworn strategy for combating androcentrism in the philosophical and literary canon. Aggrandizing the feminine, idealizing essentialist reifications like maternity, earthly, nature, etc., belong to goddesses, not to a hypostatic abstraction such as "the eternal feminine" or to any essentialist rhetoric. Remedying the injustices visited upon women in the twenty-first century lies in social action, not ancient mythology re-invented. Ideologies are mythologies and to seek social justice we must focus on reality. To quote Hesiod, at the end of what we have of the *Theogony*, "But now, oh sweet-singing Olympian Muses, (let us) … sing of mortal women" (1023).

Notes

Chapter 1

1. Philippe Borgeaud, *Mother of the Gods: From Cybele to the Virgin Mary*, trans. Lysa Hochroth (Baltimore: Johns Hopkins University Press, 2004), 121–3.
2. See Matthew Brunwasser, "The Greeks Who Worship the Ancient Gods," BBC news, June 2013. http://www.bbc.co.uk/news/magazine-22972610. accessed June 20, 2015
3. Lucy Goodison and Christine Morris, *Ancient Goddesses: The Myths and the Evidence* (Madison: University of Wisconsin Press, 1999), 11.
4. Mary Lefkowitz, "Feminist Myths and Greek Mythology," TLS (July 22-28, 1989), 804–5; "Twilight of the Goddess," *The New Republic*, vol. 8, 3 (1992), 29–35; Review of Goodison and Morris, *Ancient Goddesses: The Myths and the Evidence* in BMCR 1999.10.03.
5. Brooke Holmes, *Gender Antiquity and Its Legacy* (Oxford: Oxford University Press, 1976), 133.
6. Jann Assmann, *Cultural Memory and Early Civilization* (Cambridge: Cambridge University Press, 2011), 17.
7. Jan Assmann, *Religion and Cultural Memory*, trans. Rodney Livingston (Stanford: Stanford University Press, 2006), 179: "From the standpoint of the history of memory, these fictions are themselves facts, to the extent that they have defined the memory horizon of a society as it was and have thus put their stamp on its particular character."
8. Assmann, *Cultural Memory, Early Civilization*, 72.
9. Assmann, *Cultural Memory, Early Civilization*, 11.
10. Jan Assmann, *Moses The Egyptian* (Cambridge: Harvard University Press, 1997).
11. Umberto Eco, *Semiotics and the Philosophy of Language* (Bloomington: Indiana University Press, 1986), 24–5.
12. Tikva Frymer-Kensky, *In the Wake of the Goddesses: Women, Culture, and the Biblical Transformation of Pagan Myth* (New York: Macmillan, Free Press, 1992), 9.
13. Jenny Strauss Clay, *The Politics of Olympus* (Princeton: Princeton University Press, 1989), 3.
14. Jean-Pierre Vernant, *Mortals and Immortals: Collected Essays*, ed. F. Zeitlin (Princeton: Princeton University Press, 1991), 197.
15. Mary Lefkowitz, *Greek Gods, Human Lives: What We Can Learn from Myths* (New Haven: Yale University Press, 2003), 1.
16. Charles Martindale, "Introduction," in *Classics and the Uses of Reception*, ed. Charles Martindale and Richard G. Thomas (Malden: Blackwell Press, 2006), 7.
17. Clay, *Politics of Olympus*, 8.
18. See for example, Jean Pulvel, *Comparative Mythology* (Baltimore: Johns Hopkins University Press, 1989)
19. See Walter Burkert, *Ancient Mystery Cults* (Cambridge: Harvard University Press, 1987), Ch. 1 and *Greek Religion: Archaic and Classical* (Cambridge: Harvard

University Press, 1991), 11ff. The words *mysteria* and *teletai*, and variations of them, were used to designate festivals, initiation rites, etc., in both Mycenaean and Greek ancient ritual practices.

20 Carolina López-Ruiz, *When the Gods Were Born* (Cambridge: Harvard University Press, 2020) is an excellent source for this.
21 M.L. West, *East Face of Helicon* (Oxford: Clarendon Press, 1999), x.
22 Walter Burkert, *The Orientalizing Revolution*, trans. Margaret E. Pinder and Walter Burkert (Cambridge: Harvard University Press, 1992), 4–5 citing Albin Lesky (1950) "Hethitische Texte und griechischer Mythos," *Gesammelte Schriften* (Bern, 1966), 356–71, and F. Dornseiff, *Die archaische Mythenerzählung* (Berlin: De Gruyter, 1933), 25–7, among other works by these authors.
23 See M. L. West, Introduction: Hesiod *Theogony* (Oxford: Clarendon Press, 1966), 18–31, and G. S. Kirk, *Myth, Its Meaning and Function in Ancient and Other Cultures* (Berkeley: University of California Press, 1973), 214–20.
24 Raphael Patai, "Matronit: The Goddess of the Kabala," *History of Religions*, vol. 4 (Summer 1964), 53–68 at 53–55. Patai elaborates the similarities at length. M.L. West, *East Face of Helicon*, is an excellent source for these connections.
25 Assmann, *Cultural Memory, Early Civilization*, 102.
26 Francis Cornford, *The Unwritten Philosophy* (Cambridge: Cambridge University Press, 1950), 42, and Kirk, *Myth*, 238.
27 Kirk, *Myth*, 238ff. at 241. Martin Nilsson, *A History of Greek Religion* (Oxford, 1925);. Cornford, *Unwritten Philosophy*. W. K. C. Guthrie, *A History of Greek Philosophy* (Cambridge: Cambridge University Press, 1962).
28 See Glen W. Most, "Introduction," in *Hesiod, Theogony, Works and Days, Testimonia* (Loeb: Loeb classical Library, Harvard University Press, 2018), xxv. Most claims that it would be impossible to be more precise. See also Apostolos N. Athanassakis, *Hesiod* (Baltimore: Johns Hopkins University Press, 2004), xii.
29 Robert Lamberton, *Hesiod*. (New Haven: Yale University Press 1988), 43.
30 See Gregory Nagy, *Homeric Questions* (Austin: University of Texas Press, 1996), 113 and n. 2, citing M. M. Willcock, "Ad Hoc Invention in the Iliad," *Harvard Studies in Classical Philology*, vol. 81 (1977), 141–53.
31 Willcock, "Ad Hoc Invention," 53.
32 Jasper Griffin, *Homer on Life and Death* (Oxford: Oxford University Press, 1980), 185.
33 Nagy, *Homeric Questions*, 114.
34 Nagy concludes his study by providing the meaning of the Latin word *exemplum* from the Latin etymological dictionary of Alfred Ernout and Antoine Meillet, who define it as "an object set apart from among other objects like it, for the sake of serving as a model." Nagy, *Homeric Questions,* 136–37, 146 and n. 143.
35 Mary E. Voyatzis, "From Athena to Zeus," in *Ancient Goddesses*, ed. Goodison and Morris (Madison: University of Indiana Press, 1998), 144.
36 Clay, *Politics of Olympus,* 10.
37 See Assmann, *Cultural Memory, Early Civilization,* 24f.
38 Lamberton, *Hesiod,* xiii.
39 Athanassakis, Hesiod, xii.
40 Jean-Pierre Vernant, *Mythe et société en Grèce ancienne* (Paris: Françoise Maspero, 1974), 106, quoted by Clay, *Politics of Olympus*, 10 with n. 18.
41 See Sarah B. Pomeroy, Stanley M. Burstein, et al., *Ancient Greece, a Political, Social, and Cultural History*, 3rd edn (New York: Oxford University Press, 2012), 516.

42 Thomas A. Sebeok and Marcel Danesi, *The Forms of Meaning* (Berlin: de Gruyter, 2000), 38, 40–1. Sebeok and Danesi define a "metaform" as a "primary connective form" portraying abstractions in terms of concrete source. The source domain in this case consists of the goddesses in textual or ritual contexts, each with an individual name and "concrete" identity. The target domain is the more abstract and higher layer consisting of a conceptual entity: the goddess per se.
43 Luc Brisson, *How the Philosophers Saved Myths*, trans. Catherine Tihanyi (Chicago: University of Chicago Press, 2004).
44 Assmann, *Moses*, 45.
45 A Ptolemaic decree (218 BCE) issued by Ptolemy IV in Egyptian hieroglyphics, Egyptian Demotic, and Greek.
46 R. E. Witt, *Isis in the Ancient World* (Baltimore: Johns Hopkins University Press, 1971), 112.
47 See Morton Bloomfield, "A Grammatical Approach to Personification Allegory," *Modern Philology*, vol. 60, 3 (1963), 161–71.
48 Which commentators have named Hekate, Rhea, or Ge.
49 Athanassakis, Hesiod, 5.
50 In *Goddesses, Whores, Wives, and Slaves* (Shocken 1975, 1995), Sarah B. Pomeroy gives us the three roles of the goddess: "Athena—an intellectual sexual career woman—or an Aphrodite—frivolous sex object—or a respectable wife-mother like Hera ... the Greek goddesses represent these archetypes of female existence."
51 Plutarch *Isis and Osiris*, in Plutarch *Moralia* (Loeb, 1936).
52 Plutarch *De Animae Procreatione in Timaeo*, trans. Harold F. Cherniss, Plutarch *Moralia*, vol. 12 (Loeb, 1976).
53 See Holmes, *Gender/Antiquity*, for an extended discussion of this in her chapter "The Gender of Nature and the Nature of Gender," under the heading "The Gendering of Matter," 56ff.
54 See Emilie Kutash, "The Prevailing Circumstances: The Pagan Philosophers of Athens in a Time of Stress," *The Pomegranate*, vol. 10, 21 (2008), 84–200, and Lucas Siorvanes, *Proclus* (New Haven: Yale University Press, 1996), ch. 1.
55 Assmann, *Cultural Memory, Early Civilization*, 33.
56 Daniel Chandler, *Semiotics* (London: Routledge, 2007), 93.
57 See Erich Neumann, *The Great Mother: An Analysis of the Archetype*, Bollingen Foundation Series XLVII (New York: Pantheon Books, 1963), and Carl C. Jung, *The Collected Works of C. G. Jung*, vol. 6, Bollingen Foundation Series XX (Princeton: Princeton University Press, 1971), 443. Other popular books cited by Goodison and Morris are Gerard Lerner's *The Creation of Patriarchy* (1986) and Merlin Stone, *When God Was a Woman* (1976). See Goodison and Morris, *Ancient Goddesses,* 10ff. for an extensive bibliography of such books and ideas. See also Ruth Trigham and Margaret Conley, "Rethinking Figurines: A Critical View from Archeology, Gimbutas, the 'Goddess' and Popular Culture," 22–45 in Goodison and Morris, *Ancient Goddesses*.
58 Goodison and Morris, *Ancient Goddesses*, 11ff.
59 Lucy Goodison and Christine Morris, "Goddesses in Prehistory," in *A Companion to Gender Prehistory*, ed. Diane Bolger (Malden: Wiley-Blackwell, 2013), 272.
60 Goodison and Morris, *Ancient Goddesses*, 8.
61 Holmes, *Gender Antiquity*, 144ff and 146 citing the excavations at Çaralhöyuk in Turkey which have revised the former approaches to female figurines.
62 Helen P. Foley, *The Homeric Hymn to Demeter* (Princeton: Princeton University Press, 1994), xiii, 168.
63 John Deely, *Basics of Semiotics* (Bloomington: University of Indiana Press, 1990), 5.

Chapter 2

1. Clay, *Politics of Olympus,* 9–10 and n. 17, citing G. Nagy, *"Hesiod" in Ancient Writers,* ed. T. J. Luce (New York: Charles Scribner's Sons, 1982), 28–49.
2. While male deities, Zeus, Ares, Hephaestus, Apollo, Hermes were involved in sexual activities as well, many times aggressive in nature, goddesses as will be discussed later here, were used as exemplars of desire, seduction, fertility, and mating.
3. Jennifer Nails (ed.), *Worshipping Athena* (Madison: University of Wisconsin Press, 1996), 23.
4. *Iliad* (1. 196-223). Athena wisely advises Achilles to hold back his sword and not smite Agamemnon.
5. Wendy Elgersma Helleman, *The Feminine Personification of Wisdom* (Lewiston: The Edwin Mellen Press, 2009), 174, also see page 19.
6. López-Ruiz, *Gods were Born,* 67–8 and n. 70. She cites R. G. Edmonds III, *Myths of the Underworld Journey in Plato, Aristophanes and the "Orphic" Gold Tables* (Cambridge: Cambridge University Press, 2004).
7. Jean-Pierre Vernant, "Greek Cosmogonic Myths," in *Greek and Egyptian Mythologies,* ed. Yves Bonnefoy, trans. Wendy Donige (Chicago: University of Chicago Press, 1992), 69.
8. All citations of Hesiod's *Theogony* are from Athanassakis, *Hesiod,* 2004.
9. Kirk, *Myth,* 174.
10. Thuc. ii.15; Pausanius *Description of Greece,* vols 1–4, trans. W. H. S. Jones (Loeb, 1918-35). Paus. i.22 §3, 24 §3, 31 §2, iii.11 §8, 12 §7, v.14 §8, vii.25 §8, viii.48 §6. See *Dictionary of Greek and Roman Biography and Mythology,* ed. William Smith (Boston: Little Brown and Company, 1849) quoted on www.thoi.com/Protogonos/Gaia.html. accessed April l4, 2016.
11. All quotes from the Orphic hymns are from Apostolos N Athanassakis and Benjamin M. Wolkow, *Orphic Hymns* (Baltimore: Johns Hopkins University Press, 2013).
12. Lamberton, *Hesiod,* 75.
13. Lamberton (*Hesiod,* 72) suggests that the epithet *pelore* is a key to the characterization of Gaia and may simply mean huge or monstrous. In Homer it denotes something large or awe-inspiring, but in Hesiod this adjective is used to describe things like the sickle used to castrate Ouranos, as monstrous.
14. Athanassakis and Wolkow, *Orphic Hymns,* 24.
15. Aeschylus, *Seven against Thebes* 16ff. (Mother Ge your beloved nurse) and *Suppliant Women* (as producer of plagues and a swarming colony of serpents) 260ff. Aeschylus, *Seven Agains Thebes,* trans. H. Weir Smyth (Loeb, 1930).
16. Athanassakis and Wolkow, *Orphic Hymns,* 76.
17. Lawrence Kahn-Lyotard and Nicole Loraux, "Death in Greek Myth," in Bonnefoy, *Greek Mythologies,* 105.
18. See Robert Lamberton, *Homer, the Theologian* (Berkeley: University of California Press, 1989), 126–210.
19. Athanassakis and Wolkow, *Orphic Hymns,* 76–7.
20. Liz Locke, "Orpheus and Orphism: Cosmology and Sacrifice at the Boundary," *Folklore Forum,* vol. 28, 2 (1997), 17.
21. Mark H. Munn, *The Mother of the Gods: Athens and the Tyranny of Asia* (Berkeley: University of California Press, 2006), 31–3.
22. West, *East Face of Helicon,* 109

23 Gabor Betegh, *The Derveni Papyrus: Cosmology, Theology and Interpretation* (Cambridge: Cambridge University Press, 2004), 189–90. Athanassakis and Wolkow, *Orphic Hymns*, 102–3.
24 Athanassakis and Wolkow, *Orphic Hymns*, 103.
25 Athanassakis and Wolkow, *Orphic Hymns*, 107–8.
26 Athanassakis and Wolkow, *Orphic Hymns*, 107.
27 See Apuleius, *The Golden Ass*, trans., intro., and explanatory notes R. G. Walsh (Oxford: Oxford University Press, 1994), 6.3ff. (Samos); Herodotus *Histories* 9.61.3 (Plataia); Pausanias 9.34.3 (Boiotia); Strabo *Geography* 14.1.14 (Boiotia) (http://www.theoi.com/Cult/HeraCult.html accessed January 19, 2014).
28 John Chadwick, *The Mycenaean World* (Cambridge: Cambridge University Press, 1978), 89. Linear B dates from around 1450 BCE and the reference here is to the Pylos tablets which contain the Linear B inscriptions.
29 Walter Burkert, *Greek Religions* (Malden: Wiley-Blackwell, 1991), 132–3.
30 Joan V. O'Brien, *The Transformation of Hera: A Study of Ritual, Hero, and the Goddess in the Iliad* (Lanham: Rowman and Littlefield, 1993), 205.
31 O'Brien, *Transformation of Hera*, 14–19.
32 Ingrid E. Holmberg, review of Joan V. O'Brien, *Transformations of Hera*, in BMCR 95.02.04.
33 O'Brien, *Transformation of Hera*, 113–17, 139, 156, 185.
34 Athanassakis and Wolkow, *Orphic Hymns*, 107.
35 The fragments from the *Chaldean Oracles* discussed here can be found in *The Chaldaean Oracles: Studies in Greek and Roman Religion*, trans. And comm. R. Majercik (Leiden: Brill, 1989) and *Oracles Chaldaques aven un choix de commentaires anciens*, ed., comm., and trans. E. Des Places (Paris, 1971).
36 Sarah Iles Johnston, *Hekate Soteira* (Atlanta: Scholars Press: 1990), 66 with n. 42. Generally, Johnston points out, in the second century Hekate's syncretism with many goddesses may reflect the Chaldean system's attempt to validate itself by affiliating with the Orphic canon in which Rhea is important. Hans Lewy, *Chaldean Oracles and Theurgy* (Paris: Brepols, 1978), 481–5.
37 Athanassakis, *Hesiod*, 34.
38 Voyatzis, "From Athena to Zeus,"133–5.
39 Voyatzis, "From Athena to Zeus," 139.
40 *Il.* 5.765, 824-64; 15.121-42; 21.391-415. Jean-Pierre Darmon, "The Powers of War: Ares and Athena in Greek Mythology," in *Greek and Egyptian Mythologies*, ed. Yves Bonnefoy, trans. Wendy Doniger (Chicago: University of Chicago Press, 1992), 114.
41 The Siphnian Treasury is a marble building at the cult center of Delphi erected to hold the offerings of the wealthy city-state of Siphnios (530–480 BCE). Athena is depicted in the north frieze.
42 Heraclitus, *Homeric Problems*, ed. David Konstan and Donald A. Russell (Society of Biblical Literature, 2005), 54, 93. See also Héraclite, *Allégories d'Homère*, ed. F. Buffière (Paris, 1962), trans. Stephan R. M. Tzaskoma, R. Scott Smith, and Stephen Brunet in *Anthology of Classical Myth* (Indianapolis: Hackett, 2004), 118.
43 Athanassakis and Wolkow, *Orphic Hymns*, 129; Herodotus 8.550.
44 Callimachus *Hymns, Epigrams, Select Fragments*, trans. Stanley Lombardo and Diane Raynor (Baltimore: Johns Hopkins University Press, 1988). Athanassakis and Wolkow, *Orphic Hymns*, 131.
45 See Emilie Kutash, *Ten Gifts of the Demiurge: Proclus' Commentary on the Timaeus* (London: Bloomsbury, 2011), ch. 3.

46 Nicole Loraux, "Gods and Artisans: Hephastus, Athena, Daedalus," in Bonnefoy, *Mythologies*, 84–90 at 87.
47 See Lefkowitz, *Greek Gods*, 152–6.
48 Michael N. Nagler, *Spontaneity and Tradition: A Study in the Oral Art of Homer* (Berkeley: University of California Press, 1974), 45–59.
49 Carol Lawton, *Marbleworks in the Athenian Agora* (Athens: American School of Classical Studies at Athens, 2006), 39.
50 Patricia A. Marquardt, "A Portrait of Hecate," *American Journal of Philology*, vol. 102, 3 (1981), 243–60, 251–2.
51 Lamberton, *Hesiod*, 85.
52 George C.W. Warr, "The Hesiodic Hecate," *Classical Review*, vol. 9, 8 (1895), 300–93 at 392.
53 Athanassakis, *Hesiod*, 46.
54 Marquardt, Portrait of Hecate, 244 with n. 2. Marquardt cites Martin Nilsson, *Geschichte der griechischen Religion* (Munich: C. H. Beck, 1967), I. 722 for Hekate's beneficent function.
55 Johnston, *Hekate Soteira*, 22 with n. 4 citing J. S. Clay, "The Hekate of the Theogony," *Greek, Roman and Byzantine Studies* (1984), 27–38.
56 Johnston, *Hekate Soteria*, 23.
57 Sarah Iles Johnston, *Restless Dead: Encounters between the Living and the Dead in Ancient Greece* (Berkeley: University of California Press, 1999), 207.
58 Johnston, *Hekate Soteria*, 21.
59 See Johnston, *Hekate Soteria*, Appendix concerning the evidence for Hekate's Equation With Soul, 153ff. as well as ch. III esp. 40 discussing Proclus.
60 Johnston, *Hekate Soteria*, 49.
61 Callimachus, "Hymn to Artemis," in Callimachus, *Hymns*, 11–12.
62 See *Od.* 5.123; 11.172-73, 18.202; 20.60 and 80. Vernant, *Mortals and Immortals*, 196 with n. 5.
63 John Sallis, *The Figure of Nature: On Greek Origins* (Bloomington: Indiana University Press, 2016), 1.
64 Spyridon Rangos, "Proclus and Artemis: On the Relevance of Neoplatonism to the Modern Study of Ancient Religion," *Kernos* (2000), 13, 47–84. http://jornalss.openedition.org/kernos/1293.
65 Rangos, "Proclus and Artemis," 77.
66 Paul Ellinger, "Artemis," in Bonnefoy, *Mythologies*, 145. The Paris School and others emphasized the social use of Greek myths within their historical contexts.
67 Clay, *Politics of Olympus*, 160 with n. 25, citing Pausanus 5.154, Artemis as *agoraia*.
68 Vernant, *Mortals and Immortals*, 205.
69 Vernant, *Mortals and Immortals*, 195.
70 Lefkowitz, *Greek Gods*, 131.
71 Aeschylus *Agamemnon* 109–247, trans. Herbert Weir Smyth (Loeb, 1926).
72 Callimachus, *Hymn to Demeter*, *Hymns* 40.
73 Clay, *Politics of Olympus*, 9.
74 Nicholas Richardson, "The Homeric Hymn to Demeter," in *The Homeric Hymns: Interpretative Essays*, ed. Andrew Faulkner (Oxford: Oxford University Press, 2011), 50 and n.13.
75 Foley, *Hymn to Demeter*, 12–13.
76 See See *The Pyramid Texts* published by The Library of Alexandria, first translated by Samuel A.B. Mercer in 1952, now in the public domain.

77 Herodotus *Histories* 2.59, 61
78 Gail Paterson Corrington, *Her Image of Salvation* (Louisville: Westminster/John Knox Press, 1992), 90-1, and Herodotus *Histories* 2.59, 123.
79 *The Oxyrhynchus Papyri*, trans. B.P. Grenfels and A.S. Hunt (London: Egypt Exploration Fund, 1898), excerpted in *Woman's Religion in the Greco-Roman World*, ed. Ross Shepard Kraemer (Oxford: Oxford University Press, 2004), 455.
80 Assmann, *Cultural Memory*, 14-16.
81 Michael Tardieu, "The Cults of Isis among the Greeks and in the Roman Empire," in Bonnefoy, *Mythologies*, 245-55 and Martin Bommas "Isis and Osiris and Serapis," in *The Oxford Handbook of Roman Egypt*, ed. Christina Riggs (Oxford: Oxford University Press, 2012) 419-35 are recommended for further reading on these histories.

Chapter 3

1 Michael Frede, "Monotheism and Pagan Philosophy in Later Antiquity," in *Pagan Monotheism in Late Antiquity*, ed. Polymnia Athanassiadi and Michael Frede (Oxford: Oxford University Press, 1999), 61-7.
2 Origen, *Contra Celsum*, trans. Henry Chadwick (Cambridge: Cambridge University Press, 1953).
3 Simon Swain, *Hellenism and Empire* (Oxford: Clarendon Press, 1996), 45-65.
4 See Johnston, *Hekate Soteria*, 53ff, 68. She points out that Hekate and Reha are equated as "mother goddesses" during the second century which was a time at which Rhea, Cybele and other versions of the mother goddess gained wide popularity.
5 Garth Fowden, *The Egyptian Hermes* (Princeton: Princeton University Press, 1986), 18-19.
6 Fowden, *Egyptian Hermes*, 45-8.
7 Bloomfield, "Personification Allegory," 161-71.
8 George Boys-Stones, *Platonist Philosophy 80B.C. to AD 250* (Cambridge: Cambridge University Press, 2017. Ch. 20.
9 Xenocrates, "Fragment 15" in Richard Heinze, *Xenocrates* (Stuttgart: Teubner, 1892; repr. Hildesheim: Golms, 1965). John Dillon, *The Middle Platonists* (Ithaca: Cornell University Press, 1977), 25.
10 The best source for this is Dillon, *Middle Platonists*, as the original sources for Eudorus cannot be accessed easily and are found only in the references of other Neoplatonists: 127 and n. 1, This quote is from 347.
11 A source for Moderatus is Simplicius, *Commentaria in Aristotelem Graeca*, ed. Hermannus Diehls (Berlin, 1882),230, 34ff. Dillon, *Middle Platonists*, 347.
12 Dillon, *Middle Platonists*, 347-8.
13 Proclus, *In Tim.* I.303.27ff.: *In Platonis Timaeum commentaria*, vols 1-3, ed. E. Diehl (Leipzig: Teubner, 1903-6). Numenius, fr. 21: Numenius, *Fragments*, Boys-Stones (Des Places). Dillon, *Middle Platonists*, 366-7.
14 John D. Turner, *Sethian Gnosticism and the Platonic Tradition* (Quebec: Les Presses de l'Université Laval, 2001), 380.
15 See John Peter Kenney, *Mystical Monotheism: A Study in Ancient Platonic Theology* (Eugene: WPf and Stock Publishers, 2010 [Brown, 1991]), 60-72. Kenney considers Numenius an important influences in the tradition antecedent to Plotinus. He makes a case for a nascent "monotheism" in the Middle Platonists, as the levels of gods

seem more like aspects in descending levels of transcendence of one ultimate first principle, rather than polytheistic individual entities. It is tricky to ascribe gods' and goddesses' names to various functions in the Middle and Neoplatonist universe and at the same time maintain cosmic sympathy and emanative unity of all levels of being.

16 John Dillon, "Female Principles in Platonism," lecture given at the University of Barcelona. http://revistes.iec.cat/index.php/ITACA/article/viewFile/836/82794, accessed May 2, 2016, 108. Philo, vol. V, *On Flight and Finding*, trans. F. H. Colson and G. H. Whittaker (Loeb, 1934), Sec. 109.
17 Dillon, "Female Principles," 109.
18 Dillon, "Female Principles," 114.
19 M. L. West, *Orphic Poems* (Oxford: Oxford University Press, 1984)and Brisson's review in "Les théogonies orphiques et le papyrus de Derveni," *Revue de l'Histoire des Religions* CCII (1985), 389–420.
20 Proclus, *In Tim.* III.161ff.
21 Lamberton, *Homer*, 61 and n. 55. Scholars in the past such as Dodds, as Lamberton points out, attempted to define the "oriental element" in Numenius, who refers to the Brahmans, the Jews, the Magi, and the Egyptians (fr. 18). The recent trend, he goes on to say, is to discredit these arguments and to point to Greek sources for many of Numenius's ideas. Emilie Kutash, "The Unruliness of Matter in Numenius" (unpublished but presented to ISNS Conference at U. of Haifa, March 2011) also discusses this.
22 See Roger Miller Jones, *The Platonism of Plutarch* (Biblical Life Reproduction Series, 2009), 369–77.
23 Daniel Richter, "Plutarch on Isis and Osiris: Text: Cult, and Cultural Appropriation," *Transactions of the American Philological Association*, vol. 131 (2001), 191–216.
24 Foley, *Hymn to Demeter*, ll. 235-60, 14. Richter, "Plutarch," 201–2.
25 Sarolta A. Takács, "Initiations and Mysteries in Apuleius," *Metamorphoses*, http://scholar.lib.vt.edu/ejournals/ElAnt/V12N1/takacs.pdf, accessed May 19, 2014, 82–3.
26 See Majercik, *Chaldaean Oracles*, and Hans Lewy, *Chaldaean Oracles and Theurgy*.
27 See Polymnia Athanassiadi, "The Chaldaean Oracles," in Athanassiadi and Frede (eds), *Pagan Monotheism in Late Antiquity*,150ff.
28 Michael Psellus, *Oracles Chaldaïques avec un choix de commentaires anciens*, ed. trans. and comm. E. Des Places (Paris: Les belles Lettres, 1971).
29 Marinus *Vita Procli*, tr. M. J. Edwards, in *Neoplatonic Saints: The Lives of Plotinus and Proclus by Their Students* (Liverpool: Liverpool University Press, 2000).
30 Johnston, *Hekate Soteria*, 2 n. 5, frr. 38, 53, 72, 146, 147, 148, 219, 221, 222, 223, 224.
31 Luc Brisson, "Plato's Timaeus and the Chaldaean Oracles," in *Plato's Timaeus as Cultural Icon*, ed. G. Reydams-Schils (Notre Dame: University of Notre Dame, 2002), 111–51.
32 Athanassiadi, "*Chaldean Oracles*," 153ff.
33 Franz Cumont, *Oriental Religions in Roman Paganism* (Chicago: Open Court Publishing Co, 1911), 279 n. 66 cited by Majercik, *Chaldaean Oracles*, 2 n. 8.
34 Johnston, *Hekate Soteira*, 50–1.
35 Majercik, *Chaldaean Oracles*, 4.
36 Lewy, *Chaldaean Oracles and Theurgy*, 88–9.
37 See John F. Finamore and Sarah Iles Johnston, "The Chaldaean Oracles," in Lloyd Gerson, *The Cambridge Companion to Late Antiquity*, 162ff.
38 Finamore and Johnston, "Chaldaean Oracles," 163.

39 Athanassiadi, "Chaldaean Oracles," 159.
40 Brisson, "Plato's Timaeus and the *Chaldean Oracles*," 119.
41 See Janet H. Johnson's introduction to Hans Dieter Betz, *The Greek Magical Papyri in Translation* (Chicago: University of Chicago Press, 1992).
42 Fowden, *Egyptian Hermes*, xxi-xxii. The *Hermetica* that were transmitted in Greek or Latin were edited by A. D. Nock and A. J. Festugière (Paris 1946–54). Festugière produced four volumes entitled *La revelation d'Hermès Trismégiste* between 1944 and 1954.
43 Fowden, *Egyptian Hermes*, 24.
44 Jeremiah Genest, *The Corpus Hermetica*, (2002). www.granta.demon.co.uk/arsm/jg/corpus.html, accessed June 11, 2014, 1.
45 Hans Jonas, *The Gnostic Religion* (Boston: Beacon Press, 1963), 147.
46 Brian Copenhaver, *Hermetica* (Cambridge: Cambridge University Press, 1998), xxxii.
47 Copenhaver, *Hermetica*, 37–8.
48 Elaine Pagels, *The Gnostic Gospels* (New York: Vintage Books, 1979), xxi.
49 Wolf-Peter Funk, Paul-Hubert Poirier, and John D. Turner, *Marsenès* (*NH* X), Collection Bibliothèque copte de Nag Hammadi, section "Textes," 25 (Québec: Les Presses de l'Université Laval/Louvain: Peeters, 2000), 179.
50 Dillon, *Female Principles*, 120–1.
51 Genest, *The Corpus Hermetica*, 1.
52 Mary Lenzi, "Platonic Polypsychic Pantheism," *Monist*, vol. 80, 2 (1997), 239.
53 Turner, *Sethian Gnosticism*, 389.
54 *The Chaldean Oracles: Studies in Greek and Roman Religion*, trans. and comm. R. Majercik (Leiden: Brill, 1989), 4.

Chapter 4

1 See Gilles Quispel, "Hermes Trimegistos and the Origins of Gnosticism," *Vigilae Christianae*, vol. 46 (1992), 1–19. The bible, Quispel points out, does not know of *creatio ex nihilo*, the dogma of later Catholicism, Judaism, and Islam. The bible can be seen as mentioning a pre-existent chaos. Philo of Alexandria and Justin Martyr, among others, held that matter is pre-existent in the Hebrew tradition.
2 Bruno Snell, *The Discovery of the Mind in Greek Philosophy and Literature* (New York: Dover Publications, 1953), 229.
3 Athanassakis, *Hesiod*, 1.
4 Snell, *Discovery of the Mind*, 217, 280. Snell suggests that there are three different types of substantive: the proper noun, the concrete noun, and the abstract noun. The proper noun does not produce knowledge, its object is one that cannot be known nor understood but only recognized once it has been seen, for example, "This is Socrates." The concrete noun, of course, designates the physical phenomena of the world. "Abstractions such as 'the universal' or 'the act of thinking'" are neither proper nouns, nor concrete nouns, but are abstract nouns, an independent form of the substantive. The abstract noun "owes its origin to the development of thought, and only reaches completion with the generic definite article."
5 Fr. 50 (Hippolytus preserves this fragment in *Refutation of All Heresies*, a doxogrpahy: *Ref.* ix.9.1). S. Kirk, J. E. Raven, and M. Schofield, *The Presocratic Philosophers* (Cambridge: Cambridge University Press, 1983), 187.

6   For example on. 120 of her book, *Athena* (Routledge, 2008).
7   See Karl Kerényi, *Athene*, trans. Murray Stein (Dallas: Spring Publications, 1978).
8   Athanassakis, *Hesiod*, 14.
9   E. E. Pender, "Chaos Corrected: Hesiod in Plato's Creation Myth," in *Hesiod and Plato*, ed. G. R. Boys-Stones and J. H. Haubold (Oxford: Oxford University Press, 2010), 217–58, at 229 and n. 14, 15. M.L West, *East Face of Helicon,* 288.
10 Marija Gimbutas and Miriam Robbins Dexter, *The Living Goddess* (Berkeley: University of California Press, 2001), 112.
11 López-Ruiz, *When the Gods Were Born*, 239 n. 25 suggests that for the history of the discovery and its publication vicissitudes we see A. Laks and G. Most, *Studies in the Derveni Papyrus* (Oxford: Oxford University Press, 1997) or G. Betegh's monograph, *The Derveni Papyrus: Cosmology, Theology and Interpretation* (Cambridge: Cambridge University Press, 2004).
12 See López-Ruiz, *When the Gods Were Born*, 145 and n. 68.
13 Vernant, " Cosmogonic Myths," 67.
14 F. M. Cornford, *From Religion to Philosophy* (Mineola: Dover Edition, 2004), 67 and n. 3, citing Diehls, *Fragmente der Vorsokratiker* ii.6d, 479 and Maurice Bloomfield, *Religion of the Veda* (New York: G.P. Putnams Sons, 1908), 124. In the Babylonian cosmogony, Marduk cut in two pieces the monstrous Tihamat and "one half of her he set in place, he spread out as heaven." There are similar structures in Egyptian and Taoist literature. In the Egyptian account Shu separates the sky (*Nut*) from the earth (*Seb*), and in Taoism chaos separates into Yang and Yin, regions of light and darkness.
15 M.L. West, *East of Helicon*, 299.
16 See Homes, *Gender/Antiquity* for an extended discussion of this in her chapter, The Gendering of Matter, 56ff.
17 Pender, "Chaos Corrected," 230.
18 See A. H. Armstrong, "Dualism: Platonic, Gnostic and Christian," in *Neoplatonism and Gnosticism*, ed. Richard T. Wallis and Jay Bregman (Albany: SUNY Press, 1992) 39 and n. 13, quoting Chalcidius 298 (fr. 52 65–70, 82–7 des Places).
19 Athanassakis, *Hesiod*, 5.
20 Vernant, "Cosmogonic Myths," 69.
21 López-Ruiz, *When the Gods Were Born*, 106.
22 Joan Goodnick Westenholz, "Goddesses of the Ancient Near East," in Goodison and Morris, *Ancient Goddesses*, 68.
23 Jones, *Platonism of Plutarch*, 96–7.
24 Brisson, *Plato's Timaeus, Chaldean Oracles,* 11. Brisson points out that the Middle Platonists made this third kind into an equivalent of Aristotelian matter.
25 Kenneth Sayre, *Plato's Late Ontology* (Princeton: Princeton University Press, 1983), 248.
26 Emanuela Bianchi, "Receptacle:/Chora: Figuring the Errant Feminine in Plato's Timaeus," *Hypatia,* vol. 21, 4 (Fall, 2006), 124–46 at 125.
27 Kristeva discusses this in many places for example in Julia Kristeva, "Place Names," in *Desire in Language*, ed. Leon S. Rodiez (New York: Columbia University Press, 1980), 286. See also Introduction to *Desire in Language*, 6.
28 See, for example, Judith Butler, *Bodies That Matter: On the Discursive Limits of "Sex"* (London: Routledge Press, 1993), 39ff. discusses *chora* extensively, including the views of Luce Igriarary.
29 John D. Turner, "The Figure of Hekate and Dynamic Emanationsim in the *Chaldean Oracles*, Sethian Gnosticism and Neoplatonism," *The Second Century Journa*l, vol. 7, 4 (1991), 221–32 at 228.

30 See Finamore and Johnston, "*Chaldean Oracles,*" 162ff.) where Rhea represents Life on a higher level and Hekate on a lower one.
31 Robbert van den Berg, "Becoming like God According to Proclus' Interpretations of the *Timaeus*, the Eleusinian Mysteries, and the *Chaldaean Oracles*," in *Ancient Approaches to Plato's Timaeus, Classical Studies*, R. W. Sharples and Anne Shepard eds. (London: Bulletin of the Institute of Classical Studies, 2003), 191–4.
32 Athanassakis, *Hesiod,* 7.
33 Jones, *Platonism of Plutarch,* 99.
34 Pierluigi Donini, "Platonism, Aristotelianism and Stoicism in Plutarch's on the Face in the Moon," in *The Question of "Eclecticism"*, ed. J. M. Dillon and A. A. Long (Berkeley: University of California Press, 1988), 143 n. 28.
35 Johnston, *Hekate Soteria,* 52, 65 referring to frr. 34 and 35.
36 Brisson, *Plato's Timaeus, Chaldean Oracles,* 119.
37 Jonas, *Gnostic Religion,* 299.
38 Funk, Poirier, and Turner, *Marsanès,* 179.
39 Turner, *Sethian Gnosticism,* 368.
40 See Turner, *Sethian Gnosticism,* 140, 215, which covers the complexities of the Gnostic gospels in light of their Middle Platonic influence in great detail. See also Turner, "Figure of Hekate," 228.
41 Zeke Mazur, "Having Sex with the One," in *Late Antique Epistemology*, ed. Panayiota Vassilopoulou and Stephen R. L. Clark (London: Palgrave Macmillan, 2009), 70–1 and nn. 17, 19.
42 Mazur, "Sex with the One," 70.
43 Proclus, *Commentary on Timaeus,* III.247.26; 248.12-13; 249.27-250.8.
44 As R.M. van den Berg discusses in. *Proclus' Hymns,* 41, cited by Harold Tarrant in a note to his translation, *Commentary on Plato's Timaeus,* vol. I: *Proclus on the Socratic State and Atlantis* (Cambridge: Cambridge University Press, 2007), 264 and n. 702.
45 Lamberton, *Homer,* 208ff.
46 Kirk, Raven and Schofield, *Presocratic Philosophers,* 26.
47 In Proclus, *Commentary on Plato's Timaeus,* vol. II, book 2, trans. David T. Runia and Michael Share (Cambridge: Cambridge University Press, 2008), 312 n. 596, Runia and Share tell the reader that Phanes means "he who reveals."
48 See Kutash, *Ten Gifts,* 137–8.
49 Liz Locke, "Orpheus and Orphism," 7.

Chapter 5

1 Athanassakis, *Hesiod,* 14.
2 Homer, *The Iliad*, trans. Richmond Lattimore (Chicago: University of Chicago Press, 2011), 320.
3 Xenocrates (of Chalcedon) (396/395-314/313 BCE) was head of Plato's academy after Speusippus (c. 339/338 BCE).
4 See Charles Kahn, *Pythagoras and the Pythagoreans* (Indianapolis: Hackett, 2001), 115 and n. 45 (fr. 15 Heinze-Aethius 17.30).
5 See Dominic J. O'Meara, *Pythagoras Revived* (New York: Oxford Clarendon Press, 1989), 16f.
6 O'Meara, *Pythagoras,* 20.

7   Iamblichus, *Theology of Arithmetic*, trans. Robin Waterfield (Grand Rapids: Phanes Press, 1988), Waterfield translates from V. de Falko's Greek manuscript (Teubner Series: Leipzig, 1922).
8   Iamblichus, *Theology of Arithmetic*, 37.
9   Iamblichus, *Theology of Arithmetic*, 45-6 and n. 10.
10 Wolf-Peter Funk, Paul-Herbert Poirier, and John D. Turner, *Marsenès (NHX). Collection Bibliothèque copte de Nag Hammadi section 'Textes'*, 25 (Québec: Les Presses de l'Université Lavan/Louvain: Peeters, 2000), 179.
11 See Kahn, *Pythagoras*, 118, citing E. R. Dodds, the translator and commentator on Proclus' *Elements of Theology* (1963), 259.
12 See for example, Porphyry's *Life of Pythagoras* where he mentions better and worse opposites. Porphyry, *Life of Pythagoras, The Pythagorean Sourcebook and Library*, ed. Kenneth Sylvan Guthrie (Grand Rapids: Phanes Press, 1988), 130.
13 G. E. R. Lloyd, *Polarity and Analogy: Two Types of Argumentation in Early Greek Thought* (Indianapolis: Hackett, 1992), 36-7, and "Right and Left in Greek Philosophy," in *Methods and Problems in Greek Science*, ed. G. E. R. Lloyd (Cambridge: Cambridge University Press, 1991), 29.
14 Jones, *Platonism of Plutarch*, 3.
15 Funk, Poirier, and Turner, *Marsanès*, 179.
16 Jones, *Platonism of Plutarch*, 96-7.
17 Iamblichus, *On the Mysteries*, trans. Emma Clarke, John Dillon, and Jackson Hershbell (Leiden: Brill, 2003), 289.
18 See Lamberton, *Homer*, 106 and n. 76, citing Pépin, "Plotin et les mythes," 25, and Pierre Hadot, "Ouranos, Kronos, and Zeus in Plotinus' Treatise against the Gnostics," in *Neoplatonism and Early Christian Thought*, ed. J. J. Blumental and R. A Marcus (London: Ashgate, 1981), 124-34.
19 Majercik, *Chaldaean Oracles*, 4.
20 Iamblichus, *Theology of Arithmetic*, 46.
21 Aristotle, *Phys.* 3.6, 206a15-25, supplies a well-known definition of the infinite as existing potentially not actually, endlessly changing into something else, like a day or the Olympic games. "It is not that which has nothing outside it, but which always has something outside it" (206b33-207a1).
22 T. L. Heath, Euclid, *The Elements*, vol. I (New York: Dover, 1956), 413.
23 The precedents for motion and particularly the irrational component and its agency can be found in Plato's *Statesman* (269C-274D) and *Laws* X (896D-E). Plutarch and Numenius tie the irrational component with the lower aspect of the Cosmic Soul. See Turner, *Sethian Gnosticism*, 362.
24 Jones, *Platonism of Plutarch*, 98.
25 Augustine, *On Free Choice of the Will*, book I, trans. Thomas Williams (Indianapolis: Hackett, 1993), 1-28.
26 Dennis O'Brian, "Plotinus on Matter and Evil," in *The Cambridge Companion to Plotinus*, ed. Lloyd Gerson (Cambridge: Cambridge Companion to Plotinus, 1996), 171-95.
27 See G.S. Kirk, *Heraclitus: The Cosmic Fragments* (Cambridge: Cambridge University Press, 1954), 133.
28 See Johnston, *Hekate Soteira*, 153 and n. 1. She cites Hans Lewy, *Chaldaean Oracles and Theurgy*, 356 n. 168 for supporting evidence for the equation of life and soul from Plato and the Platonists.

29 "Concerning the Indestructibility of the Soul," fr. 44 in *The Neoplatonic Writings of Numenius*, ed. Kenneth Guthrie (Lawrence: Selene Books, 1987).
30 See Johnston, *Hekate Soteria*, 153 n. 1 and 154 n. 7. She cites Hans Lewy who identifies Hekate with Soul throughout his book (e.g., 85–95, 353–66), and Dillon, *Middle Platonists*, 364–95. Johnston herself has modified her position (see Chapter 4 here).
31 Porphyry, *Philosophy from the Oracles* (Eusebius, *Praeparatio Evangelica*, ed. comm., and trans. E. H. Gifford, V.7, 191 (Oxford, 1903). Psellus, *Oracles Chaldaïques avec un choix de commentaires anciens*.
32 Proclus, *Commentary on Plato's Republic: In Platonis rem publicam, commentaire sur la République*, trans. A.J. Festigière (Paris: Vrin, 1970).
33 Johnston, *Hekate Soteria*, 156–7, 158 and n. 19 where Johnston mentions that Rhea is also described as having a womb in fr. 56 of the *Oracles*.
34 Plotinus, *Enneads, Enn*. VII, trans. A. H. Armstrong (Loeb, 1988).
35 Proclus, *In Tim*. III.246.18-19, 248.12-20-249.6, for example.
36 See Emilie Kutash, "Oikoumene, Ouranos, Ousia and Outside: An Analogy across Three Ancient Disciplines," In *Graduate Faculty Philosophy Journal*, vol. 22, 2 (2001), 115–45.
37 Athanassiadi, *Chaldean Oracles*, 159.
38 Walter Burkert, *Babylon, Memphis, Persepolis: Eastern Contexts of Greek Culture* (Cambridge: Harvard University Press, 2004), 35–7, quotes from W. G. Lambert and A.R. Millard, *Atra-hasis: The Babylonian Story of the Flood* (Oxford: clarendon Press, 1969), 129.
39 Burkert, *Babylon*, 35–7.
40 López-Ruiz, *When the Gods Were Born*, 113 and n. 9.
41 As Athanassakis points out in a note on *Theogony* 133–8 (40).
42 López-Ruiz, *When the Gods Were Born*, 118.
43 John Palmer, "Parmenides," in *Stanford Encyclopedia of Philosophy* (summer 2012 edition), ed. Edward N. Zalta http://plato.stanford.edu/archives/sum2012/entries/parmenides/, accessed November 12, 2013.
44 He also was the first Platonist to comment on the *Chaldaean Oracles*.
45 Lamberton, *Homer*, 120–33. See P.T. Struck "Allegory and Ascent in Neoplatonism," in *The Cambridge Companion to Allegory*, ed. R. Copeland and P.T. Struck (Cambridge: Cambridge University Press, 2010), 60 and n. 4. Stuck recommends Robert Lamberton's translation of Porphyry, *On the Cave of the Nymphs* (Barryton: Station Hill Press, 1983). See also Emilie Kutash "Myth Allegory and Inspired Symbolism in Early and Late Platonism," in *International Journal of the Platonic Tradition*, vol. 14 2020, 1–25, 11.
46 Struck Allegory, (2010) 60.
47 Rangos, "Proclus and Artemis," 50.
48 Susan Bordo, "The Cartesian Masculinization of Thought," *Signs*, vol. 11, #3 (Spring, 1996), 439–56.

Chapter 6

1 See Edward J. Watts, *City and School in Late Antique Athens and Alexandria* (Berkeley: University of California Press, 2006), 131ff.

2   Julian, *Oration 5: Hymn to the Mother of the Gods* 475, 7.2.7-10, trans. Wilmer Cave Wright (Loeb Classical Library. Cambridge: Harvard University Press, 2014), 435.
3   Eunapius, *Lives of the Philosophers* 475.19-23, trans. Wilmer Cave Wright (Loeb Classical Library. Cambridge: Harvard University Press, 1998), 435.
4   Pierre Chuvin, *A Chronicle of the Last Pagans*, trans. B. A. Archer (Cambridge: Harvard University Press, 1990), 26–32.
5   Chuvin, *Last Pagans*, 29.
6   Averil Cameron, *The Later Roman Empire* (Cambridge: Harvard University Press, 1993), 68–9.
7   Eusebius *Vit. Cons.* 3.55.1-5, 358.1-4 in *A Companion to Greek and Roman Sexualities,* ed. Thomas K. Hubbard (Hoboken: John Wiley and Sons, 2014), 559.
8   Stephen Williams and Gerard Friell, *Theodosius* (New Haven: Yale University Press, 1994), 121–3 and n. 20 (citing Theodosius' edict C.TH XVI. 10.10-11).
9   Williams and Friell, *Theodosius*, 130–5.
10 See Watts, *City and School,* 85 and n. 32, citing Damascius *Life of Isidore* (*Vit. Is. Ath.* 105A).
11 For much of what follows here see Kutash, "The Prevailing Circumstances", 185–94.
12 See Garth Fowden, "The Pagan Holy Man in Late Antique Society," *JHS* (1982), 33–59, at 53, 43 n. 79 (Marinus *Vit. Proc.* 36), 43 n. 82.
13 Paul Oskar Kristeller, *Renaissance Thought and Its Sources* (New York: Columbia University Press, 1979), 224–6.
14 Julian, "Mother of the Gods," in *Orations 1–5*, 463. Wright, *Orations,* 463 n. 2.
15 Iamblichus, *On the Mysteries,* 3.
16 Lewy, *Chaldean Oracles and Theurgy,* 69 n. 9.
17 Alan Cameron, "The Last Days of the Academy at Athens," *PCPS,* vol. 15 (1969), 7–29 at 16 n. 3; Proclus *In Crat.* 264.7; Proclus *In Tim.* III.44.6.
18 Van den Berg, *Proclus' Hymns* (Leiden: Brill, 2001), 241, 307.
19 See Vered Lev Kanaan, "Aphrodite the Goddess of Appearances," in *Brill's Companion to Aphrodite*, ed. Amy C. Smith and Sadie Pickup (Leiden: Brill, 2010).
20 This information is taken from Tuomo Lankila's article "Aphrodite in Proclus' Theology," *Journal for Late Antique Religion and Culture,* vol. 3, (2009), 21–43 at 23. This study cannot be given due justice here as it identifies all of Proclus' usages of Aphrodite in his complex triadizing metaphysics.
21 Lankila, "Aphrodite," 32.
22 See Kutash, "Myth, Allegory and Inspired Symbolism, 15."
23 Proclus *In Crat.* 109C2, 71 30, 8-10i in *The Philosophy of the Commentators* 200–600, vol. I, ed. Richard Sorabji (Ithaca: Cornell University Press, 2005),387.
24 These depictions came to be called Hekataia; according to Pausanias, *Descriptions of Greece* (II.30.2), this is the first triple Hekate that was known.
25 Ovid, *Selected Works,* ed. Frank J. Miller (New York: American Book Company, 1904), 281. See *The Works of Virgil with a Commentary* (1865). com. Jon Collington (Kesinger Publishing, 2010) 312,n. 511. The same goddess was supposed to be Artemis, the moon and Hekate or Persephone.
26 Athanassakis, *Hesiod,* 46.
27 Betz, *Greek Magical Papyri,* 332 (*PGM* 2441–2621).
28 See Lamberton, *Homer,* 115. This is a quote from an extensive passage from Porphyry preserved by Stobaeus from an unidentified lost work.
29 Foley, *Hymn to Demeter,* 40 and 55.

30 Philo, *Questions and Answers on Genesis*, trans. Ralph Marcus (Loeb Classical Library. Cambridge: Harvard University Press, 1953). Lamberton, *Homer*, 52.
31 Majercik, *Chaldean Oracles*, 71.
32 Brisson, *Philosophers Saved Myths*, 97–8.
33 Xenocrates' views on triads are derived from an account by Sextus Empiricus, *Adv. Math.* VII, 147ff. Dillon, *Middle Platonists*, discusses Xenocrates' and other Middle Platonists' views on triads on 30, 214, 356ff.
34 See J. Gwyn Griffiths, *Triads and Trinity* (Cardiff: University of Wales Press, 1900), 74.
35 Turner, "Figure of Hecate," 221.
36 In other Sethian Gnostic literature, *Trimorphic Protenoia*: "I, the thought of the Father, Protenoia that is Barbelo. the Invisible One who is hidden. (I am) the Mother. the light which she appointed as virgin, she who is called Merothea, the incomprehensible the womb."
37 Turner, "Figure of Hecate," 221. Damascius *Dub. et Sol.* 61 & 221 = 1.131,17 & 2.101,25 Ruelle.
38 There are striking parallels, according to Majercik, between the Oracles and Sethian Gnosticism. See Majercik, *Chaldean Oracles* 3, 3 n. 9; Lewy, *Chaldean Oracles and Theurgy*, 311–98; Dillon, *Middle Platonists*, 197, 384–9.
39 Turner, "Figure of Hecate," 222. "In the Platonizing Sethian treatises, the members of this triad are named Existence (*hyparxis*) or Being (Greek *ousia* or Coptic *pet* = Greek *to on* or *ontotês*), Life (Coptic *pônh* = Greek *zôê*) or Vitality (Coptic *timntônh* = Greek *zôotês*) and Mentality (Coptic *timnteime* or the Greek neologism *noêtês*), attributes which the Unknowable deity, although it exists, lives and thinks, does not itself possess."
40 Turner, "Figure of Hecate," 224.
41 In the *Oracles* a triad is identified with Hekate, who is called a "membrane" which separates the first and second fires (fr. 6 Des Places), that is, the Father and the Intellect (fr. 50 Des Places). In effect, the *Oracles* depict an ennead: a first triad of the Father together with his power and potential intellect, a third triad of the dyadically oriented (above and below) demiurgic Intellect, and between these two a second "measured triad" identified with Hekate representing the multiplicity that proceeds from the Father.
42 Turner, "Figure of Hecate," 222. Damascius *Dub. et Sol.* 61 & 221 = 1.131,17 & 2.101,25 Ruelle. Turner identifies Proclus, perhaps Porphyry, and the author of the Anonymous Parmenides Commentaries as holding to a doctrine in which there are three stages of the process of "Being" (as opposed to the One whose hypostasis is unknown and transcendent): Permanence, Procession, and Reversion. During this process Existence, Life, and Mind are the successive modes of productive existence.
43 Lamberton, *Homer*, 104–5. Lamberton cites Plotinus, *Opera*, ed. Paul Henry and Hans-Rudolf Schwyzer, 3 vols (Paris, 1951–73).
44 Hadot, "Ouranos, Kronos, and Zeus," 124–37.
45 Turner, *Gnosticism and Platonism*, 432ff.
46 Rangos, "Proclus and Artemis," 47.
47 Proclus, *Elements of Theology*, ed. and trans. E. R. Dodds, Proposition 103.
48 Rangos, "Proclus and Artemis," 62.
49 Brisson, *Philosophers Saved Myths*, 97–8.
50 Majercik, *Chaldean Oracles*, 71. In the *Oracles*, Hekate is found among the triad of intellective gods (Kronos, Hekate, and Zeus) where she intermediates on the

higher level. When she is found in the hypostasis of Soul (Hekate, Soul, Virtue), she becomes more worldly. Traditionally Rhea is the mother of Zeus—here she assimilates to Hekate, she is the spouse of the First Father and mother/sister of the Demiurge. Hekate's womb generates the World Soul and also represents nature.

51 See Brisson, *Philosophers Saved Myths*, 97–8.
52 Jan Opsomer, "Proclus on Demiurgy and Procession in the Timaeus," in *Reason and Necessity: Essays in Plato's Timaeus*, ed. M. R. Wright (London: Duckworth, 2000), 131.
53 Rangos, "Proclus and Artemis," 61.
54 Opsomer, "Proclus on Demiurgy," 114. See S. E. Gersh, *Kinesis Akinetos* (Leiden: Brill, 1973).
55 Rangos, "Proclus and Artemis," 57, translates from the Porus edition of *Platonic Theology*, Budé edition.
56 Much of the preceding account and what follows is that of Rangos, "Proclus and Artemis," 57–9.
57 Rangos, "Proclus and Artemis," 61ff.
58 As R.M. van den Berg discusses in *Proclus' Hymns,* 41, cited by Harold Tarrant in a note to his translation, *Commentary on Plato's Timaeus,* vol. I: *Proclus on the Socratic State and Atlantis* (Cambridge: Cambridge University Press, 2007), 264 and n. 702. See Kutash, *Ten Gifts*, 186. *In Tim.* III.247.26, 248.12-13, 249.27, 250.8. Tarrant *Commentary on Plato's Timaeus,* vol. I, 97 n. 28 commenting on Proclus *In Tim.* I.5.15, the reference to the "life-giving goddess."
59 Peter Manchester in his article, "The Noetic Triad in Plotinus, Marius Victorinus and Augustine," in *Neoplatonism and Gnosticism*, ed. Richard T. Wallis (Albany: State University of New York Press, 1992), 217 ff., finds it doubtful that the Plotonian hypostases were an exemplar for Christian Trinitarian metaphysics and finds no real parallels between the One and Nous and father and son in, for example, Origen.
60 See Michael Brabazon, "Carl Jung and the Trinitarian Self," *Quodilbet Journal*, vol. 4, 2–3 (Summer, 2002).

Chapter 7

1 Moshe Halbertal and Avishai Margalit, *Idolatry*, trans. Naomi Goldblum (Cambridge: Harvard University Press, 1992), 138–9.
2 Saul Kripke, *Naming and Necessity* (Cambridge: Harvard University Press, 1980). Kripke famously argues with Frege's idea that naming and any variety of descriptions can pertain to a name.
3 Michael Chase, "What Does Porphyry Mean by Theōn patēr?" *Dionysius,* 85 and n. 30.
4 Assmann, *Moses*, 3.
5 Chiara Bottici, "Mythos and Logos: A Genealogical Approach" in *Epoché* 13:1 (Fall, 2008), 1–24, at 3 and n. 16, citing J. P. Vernant, *Mythe et pensée chez les grecs. Etudes de psychologie historique* (Paris: La Découverte, 1990), 374.
6 Marquardt, Portrait of "Hecate," 251.
7 West, *East Face of Helicon*, 209.
8 Jan Assmann, "Translating Gods: Religion as a Factor of Cultural (Un) Translatability," in *Religion, beyond a Concept*, ed. Henri de Vries (New York: Fordham University Press, 2008), 139 and n. 1.

9   Assmann, *Moses*, 45.
10 Kripke, *Naming and Necessity*, 190.
11 These manuscripts discovered in Egypt by papyrologists came from Ptolemaic and Roman periods (32 BC to as late as 640 CE).
12 Assmann, *Moses*, 50.
13 Assmann, *Moses*, 50 and n. 67, citing B. P. Grenfell and A. S. Hunt, *The Oxyrhynchos Papyri*, vol. 11 (London, 1915), 190–202, no. 1380.
14 Assmann, *Moses*, 49, citing a hymn of Isidorus of Marmuthis engraved on pillars in the temple of Thermuthis at Medinet Madi.
15 Gail Corrington Streete, "An Isis Aretalogy from Kyme in Asia Minor, First Century BCE," in *Religions of Late Antiquity in Practice*, ed. Richard Valantasis (Princeton: Princeton University Press, 2000), 369–70: 69.
16 Robert Turcan, *The Cults of the Roman Empire* (Hoboken: Wiley-Blackwell, 1997), 76.
17 Corrington Streete, "Isis Aretalogy," 369–70.
18 Copenhaver, *Hermetica*, xxii–xxiiii.
19 Turcan, *Cults*, 76 and n. 5, citing F. Dumand, *Le culte d'Isis dans le bassin oriental de la Méditerranée* (EPRO 26) (Leiden: Brill, 1973), II, 48.
20 Turcan, *Cults*, 76 and n. 12 citing Pausanias *Description of Greece* I.18.4.
21 Turcan, *Cults*, 88.
22 Copenhaver, *Hermetica*, xxii–xxiiii.
23 Herodotus, *Histories* 2.42 and 1.56.
24 Witt, *Isis*, 121–2.
25 John Gwyn Griffiths, *Apuleius of Madaura: The Isis-Book (Metamorphoses*, Book XI) Etudes Préliminaires des Religions Orientales 39 (Leiden: Brill, 1975), 70f,114ff. Assmann, *Moses*, 47–8, n. 62.
26 Streete, "Isis Aretalogy," 70.
27 Corrington, *Image of Salvation*, 85–7.
28 Witt, *Isis*, 112.
29 Frederick Solmsen, *Isis among the Greeks and Romans* (Cambridge: Harvard University Press, 1979), 7.
30 Marcel Le Glay, Jean-Louis Voisin, and Yann Le Bohec, *A History of Rome* (Malden: Blackwell Publishers, 1997), 222.
31 Karl Galinsky, *Augustan Culture* (Princeton: Princeton University Press, 1996), 333 (Pliny *HN* 34.54).
32 See Lynn Emrich Roller, *In Search of God the Mother, the Cult of Anatolian Cybele* (Berkeley: University of California Press, 1999), 145.
33 Roller, *God the Mother*, 125 citing Pindar fr. 80, the earliest known equation of Kybele with the word Meter.
34 Roller, *God the Mother*, 270–1 citing Ovid and Virgil in nn. 40 and 41 (Ovid *Fast.* 4.179-372 and throughout Virgil's *Aeneid*, e.g., 2.693-97).
35 Lamberton, *Homer*, 45.
36 Ramsey McMullan, *Paganism in the Roman Empire* (New Haven: Yale University Press, 1981), 86–90, 188 nn. 51, 54. McMullan cites Alex. Rhet. in L. Speigel, *Rhet. Graeci* 3 4f. for Dio Chrysostom and for Maximus of Tyre, *Philos.* 17 (1).5.
37 Assmann, *Moses*, 47–8, 50.
38 Le Glay, Voisin, Le Bohec, *History of Rome*, 249.
39 Corrington, *Image of Salvation*, 81–98.
40 Celsus, *On the True Doctrine*, trans. R. Joseph Hoffmann (New York: Oxford University Press, 1987), 35.

41 Assmann, *Moses,* 51 and n. 71 citing an Orphic fragment and Macrobius *Saturnalia* I.18.17.
42 McMullen, *Paganism,* 86. He is "Zeus Greatest Helios Olympian, the Savior" in an inscription from Pergamon, "Zeus Sarapis" often on gems and amulets, "Zeus Dionysius" in Phrygia and Rome.
43 Gregory Shaw, *Theurgy and the Soul: The Neoplatonism of Iamblichus* (University Park: Pennsylvania State University Press, 1995), 203.
44 Assmann, "Translating Gods," 145.
45 Proclus, *Commentary on Plato's Timaeus,* vol. II: *Proclus on the Causes of the Cosmos and Its Creation,* trans. D. T. Runia and M. Share (Cambridge: Cambridge University Press, 2008), 123.
46 Proclus, *Theol. Plat.* I.29, 124.12-125.2, quoted in H. D. Saffrey, "New Objective Links between the Pseudo-Dionysius and Proclus," in *Neoplatonism and Christian Thought,* ed. D. J. O'Meara (Norfolk: International Society for Neoplatonic Studies, 1982), 65–74 at 68.
47 Saffrey, "Pseudo-Dionysus," 70 and n. 20, citing Marinus *Vita Procli* 30.
48 Robert Maarten van den Berg. *Proclus Commentary on the Cratylus in Context* (Leiden: Brill, 2007), 111, 175. See also *In Crat.* 51, 18.27-19.17 where Proclus says names are like statues of the realities.
49 Dylan Burns, "Apophatic Strategies in *Allogenes,*" *Harvard Theological Review,* vol. 1032 (2010), 161–79 n. 73.
50 Kutash, *Ten Gifts,* 206 and Proclus *Commentary on Parmenides,* 1171ff.
51 Jacques Derrida, "Sauf le nom," in *On the Name,* ed. Thomas Dutoit (Stanford: Stanford University Press, 1993), 62.
52 Assmann, "Translating Gods," 145.

Chapter 8

1 Leah Novick, *On the Wings of the Shekinah: Judaism's Divine Feminine* (Wheaten, Il.: Quest Books, 2008).
2 Rafael Patai, *The Hebrew Goddess* (Detroit: Wayne State University Press, 1967), 28–9.
3 See Ephraim E. Urbach, *The Sages,* trans. Israel Abrahams (Cambridge: Harvard University Press, 1979).
4 Karel van der Toorn, "Goddesses in Early Israelite Religion," ed. Goodison and Morris, *Ancient Goddesses,* 91.
5 Julia Friedman, "Archeologists Discover God's Wife?" *Ha'aretz* 15/09/13.
6 Amihal Mazaar and Nava Panitz-Cohen, "To What God?" www.Regov.org/Rehovpublications/mazar-Panitz-Cohen-BAR0608.pdf. accessed July 20, 2015
7 James B. Pritchard, *Palestinian Figurines in Relation to Certain Goddesses Known through Literature* (Philadelphia: University or Pennsylvania, 1943), 1, 87. Patai, *Hebrew Goddess,* 59–60 and n. 33. Seals with Hebrew names, such as Leyaquin, Yoyakhimn, etc., prove to Patai, on the other hand, that they were of Israelite origin.
8 West, *East Face of Helicon,* 34.
9 See Ze'ev Meshel, "Did Yahweh have a Consort?" *Biblical Archeology Review* 5:02 Mar./Apr. 1979). The first photos and announcements of this find were published in 1976: "Cache of Hebrew and Phoenician Inscriptions Found in the Desert," *BAR* 02:01.1976.

10 See Hershel Shanks, "The Persisting Uncertainties of Kuntillet Ajrud," *Biblical Archeology Review* Nov/Dec. 2012. William G. Dever, "Asherah, Consort of Yahweh? New Evidence from Kuntillet Ajrud," *Bulletin of the American Schools of Oriental Research*, vol. 255 (1984), 29–37.
11 Ziony Zevit, "The Khiber el-Qōm Inscription Mentioning a Goddess," *Bulletin of the American Schools of Oriental Research*, vol. 255 (1984), 39–47.
12 Frymer-Kensky, *Wake of the Goddesses*, 86, 244 n. 13.
13 Frymer-Kensky, *Wake of the Goddesses*, 157, 158 and n. 27. The inscription is found in Moshe Weinfeld, 'Further Remarks on the "Ajrud inscriptions," *Shnaton*, vol. 5-6 (1978–79), 23–33 (in Hebrew).
14 See Cyrus H. Gordon "The Origins of the Jews in Elephantine," *Journal of Near Eastern Studies*, vol. 14, 1 (Jan 1955), 55–8. The Jewish temple had already been established before Cambyses conquered Egypt in 525 BCE. See also John Day, *Yahweh and the Gods and Goddesses of Canaan* (London: Sheffield Academic Press, 2002), 143.
15 Van der Toorn, "Goddesses," 85.
16 Van der Toorn, "Goddesses," 87 and n. 1; N. H. Walls, *The Goddess Anat in Ugarit Myth* (Atlanta: Scholars Press, 1992), 152–4.
17 K. L. Noll, *Canaan and Israel in Antiquity* (London: Bloomsbury, 2013), 392 cites R. G. Kratz, "The Second Temple of Jeb and of Jerusalem," in *Judah and Judeans in the Persian Period*, ed. Oded Lipschitz and Manfred Oeming (Winona Lake: Eisenbrauns, 2006), 247–64.
18 Frymer-Kensky, *Wake of the Goddesses,* 153ff. and n. 1, citing W. L. Halladya, "On Every Lofty Hill and under Every Leafy Tree," *VT*, vol. 11 (1961), 170–6.
19 *The Jerusalem Bible*, ed. Harold Fish (Jerusalem: Koren Publishers, 1997), 597.
20 Mark S. Smith, *Memoirs of God* (Minneapolis: Augsburg Fortress Press, 2004), 63.
21 John Day, "Asharah in the Hebrew Bible and Northwest Semitic Literature," *JBL*, vol. 105 (1986), 335–408.
22 Patai, *Hebrew Goddess,* 38 and n. 9.
23 In a review of Patai's book, *The Hebrew Goddess*, Seger finds the premise that the prophets railed against worship of the queen of heaven and other such allusions are not adequate evidence to support the presence of a Hebrew goddess. While it may have been popular cult practice, that does not make it a core belief of Israelite religion. Patai answers that there is no hard and fast line between official and non-official versions of faith. This seems a poor argument for the fact that goddess worship was clearly not a mainstream Judaic practice. See Joe D. Seger, "Review of *The Hebrew Goddess*," *American Anthropologist*, vol. 72 (1970), 205–7; Raphael Patai, "Seger's Review of *The Hebrew Goddess*," *American Anthropologist*, vol. 72, (1970).
24 Van der Toorn, "Goddesses," 90.
25 Frymer-Kensky, *Wake of the Goddesses,* 159.
26 Yehezkel Kaufman, *The Religion of Israel*, trans. Moshe Greenberg (Chicago: University of Chicago Press, 1990).
27 Peter Schäfer, *Mirror of His Beauty: Feminine Images of God from the Bible to the Early Kabbalah* (Princeton: Princeton University Press, 2002), 6–7.
28 See Jane S. Webster "Sophia: Engendering Wisdom in Proverbs, Ben Sira and the Wisdom of Solomon," *Journal for the Study of the Old Testament*, no. 78 (1998), 63–79 at 63.
29 Corrington, *Image of Salvation,* 107.
30 www.jewishencyclopedia.com/articles/14971-wolf-aaron-benjamin. accessed 6 June, 2016

31 Griffiths, *Triads*, 199–200 and n. 20.
32 Corrington, *Image of Salvation*, 104–5.
33 Corrington, *Image of Salvation*, 104 cites Burton Mack, *Logos und Sophia*, Studien zur Umwelt des Neuen Testaments 10 (Göttingen: Vandenhoeck & Ruprecht, 1973), 21.
34 Corrington, *Image of Salvation*, 107 citing John Kloppenborg, "Isis and Sophia in the Book of Wisdom," *HTR*, vol. 75 (1982), 81–2.
35 Philo, *On the Cherubim* XIV, Loeb Classical Library (Harvard University Press), 39; Patai, *Hebrew Goddess*, 97–8 and n. 17.
36 Barbara Newman, *God and the Goddesses* (Philadelphia: University of Pennsylvania Press, 2005), 373 n. 1. Barbara Newman points out that a vast bibliography of Hebrew Wisdom literature exists, and cites some of the sources.
37 Gershom Scholem, *Origins of Kabbalah*, trans. Allan Arkush (Princeton: Princeton University Press, 1987 (1967), 88–95. See also Halbertal and Margalit, *Idolatry*, 198 n. 14, in which they cite Scholem, *Major Trends in Jewish Mysticism* (New York: Schocken, 1961), 18–39 and Scholem, *On the Kabbalah and Its Symbolism* (New York: Schocken Books, 1996), ch. 3.
38 See Urbach, *The Sages*, 190, 166, 193.
39 Arthur Green, "Shekhinah, The Virgin Mary, and the Song of Songs," *AJS Review*, vol. 26, 1 (2002), 1–52.
40 Arthur Green, *A Guide to the Zohar* (Stanford: Stanford University Press, 2004), 49.
41 Scholem, *On the Kabbalah and Its Symbolism*, ch. 3 on "Kabbalah and Myth," 100ff elaborates Scholem's contention that myth is a prevalent modality in Kabbalah.
42 Scholem, *Origins of the Kabbalah*, 2ff.
43 Scholem, *Origins of the Kabbalah*, 85.
44 This description is taken from Lawrence Fine, "Kabbalistic Texts," in *Back to the Sources*, ed. Barry Holz (New York: Summit Books, 1994), 322ff. and Schäfer, *Mirror of His Beauty*, 4–5.
45 Fine, *Kabbalistic Texts*, 310.
46 Urbach, *Sages*, 40 ff.
47 Schaffer, *Mirror of His Beauty*, 137.
48 Green, "Shekhinah," particularly 37ff.
49 Scholem, *Kabbalah and Its Symbolism*, 104.
50 "Let them make me a sanctuary that I may dwell (*w'shakhanti*) among them" is translated in the *Targum* Onkoles (the Aramaic translation of the Bible) as "I will let my Shekhinah dwell among the Children." There is room, apparently, for ambiguity in treating the term in a personified form.
51 Patai, *Hebrew Goddess*, 96.
52 Scholem, *Kabbalah and Its Symbolism*. 105.
53 See Green, "Shekhinah," 37. More on Chrisman in influence can be found in Yehuda Liebes, *Christian Influence in the Zohar* (Albany: SUNY Press, 1993), 139–61, cited by Green, "Shekhinah," 36.
54 Halbertal and Margalit, *Idolatry*, 240.
55 Eliot Wolfson, *Along the Path* (Albany: State University Press, 1995), 108.
56 Eliot Wolfson, *Circle in the Square: Studies in the Use of Gender in Kabbalistic Symbolism* (Albany: State University of New York Press, 1995), 1.
57 Wolfson, Circle, 103 and 103, n. 134 and 132.
58 Scholem, *Kabbalah*, 105.
59 See Wolfson, *Along the Path*, 65–6 and nn. 12 and 13. Wolfson devotes ch. 2 to specifying Jewish-Christian roots of one of the Kabbalist symbols, the tree, but

questions if indigenous Jewish-Christian sources, in general, might be more pertinent to the Bahir than Gnostic sources.
60 Pagels, *Gnostic Gospels*, 55.
61 Patria Cox Miller, "Plenty Sleeps There": The Myth of Eros and Psyche in Plotinus and Gnosticism," in *Neoplatonism and Gnosticism*, ed. Wallis and Bregman, (Albany: State University of New York Press, 1992), 223–38.
62 Schäfer, *Mirror*, 138–9, citing Scholem, *Origins of the Kabbalah*, 93.
63 Schäfer, *Mirror*, 219–21, citing Scholem, *Origins of the Kabbalah*, 66f and Wolfson, *Along the Path*, 70.
64 *The Nag Hammadi Scriptures*, ed. Marvin Meyer (New York: Harper Collins, 2007), 60–51; Birger A. Pearson, *Gnosticism, Judaism and Egyptian Christianity* (New York: Fortress, 2006).
65 Halbertal and Margalit, *Idolatry*, 198–9 and n. 17. See also M. Idel, *The Mystical Experience in Abraham Abulufia* (Albany: SUNY Press, 1988), 7–10.
66 Wolfson, *Circle in the Square*, 79.
67 Wolfson, *Circle in the Square*, 80–5.
68 Elizabeth A. Johnson, *She Who Is: The Mystery of God in Feminist Theological Discourse* (Chestnut Ridge, NY: Crossroad Publishing Company, 2002) and her article, "The Incomprehensibility of God as the Image of God, Male and Female," *Theological Studies*, vol. 45 (1984), 447.

Chapter 9

1 Foley, *Hymn to Demeter*, 150.
2 Newman, *God and the Goddesses*, 1–3.
3 Bertrand Russell, *History of Western Philosophy* (London: Routledge, 2006), 305.
4 Witt, *Isis*, 188.
5 See Witt, *Isis*, 255–61. The quote is from Ephesians 6:12.
6 This litany was discovered in Egypt in 1905 by Renfell and Hunt and contains an invocation of the goddess Isis thought to date to the second century. See Marvin Bascom Norwood's 1926 dissertation on the Hymn of Clement and the Isis Litany for University of Chicago, accessible on line (archive.org/stream/MN41655 umf-2/MN41655umf-2-djvu.txt). Accessed May 14, 2016.
7 Borgeaud, *Mother of the Gods*, 121–3.
8 Chuvin, *Last Pagans*, 74–5.
9 Marinus, "*Vita Procli*," 130.
10 Witt, *Isis*, 275.
11 Damascius, *The Philosophical History*, ed. Polymnia Athanassiadi (Athens: Apamea Cultural Association, 1999) (aka *Life of Isidore*).
12 Watts, *City and School*, 224–6; Polymnia Athanassiadi, "Persecution and Response in Late Paganism: The Evidence of Damascius," *JHS* (1993), 1–29; Kutash, "Prevailing Circumstances", 84–200.
13 Mark J. Edwards, "Origen," in *The Stanford Encyclopedia of Philosophy* (Spring 2014 edition), ed. Edward N. Zalta, https://plato.stanford.edu/archives/spr2014/entries/origen/.
14 See Hyam Maccoby, *Paul and the Invention of Christianity* (New York: Harper & Row, 1986) and Elaine Pagels, *The Gnostic Paul: Gnostic Exegesis of the Pauline Letters* (Philadelphia: Fortress Press, 1992).

15 Newman, *God and the Goddesses,* 90–192.
16 McMullen, *Paganism,* 131.
17 Corrington, *Image of Salvation,* 82 and n. 2; James M. Fennelly, "The Primitive Christian Values of Salvation and Patterns of Conversion," in *Man and His Salvation: Studies in Honor of S. G. F. Brandon*, ed. Eric J. Sharpe and John R. Hinnells (Manchester, Iowa: Manchester University Press, 1973), 107–23.
18 Corrington, *Image of Salvation*, 82 and n. 3; H. Haerenus, "Soter et Soteria," *Studia Hellinstica*, vol. 5 (1948), 58 n. 5 citing C. J. Bleeker, "Isis as Savior Goddess," in *The Savior God: Comparative Studies in the Concept of Salvation Presented to Edwin Oliver James*, ed. S. G. F. Brandon (Manchester: Manchester University Press, 1963), 2.
19 See Sharon Kelly Heybob, *The Cult of Isis among Woman in the Graeco-Roman World*, EPRO 51 (Leiden: Brill, 1975), 14–22 and Corrington, *Image of Salvation,* 85.
20 Athanassakis and Wolkow, *The Orphic Hymns*, 17.
21 Borgeaud, *Mother of the Gods*, 128–9 and n. 33.
22 Sarah Jane Boss, *Mary: The Complete Resource* (Oxford: Oxford University Press, 2007).
23 Green, "Shekinah," 27, 39, 47. On p. 47 he gives the example of a classic Mariological commentary on the Song of Songs by Honorius, an early twelfth-century monk who wrote *Sigillum Beatae Mariae* (c. 1100–1110). On p. 27 Green cites E. Ann Mathrer, "The Virgin Mary—A Goddess," in *The Book of the Goddess: Past and Present*, ed. C. Olson (New York: Crossroad Books, 1995), 6 for examples of cathedrals dedicated to Notre Dame, etc.
24 One example (among many) is the website of the Esoteric Interfaith Church (www. noretherneway.org, accessed July 9, 2013), "Putting the Goddess, the Sacred Feminine back into Judeo Christianity" which is typical of these popular sites. The website gives a long list of references to popular literature along these lines, such as Marina Warner, *Alone of Her Sex: The Myth and Cult of the Virgin Mary* (NY: Random, 1976); Clysta Kinstler, *The Moon under Her Feet: The Story of Mary Magdalene in the Service of the Greet Mother* (SF: Harper, 1989), and Elinor Gadon (ed.), *The One and Future Goddess* (SF: Harper, 1989).
25 Corringdon, *Salvation*, 172, citing Rosemary R. Ruether, *Mary, the Feminine Face of the Church* (Philadelphia: Westminster Press, 1977), 50
26 John van den Hengel, "Miriam of Nazareth," in *A Feminist Companion to Mariology*, ed. Amy-Jill Levine and Maria Mayo Robbins (London: Bloomsbury/T & T Clark, 2005), 133.
27 Michael P. Carroll, *The Cult of the Virgin Mary: Psychological Origins* (Princeton: Princeton University Press, 1996), 77–8.
28 See Stephen Benko, *The Virgin Goddess: Studies in the Pagan and Christian Roots of Mariology* (Leiden: E. J. Brill, 1993), 2 n. 4. Benko cites Leonhard Fendt, Gnostische Mysterien: ein beitrag zur Geschichte des Christlichen Gottesdienstes (Munich: Keiser, 1922) and Karl Prüm, Die Christliche Glaube und die altheidrische Welt, 2 vols (Leipzig), vol. 1, 285–333, both of whom provide criticisms of the idea that the Virgin Mary has pagan roots.
29 Andrew M. Greeley, *The Mary Myth, on the Femininity of God* (New York: Seabury Press, 1917), 49.
30 See Benko, *Virgin Goddess,* 6 n. 13, quoting Greeley, *Mary Myth,* 13; Phyllis Treble, *God and the Rhetoric of Sexuality* (Philadelphia: Fortress 1978), 17. In his ch. 3, "The Androgyny of God," Benko cites an extensive literature on androgyny including Pierre Teilhard de Chardin's elevation of the feminine and Mary and the need to

31. See O.S. B Kilian McDonnell, "Feminist Mariology: Heteronomy/Subordination and the Scandal of Christology," *Theological Studies*, vol. 66 (2006), 527–67.
32. Corrington, *Image of Salvation*, 148.
33. Benko, *Virgin Goddess*, 6-7 and n. 13.
34. Randall Collins, *The Sociology of Philosophy* (Cambridge: Belknap Press, 1998), 125.
35. Taken from the website of Wisconsin Lutheran College, Arius' Translation of the Thalia by Rowen W. William. www.fourthcentury.com/index.php/ariusthalia-intro. Accessed 2 May 2014.
36. See Ralph De Colle, "The Triune God," in *Cambridge Companion to Christian Doctrine*, ed. Colin E. Gunton (Cambridge: Cambridge University Press, 1997), 129 (see for example Basil of Caesarea *On the Holy Spirit* XV, 36, 38).
37. Clement *Miscellanies* 6.4 (see Copenhaven, *Hermetica*, xxxiii).
38. Russell, *Western Philosophy*, 307.
39. See John D. Turner, "The Gnostic Threefold Path to Enlightenment," (jdt.unl.edu./3fold.htm) or Turner, "Figure of Hecate," 221ff.
40. Antonia Tripolitis, *The Doctrine of the Soul in the Thought of Plotinus and Origin* (New York: Libra Publishers, 1978), 94.
41. Origen *On First Principles* 1.37, trans. G. W. Butterworth (London: SPCK, 1936).
42. See John Dillon, "The Philosophy in Christianity: Arius and Athanasius," in *The Philosophy in Christianity*, ed. G. Vesey (Cambridge: Cambridge University Press, 1990).
43. Mary T. Clark, "A Neoplatonic Commentary on the Christian Trinity: Marius Victorinus," in *Neoplatonism and Christian Thought*, ed. Dominic J. O'Meara (Albany: State University of New York Press, 1982), 25 and n. 2, citing Pierre Hadot, *Marius Victorinus* (Paris: Etudes Augustiniennes, 1971), 239.
44. Clark, "Neoplatonic Commentary," 26; Victorinus, *Adversus Arium* III.14.20, trans. Mary T. Clarke.
45. See Cornelio Fabro, "The Overcoming of the Neoplatonic Triad of Being, Life and Intellect by Thomas Aquinas," in *Neoplatonism and Christian Thought*, ed. O'Meara, 107 and n. 49, quoting Thomas Aquinas, *Super librum de causis expositio*, ed. H. D. Saffrey (Fribourg and Louvain, 1954), 8, line 8 to 9, line 1.
46. Fabro, "Overcoming," 108.
47. Fabro, "Overcoming," 106-8.
48. See Hilary Armstrong, "Negative Theology, Myth and Incarnation," in *Neoplatonism and Christian Thought*, ed. O'Meara, 213-22.
49. Armstrong, "Negative Theology," 218.
50. Johnson, *She Who Is* and "The Incomprehensibility of God as the Image of God Male and Female," 441-65 at 441.
51. John B. Cobb, "God and Feminism," in *Talking about God*, ed. J. B. Cobb and David Tracy (New York: Seabury, 1983), 79: Rosemary Radford Ruether, *Sexism and God-Talk: Toward a Feminist Theology* (Boston: Beacon, Press, 1983), 22–7; Mary Daly, *Beyond God the Father* (Boston: Beacon, 1973); Elisabeth Schüssler Fiorenza, "Feminist Spirituality, Christian Identity, and Catholic Vision," in *Womanspirit Rising*, ed. C. Christ and J. Plaskow (San Francisco: Harper & Row, 1979), 139; Anne Carr, "Is a Christian Feminist Theology Possible?" *Theological Studies*, vol. 43 (1982), 296; Gail Ramshaw Schmidt, "De divinis nominibus: The Gender of God," *Worship*, vol. 56 (1982), 117–31.

correct "a dreadfully masculine conception of the godhead," 126. See Henri de Lubac, *The Eternal Feminine* (London: Collins 1970) for a discussion of Teilhard de Chardin's views on the Eternal Feminine.

52 St Augustine, "*On the Psalms,*" in *Ancient Christian Writers* no. 30, ed. Johannes Vasten and Walter Burgha (Westminster: Newman Press, 1961), II.20–1. This is quoted by Bridget Mary Meehan, *Delighting in the Feminine Divine* (Kansas city: Sheed and Ward, 1994), 63–4. She gives examples along these lines from Clement, John Chrysostom, Augustine, Anselm of Canterbury, Aquinas, and others.
53 See Newman, *God and the Goddesses*, Ch. 2.

Chapter 10

1   Alfred North Whitehead, *The Concept of Nature* (Ann Arbor: University of Michigan Press, 1957), 3.
2   Goodison and Morris, *Ancient Goddesses,* 119 n. 17 cite P. Williams, *Problems in Materialism and Culture: Selected Essays* (London: Verso, 1980), 68–9.
3   Macrobius *Commentary on Scipio's Dream* I, 2, 17, 8 (Armisen-Marchetti) cited in Pierre Hadot, *The Veil of Isis* (Cambridge: Harvard University Press, 2006), 61 n. 12.
4   See Cornford, *Religion*, 166–7 and n. 1. Fragments are preserved in Stobaeus. Hippodamus the Pythagorean, Stob. *Flor.* 98, 71.
5   Hadot, *Veil of Isis*, 17.
6   See F. E. Peters, *Greek Philosophical Terms* (New York: New York University Press), 158–9.
7   Pierre, *The Veil of Isis*, 10–11;. citing for the Greek, G. Quandt, *Orphei Hymni* (Berlin, 1955)
8   Newman, *God and the Goddesses,* 292.
9   Newman, *God and the Goddesses*, 190–1.
10 Ernest Robert Curtius, *European Literature and the Latin Middle Ages* (Princeton: Princeton University Press, 2013), 104ff., 106, 111.
11 Claudian, *De Raptu Proserpinae* can be found in *Claudian*, trans. Maurice Platnauer (Loeb, 1922).
12 Edgar K. Knowlton, "The Goddess Natura in Early Periods," *Journal of English and Germanic Philology*, vol. 19, 2 (April 1920), 224–53.
13 George D. Economou, *The Goddess Natura in Medieval Literature* (Cambridge: Harvard University Press, 1972), 1–2.
14 Knowlton, "Natura," 241.
15 Economou, *Goddess Natura*, 54–9.
16 Economou, *Goddess Natura*, 46–7.
17 John Whitman, "Twelfth-Century Allegory: Philosophy and Imagination," in *Cambridge Companion to Allegory*, ed. Rita Copeland and Peter T. Struck (Cambridge: Cambridge University Press: 2010), 102.
18 Economou, *Goddess Natura*, 188–9 n. 15 citing Étienne Gilson, "La cosmogonie de Bernardus Silvestris," *Archives d'histoire doctrinale et littéraire du moyen âge*, vol. III (1938), 5, 7–9, 19–20, 23.
19 Theodore Silverstein, "The Fabulous Cosmogony of Bernardus Silvestris," *Modern Philology*, vol. 46, 2 (Nov. 1948), 92–116. Silverstein argues strongly against Gilson's dualism theory.
20 Wintrop Wetherbee, *The Cosmographia of Bernardus Silvestris* (New York: Columbia University Press, 1990), 6.
21 Economou, *Goddess Natura*, 66.

22 Whitman, "Twelfth-Century Allegory," 109.
23 Geoffrey Chaucer, *The Parlament of Foules*, ed. T. R. Lounsbury (Boston: Ginn & Company, 1886).
24 See Evy Johanne Haland, "Athena's Peplos: Weaving as a Core Female Activity in Ancient and Modern Greece," *Cosmos*, vol. 20 (2004), 155–82.
25 Also referred to by Proclus *In Tim.* I.167.9.
26 See Assmann, *Moses*, 86-7 and nn. 126, 127 citing Ralph Cudworth, *The True Intellectual System of the Universe* (London, 1678 (1st edn); 1743 (2nd edn), 320–4.
27 Hadot, *Veil of Isis*, 265. Proclus *In Tim.* I.140.10-14. Plutarch *De Iside* 372e.
28 Hadot, *Veil of Isis*, 62 n. 14 citing Macrobius *Commentary on Scipio's Dream* I.2, 8 (Armisen-Marchetti).
29 Hadot, *Veil of Isis*, 234–7.
30 Immanuel Kant, Footnote to Section 49 of the Third Critique. See Hadot, *Veil of Isis*, 270 and n. 31.
31 Assmann, *Moses*, 118–19; Karl Leonhold Reinhold, *Die Hebraischen Mysterien* (Mnemosyne: 2006; reprint. Charleston, SC: :Nabu Press, 2011), 54.
32 Paul Reid-Bowen, *Goddess as Nature: Towards a Philosophical Thealogy* (Burlington: Ashgate, 2007), 83, 48ff.
33 See Kune Biezeveld's review of Reid-Bowen, "*Goddess as Nature*," in *Ars Disputandi*, vol. 8, (2008), 54–6.
34 Charlene Spretnak, "Ecofeminism," *Ecospirit Quarterly*, vol. III, no 2 (1987) (a journal published by the Institute for Ecophysical Studies). Ecofeminist classics of the late 1970s and 1980s are Susan Griffin, *Women and Nature* (1978) (New York: Open Road, 2015) and Carolyn Merchant, *Death of Nature: Women, Ecology and the Scientific Revolution* (New York: HarperCollins: 1983).
35 Hellerman, *The Feminine Personification of Wisdom*, x1.
36 Newman, *Gods and Goddesses*, 23.
37 Newman, *Gods and Goddesses*, 293.
38 Newman, *Gods and Goddesses*, 2–3.
39 Hellerman, *Feminine Personification*, 273.
40 James J. Paxson, *The Poetics of Personification* (Cambridge: Cambridge University Press, 1994) and Jon Whitman, *Allegory, the Dynamics of an Ancient and Medieval Technique* (Oxford: Clarendon Press, 1987).
41 Much of what follows here in reference to Hellerman comes from Emilie Kutash, Review Essay: Wendy Elgersma Hellerman: *The Female Personification of Wisdom*, in *Journal of the Platonic Tradition*, no. 2 (2013), 138–41.
42 Hellerman, *Feminine Personnification*, 69 n. 37.
43 Boethius, *Consolation of Philosophy*, trans. H. F. Stuart, E. K. Rand, S. J. Tester (Loeb, 1973).
44 Hellerman, *Feminine Personnification*, 215–21.
45 Charles S. Singleton, *Dante Studies*, vol. 2 *Journey to Beatrice* (Cambridge: Harvard University Press, 1977).
46 Hellerman, *Feminine Personification*, 243, 277.
47 John Meyendorff, "Wisdom-Sophia: Contrasting Approaches to a Complex Theme," *Dumbarton Oaks Papers*, vol. 41 (1967), 391–401 at. 393.
48 Newman, *Gods and Goddesses*, 192–4. Hellerman gives the examples of the tradition surrounding Sophia/Mary in fifteenth-century esoteric tradition, for example *Buch der heiligen Dreifaltigkeit (Book of the Holy Trinity)*, attributed to Frater Ulmannus (a German Franciscan). It is a later alchemical text that draws on Sapientia Mariology to make the Virgin, in effect, a fourth member the Trinity.

49 https://www.boundless.com/art-history/textbooks/boundless-art-history-textbook/romanesque-art-19/romanesque-sculpture-126/romanesque-sculpture-mary-as-the-throne-of-wisdom-537-4725/accessed10 May 2014

50 Nikolai Berdyaev, *Studies Concerning Jacob Boehme*, Etude II. "The Teaching about Sophia and the Androgyne," trans. Fr. S. Janos (2002) of the article in *Put'* 21 (April 1930), 21, 34–62. http://www.berdyaev.com/berdiaev/berd_lib/1930_351.html. accessed July 24, 2013). He quotes from Jacob Boehme, *Mysterium Magnum*.

51 See Vladamir Solovyov, Judith Deutsch Kornblatt and Larry Magnus, *Divine Sophia: The Wisdom Writing of Vladamir Solovyov* (Ithaca: Cornell University Press, 2009).

Chapter 11

1 Assmann, *Cultural Memory*, 160 and n.16, citing Thomas Mann, *Die Einheit des Menschengeistes* in *Gesammelte Werke*, vol. II (Frankfort am Main, 1960–74), 751–6. See Adele Bloch, "Mythological Syncretism in the Works of Four Modern Novelists," *International Fiction Review*, vol. 8, 2 (1981).

2 Sigmund Freud, *The Standard Edition of the Complete Psychological Works of Sigmund Freud*, vol. 22, ed. and trans. James Strachey (London: Hogarth Press, 1964), 95. Ludwig Wittgenstein, *Culture and Value*, trans. Peter Winch, 2nd edition (Oxford: Blackwell, 1988), 55.

3 Christine Downing, "Sigmund Freud and the Greek Mythological Tradition," *Journal of the American Academy of Religion*, vol. 43, 1 (1975), 3–14 at 6.

4 Freud, *Standard Edition*, vol. 18, 273–4.

5 Marilyn Arthur, "Politicos and Pomegranates: An Interpretation of the Homeric Hymn to Demeter," *Arethusa*, vol. 10 (1977), 7–47, reprinted in Foley, *Hymn to Demeter*, 214–2 at 231.

6 Downing, *Sigmund Freud*, 8, n. 13; Sigmund Freud, "Why War?" in *Character and Culture*, ed. Philip Rieff (Springfield, OH: Collier Books, 1976), 143.

7 Sigmund Fred, "The Theme of the Three Caskets," in *Character and Culture*, 78–9; Downing, *Sigmund Freud*, 13.

8 Paul Ricoeur, *Freud and Philosophy: An Essay on Interpretation*, trans. Denis Savage (New Haven: Yale University Press, 1970), 243 and 535.

9 Sigmund Freud, "The Question of Lay Analysis," in *Standard Edition*, ed. Freud (London: Hogarth Press, 1959), 212.

10 Carl G. Jung, *Symptoms of Transformation* (New York: Pantheon Books, 1958), 310, cited by Downing, *Sigmund Freud*, 14 and n. 16.

11 Foley, *Hymn to Demeter*, 119f discusses Jung in this regard.

12 Carl G. Jung, *Aspects of the Feminine*, trans. R. F. C. Hull (Princeton: Princeton University Press, 1982), 79 and 86.

13 Foley, *Hymn to Demeter*, 122–3. Nancy Chodorow, "Family Structure and Feminine Personality," in Foley, *Hymn to Demeter*, 256–7.

14 Luce Irigaray, *Sexes and Genealogies* (New York: Columbia University Press, 1993), 79, 131ff, for example. See also Holmes, *Gender, Antiquity*, 136ff.

15 Nancy Chodorow, "Family Structure and Female Personality," in *Woman, Culture and Society*, ed. M.E. Rosaldo and L. Lamphere (Stanford: Stanford University Press, 1974), 43–66, 256–7, described by Foley in her "Interpretive Essay on the Homeric Hymn to Demeter," 122, both in Foley, *Hymn to Demeter*.

16 See Derek Hook, "Lacan, the Meaning of the Phallus and the 'Sexed' Subject," in *The Gender of Psychology*, ed. Floretta Boonzaier, Peace Kiguwa, and Tamara Shefer (Lansdowne, South Africa: Juta Academic Publishing, 2006), 60–84.
17 Jacques Lacan, *Écrits*, trans. Bruce Fink (New York: WW. Norton, 2006), 853ff.
18 Hook, "Meaning of the Phallus," 83.
19 Elizabeth A. Grosz, *Jacques Lacan: A Feminist Introduction* (London: Routledge, 1990).
20 Hook, "Meaning of the Phallus," 84.
21 Julia Kristeva, "From One Identity to the Other," in *Desire in Language*, ed. Leon S. Roudiez (New York: Columbia University Press, 1980), 134–6.
22 Luce Irigaray, similarly, situates sexual differences in the female bodily rhythms that suggest that an attunement with nature comes naturally to women See Luce Irigaray, *Thinking the Difference*, trans. Karin Martin (London: Routledge, 1994), 24–6.
23 Toril Moi, "Introduction to Julia Kristeva," in *The Kristeva Reader*, ed. Toril Moi (New York: Columbia University Press, 1986), 11. Moi has discussed the feminist debate around Kristeva's theories of women, feminism etc. in a chapter in *Sexual/Textual Politics: Feminist Literary Theory* (London: Methuen, 1985) and other places.
24 Jea Suk Oh, "A Study of Kristeva and Irigary's Critique of Phallologocentrism: An Interdisciplinary Research of Theology and Psychoanalysis" www.cerebratio.org./jeasukoh.html., 2014. accessed May 18, 2014.
25 Tamar Rudavsky, "Feminism and Modern Jewish Philosophy," in *The Cambridge Companion to Modern Jewish Philosophy*, ed. Michael L. Morgan and Peter Eli Gordon (Cambridge: Cambridge University Press, 2007), 340–1.
26 Julia Kristeva, "Woman's Time," *Signs: Journal of Women in Culture and Society*, vol. 7, 1 (1981), 13-35.
27 Holmes, *Gender Antiquity*, 67–70. Butler, *Bodies That Matter*, 42.
28 Elizabeth Stephens, "Feminism and New Materialism: The Matter of Fluidity," *Inter/alia: A Journal of Queer Studies*, vol. 9 (2014), 186–202. Luce Irigaray, The Mechanics of Fluids ….
29 Bianchi, "Receptacle," 126.
30 Bianchi, "Receptacle," 136.
31 Bianchi, "Receptacle," 135 (sorting grain analogy); 129 citing Julia Kristeva, *Revolution in Poetic Language*, in *The Portable Kristeva*, ed. K. Oliver (New York: Columbia University Press, 2002), 35.
32 Bianchi, "Receptacle," 139 for relation to Levinas, 142 for relation of *chôra* to the law of the polis; she cites Drucilla Cornell, *Beyond Accommodation: Ethical Feminism, Deconstruction and the Law* (New York: Routledge, 1991).
33 Rudansky, "Feminism," 330.
34 Jacques Derrida, *Spurs*, trans. Barbara Harlow (Chicago: Chicago University Press, 1979), 100.
35 John Caputo, *More Radical Hermeneutics* (Bloomington: Indiana University Press, 2000), 142.
36 Holmes. *Gender, Antiquity*, 59 and 61.
37 See Holmes, *Gender, Antiquity* citing Irigaray's Plato's Hysteria, the last chapter in *Speculum of the Other Woman* (Ithaca: Cornell University Press, 1985). Holmes provides an extensive bibliography for further reading on gender and ancient thought, 184–95.
38 See, for example Charlotte Witt, "Form, Normativity and Gender in Aristotle: A Feminist Perspective," in *Interpretations of Aristotle*, ed. Cynthia Freeland (University Park: Penn State University Press, 1998) or Emanuela Bianchi, "Aristotle and the

Masculinization of Phusis," *Yearbook of Comparative Literature*, vol. 58 (2012), 7–34. Susan Bordo, *Feminist Interpretations of René Descartes* (University Park: Penn State University Press, 1999).

39 Irigaray, *Speculum,* 204. See also Laura K. Green, "Bodiless Bodies: Perception and Embodiment in Kant and Irigaray," *Perspectives: International Postgraduate Journal of Philosophy* 1, 1 (2008), 23–37.
40 Donna Wilshire, "The Uses of Myth, Image and the Female Body in Re-visioning Knowledge," in *Gender, Body, Knowledge: Feminist Reconstructions of Being and Knowing*, ed. Alison Jaggar and Susan K. Bordo (New Brunswick: Rutgers University Press, 1989), 95–6.
41 Wilshire, "Uses of Myth," 93.
42 Wilshire, "Uses of Myth," 97–100.
43 Rudavsky, "Feminism," 330.
44 Daniel Boyarin, *Carnal Israel: Reading Sex and Talmudic Culture* (Berkeley: University of California Press, 1993), 5, and Rudavsky, "Feminism," 331.
45 See Susan Bordo, *Flight to Objectivity: Essays on Cartesianism and Culture* (Albany: State University of New York Press, 1987); *Feminist Interpretations of Descartes* (University Park, Pa.: Pennsylvania State University Press, 1999).
46 Judith Grant, "I Feel Therefore I Am: A Critique of Female Experience as a Basis for Feminist Epistemology," *Women and Politics*, vol. 7, 3 (1987), 99–114.
47 Linda Alcoff and Elizabeth Potter, *Feminist Epistemologies* (London: Routledge, 2013), 20; Sandra G. Harding, *The Feminist Standpoint Theory Reader: Intellectual and Political Controversies* (London: Routledge, 2004).
48 Elizabeth Anderson, "Feminist Epistemology: An Interpretation and Defense," *Hypatia*, vol. 10, 3 (1995), 50–84. Patrica Hill Collins, Sandra Harding, "Standpoint Theories: Productively Controversial," *Hypatia*, vol. 24, 4 (1990), 194–200 Alcoff and Potter, "Feminist Epistemologies," 2.
49 Adriana Cavarero, *In Spite of Plato: A Feminist Rewriting of Ancient Philosophy* (New York: Routledge, 1995), 2.
50 Emanuela Bianchi, "Natal Bodies, Mortal Bodies, Sexual Bodies: Reading Gender, Desire and Kinship through Reiner Schurmann's Broken Hegemonies," *Graduate Faculty Philosophy Journal*, vol. 33, 1 (2012), 57–84, 63.
51 Stuart Gardner, "Review of Adriana Cavarero," *In Spite of Plato*, in *Literature and Theology*, vol. 11, 2 (June 1997), 224–6 at 224.
52 Cavarero, *In Spite of Plato*, 70.
53 Bianchi, "Natal Bodies, Mortal Bodies," 61.
54 Chandler, *Semiotics,* 143.
55 See for example Marilyn Gottschalk, "The Ethical Implications of the Deconstruction of Gender," *Journal of the American Academy of Religion*, vol. 70, 2 (2002), 279–99. On the contribution of Judith Butler on this issue, Ellen T. Armour, *Deconstruction, Feminist Theology, and the Problem of Difference: Subverting the Race/Gender Divide* (Chicago: University of Chicago Press, 1999).

Chapter 12

1 Annis Pratt's book, *Dancing with Goddesses* (Bloomington: Indiana University Press, 1994), is largely devoted to this poetry.

2   See Chapter 1 here, note 3.
3   Assmann, *Cultural Memory, Early Civilization*, 17.
4   Assmann, *Moses*, 217–18.
5   Nagy, *Homeric Questions*, 298.
6   Katya Silverman, *The Subject of Semiotics* (New York: Oxford University Press, 1989), 36.
7   Brooke Holmes discusses this in *Gender, Antiquity*, 49ff. and cites Rebecca Jordan-Yong, *Brainstorm: The Flaws in the Science of Sex Difference* (Cambridge: Harvard University Press, 2019) for a review of this literature.
8   Athanassakis, *Hesiod*, 1.
9   Richter, *Plutarch*, 212.
10 Marc-Alain Ouaknin, *The Burnt Book: Reading the Talmud* (Princeton: Princeton University Press, 1995), 69.
11 Carol P. Christ and Judith Plaskow, *Womenspirit Rising* (SanFrancisco: HarperSanFranscisco, 1992) and Judith Plaskow and Carol P. Christ, *Weaving the Visions: New Patterns in Feminist Spirituality* (HarperCollens UK edition. London: HarperSanFrancisco, 1989).
12 Carol P. Christ, "Why Women Need the Goddess," in Christ and Plaskow, *Womanspirit Rising*, 286.
13 Christ and Plaskow, *Womanspirit Rising*, Sheila Collins, *Reflections*, 68–73, 71.
14 Nikki Bado-Fralick, Review of Carol P. Christ, *She Who Changes: Re-Imagining the Divine in the World* (New York: Palgrave MacMillan, 2003), in *NWSA Journal*, vol, 17, 2 (2005), 243–5.
15 Christ, *She Who Changes*, 44.
16 Johnson, "The Incomprehensibility of God and the Image of God Male and Female," 441–65.
17 See Goodison and Morris, *Ancient Goddesses*, 113–14 citing Martin Nilsson, *The Minoan-Mycenaean Religion, and Its Survival in Greek Religion*, 2nd edition (London: C. W. K Gleerup, 1950).
18 Lefkowitz, Review of Goodison and Morris; Cynthia Eller, *The Myth of Matriarchal Prehistory* (New York: Beacon Press, 2006).
19 Vernant, "Cosmogonic Myths," 68.
20 J. R. R. Tolkien, *On Fairy Stories*, ed. Verlyn Flieger and Douglas Anderson (Chicago: Harper Collins, 2008), 148.
21 Kutash, "Myth, Allegory," 1`: Luc Brisson, *Plato the Myth Maker* (Chicago: University of Chicago Press, 2000). See Chapter 9.
22 Paul Davies, *God and the New Physics* (New York: Simon and Schuster, 1984), 218.

Select Bibliography

The works listed here are those most helpful to pursuing further reading on this subject. More minor references appear in full in the endnotes.

Primary Sources and Commentary

Apuleius
Apuleius. *The Golden Ass*, trans., intro., and explanatory notes R. G. Walsh. Oxford: Oxford University Press, 1994.

Callimachus
Hymns, Epigrams, Select Fragments, trans. Stanley Lombardo and Diane Raynor. Baltimore: Johns Hopkins University Press, 1988.

Celsus
On the True Doctrine, trans. R. Joseph Hoffmann. New York: Oxford University Press, 1987.

Chaldean Oracles
The Chaldean Oracles: Studies in Greek and Roman Religion, trans. and comm. R. Majercik. Leiden: Brill, 1989.

Gnostics
The Nag Hammadi Scriptures, ed. Marvin Meyer. New York: Harper Collins, 2007.

Hermetica
Hermetica, trans. and comm. Brian Copenhaver. Cambridge: Cambridge University Press, 1998.

Hesiod
Theogony, trans. and comm. Apostolos N. Athanassakis. Baltimore: Johns Hopkins University Press, 2004.

Herodotus
Histories II, trans. A. D. Godley. Loeb Classical Library. Cambridge: Harvard University Press, 1975.

Homer
The Iliad, trans. Richmond Lattimore. Chicago: University of Chicago Press, 2011.

The Homeric Hymn to Demeter
The Homeric Hymn to Demeter, trans., comm. and interpretive essays. Helene P. Foley. Princeton: Princeton University Press, 1993.

Iamblichus
Theology of Arithmetic, trans. Robin Waterfield. Grand Rapids: Phanes Press, 1988.
On the Mysteries, trans. and comm. Emma Clarke, John Dillon and Jackson Hershbell. Leiden: Brill, 2003.

Julian
"Mother of the Gods," In *Orations 1-5*. trans. Wilber C. Wright. Loeb Classical Library Cambridge: Harvard University Press, 1913.

Magical Papyri
The Greek Magical Papyri in Translation, ed. Hans Dieter Betz. Chicago: University of Chicago Press, 1992.

Orphic Hymns
Orphic Hymns, trans. intro., and notes, Apostolos N. Athanassakis and Benjamin M. Wolkow. Baltimore: Johns Hopkins University Press, 2013.

Pausanias
Descriptions of Greece, trans. W. H. S. Jones. Loeb Classical Library. Cambridge: Harvard University Press, 1918.

Plato
Cratylus, trans. H. N. Fowler, Loeb Classical Library. Cambridge: Harvard University Press, 1997.

Presocratics
The Presocratic Philosophers, ed. and comm. G. S. Kirk, J. E. Raven and M. Schofield. Cambridge: Cambridge University Press, 1983.

Proclus
Commentary on Plato's Timaeus: In Platonis Timaeum commentaria, 1-3, ed. and trans. Diehl. Leipzig: Teubner, 1903-06.
Proclus Commentary on Plato's Timaeus, trans. and comm. Harold Tarrant (vol. 1), David T. Runia and Michael Share (vol. 2), Dirk Baltzly (vols 3 & 4). Cambridge: Cambridge University. Press, 2007-09.
Proclus' Hymns, essays, trans. and comm. R. M. van den Berg. Leiden: Brill, 2001.

Plutarch
Isis and Osiris: Obsolescence of the Oracles, trans. Frank Cole In *Plutarch: Moralia*, Loeb Classical Library. Cambridge, MA: Harvard University Press, 1936.

Bernardus Silvestris
The Cosmographia of Bernardus Silvestris, intro., trans. and notes Winthrop Wetherbee. New York: Columbia University Press, 1990.

Secondary sources

Addey, Crystal. "Oracles of Orpheus? The Orphic Gold Tablets." *International Journal of the Platonic Tradition* 6, 1 (2012), 115–27.
Armstrong, A. H. "Dualism: Platonic, Gnostic and Christian." In *Neoplatonism and Gnosticism*, ed. Richard T. Wallis and Jay Bregman, 33–54. Albany: SUNY Press, 1992.
Assmann, Jan. *Moses the Egyptian*. Cambridge: Harvard University Press, 1997.
Assmann, Jan. *Religion and Cultural Memory*. Stanford: Stanford University Press, 2006.
Assmann, Jan. "Translating Gods: Religion as a Factor of Cultural (Un)Translatability." In *Religion, Beyond a Concept*, ed. Henri de Vries, 139–49. New York: Fordham University Press, 2008.
Assmann, Jan. *Cultural Memory and Early Civilization*. Cambridge: Cambridge University Press, 2011.
Athanassiadi, Polymnia. "Dreams, Theurgy and Freelance Divination: The Testimony of Iamblichus." *Journal of Roman Studies* 63 (1993a), 114–30.
Athanassiadi, Polymnia. "Persecution and Response in Late Paganism: The Evidence of Damascius." *Journal of Hellenic Studies* 113 (1993b), 1–29.
Athanassiadi, Polymnia "The Chaldaean Oracles: Theology and Theurgy." In *Pagan Monotheism in Late Antiquity*, ed. P. Athanassiadi and M. Frede, 149–84. Oxford: Oxford University Press, 1999.
Benko, Stephen. *The Virgin Goddess: Studies in the Pagan and Christian Roots in Mariology*. New York: E. J. Brill, 1993.
Bianchi, Emanuela. "Receptacle/Chora: Figuring the Errant Feminine in Plato's *Timaeus*." *Hypatia* 21, 4 (Fall 2006), 124–46.
Bianchi, Emanuela. "Natal Bodies, Mortal Bodies, Sexual Bodies: Reading Gender, Desire and Kinship through Reiner Schurmann's Broken Hegemonies." *Graduate Faculty Philosophy Journal* 33,.1 (2012), 57–84.
Bloomfield, Morton. "A Grammatical Approach to Personification Allegory." *Modern Philology* 60, 3 (1963), 161–71.
Bottici, Chiara, "Mythos and Logos: A Genealogical Approach." *Epoché* 13, 1 (Fall 2008), 1–24.
Boedeker, Deborah. "Hecate: A Transfunctional Goddess in the Theogony?." *Transactions of the American Philological Association* 113 (1983), 79–93.
Bordo, Susan. "The Cartesian Masculinization of Thought." *Signs* 11, 3 (Spring 1986), 439–56.
Boss, Sarah Jane. *Mary: The Complete Resource*. Oxford: Oxford University Press, 2007.
Boys-Stones, George. *Platonist Philosophy 80BC to AD250*. Cambridge: Cambridge University Press, 2017
Brisson, Luc. "Plato's Mythology and Philosophy." In *Greek and Egyptian Mythologies*, ed. Yves Bonnefoy, trans. Wendy Doniger, 52–60. Chicago: University of Chicago Press, 1992.
Brisson, Luc. "Plato's Timaeus and the *Chaldean Oracles*." In *Plato's Timaeus as Cultural Icon*, ed. G. Reydams-Schils, 111–51. Notre Dame: University of Notre Dame, 2002.
Brisson, Luc. *How Philosophers Saved Myths*. trans. Catherine Tihanyi. Chicago: University of Chicago Pres, 2004.
Burkert, Walter. *Ancient Mystery Cults*. Cambridge: Harvard University Press, 1987.
Burkert, Walter. *Greek Religion: Archaic and Classical*. Cambridge: Harvard University Press, 1991.
Burkert, Walter. *The Orientalizing Revolution*. trans. Margaret E. Pinder and Walter Burkert. Cambridge: Harvard University Press, 1992.

Cameron, Averil. *The Later Roman Empire*. Cambridge: Harvard University Press, 1993.
Cavarero, Adriana. *In Spite of Plato: A Feminist Rewriting of Ancient Philosophy*. New York: Routledge, 1995.
Chuvin, Pierre. *A Chronicle of the Last Pagans*. trans. B. A. Archer. Cambridge: Harvard University Press, 1990.
Clay, Jenny Strauss. "The Hekate of the Theogony." *Greek, Roman, and Byzantine Studie* 25,.1 (1984), 27–38.
Clay, Jenny Strauss. *The Politics of Olympus*. Princeton: Princeton University Press, 1989.
Clark, Mary T. "A Neoplatonic Commentary on the Christian Trinity: Marius Victorinus." In *Neoplatonism and Christian Thought*, ed. Dominic J. O'Meara. Albany: State University of New York Press, 1982.
Cornford, F. M. *From Religion to Philosophy*. Mineola: Dover Edition, 2004.
Corrington, Gail Peterson. *Her Image of Salvation*. Louisville: Westminster John Knox Press, 1992.
Dillon, John. "Image, Symbol and Analogy: Three Basic Concepts of Neoplatonic Allegorical Exegesis." In *The Significance of Neoplatonism*, ed. B. Harris, 247–63. Norfolk: Old Dominion University Press, 1976.
Dillon, John. *The Middle Platonists*. Ithaca: Cornell University Press, 1996.
Downing, Christine. "Sigmund Freud and the Greek Mythological Tradition." *Journal of the American Academy of Religion* 43, 1 (1975), 3–14.
Economou, George D. *The Goddess Natura in Medieval Literature*. Cambridge: Harvard University Press, 1972.
Ellinger, Paul. "Artemis." In *Greek and Egyptian Mythologies*, ed. Yves Bonnefoy, trans. Wendy Doniger, 145–49. Chicago: University of Chicago Press, 1992.
Fabro, Cornelio. "The Overcoming of the Neoplatonic Triad of Being, Life, and Intellect by Saint Thomas Aquinas." In *Neoplatonism and Christian Thought*, ed. Dominic J. O'Meara, 97–109. Albany: SUNY Press, 1982.
Faulkner, Andrew. *The Homeric Hymns: Interpretative Essays*. Oxford: Oxford University Press, 2011.
Finamore, John F. and Johnston, Sarah Iles. "The Chaldaean Oracles." In *The Cambridge Companion to Late Antiquity*, ed. Lloyd Gerson, 161–73. Cambridge: Cambridge University Press, 2016.
Fowden, Garth. "The Pagan Holy Man in Late Antique Society." *JHS* 102 (1982), 33–59.
Fowden, Garth. *The Egyptian Hermes*. Princeton: Princeton University Press, 1986.
Frymer-Kensky, Tikva. *Wake of the Goddesses: Women, Culture, and the Biblical Transformation of Pagan Myth*. New York: Macmillan, Free Press, 1992.
Funk, Wolf-Peter, Poirer, Paul-Hubert. and Turner, John D. *Marsanès* (NH X). Bibliothèque copte de Nag Hammadi, Section "Textes" 27. Québec: Les Presses de l'université Laval; Louvain, Peeters, 2000.
Glinsky, Karl. *Augustin Culture*. Princeton: Princeton University Press, 1996.
Goodison, Lucy. and Morris, Christine. *Ancient Goddesses*. Madison: University of Wisconsin Press, 1998.
Green, Arthur. "Shekhinah, The Virgin Mary, and the Song of Songs." *AJS Review* 26, 1 (2002), 1–52.
Green, Arthur. *A Guide to the Zohar*. Stanford: Stanford University Press, 2004.
Griffiths, J. Gwyn. *Plutarch' de Iside et Osiide*. Swansea: University of Wales Press, 1970.
Griffiths, J. Gwyn. *Triads and Trinity*. Cardiff: University of Wales Press, 1996.
Grosz, Elizabeth A. *Jacques Lacan: A Feminist Introduction*. London: Routledge, 1990.
Hadot, Pierre. *The Veil of Isis*. Cambridge: Harvard University Press, 2006.

Halbertal, Moshe. and Margalit, Avishai. *Idolatry*, trans. Naomi Goldblum. Cambridge: Harvard University Press, 1992.
Helleman, Wendy Elgersma. *The Feminine Personification of Wisdom*. Lewiston: Edwin Mellen Press, 2009.
Holmes, Brooke. *Gender: Antiquity and Its Legacy*. London: I. B. Taurus, 2012.
Hook, Derek. "Lacan, the Meaning of the Phallus and the 'Sexed' Subject." In *The Gender of Psychology*, ed. Tamara Shefer, Floretta Boonzaier, and Peace Kiguwa. Lansdowne, South Africa: Juta Academic Publishing, 2006.
Irigaray, Luce. *Sexes and Genealogies*. New York: Columbia University Press, 1993.
Idel, Moshe. "Jewish Kabbalah and Platonism." In *Neoplatonism and Jewish Thought*, ed. Lenn E. Goodman. Albany: State University of New York Press, 1992.
Johnson, Elizabeth A. "The Incomprehensibility of God and the Image of God Male and Female." *Theological Studies* 45, 3 (1984), 441–65.
Johnson, Elizabeth A. *She Who Is: The Mystery of God in Feminist Theological Discourse*. New York: Crossroad Publishing Company, 2002.
Johnston, Sarah Iles. *Hekate Soteira*. Atlanta: Scholars Press, 1990.
Jonas, Hans. *The Gnostic Religion*. Boston: Beacon Press (1958) 1991.
Jung, Carl. G. *Aspects of the Feminine*, trans. R. F. C. Hull. Princeton: Princeton University Press, 1982.
Kerényi, Karl. *The Gods of the Greeks*. London: Thames and Hudson, 1980.
Kirk, G. S. *Myth, Its Meaning and Function in Ancient and Other Cultures*. Berkeley: University of California Pres, 1973.
Knowlton, Edgar K. "The Goddess Natura in Early Periods." *Journal of English and Germanic Philology* 19, 2 (April 1920), 224–53.
Kristeva, Julia. *Desire in Language*, ed. Leon S. Roudiez. New York: Columbia University Press, 1980.
Kristeva, Julia, Alice Jardine and Harry Blake. "Woman's Time." *Signs: Journal of Women in Culture and Society* 7, 1 (Autumn 1981), 13–35.
Kutash, E. F. "*Oikoumene, Ouranos, Ousia*, and Outside: An Analogy across Three Ancient Disciplines." *Graduate Faculty Philosophy Journal* 22, 2 (2001), 115–45.
Kutash, E. F. "The Prevailing Circumstances: The Pagan Philosophers of Athens in a Time of Stress." *The Pomegranate* 10, 2 (2008), 184–200.
Kutash, E. F. *Ten Gifts of the Demiurge: Proclus on the Timaeus*. London: Bloomsbury, 2011.
Kutash, E. F. "Myth, Allegory and Inspired Symbolism in Early and Late Platonism." *International Journal of the Platonic Tradition* 2 (June, 2020), 1–25.
Lacan, Jacques. *Écrits*, trans. Bruce Fink. New York: W. W. Norton, 2004.
Lankila, Tuomo. "Aphrodite in Proclus' Theology." *Journal for Late Antique Religion and Culture* 3 (2009), 21–43.
Lamberton, Robert. *Hesiod*. New Haven: Yale University Press, 1988.
Lamberton, Robert. *Homer the Theologian*. Berkeley: University of California Press, 1989.
Lefkowitz, Mary. *Women in Greek Myth*. London: Duckworth, 1986.
Lefkowitz, Mary. "Feminist Myths and Greek Mythology." *Times Literary Supplement* (July 22–28, 1989), 804–5.
Lefkowitz, Mary. "Twilight of the Goddess." *The New Republic* 8, 3 (1992), 29–35.
Lefkowitz, Mary. *Greek Gods, Human Lives: What We Can Learn From Myths*. New Haven: Yale University Press, 2003.
Lenzi, Mary. "Platonic Polypsychic Pantheism." *Monist* 80, 2 (1997), 232–20.

Lewy, Hans. *Chaldaean Oracles and Theurgy: Mysticism, Magic and Platonism in the Later Roman Empire*. Paris: Études Augustiniennes, 1956.
Locke, Liz. "Orpheus and Orphism: Cosmology and Sacrifice at the Boundary." *Folklore Forum* 28, 2 (1997), 3–29.
López-Ruiz, Carolina. *When the Gods Were Born*. Cambridge: Harvard University Press, 2010.
Maccobby, Hyman. *Paul and the Invention of Christianity*. New York: Harper & Row, 1986.
MacMullen, Ramsey. *Paganism in the Roman Empire*. New Haven, Yale University Press, 1981.
Manchester, Peter. "The Noetic Triad in Plotinus, Marius Victorinus and Augustine." In *Neoplatonism and Gnosticism*, ed. Richard T. Wallis, Albany: State University of New York Press, 1992.
Marquardt, Patricia. A. "A Portrait of Hecate." *American Journal of Philology* 102, 3 (1981), 243–60.
Miller, Roger Jones. *The Platonism of Plutarch*. Biblical Life Reproduction Series, 2009.
Meyendorff, John. "Wisdom-Sophia: Contrasting Approaches to a Complex Theme." *Dumbarton Oaks Papers* 41 (1967), 391–401.
Nagy, Gregory. *Homeric Questions*. Austin: University of Texas Press, 1996.
Neumann, Erich. *The Great Mother: An Analysis of the Archetype*. Bollingen Foundation Series XLVII. New York: Pantheon Books, 1963.
Newman, Barbara. *God and the Goddesses: Vision, Poetry and Belief in the Middle Ages*. Philadelphia: University of Pennsylvania Press, 2005
O'Brien, Joan V. *The Transformation of Hera: A Study of Ritual, Hero, and the Goddess in the Iliad*. Lanham: Rowman and Littlefield, 1993.
Opsomer, Jan. "Proclus on Demiurgy and Procession in the *Timaeus*." In *Reason and Necessity: Essays in Plato's Timaeus*, ed. M. R. Wright. London: Duckworth, 2000.
Pagels, Elaine. *The Gnostic Gospels*. New York: Random House, 1979.
Parisinou, Eva. *The Light of the Gods: The Role of Light in Archaic and Classical Greek Cult*. London: Duckworth, 2000.
Patai, Rafael. *The Hebrew Goddess*. Detroit: Wayne State University Press, 1967.
Pomeroy, Sarah (1975). *Goddesses, Whores, Wives and Slaves*. New York: Schocken Books, 1995
Ramnoux, Clémence. "Philosophy and Mythology from Hesiod to Proclus." In *Greek and Egyptian Mythologies*, ed. Yves Bonnefoy, trans. Wendy Doniger, 46–52. Chicago: University of Chicago Press, 1992.
Reid-Bowen, Paul. *Goddess as Nature: Towards a Philosophical Thealogy*. Burlington: Ashgate, 2007.
Richter, Daniel S. "Plutarch on Isis and Osiris: Text: Cult, and Cultural Appropriation." *Transactions of the American Philological Association* 131 (2001), 191–216.
Rangos, Spyridon. "Proclus and Artemis: On the Relevance of Neoplatonism to the Modern Study of Ancient Religion." *Kernos* 13 (2000), 47–84.
Roller, Lynn E. *In Search of God the Mother: The Cult of Anatolian Cybele*. Berkeley: University of California Press, 1999.
Rudavsky, Tamar. "Feminism and Modern Jewish Philosophy." In *The Cambridge Companion to Modern Jewish Philosophy*, ed. Michael L. Morgan and Peter Eli Gordon, 324–48. Cambridge: Cambridge University Press, 2007.
Schafer, Peter. *Mirror of His Beauty: Feminine Images of God From the Bible to the Early Kabbalah*. Princeton: Princeton University Press, 2002.
Scholem, Gershom. *Origins of the Kabbalah*. Princeton: Princeton University Press, 1987.

Shaw, Gregory. *Theurgy and the Soul: The Neoplatonism of Iamblichus*. University Park: Pennsylvania State University Press, 1995.
Snell, Bruno. *The Discovery of the Mind in Greek Philosophy and Literature*. New York: Dover Publications, 1953.
Solmsen, Friedrich. *Isis among the Greeks and Romans*. Cambridge: Harvard University Press, 1979.
Swain, Simon. *Hellenism and Empire*. Oxford: Clarendon Press, 1996.
Takács, Sarolta A., "Initiation and Mysteries in Apuleius' Metamorphoses." https://scholar.lib.vt.edu/ejournals/ElAnt/V12N1/takacs.pdf
Turcan, Robert. *Cults of the Roman Empire*. Oxford: Blackwell, 1996.
Turner, John D. "The Figure of Hecate and Dynamic Emanationism in the *Chaldean Oracles*, Sethian Gnosticism and Neoplatonism." *The Second Century Journal* 7, 4 (1991), 221–32.
Turner, John D. *Sethian Gnosticism and the Platonic Tradition*. Quebec: Les Presses de l'Université Laval, 2001.
Van den Berg, R.M. *Proclus' Commentary on the Cratylus in Context*. Leiden: Brill, 2007.
Van der Toorn, Karen. "Goddesses in Early Israelite Religion." In *Ancient Goddesses*, ed. Lucy Goodison and Christine Morris, 83–97. Madison: University of Wisconsin Press, 1998.
Vernant, Jean-Pierre. *Mortals and Immortals*: *Collected Essays*, ed. F. Zeitlin. Princeton: Princeton University Press, 1991.
Vernant, Jean-Pierre. "Greek Cosmogonic Myths." In *Greek and Egyptian Mythologies*, ed. Yves Bonnefoy, trans. Wendy Doniger, 66–75. Chicago: University of Chicago Press, 1992.
Voyatzis, Mary E. "From Athena to Zeus." In *Ancient Goddesses*, ed. Lucy Goodison and Christine Morris, 133–47. Madison: University of Wisconsin Press, 1998.
Watts, Edward J. *City and School in Late Antique Athens and Alexandria*. Berkeley: University of California Press, 2006.
Webster, T. B. L. "Personification as a Mode of Greek Thought." *Journal of the Warburg and Courtland Institutes* 17, 1/2 (1954), 10–21.
West, M. L. *The East Face of Helicon*. Oxford: Clarendon Press, 1999.
Wilshire, Donna. "The Uses of Myth, Image and the Female Body in Re-visioning Knowledge." In *Gender, Body, Knowledge: Feminist Reconstructions of Being and Knowing*, ed. Allison Jagger and Susan K. Bordo, 92–114. New Brunswick: Rutgers University Press, 1989.
Westenholz, Joan Goodnick. "Goddesses of the Ancient Near East 3000–1000 BCE." In *Ancient Goddesses*, ed. Lucy Goodison and Christine Morris, 63–82. Madison: University of Wisconsin Press, 1998.
Witt, R. E. *Isis in the Ancient World*. Baltimore: Johns Hopkins University Press, 1971.
Wolfson, Eliot. *Circle in the Square: Studies in the Use of Gender in Kabbalistic Symbolism*. Albany: SUNY Press, 1995.

Index

academies 43, 63, 75, 77, 90, 92
    Alexandrian School 89, 92, 141
    Athenian School (revival of Plato's academy) 10, 26
    Justinian edict to forbid teaching 91
    matter devalued 59, 63, 75, 77, 89, 90
    Old Academy 40–1, 55, 74
    politically contentious 93, 107, 121, 209
Akkadian (texts) 5
    Atrahasis text 84
    Ishtar 145
    lists of gods 110
    mother of the gods 22
Alexander the Great 37
Alexandria
    early Christians and 105
    library of 39, 91, 92
    Serapeum 112, 141
allegory
    interpretation myth 38, 54
    Middle Platonists 94
    personification of wisdom 162
    Sophia in medieval 12, 15
Apollo
    and Constantine 90
    Delian Hymn to Apollo 22, 36
    temple at Delphi 43
    in triad 102
Antigone 17
    Emanuela Bianchi's interpretation 186
Aphrodite 55, 169
    in aretalogies 111–12, 166
    blatant eroticism 32, 38, 56, 155, 189
    Christian hostility to 91
    Hymn to Aphrodite 31
    Plotinus' view 67
    Proclus views 93–4
    seduction of Zeus 23
    in triads 102, 209
Apuleius 44
    on being and becoming 77
    Metamorphosis: Isis as Lucius' savior 34, 116
    as worshipper of Isis 45, 114
Aquinas
    apophatic theology 151
    Christian theology and Neoplatonism 150
    masculine nature of deity 71, 146
    many named goddesses 38
Archaic Period 3, 4, 55, 59
    and Hekate 39
archeology 5
    current approaches 3
    Jung 174
Ares 94, 199
    compared to Athena re. war 25
    triads 102
aretalogies 3, 5, 8, 111
    intertranslatable names 39–40
    Isis 112, 114, 143
Artemis 3, 11, 25, 112, 142
    attached to nature and the wild 18, 30–2, 38, 94, 123, 155, 160, 161, 178
    Greek drama 32
    in Hermetica 48
    many-named 113
    mistress of animals 18
    in sixteenth-century allegory 162
    temple of Artemis 91
    triads 95, 101, 102, 103–4
    virgin 55, 68, 145
Aristotle 54, 89, 141, 155
    Chaos 60
    feminist epistemology 12, 87, 182, 183, 184
    the infinite 207
    matter and form 10, 59, 76, 77
    nature (*physis*) 157
    Proclus 92
    sublunary world 84

Asharah 124, 125-6, 127-8
    Canaanite 133
Assmann, Jann 5, 163, 172
    cultural memory 2, 190, 196
    idolatry 134
    intertranslation of god's names 8, 109, 111-14, 116, 118, 119
Athanassakis, Apostolos N. (and Benjamin M. Wolkow, *The Orphic Hymns*) 6, 9, 25, 54, 64, 191
    Demeter 20
    Gaia 59
    Hekate 95
    Nyx 21
    Rhea 22
Athena 3, 24-8, 120, 171. *See also* wisdom
    born from Zeus's head 20, 21-4, 57, 58, 18
    Cave of the Nymphs 85
    coup against Zeus 22
    in *Iliad* 36
    and Lady philosophy, Boethius 167
    and Mary 145
    as mother 56
    peplos 155, 161
    Plutarch, Isis and 44
    in Proclus 11, 26, 81, 93
    in triads 90, 102, 103-4
    virgin 31, 55, 68
Athens 20, 24, 25, 89, 91-2, 143
    Proclus 26, 93, 120, 140, 141
Augustine 81, 141, 146, 152

Babylonian 46, 59, 95, 109, 205
    pantheon 84
    and primal waters 60, 178
Barbelo 43, 50, 63, 98-9, 138, 210
    as Dyad 66, 75
    as Sophia 138, 148
Bianchi, Emanuela
    chora 179-80, 205
binary oppositions 13, 49, 54, 76, 163, 191
    and dualism 13, 50
    in feminism 12, 184
    of gender 8, 10, 171, 190, 195
    psychoanalytic theory 172
    in theology 192

Boethius
    Lady Philosophy 18, 167
Bordo, Susan
    Cartesianism 87, 182
Brisson, Luc
    Chaldean Oracles 46
    Hekate 47, 65
    myth 8, 194
    triads 101-2
Burkert, Walter
    Atrahasis text 84
    Hera 23
    Near East influence 5
Butler, Judith
    chora 63
    gender, body and identity 179

Canaanite 84, 124, 145
    figurines 125, 126, 128
Callimachus *(Hymns)* 17, 25, *32*
Cavarero, Adriana, *In Spite of Plato* 185-6
Celsus 37, 117
Chaos 53, 60, 61-2, 77, 79
    ancient cosmography 46, 109
    Athena subdues 81
    and chora 71
    and goddess Natura 159-60
    in Hesiod (Chaos) 19-21, 54, 56, 58, 60, 69, 178
    in Isis and Osiris 80
    and Orphic egg 70
Chaldean Oracles 9, 11, 39, 40, 45-8, 50, 51, 64, 78, 141, 191
    and Athenian academy 92-3
    and Gnosticism 43, 50, 66, 191
    Hekate in 8, 9, 24, 29, 30, 38, 47, 51, 63, 65, 66, 67, 68, 77, 79, 86, 194
    and Numenius 82
    triads 96, 98, 101, 102, 149
Chora. *See also* Bianchi
    Plato's receptacle or *krater* 42, 61-3, 65, 180, 182
    in feminism 62-3, 177
Clay, Jenny Strauss 4, 5
    Artemis 32
    Demeter myth 33
    Panhellenic era 6, 17
classical period 55, 76, 161
Clement of Alexandria 49, 149, 151, 152

Christ, Carol 1, 192
Christ, Jesus
  androgyny 169
  Constantine 90
  Hymn to Christ 140
  in John 142
  Paul 139
  and Sophia 11, 141, 142, 165, 166, 168
  trinity 147–9
  Victorians 150
Christianity 1, 10, 11, 12, 37–8, 52, 75, 91, 107, 139, 151, 158, 192
  and Athenian School 93
  Celsus, see also 149
  and Gnosticism 150
  Hellenism threat to 117
  and Isis 142
  medieval allegory and 192
  and Platonism 142
  in Roman Empire 90, 91–2, 113, 117, 140, 141
Constantine 89, 90–1, 141, 143, 147
conversion 91, 118, 141
cosmotheism 139, 143, 145
Council of Nicaea 90–1, 147–8
cultural memory 2, 12, 13, 53, 89, 186, 190, 193
  allegory 152
  binary oppositions of gender 76, 87
  feminists and 179
  Freud 174
  Gerard Manley Hopkins 144
  Lacan 176
  nature 158
  Sophia 166, 168
  triads 104, 105

Damascius (*Philosophical History*) 46, 70, 92, 98
  and *Chaldean Oracles*, triads 99
  Philosophical History 141
Demeter 7, 8, 20, 30, 33–4, 44, 162
  as Dyad 75
  feminists (*see* Persephone)
  and Hekate 29
  Hymn to Demeter 14, 96
  and Isis 34, 40, 112, 114
  life giving goddess 101, 117
  and nature 156

  nursing Demophon 56
  and Rhea
  triads 90, 101–2, 103, 104
demiurge 52, 142
  in *Chaldean Oracles* 65, 96, 210–11
  in gnostic texts 66, 99
  in Plato's *Timaeus* 62, 71, 108
Derveni Papyrus 109
  Rhea, blending goddess identities 22
  role of Zeus 57–8
Descartes. *See* Susan Bordo
  dualism 87
  feminist epistemology 12, 87, 182, 183–4
Derrida, Jacques
  "belongs différance" as woman's truth 180–1
  "phallologocentrism" 180
Dillon, John
  Female Principles in Paganism 42
  Middle Platonists 41
  triads 50, 97
divine feminine 53, 123, 145
Downing, Christine 173, 174
dualism 10, 55, 71, 73–9, 87
  Arianism and 147–8
  Cosmographia and 160
  Descartes, and 184
  dyad and goddesses 75, 79
  form and matter 81–2
  gender binary and 13, 50, 59
  Isis and Osiris 77
  Kristeva and 178
  topographic regions 83–5
  triplicate structures, and 105
  Wilshire and 183

Economou, George 159–60
Elephantine Jews 124, 126–7, 128, 129
Eusebius 90–1, 142

feminism 2, 21, 63, 187
  Chora 62, 63, 177, 178, 179–80, 205
  gender binaries (essentialism) 12, 71, 163, 170, 191
  goddess movement 1
  and Hymn to Demeter 173
  and material and bodily 179
  spiritual feminism 133
  and theology 146, 192, 218

wisdom, personification of 165
feminist epistemology 12, 182-5
    Bordo, Susan and Descartes 182
    Charlotte Witt and Aristotle 182
    standpoint theory 184
fertility 3, 9, 10, 53, 55, 64, 68, 199
    Artemis 32
    Athena 25
    figurines 128
    gender, opposition 71
    Hymn to Demeter in feminist studies 179
    Isis 114
    Natura 11, 18, 22
    Neoplatonism, in 117
    Yahweh and 128
figurines, female 14, 57, 123, 124-5, 128, 193, 198
    Freud's collection 173
fluidity 51, 171, 176, 179
Foley, Helene (*Homeric Hymn to Demeter*) 14, 33, 96, 139, 175, 179
Frymer-Kensky, Tikva (*In the Wake of the Goddess*) 126, 127, 128
Freud, Sigmund 172-4
    penis envy 173, 174, 177

Gaia 3, 11, 18, 19-21, 22, 38, 54, 57, 58, 61, 62, 78, 81, 178, 191, 193
    castration of Ouranos 164
    mother goddess 22, 56, 59-60, 193
    nature, associated with 155
    in Proclus 68
gender. *See* binary oppositions of gender
Gimbutas, Maria 14, 57, 174, 183, 193. *See also* goddess movement
goddess movement 1, 14, 18, 174
Gospels (Mathew, Luke, Mark, John) 140, 142
Gnosticism 2, 11, 50, 71, 98-9, 105
    Allogenes 43, 50, 98-9, 100, 136
    Apocryphon of John 43, 50, 66, 75, 98, 99, 136
    Gnostic Gospels 9, 45, 50, 206
    Jewish Gnosticism 130, 132
    Kabbalah and 134-6
    Marsanès 79, 136, 191
    Origen and Clement and 148-9
    Paul and 142

Sethian 50, 66, 98, 99, 136, 193
triads 148, 149
trinity and 147
triple powered one 50, 98-9
Valentinian 42, 50, 66
Zostrianos 50, 98, 99, 136
Gold Tablets 19, 50, 54, 85
Great Mother (*Magna Meter*) 1, 22, 92
    Freud on 174
    Gaia as 59
    Kybele 116
Greek drama 4, 27, 35, 190
Green, Arthur 131, 132, 135, 145
Greek Magical Papyri 48-9
    and triplicity 95
Griffiths, John Gwyn 44, 104, 105, 129
    Triads and Trinities 146

Hades 3, 21, 29, 84, 95, 96, 118
    And Persephone 175
Hadot, Pierre (*The Veil of Isis*)
    Isis veiled 27, 28, 155
Halbertal, Moshe (*Idolatry*) 121, 122, 124, 135
Halbwachs, Maurice 2, 190
    and Kabbalah 133
Hebrew tradition 84, 110, 121, 137-8, 140, 142
    and chaos (*tohu va bohu*) 61
    Christianity and 139
    goddess 11, 123, 124, 125-6
    name of God 122, 163
    Prophets 124, 214
    Sirach (*Ecclesiasticus*) 142
    Yahwah 124
Hekate 3, 8, 9, 11, 18, 28-30, 109, 116, 193
    Chaldean Oracles 43, 46-7, 66, 82
    Gnosticism 50, 63, 79, 149
    guide 85, 86, 96
    life giving goddess 68, 104, 117
    life giving womb 38, 65, 99
    mediator 38, 39, 41, 48, 51
    triplicate/triads 90, 95, 98, 102-3
    as World Soul 46-7, 77, 82, 99
Helleman, Wendy (*The Feminine Personification of Wisdom*)
    See also wisdom, personifications of
Hellenism 37, 39, 52, 91, 92, 117, 190

Hera 3, 11, 21–4, 36, 73, 156, 198
　in aretalogy 111, 112
　and Artemis in *Iliad* 31
　Derveni papyrus 22
　and Dyad 74
　life generating triad 101, 102
　Orphic Hymn to Hera 144
　Proclus 67
　triads 103, 104
　and Zeus 74
Hermetica 45, 48–9, 79, 110, 204
　Hermeticism 2
　Poimandres 49, 66
Hesiod 5, 6, 9, 10, 40, 54, 191–3
　Chaos in 60, 96, 109
　cosmogony 53
　divine couple 58, 109
　family tree 118
　Herodotus 122
　for Jung 175
　mortal women 195
　Panhellenic construct 17
　and Tartarus 84
Holmes, Brooke (*Gender, Antiquity & Its Legend*) 2, 14, 171
　Irigaray 182
　Judith Butler 179
　matter 10, 182, 198
Homer 3, 4, 5, 6, 54, 86, 92, 109
　Athena beats Ares 25
　Hera's role Zeus coup 22
　Iliad 23, 31, 69, 84
　Odyssey 4, 17, 85, 161
　Okeanos 58
　Neoplatonist reading of Homer 190, 194
　Nyx 21
　Penelope 166
Homeric Hymns 3, 5, 17, 31, 56, 193
Herodotus 8, 23, 34, 110, 112, 122
　Isis 113
Hymn to Demeter 14, 22, 32, 33, 34, 44, 56, 96, 103
　and gender identity 175
　Hekate's role as guide 29
　Marilyn Arthur interpretation 173
　and two world ontologies 85
Hypatia 91, 141, 167

Iamblichus 48, 74, 75, 78, 90
　on Chaldean Julians 45
　and emperor Julian 93
　Life of Pythagoras 167
　names of gods 119, 120
　Oracles 46
Irigaray, Luce 163, 180
　allegory of the cave 182
　Demeter/Persephone 175, 185
　Kant 182
　Lacan 177
　Mechanics of Fluids 172, 176
Isis 7, 8–9, 14, 18, 34–5, 39–40. *See also* Plutarch *Isis and Osiris*
　in Apuleius, *Metamorphosis* 44–5, 116
　Christian attack on 147
　and Hekate 5
　in Hellenic and in Roman Empire 111–15
　and Mary 145–6
　and matter 42
　myrionymos (many-named)
　Old and New Kingdom 34, 113
　and Paul 139–40
　as savior 117, 143
　and wisdom 121, 130
　and World Soul 62

Johnson, Elizabeth (*She Who Is*) 137
　apophatic theology, and gender 152, 193
Johnston, Sarah Iles (*Hekate Soteria*) 24, 29, 30, 46
Jonas, Hans 49, 66
Jones, Roger Miller (*Platonism of Plutarch*) 64, 76, 77, 80
Julian, emperor 52, 89–90, 93, 143, 191
　the Chaldean Julians 45
Jung, Carl 34, 56, 105, 172, 174–5, 193

Kabbalah 2, 87, 131, 169. *See* Shekhinah
　androgyny in (Elliot Wolfson) 134, 137
　Bahir and Zohar 130–1, 132, 134, 135
　and gender 137
　and Gnosticism 134–6
　idolatry (Moshe Halbertal) 133
　in Jewish religion and history 130, 131–2
Knowlton, Edward 159–60
Kristeva, Julia 12
　chora 63, 177, 178
　semiotic and symbolic 177–8

thinking with the body 180
Kronos 5, 19, 25, 56, 60, 67, 84
   overthrow of 20, 22, 60
   Plotinus 99–100
   Proclus, as Intellect 63
   triads 102
Kybele 3, 22, 24, 35, 90, 109, 115, 116
   Mary and 144–5

Lacan, Jacques 172
   Imaginary, Symbolic and Real 176
   the Name of the Father 176
Lamberton, Robert 6, 78
   Athena's *peplos* 161
   Cave of the Nymphs 85
   Hera's deception of Zeus (*Iliad*) 69
   Nyx 21
   on interpretation 190
   Ouranos and Gaia 20
Lefkowitz, Mary
   goddess revivals 2, 193
   Greek drama 4
Limit and unlimited
   and gender 42, 191
   and mating 167
   necessary in being 80, 82
   Neoplatonism 59, 68, 70
   in *Philebus* 79, 101
   table of opposites 78, 184
   triads 102
Lopez-Ruiz, Carolina (*When the Gods Were Born*) 5, 57
   chaos in Phoenician texts 84
   Northwest and Semitic tradition 60

Magna Mater. *See* Kybele and Great Mother
Mary 11, 91, 131, 144–6, 169, 172
   Christian Kabbalists and 133
   and Jung 175
   Queen of Heaven 143
   virgin 169
   wisdom and 167, 168
mathematical Numbers 73–4
   Theology of Arithmetic 74–5, 79
monad and dyad 55
   and Arian doctrine 148
   Aristotle's *Physics* 10
   and dualism 87
   as god and goddess 69, 74
   as paternal monad in Plotinus 98–9
   in middle Platonism 97
   in Plutarch, as Isis and Typhon 77
   in Proclus 103
   in *Theology of Arithmetic* 75
matter
   binary: form as male, matter as female 59, 62–7
   and dualism 87, 97
   feminist readings of Aristotle and 182–3
   goddess Nammu 61
   Gnosticism 50, 66
   in Isis and Osiris 27, 76, 78, 80
   in life-giving triad 101
   matter and evil 80–2, 157–8
   matter desires form 76, 77, 79
   middle Platonists 41–2, 59
   Numenius 57–8
   in Silvestris *Cosmographia*: Natura 160
   womb of Hekate 47, 65
Maximus 90, 92
Middle Platonists 41, 121, 157, 202. *See also* Numenius
   Albinus 42
   apophatic tradition 151
   Eudorus of Alexandria 41
   Moderatus of Gades 41, 59, 66, 98
   Philo 42, 121, 130, 132
mythology 2, 4, 5, 6, 53, 194
   allegory and 38
   Derrida 86, 181
   Freud and 172–3
   and gender binary 163, 171, 184
   Jung and 175
   and Kabbalah 130, 136–7
   in late antiquity 7–8
   modern reception 12, 13–14
   mystical literature 2nd c., 43, 44, 50
   Origen and 149
   Orphic 70
   Proclus 93

Natura 11, 153, 158–60, 164, 165, 192
   Chaucer 159, 160
   Claudian 158–9
   Cosmographia, Bernard Silvestris 159–60
nature 9, 10, 11, 18, 30, 35, 53, 78, 155–8. *See also* Artemis, feminism,

Hadot, Pierre, Natura, Reid-
  Bowen
 Aquinas 150
 Demeter and 33
 and divine feminine 163–4
 Dyad and 75
 evil and 8, 83
 and gender 12, 13, 38, 40, 51, 55, 71, 76
 Gnosticism 9
 and goddesses 38, 40, 51, 55
 mediation 79–81, 85, 87, 104
 Metamorphosis 45
 personification of 169, 189–193
 Plato, Platonism and Neoplatonism 42, 48, 54, 86, 96, 97
negative theology 118, 121, 151–2
Neoplatonism
 emanation 100
 gender dualism 13
 life 82, 99
 and nature 162
 and origin and clement 148–9
 Sophia 164, 169
 Victorinus 15
 and Zohar 132, 135, 136
Newman, Barbara (*God and Goddesses*) 139, 142, 152, 158, 165, 166
 Wisdom and Mary 168
Numenius 40, 41, 42, 47, 77
 and *Chaldean Oracles* 5, 82
 matter 59, 81, 157–8
 and Plotinus 100

Okeanos 21, 56, 58, 60, 70, 73
Origen 142, 146, 148–50, 211
 Against Celsus 117
 and Proclus 92
Orphic egg 69–70, 178
Orphic Hymns 19, 20, 24, 33
 and goddess Natura 159
Orphism 2, 54, 70, 78
Ouranos 5, 19, 20, 54, 57–8, 60, 81, 191
 castration of 164
 planets and 78
 in Plotinus 99, 100
 in Theogony 28, 56

Pagels, Elaine 50

 and Trimorphic Protanopia 135
Parthenogenesis 53, 54, 57, 61, 71, 108, 144
Paul of Tarsus 8, 114, 139
 and Isis 139, 40, 142
 and Mary 146
Pausanias 20, 2
Peplos, veiled or robed goddess 18, 23, 27, 165. *See also* Hadot, Pierre, *The Veil of Isis*
 secrets of nature 161
Persephone 3, 11, 29, 30, 32, 39, 44, 48, 96
 and Demeter 32–4, 155
 for feminists 175, 179, 183, 192
 Freud, Jung 175
 and Isis 114
 nature 156
 triads 103–4
 underworld 155
Plato 70. *See also Chora*
 Athena 81, 165
 and Athenian Academy 92
 Commentary tradition 89
 Cratylus 19, 2
 denigration of myth 7 23, 44, 51, 172, 186, 190
 feminist epistemology 182, 184
 as logocentric 12
 Phaedo 10
 Philebus, limit and unlimited 79
 Republic 23
 same and other 32
 the Good 65
 Timaeus 26, 64, 78, 97, 110, 157
Platonism 13, 37–8, 40, 54, 77, 85, 89, 163, 164, 171. *See also* Middle Platonism
 being and becoming 78
 Chaldean Oracles and 39, 46
 Christianity and 141, 142, 190
 and Egyptian lore 64
 and Hermetica 43
 and matter 81, 157
 nature 86, 150, 157
 Old Academy 55
 triads 96
 Trinity 147, 148
Plotinus 78, 82, 92, 99–100, 149, 157, 207
 on evil and matter

negative theology 121
Numenius, influence 81
reproductive imagery 67
triads 149
Plutarch of Athens 92, 93, 121
Plutarch, of Chaeronea 1, 9, 27, 29, 45, 161
   Isis and Osiris 34, 42-4, 64, 74, 80, 97, 113, 116, 129, 149, 174
   in late antiquity 7-8
   Middle Platonists 41, 59, 77
   peplos 161
   philosophical goddess 191
   and receptacle 62
polis 3, 6, 17
   and Athena 24, 25, 26, 165
   chora and law of 180
   and patriarchy, and law of 185-6
polytheism 37, 94, 101, 107, 110
Porphyry 46, 78, 82, 96, 99, 100
   Cave of the Nymphs 85
   Isagoge 118
   Zeus 108
Poseidon 21, 69, 84, 74
   and Athena 25
   coup against Zeus 22
   triads, in 102 94, 96
PreSocratics 5, 54, 59, 60, 108, 109
   Heraclitus 161
   and nature 155, 156
Proclus 9, 10, 67, 74, 84, 108, 117. *See also* Athenian school
   and Aphrodite 93-4
   and Athena 26, 39, 81, 93, 140
   Chaldean Oracles 45, 48
   Commentary on Timaeus 68, 83
   deception of Zeus 69
   and Hekate 82
   life, and disorderly motion 83
   life producing goddess 9, 68, 103, 104
   limit and unlimited 59, 67
   myth as philosophical argument 190
   names of gods 119-20
   negative theology 121
   Okeanos 58
   Orphic egg 70
   Orphic theogony 43
   peplos (veil) 161
   political danger 141
   receptacle 63

theurgy 90
triads 94, 101-4
soul 97
psychoanalysis 172-7. *See also* Freud, Jung, Lacan
Ptolemy 8, 39, 49, 51, 112, 198
Pyramid Texts 34, 113
Pythagorean 38, 70, 163, 171
   arithmetologies 75
   and Christianity
   evil 158
   and gender 76
   limit and unlimited 79
   and Plotinus 81
   table of opposites 8, 10, 13, 59, 69, 76, 82
   Wilshire and 183

Queen of Heaven 23, 172, 214
   Elephantine 126-7
   in Jeramiah 124
   and Mary 145
   in *Metamorphosis* 45, 114, 143

Rangos, Spyridon 31, 101, 102, 103
Rhapsodic Theogony 43
Rhea 3, 11, 19, 20, 21-4, 42, 56, 73
   in aretalogy 112
   Chaldean Oracles 46-7
   and Demeter 115
   fluid 193
   and Hekate 38, 63, 65
   Iamblichus 75
   life producing 104, 117
   and nature 155-6
   Plotinus 100
   in *Theogony* 56-60
   triads 90, 96, 102
reception (theory) 1, 3, 4, 9, 13, 34, 59
   and gender stereotypes 12, 171
Richter, Daniel 43, 44
Reid-Bowen, Paul 163-4
Roman Empire 7, 8
   and Christianity 140-1, 143
   cult of Isis 34, 35, 45, 111-14, 143
   Greco-Roman 52, 89, 91
   Hermetica in 48-9
   intertranslatable gods' names in 110, 115, 117

Kybele in 116
Rudavsky, Tamar 180
  nongendered arguments to Descartes 184

salvation (savior goddess) 33, 38, 52, 80, 161
  Arius and 147
  Holy Spirit and 150
  Isis as savior 117, 130
  Paul preaching salvation 139
  in Roman empire 143
second century 1, 7, 8, 37, 90
Serapis 91, 112–13, 116, 118
Shekhinah 123, 131, 136, 165, 189, 215
  personification of God's presence in the world 132–4
  in Zohar, as lower mother 132, 134
Simplicius 4, 41, 47, 80, 92, 141
Snell, Bruno (*The Discovery of the Mind*)
  personifying nouns 54
  prose writing, in Greek world 54
Sophia 11, 27. *See also* wisdom
  Barbelo 136 as
  Byzantine church 168
  Gnosticism 42, 50, 66, 75, 79, 98, 99, 136, 149
  Hebrew 129, 130, 136, 142, 165
  Jacob Boehme 169
  medieval allegory 158
  personification of wisdom (Wendy Helleman) 166–168
  Sirach, Wisdom of Solomon 129, 130
  Russian sophrology 165
Soul 41, 51–2, 55, 65, 149
  Barbelo and 63
  Cosmic Soul 30, 78, 82, 86
  female principle 71
  Isis and 62, 77, 80
  Persephone as 11
  Plato and 157, 167
  Plotinus 81, 99, 149
  Porphyry 96
  Porphyry's cave 85
  and Shekhinah 134
  triads 97, 102
  World Soul 37, 38, 42
    Hekate and World Soul 46–7, 51, 65, 77, 78, 82
    Xenocrates and 74

Speusippus 40, 42, 74, 86
statues 3, 20
  animation of, in Neoplatonism 90, 93, 120, 121
  Christian destruction of 89
  of Isis and Horus 65
Stoics 18, 24
  and Chaos 60
  interpretation of Penelope as wisdom 166
Syrianus 92, 93, 120, 121

Tartarus 56–7, 60, 61, 84, 95
  and Gaia 20
Titans 19, 20, 22, 29, 57, 58, 81
Theodosius I 91
  Theodosian code 141
  Theodosius II 92
Triads 11, 38, 44, 89, 91, 96–8, 149. *See also* Trinity
  in *Chaldean Oracles* 47
  in Gnostics 99
  Plotinus 99–100
  Proclus, Neoplatonism 101–4
Trinity 11
  in Clement and Origin 149–50
  disputes over ontological status in church 147–8
  and female divinity 151
  John Gwyn Griffiths's book *Triads and Trinities* 104–5
  as masculine 139, 141, 152
  Nicene council 147
  and triads 91, 114, 141, 142, 149, 192
Turner, John 43, 50, 51, 63, 77, 79, 100
  Barbelo 98
  goddess function in *Marsanès* 79
  Hekate 63, 99
Typhon 20, 22
  in Plutarch *Isis and Osiris* 34, 42, 44, 77, 80–1

Ugarit 5, 19, 22, 84, 124
underworld 3, 83–5, 96, 113, 173
  in *Hymn to Demeter* 29, 33, 155–6

Van den Berg, Robert 63, 68, 93
  life-producing goddess 104
Van den Toon, Karel
  Hebrew goddess 124, 126–8

Vernant, Jean-Pierre 4, 7, 19, 31, 32, 58, 60, 109, 193
Virgin Goddesses 5, 10, 18, 31, 55, 68, 145
　associated with Mary 144–5
　Athena 24, 156
　in Gnosticism 98, 210
　in Proclus 68
　Sophia 169
Voyatzis, Mary E. 6, 24, 25

West, M. L. 5, 22, 57, 109, 125, 197
wisdom. *See* Athena, Isis and Sophia
　Athena 3, 18, 24, 25, 26, 27, 39, 81, 86, 165
　and Christ 138, 149, 165, 166, 168
　in Gnostic gospels 50, 66, 98, 99, 131
　in Hebrew literature 129–30, 132, 142
　in Kabbalah 130, 131, 133
　and Mary 168
　personifications of wisdom
　　Beatrice 167–8, 192
　　Lady Philosophy (*see* Boethius) 167
　　Macrina 166–7
　　Penelope 166
　in Proclus 81, 83
　in triads 96, 100, 102
Witt, R. E. (*Isis in the Ancient World*) 8, 113, 139, 140

Xenocrates 41, 42, 74, 86, 97

Yahweh 118, 213
　and Asharah 124–8, 129

Zeus 47, 84, 93, 96, 108
　and Artemis 31
　birth of Athena from Zeus' head 3, 21, 24, 27, 57, 58, 183
　deception of Zeus in Iliad 69
　demiurge as 63, 108
　dominant god 22, 59
　Hera and 3, 22, 67
　honors Hekate 28, 29
　in Hymn to Demeter 33
　Irigaray: Zeus and Persephone 175, 185
　in Julian oration 93
　and life-producing goddesses 68
　in medieval allegory 159
　and Monad 41, 42, 74
　Nyx and 21
　in Orphic cosmogony 57
　Orphic Hymn to Hera 144
　overthrow of Kronos 19–20
　in Plotinus 99–100
　and Sarapis 112, 116, 118
　triads 102

www.ingramcontent.com/pod-product-compliance
Lightning Source LLC
Chambersburg PA
CBHW062138300426
44115CB00012BA/1975